Company Law
in the
Republic of Ireland

Company Law
in the
Republic of Ireland

The Hon Mr Justice Ronan Keane
BA (NUI), of Lincoln's Inn, Barrister
Judge of the High Court

London
Butterworths
1985

United Kingdom | Butterworth & Co (Publishers) Ltd, 88 Kingsway, LONDON WC2B 6AB and 61A North Castle Street, EDINBURGH EH2 3LT

Australia | Butterworths Pty Ltd, SYDNEY, MELBOURNE, BRISBANE ADELAIDE, PERTH, CANBERRA and HOBART

Canada | Butterworth & Co (Canada) Ltd, TORONTO and VANCOUVER

New Zealand | Butterworths of New Zealand Ltd, WELLINGTON and AUCKLAND

Singapore | Butterworth & Co (Asia) Pte Ltd, SINGAPORE

South Africa | Butterworth Publishers (Pty) Ltd, DURBAN and PRETORIA

USA | Butterworth Legal Publishers, ST PAUL, Minnesota, SEATTLE, Washington, BOSTON, Massachusetts, AUSTIN, Texas and D & S Publishers, CLEARWATER, Florida

© Ronan Keane 1985

All rights reserved. No part of this publication may be reproduced or transmitted in any form or by any means, including photocopying and recording, without the written permission of the copyright holder, application for which should be addressed to the publisher. Such written permission must also be obtained before any part of this publication is stored in a retrieval system of any nature.

This book is sold subject to the Standard Conditions of Sale of Net Books and may not be re-sold in the UK below the net price fixed by Butterworths for the book in our current catalogue.

ISBN 0 406 27290 5

Typesetting by Text Processing Ltd., Co. Tipperary, Ireland
Printed and Bound in Great Britain by
Butler & Tanner Ltd., Frome and London.

To the Hon Mr Justice John Kenny,
former Judge of the High Court and of the Supreme Court,
this book is dedicated with respect and affection.

Preface

When the Cox Committee on Company Law Reform presented its report in 1958, it had this to say in support of its recommendation that company legislation in Ireland should not depart too far from company legislation in the United Kingdom:

'The legal and accountancy professions here must rely largely upon English textbooks, the value of which would be considerably diminished if the two systems of law did not correspond in broad outline.'

Attitudes have changed since then: there has been a steadily increasing supply of Irish textbooks on law, due not least to the pioneering work of the Incorporated Law Society and the Arthur Cox Foundation. Irish lawyers have developed a more robust and mature reliance on their own corpus of law, undaunted by a system of law reporting which, one can be sure, no other common law jurisdiction would tolerate. (The reader who thinks I exaggerate need only consult the index of cases in this book to discover for himself how many of the modern Irish cases referred to have been reported and, of those, how many have achieved the privilege of being recorded in the Irish Reports.)

The inadequacy of our law reporting system is, of itself, probably a sufficient justification of an Irish textbook on company law. But it is by no means the only one. While the Oireachtas heeded the advice of Cox to keep our company law in step with the neighbouring jurisdiction, the changes wrought by the years have rendered it an increasingly perilous exercise to rely uncritically on the leading English textbooks.

This book is an attempt to supply practitioners and students with a readable and, it is hoped, reliable guide to the essential features of Irish company law. In order to make it as accessible as possible to the general reader, I have avoided lengthy and detailed discussions of the more abstruse topics; but I have not hesitated to provide the reader with signposts to the places in the classic English textbooks where he will find more detailed treatment of the particular subject.

I have also abridged the treatment of some areas which bulk less large in the Irish context: eg public flotations, take-overs and mergers. On the other hand, I have thought it reasonable to adopt a more detailed approach to the whole area of borrowing, receiverships and liquidations since this is clearly of pressing practical concern particularly in these sombre times.

The task of the writer on company law is not rendered easier by the ceaseless torrent of new legislation and decisions. The Companies (Amendment) Bill 1985 was published too late to be dealt with in any detail.

It is planned, however, to publish supplements at intervals with the object of keeping the text as up to date as possible.

I am grateful to my publishers for being constantly ready with advice and for their patience in awaiting a somewhat belated manuscript. Mr Justice Frank Murphy, Mr Oliver Fry and Mr Brian O'Connor read a number of chapters and made most helpful comments. The chapters on types of capital, accounts, auditing, receiverships and liquidations benefited from the expert comments of Mr John Donnelly FCA. Mr Colm O'Briain, former President of the Dublin Stock Exchange and Mr Patrick Gowran, its general manager, performed a similar service for the chapter on flotations. Professor Kevin B Nowlan made some helpful suggestions on the chapter dealing with the history of company law in Ireland. Much as lawyers may deplore the fact, company law is in the end of most importance to those who have to operate within its confines, and I am grateful to Mr Niall Higgins and Mr Kenneth O'Reilly-Hyland of the Institute of Directors for helpful advice. The responsibility for any errors or omission is entirely mine.

I am also indebted, for their courtesy and assistance, to the librarians and staffs of Judges' Library, Dublin, the Law Library, Dublin, the King's Inns Library, Dublin and the library of Lincoln's Inn. A difficult manuscript was prepared for the printers with exemplary efficiency by Miss Croasdella Cruess Callaghan. I should also like to thank the Incorporated Law Society of Ireland for arranging a grant in aid of the publication.

I have referred throughout to 'Ireland' instead of the 'Republic of Ireland' and to 'England' instead of 'England and Wales' when dealing with the territorial jurisdiction of the relevant legislation. References to articles are to the appropriate regulations in Table A of the First Schedule to the Companies Act 1963. References to Buckley, Gore-Browne, Gower, Palmer and Pennington are in each case to the latest edition of the relevant company law textbook.

The law is stated as of 1 April 1985. The shade of Sir Winston Churchill and the living presence of Mr Jack Lynch will forgive me for recalling that it was also on April Fools' Day that the two statutes introduced by them on which so many Irish company lawyers have grown up – the 1908 Act and the 1963 Act – became law.

Ronan Keane
Four Courts
Dublin
7 July 1985

The Companies (Amendment) Bill 1985

This bill was published after the text of the present work had been sent to the printers. As expected, it implements in its present form the requirements of the Fourth EEC Directive on Company Law (see paras 2.24 and 30.01).

The major change introduced by the bill is the requirement that private companies furnish their accounts with their annual returns to the Registrar of Companies, thereby ending the immunity from public scrutiny of such accounts which has been a feature of Irish company law since 1908.

In its present form the bill affords a measure of relief from this requirement to what are described as 'small' and 'medium-sized' companies. The former must meet at least two of the following criteria:

(i)   the balance sheet total must not exceed £1,250,000;
(ii) the turnover must not exceed £2,500,000;
(iii) the company must not employ more than 50 people.

The latter msut meet two of the following criteria:

(i)   the balance sheet total must not exceed £5,000,000;
(ii) the turnover must not exceed £10,000,000;
(iii) the company must not employ more than 250 people.

Small companies need furnish an abridged balance sheet only. A similar exemption is afforded to medium-sized companies, the relaxation being less comprehensive in their case.

The bill also imposes important new obligations on companies in relation to the format of the accounts. Companies will now be required for the first time to include details of turnover and operating costs inter alia in the account furnished to the Registrar.

Contents

xi

Table of statutes

Table of statutes

Table of cases

Part one

Introduction

Chapter 1

Companies and other forms of business organisations

What is a company?

1.01 The word 'company' has no strictly technical meaning in law.[1] In everyday language it is normally taken to mean a number of people combined for some common object. Where the object is gain, no group of this sort consisting of more than twenty members can be lawfully formed unless it is registered as a company under the Companies Acts 1963 to 1983 (which are referred to in this book as 'the Acts'[2]) or formed pursuant to some other statute.[3] It is with companies registered under the Acts that this book is principally concerned.

It should be borne in mind at the outset that, in the context of the Acts, a company need not consist of a significant number of people. It is common to find companies registered under the Acts which consist of as few as two people and, as we shall see, a company may have its membership reduced to one and still remain in law a company.[4]

1. *Re Stanley* [1906] 1 Ch 131 at 134 per Buckley J.
2. Three Acts have been passed amending the Act of 1963 (which is the principal Act) in 1977, 1982 and 1983. In this book references to 'the Principal Act' are to the Act of 1963.
3. S 376 of the Principal Act. For banking groups, see para 1.16 below.
4. See para 3.01 below.

Companies, single traders and partnerships

1.02 The most popular form of business organisation in Ireland is the limited liability company formed and registered under the Acts. While there are still many people who carry on business as single traders or in partnership with others, the benefits of forming a limited liability company are so overwhelming that businesses of any size almost inevitably take advantage of them.

1.03 The advantages of a company, as contrasted with other forms of business organisations such as partnerships, may be summarised as follows:

(1) *A company can be incorporated with limited liability*. The liability of the members for the debts and wrongs of the company can be limited to the amount unpaid on the shares which they own in the company (in which case it is known as a *company limited by shares*) or to the amount which they undertake to pay in the event of the company ceasing to exist (in which case it is known as a *company limited by guarantee*). In the case of a

3

partnership or an unlimited company, there is no such limitation on the liability of the partners or members.

(2) *A company is a legal entity distinct from its members*. This means that the company continues to exist despite any changes in its membership: in other words, it enjoys *perpetual succession*. It also means that the company can own property and sue and be sued in its own name. The company is, as a result, afforded a flexibility in its activities denied to other organisations. For example, when the shares in a company change hands, its property does not have to be separately transferred to the new members. Since it is vested in the company and not in the individual members, it remains vested in the company and this is the case even where the majority of the shares changes hands. By contrast, when one partner assigns his rights in the partnership to another, the property remains vested in the original partners. This flexibility may also provide certain tax advantages.

(3) *The shares in a company are freely transferable unless the constitution provides otherwise and a person who acquires shares becomes a member with all the rights of the person who transferred the shares to him*. When a partner assigns his share, the assignee does not become a partner unless the other partners agree.[1]

(4) *The affairs of a company are managed by its directors and not by the members*. By contrast, each partner is entitled to participate in all the partnership activities. Management by directors on behalf of the members is generally regarded by businessmen as preferable to the partnership system.

1. Partnership Act 1890, s 24 (7).

Reasons for not forming a company

1.04 The advantages for business organisations of forming a company are so clear that it may well be asked why people still carry on business as single traders or in partnership. In the case of very small businesses, the cost of incorporation, though not great, sometimes acts as a deterrent. Some activities of their nature–and this applies particularly to certain professions such as the law and accountancy–can only be carried on individually or in partnership.[1]

As we have seen, there cannot be more than twenty members in a partnership and each partner is the agent of the others. It provides, accordingly, a suitable legal basis for 'an association of a small body of persons having trust and confidence in each other'.[2] It should be noted, however, that the limitation on the number of members in a partnership has been removed in the case of accountants and solicitors by the 1982 Act.[3]

1. In the case of barristers, not even partnerships are allowed.
2. Gower, p 3.
3. S 13. The Minister for Industry, Trade, Commerce and Tourism may add to the categories of such partnerships by order.

Companies not formed under the Acts

1.05 While this book is principally concerned with companies formed and registered under the Acts, there are other forms of companies in existence which will be referred to from time to time. The three principal types of such companies are now considered in more detail.

1.06 (1) *Chartered companies or corporations*. There are many such bodies in Ireland but very few of them carry on business for gain. They include learned and professional bodies such as the King's Inns and the Incorporated Law Society, the universities, the Royal Irish Academy, the Royal Colleges of Surgeons and Physicians, voluntary hospitals etc. They were incorporated by charters or grants of letters patent from the British Crown and preserve their corporate existence by virtue of the transitional provisions of the Constitution and the relevant adapting legislation.[1] Although they have many of the features of companies registered under the Acts, they lie outside the scope of this book.

(2) *Companies incorporated by statute*. In the Victorian era when railways and similar undertakings were being promoted by private enterprise, parliament passed a number of special Acts, some of them applicable to Ireland, providing for the incorporation of such undertakings as companies. Since 1921 most of the companies so formed have been dissolved and their assets and functions transferred to other bodies.[2] Thus, railways and canals are vested in Coras Iompair Eireann which is not a company but a board established by statute.

It has also been a frequent practice since 1921 for the Oireachtas to provide for the establishment of companies intended to carry out certain functions considered to be of national importance. The companies concerned include Aer Rianta Teoranta, Aer Lingus Teoranta, Comhlucht Suicre na hEireann (the Irish Sugar Company), the Industrial Credit Company, Telecom Eireann and An Post. (While such companies are often referred to as 'semi-state bodies', they should be carefully distinguished from other bodies also so described, such as Coras Iompiar Eireann and the Electricity Supply Board, which are *not* companies.) The Act usually empowers the relevant Minister to obtain the incorporation of a company under the Acts with the appropriate objects. The enabling Act and subsequent amending legislation generally contain special provisions relating to the Minister's shareholding in the company, the composition of the board of directors, its authorised capital etc.

Companies of this nature play a major role in the Irish economy, accounting for a significant proportion of business activity and employment. It should always be borne in mind that, while they are normally incorporated under the Acts and many of the legal principles explained in this book are accordingly applicable to them, the Acts providing for their establishment contain many special provisions relating exclusively to them. In considering the legal powers and duties of such companies, therefore, it is not sufficient to have regard to the constitution of the company under the Acts (the memorandum and articles of association): the special provisions of the enabling Act and any amending legislation must also be taken into account.

(3) *Bodies with special objects*. There are certain bodies with special objects which can be formed under statutes other than the Acts. While in some respects, they resemble companies registered under the Acts, their primary objects are not normally the making of profit for their members. They include friendly societies, industrial and provident societies, building societies, trade unions and trustee savings banks. While they are occasionally referred to, they lie outside the scope of this book.

1. Constitution of Saorstat Eireann, Article 73; Constitution of Ireland, Article 50.1; Adaptation of Charters Act 1926.
2. But some survive, e.g. the Alliance and Dublin Consumers Gas Company incorporated under 37 & 38 Vict cxxxv.

Semi-state bodies which are not companies

1.07 As has been pointed out in the preceding paragraph, many semi-state bodies in Ireland take the form of companies established under Acts of the Oireachtas but incorporated under the Acts. There is, however, a number of semi-state bodies which are not companies of this type. They take the form of bodies corporate with all the usual features of corporations, such as perpetual succession, the capacity to sue and be sued, the power to hold property etc. They do not, however, have any share capital or shareholders: all their funds are provided by the state or by borrowing guaranteed by the state. They are the exact equivalent of the 'public corporations' in the UK.[1] They are usually described as a 'Board' or 'Authority'. Examples of such bodies in Ireland are:

   (i) the Electricity Supply Board,
  (ii) Coras Iompair Eireann,
 (iii) Bord na Mona,
 (iv) Radio Telefis Eireann,
  (v) An Bord Gais,
 (vi) Bord na gCapall,
(vii) Bord Failte,
(viii) the Racing Board,
 (ix) Udaras na Gaeltachta.

1. As to which see Palmer Vol. I pp 1345/6; Gower pp 285/292.

Partnerships

1.08 Partnerships, which do not have a separate legal personality, are an important feature of Irish life, particularly in the field of the professions. As they are wholly different in their legal nature from companies, any extended discussion of them would be outside the scope of this book. It may be noted, however, that it is still possible to form a partnership which extends to one or more of the partners the privilege of limited liability. This can be done under the Limited Partnerships Act 1907 but there are severe restrictions on the application of limited liability. In addition to the partners whose liability is limited to the assets which they have contributed, there must be one or more 'general partners' whose liability is unlimited. Moreover, a limited partner cannot take part in the management of the business without losing his immunity from liability. In practice, very few such limited partnerships are formed in Ireland.[1]

1. Their numbers have increased slightly in recent years, perhaps because of certain tax advantages.

1.09 As we have seen,[1] any association with more than twenty members whose object is gain must be incorporated as a company under the Acts: if this does not happen, the association in the eyes of the law does not exist. There are, of course, quite a number of bodies in Ireland which do not have gain as their object. Some of them find it convenient to become companies under the Acts, usually in the form of a company limited by guarantee. Others remain unincorporated, in which case the individual members are regarded in law as having entered into a contract with each other, the terms of which are usually to be found in the rules. The many clubs, social, educational and recreational, which flourish in Ireland are examples of bodies not established for gain, some of them being incorporated under the Acts as companies limited by guarantee, others remaining unincorporated.

1. Para 1.01 above.

Companies formed and registered under the Acts

1.01 It is with such companies that this book is principally concerned. As we have seen,[1] companies can be registered under the Acts either with or without limited liability; and, where liability is limited, it may be limited either by *shares* or by *guarantee*.

When a company is limited by shares, the liability of the members for the debts and wrongs of the company is limited to the amount which they have agreed to pay for the shares which they own in the company. Those shares collectively represent the *share capital* of the company. The members, or *shareholders*, as they are more often called, effectively own the company by virtue of their ownership of the share capital, although the property and assets of the company are vested in the company itself and not in the members. Their ownership of shares usually gives certain important rights to the shareholders, i.e.

(i) the right to receive a share at fixed intervals of the company's profits, where the company decides to distribute its profits, in the form of a money payment called a *dividend*;

(ii) the right to attend meetings of the company and, in the case of those holding voting shares, to vote at the meetings;[2]

(iii) the right to receive copies of certain important documents, i.e. the balance sheet, profit and loss account and directors' and auditors' reports;

(iv) the right to participate in the surplus assets of the company in the event of its ceasing to exist or being *wound up*, as the process is generally known.

1. Para 1.03 above.
2. But note that these rights may be abridged or altogether abolished by the company's constitution.

1.11 A further distinction of great importance among companies registered under the Acts exists. They can be either *public* or *private* companies. In practice, the most important distinction between the two forms of company is that the shares in a public company are offered for subscription to the public: those in a private company are not. Accordingly, there is, in general terms, no restriction on the right to transfer shares in a public company. By contrast, shares in a private company cannot be sold to the public and, in particular, cannot be quoted or dealt in on the stock exchange. Moreover, while there is no limit to the number of members of a public company, a private company cannot have more than fifty.[1]

1. S 33 (1)(b) of the Principal Act.

1.12 One of the major differences between a company and a partnership is that in the case of a company there is a separation between the ownership of the company, which is vested in the shareholders, and the day to day management of the company, which is carried on by the directors. (In the case of a partnership, each of the partners is usually concerned in the management of the business in addition to owning it in part.) But the shareholders–or in the case of a company not limited by shares, the members–may remove the directors at any time, so that the ultimate control of the company is in their hands. In the apt analogy of Gower, the members are the legislature of the company and the board of directors is the government.

Any decision of the members at a general meeting of the company is accordingly regarded as the act of the company itself. Similarly, any decision of the board of directors acting within the powers vested in them under the company's constitution is regarded as the act of the company. For this reason, the members in general meeting and the board of directors are frequently referred to as the *organs* of the company. By contrast, an officer or employee is at best no more than an *agent* of the company and his actions are not the actions of the company itself, although they may involve the company in legal liability where he is acting within the scope of his authority as such an agent.

1.13 The procedure for forming companies under the Acts is straight-forward and is explained in greater detail in the next chapter. It is sufficient to say at this point that the persons wishing to form the company–the *promoters*, as they are usually called–lodge with a government official called the *Registrar of Companies*[1] a document setting out the name and objects of the company (the *memorandum*) and its rules (the *articles of association*). If the registrar is satisfied that the document is in order, he issues a *certificate of incorporation* and the company is thereupon in existence. It is then in general terms entitled to avail of the various benefits conferred by law on such companies but must also comply with the requirements of the Acts and the regulations.

1. Referred to in this book as 'the Registrar'.

1.14 The law governing such companies is to be found principally in the Acts and the regulations made by the relevant authorities under the Acts. These authorities are the Minister for Industry, Trade, Commerce and Tourism (usually referred to in this book as 'the Minister') who has a general supervisory jurisdiction over companies and the Superior Courts Rules Committee which is the rule making authority for the High Court and the Supreme Court.

The interpretation of the Acts and regulations is the exclusive province of the courts established under the Constitution. This jurisdiction belongs to the High Court alone; but its decisions are subject to an appeal to the Supreme Court whose decisions are final. This is subject to one important qualification: the ultimate authority on the interpretation of any provisions of the Treaty of Rome under which the European Economic Community was established is the Court of Justice established under the Treaty. That court is also the ultimate authority on the interpretation of any directive issued by the Council established under the Treaty.

One other Act of special significance in the context of company law should be mentioned. The Mergers Take-overs and Monopolies (Control) Act 1978 contains important provisions designed to ensure among other things that mergers and take-overs do not take place which are inimical to the public interest.

1.15 While it is not part of the law of the State, the rules of the Stock Exchange are also relevant to the student of company law, as they affect public companies. Since the merger of all the stock exchanges in the United Kingdom and Ireland into one stock exchange in 1973, the relevant rules in this country have been the rules for the *Admission of Securities to Listing*.[1] The City Code on Take-overs and Mergers drawn up by a panel representative of the City of London is also applicable in Ireland.

1. The minimum requirements of the stock exchange have now been given the force of law: see para 7.06 below.

Banks and Insurance Companies

1.16 No company, association or partnership consisting of more than ten members may be formed for the purpose of carrying on the business of banking unless it is registered as a company under the Acts or is formed in pursuance of some other statute.[1]

There is no definition of 'banking' in the Acts, but it is generally recognised that the usual features of a banking business are

(1) the collection of cheques for customers;
(2) the payment of cheques drawn on the bank by customers; and
(3) the keeping of current accounts.[2]

In addition, banking business is defined by s 2 of the Central Bank Act 1971 (which requires the obtaining of licences from the Central Bank by all persons carrying on banking business) as including, subject to certain exceptions, the business of accepting deposits payable on demand or on notice or at a fixed or determinable future date.

1. S. 372 of the Principal Act.
2. But note that a person may be in law a 'banker' although he does not keep current accounts or issue cheque books; per FitzGibbon LJ in *Re Sheilds* (1901) 1 IR 172 at 199. It will comfort some to know that the learned judge virtually equated the terms 'banker' and 'gombeen man'.

1.17 Section 15 of the Central Bank Act 1971 requires the Registrar to notify the Central Bank of the delivery to him of any memorandum and articles of any company which would, in his opinion, be holding itself out as a banker or have as one of its objects the carrying on of banking business. A certificate of incorporation may not be granted by the Registrar in respect of such a company unless and until the Bank indicates to the Registrar its willingness to grant a licence to the company or to exempt it from the requirements as to a licence. The Registar must also notify the Bank of the delivery to him of any documents by an overseas company establishing a place of business in Ireland which would have a similar effect. There is a similar provision where the constitution of a company is being altered to the same effect.

1.18 Insurance companies, in addition to being subject to the provisions of the Acts, are also subject to the provisions of the Insurance Acts 1908 to

1983 which deal with such matters as the granting of licences to insurance companies by the Minister, the maintenance of deposits in the High Court by such companies, the monitoring by the Minister of their accounts (and, in particular, the ratio between their reserves and their actual and contingent liabilities) and the appointment of an administrator by the court where such a company gets into difficulties.

Chapter 2

The development of company law in Ireland[1]

2.01 The general structure of Irish company law is closely modelled on that of England. The reason is obvious: the two countries had a common legal tradition and, after the Act of Union in 1800 and until 1921, all statute law affecting Ireland was enacted at Westminster. While there have been substantial changes in Irish company law since 1921, it was thought better to preserve the general structure inherited from the English, and such changes as have been made since 1921 have in many instances been based on changes in the neighbouring jurisdiction. Since the accession of Ireland to the European Economic Community in 1973, however, changes have largely resulted from compliance with directives of the community requiring the harmonisation of company law in the member states.

1. For readable accounts of the history of English company law see Gower, chapters 2 and 3 and Hahlo, *Cases in Company Law,* 2nd edition, chapter one. A more detailed account will be found in Holdsworth, *History of English Law*, vol. 8, pp 192–222, vol. 13, pp 365–370 and vol. 15, pp 44–61. There is no Irish work dealing specifically with the topic of which I am aware but useful background information will be found in Lyons, *Ireland since the Famine,* pp 42–58, Lynch & Vaisey, *Guinness's Brewery in the Irish Economy* 1759/1876, chapter one, *The Formation of the Irish Economy* (ed. L.M. Cullen), particularly the chapter by J. Lee on *Capital in the Irish Economy,* Robinson, *A History of Accountants in Ireland* and Meenan, *The Irish Economy since 1922.*

The joint stock company

2.02 The modern Irish companies with which this book is concerned are descended from the *joint stock companies* which first became a feature of English commercial life in the seventeenth century. Legal historians have seen shadowy prototypes of such companies in the gilds of the middle ages, but the medieval institution with which they had more in common was the *commenda*.[1] This had its origin partly in the medieval dislike of usury: the *commendatores* advanced money to the commendatarii so that the latter might use it in their trade, but no interest was charged. Instead the commendatores were entitled to participate in the profit of the venture. Since they took no part in the management, leaving that to the commendatarii, one can discern in the commenda the development of the division, familiar to us in company law today, between ownership and management. The interest of the commendatores was confined to their financial investment, as was their liability.

From this institution there evolved in turn the structure, familiar on the continent, of the *societe en commandite*, whose nearest equivalent in our law

11

was the limited partnership. But the limited partnership concept never really became established in England or Ireland, although it is of interest to note that the first statute which recognised its existence was the Irish Anonymous Partnership Act of 1781.

1. Holdsworth, vol. 8, pp 193–7.

2.03 English commercial development initially took the form of the 'regulated companies', the individual members of which traded with their own stock. Since each member was responsible for his own trade, it might have been thought that there were no advantages to be derived from forming any sort of corporation. In fact there were: the benefits which the members of such companies derived from the charters under which they were incorporated consisted of monopolies and similar privileges then in the gift of the crown. This was particularly the case with the great overseas companies, of which the most celebrated was the East India Company.[1]

The merchant adventurers, who were the members of such companies, developed the practice during the seventeenth century of forming a 'joint stock' for a particular venture. At the end of the venture, the stock and the profits were divided between the members. From this it was a short step to having a permanent joint stock which was the property of all the members and hence the name 'joint stock company', still sometimes used to describe the limited liability company of today.[2]

Although the concept that the members were not responsible for the debts of the company developed at an early stage in the history of the joint stock companies (the concept of 'limited liability'),[3] it did not have the practical significance that it does today, since the company could exact from the members *leviations* (calls to meet the liability), at least where it was authorised so to do by its charter.

1. Holdsworth, vol. 8, p 209.
2. Thus one of the best known text books is still called Gore Browne's *Handbook of Joint Stock Companies*.
3. *Edmunds v Brown & Tillard* (1668) 1 Lev 237, Hahlo p 11.

2.04 There also developed during the seventeenth century the practice of raising funds from the public for such ventures and in the early decades of the eighteenth century such *flotations*, as they came to be called, became extremely common. Many of the new ventures came to grief and ultimately parliament felt obliged to intervene when the speculative frenzy which accompanied the launching of such schemes reached fever pitch with the remarkable project of the South Sea Company to acquire virtually the whole of the English national debt. The resultant legislation, passed in 1720 and known as the 'Bubble Act', prohibited the formation of joint stock companies in the future except under Act of Parliament or by the grant of a royal charter. The Bubble Act, although well intentioned, has been generally regarded as having seriously impeded the development of a proper framework of company law in the United Kingdom.

2.05 The passing of the Bubble Act did not mean that joint stock companies ceased to be formed. It was still possible to obtain a royal charter for that purpose; but this was a difficult and expensive process. If the project was thought to be of sufficient importance, parliament was prepared to permit the incorporation of a company by a special Private Act and this was the statutory framework for the establishment by private enterprise of the various railway and canal undertakings in both England and Ireland. The many smaller traders, however, who could not make use of such elaborate machinery were driven to form a new sort of association to obtain some at least of the advantages of carrying on business in combination. This was the 'deed of settlement' company and in it we can see many of the features of the private commercial company of our own time. It was not an incorporated body like our modern companies: instead the individual members entered into a deed of settlement with one or more trustees which declared that the individuals constituted a company with a specified name, in the capital of which they all held shares. The deed also provided that the affairs of the company should be managed by a committee of directors and that the property of the company should be vested in them. This arrangement secured to traders one of the great advantages of incorporation, continuity of existence, but the members continued to be liable for the debts of the company.

2.06 The Bubble Act was repealed in 1825 but it continued to be difficult to obtain the necessary charters and the case for radical reform was strengthened by the confusion and uncertainty surrounding the formation and composition of the numerous incorporated and unincorporated bodies seeking funds from the public for a wide range of enterprises. Investors found it extremely difficult to discover who the real promoters and managers of fraudulent schemes were and to bring home legal responsibility for the losses they sustained against anyone.[1] Dickens pilloried the dubious enterprises that flourished in those days in *Nicholas Nickleby*

> ' "It's the finest idea that was ever started. "United Metropolitan Improved Hot Muffin and Crumpet Baking and Punctual Delivery Company". Capital, five million in five hundred thousand shares of £10 each. Why, the very name will get the shares up to a premium in ten days. "
> "And when they are at a premium", said Mr Ralph Nickleby smiling.
> "When they are, you know what to do about them as well as any man alive, and how to back quietly out at the right time", said Mr Bonney, slapping the capitalist familiarly on the shoulder. '

It was against this background that the first modern companies legislation appeared on the statute book in 1844. The Joint Stock Companies Act 1844, the enactment of which owed much to the energy of the young Gladstone as president of the Board of Trade, was primarily designed to curb fraudulent enterprises and introduce some degree of order into the affairs of joint stock companies. With this object in view, it established the requirements as to publicity in the formation and management of such enterprises which have been a feature of company law since then.

The office of Registrar of Companies was established in both England and Ireland, provision was made for the registration of the names of the promoters, for the execution of a deed by the shareholders and the appointment of named directors before the company commenced business and for defining the rights of shareholders and powers of directors. The company could now own property and sue and be sued itself. In the same year legislation was introduced, which again applied to Ireland, providing a machinery for the *winding up* of insolvent companies, in many respects similar to the well established bankruptcy procedures applicable to individuals. The advantages of limited liability was still withheld but was ultimately granted by the Limited Liability Act 1855, which also introduced the requirement that the names of companies availing of such a privilege had to end with the word 'limited'.

The 1855 Act was replaced in less than a year by the Joint Stock Companies Act 1856, which has generally been seen as representing the highwater mark of the Victorian *laissez faire* philosophy as applied to company law. The principle that the company's name had to end in the word 'limited' when limited liability was availed of was maintained. But a much simpler process of registration was introduced, the deed of settlement was replaced by the now familiar memorandum and articles as the constitution of the company, and many of the restrictions imposed by the earlier legislation on those seeking the benefits of incorporation and limited liability were swept away.

Other legislation followed the 1856 Act and ultimately the Acts were consolidated in the Companies Act 1862, the first statute to bear that short title.

1. Holdsworth, vol. 15, pp 45–60.

Economic development in Ireland

2.07 The new companies legislation was also applicable in Ireland. Conditions were, however, very different in the neighbouring island. Ireland had enjoyed a significant degree of economic development in the seventeenth and eighteenth centuries, characterised by the emergence of a number of crafts and industries and the growth in size and prestige of some of the cities and towns, most notably Dublin. But its history in the nineteenth century was overshadowed by the catastrophe of the great famine and there was no real counterpart to the massive expansion of trade and industry in England. Such significant commercial developments as there were tended to be confined to the north-east of Ulster and certain major ports, cities and towns.[1] In this period the most important expansion was in the north-east with the development of ship building and linen, while in other areas such industry as there was tended to be dominated by brewing and distilling. Ironically, Ireland was also the scene at this period of a rapid expansion of two services which would have been an important asset to industrial development on the English scale, if it had ever occurred: with the end of the monopoly of the Bank of Ireland, other banks began to flourish, and an extensive railway network was built throughout the country.

Thus, while the new legislation undoubtedly had its effect in Ireland, one of its by-products being a substantial growth in the numbers and respectability of the relatively new profession of accountancy,[2] there was no equivalent in Ireland to the vast number of public flotations in England.

1. Lynch & Vaisey, chapter one.
2. Thus shortly after the enactment of 7 & 8 Vic. c III providing for the winding up of insolvent companies, a Mr Henry Brown became the first of a long and illustrious line of official liquidators appointed by the Irish courts. The firm of which he was a member subsequently became the well known firm of Craig Gardner & Co. See Robinson, *A History of Accountancy in Ireland*, pp 17–21.

The private company

2.08 The new legislation had obviously been framed with relatively large public companies in mind. But it did not take lawyers long to realise that it also could be used to give the ordinary trader, who did not wish to seek funds from the public, the benefits of incorporation and limited liability. This paved the way for the development of the 'private company', as it came to be called, which was to be the central institution of Irish company law. It was only a short step from this to the formation of 'one man companies', in which virtually all the shares were held by one trader who also nominated the directors. Their validity was recognised by the House of Lords in 1897 in the great case of *Salomon v Salomon & Co.*[1] in which the Court of Appeal had reacted with shocked disbelief to the proposition that such bodies were perfectly lawful. No less a judge than Lindley LJ thundered that companies of this nature

'do infinite mischief; they bring into disrepute one of the most useful statutes of modern times by perverting its legitimate use and by making it an instrument for cheating honest creditors...'[2]

The House of Lords, however, made it clear that the benefits of the Acts were no less available to the small businessman than to the large public enterprises and, when the Companies Act 1907 became law, it not merely gave statutory recognition to private companies, but also exempted them from the requirments of the Acts as to the filing with the Registrar of balance sheets. This exemption, which effectively removed from public scrutiny the financial affairs of such companies, has remained a feature of Irish company law until the present day.

The 1907 Act was followed by the second great consolidating measure, the Companies (Consolidation) Act 1908 which was to be for Irish lawyers the bedrock of company law for over half a century.

1. [1897] AC 22.
2. [1895] 2 Ch 323 and 339

Company law in Ireland after 1921

2.09 The pattern had been established in the United Kingdom during the nineteenth century of setting up committees at intervals of approximately twenty years to consider what changes might be required in the legislation dealing with companies. Due in part perhaps to the lesser role played by industry and business in a predominantly agricultural economy, this pattern was not reflected in the legislation of the new Irish State after 1921. A committee was appointed in 1927 to investigate the law and procedure relating to bankruptcy and winding up of companies and duly reported, but no legislation was introduced as a result of its recommendations. There was no Irish equivalent to the English Acts of 1929 and 1948.

In 1951 a committee was appointed to report on the reform of company law. The first chairman of the committee was Mr H. Vaughan Wilson SC who was replaced on his death in 1956 by Mr Arthur Cox. The secretary of the committee was Mr John Kenny, subsequently a Judge of the High Court and of the Supreme Court, with whom much of the development of modern Irish company law is associated.

2.10 The most significant feature of Irish Companies since the enactment of the first companies' legislation in the nineteenth century was the vast number of private companies formed as opposed to the relatively small number of public companies. This obviously raised the question, with which Cox dealt as to whether the continued exemption of such companies from the requirement to file a balance sheet was justified. In England, following the recommendation to that effect of the Cohen Committee, the 1948 Act had confined the privilege to exempt private companies. There was the further problem in this context presented by the growth of subsidiary companies: the requirement that a public company should file a balance sheet was rendered almost meaningless by the fact that its wholly owned private subsidiaries were under no such obligation.

The Cox Committee, whose report[1] was presented in 1958, recommended that the exemption of private companies in this area should continue. They considered that any harm that might result for creditors and investors was more than outweighed by the difficulties which would be caused to small businesses if they were compelled to disclose their trading situation to competitors. They also considered that the legislation required to define the type of private companies which should file balance sheets would be of necessity highly technical and complex and that in the Irish context this sort of legislation should be avoided where possible. To deal with the problem of public companies which owned private subsidiaries, they recommended the adoption of the practice which had existed in England since the 1929 Act of requiring holding companies to file group accounts which would show the financial position of both the parent company and its subsidiaries taken as a whole. In the case of a private company owning subsidiaries, however, they recommended that the obligation to file group accounts should not be imposed: it would be sufficient if the private subsidiaries had the right to obtain a copy of the balance sheet of all the subsidiaries in the group. All of the committee's recommendations in this area were embodied in the Principal Act.

1. *Report of the Company Law Reform Committee,* 1958 (pl 4523).

2.11 Another major change recommended by Cox related to the keeping and publication of accounts generally. It is a remarkable fact that, until the committee's recommendations in this area were implemented by the Principal Act, there was no general obligation on companies to keep proper accounts or to present their shareholders with a picture of the financial situation of the company in which they had invested their money. The only requirement of the 1908 Act was that public companies should include in their annual report to the shareholders a statement in the form of a balance sheet. The Principal Act gave effect to Cox's recommendation that all companies, public and private, should be required to keep proper accounts and should be obliged to present the shareholders each year with an audited balance sheet and profit and loss account.

2.12 Another development which had given rise to concern since the enactment of the 1908 Act related to the position of minority shareholders. Short of putting an end to the company's existence by obtaining a winding up order from the court, no remedy was available to such shareholders and their interests could be disregarded almost with impunity by the majority. The English 1929 Act had enabled shareholders who found themselves in this position to obtain relief from the court, and the Cox recommendation that a similar reform should be introduced in Ireland was implemented by the Principal Act. Recommendations intended to ensure that the practice of giving loans to directors was not abused were also implemented, but Cox advised against any general prohibition on such loans and this advice was also accepted by the legislature.

2.13 In the area of winding up, two of the most important recommendations of Cox were not implemented. Although the committee was not unanimous on the matter, some at least of the members were in favour of the proposal that in the case of the winding up of companies, there should be an official receiver attached to the High Court who would perform functions roughly analogous to those of the official assignee in bankruptcy. They thought that the delays associated with the existing system, under which a winding up by the court was carried out by a liquidator (almost invariably an accountant) under the control of the court, would be reduced by the adoption of this system which had been in existence in England since 1890. Other members of the committee, however, were opposed to this suggestion which had also been considered by the committee established in 1927 and rejected by them.[1]

Cox also recommended (and here there was no indication of any dissent) that the priority given to debts due to the State in a winding up should be abolished. That priority is, of course, of far greater significance in modern conditions than it was when the comittee reported: the huge increase in the volume of taxation and the introduction of PAYE and Value Added Tax means that in the vast majority of winding ups conducted by the court the Revenue Commissioners are the largest single creditor.

On another topic, however, which has also become of critical importance in modern conditions, Cox's recommendation was adopted in the Principal Act. The committee was seriously concerned by the abuses which had developed of the protection of limited liability. The report recommended that where in the course of a winding up it appeared that the business of the company had been carried on with intent to defraud creditors or for any fraudulent or dishonest purpose, the court should have power to declare that any persons who were knowingly concerned in the carrying on of the business in that manner should be personally responsible for the debts of the company. The relatively more frequent use of this power by the High Court has been a feature of company law in recent times.[2]

Cox also recommended that the power given to the relevant Minister under the 1908 Act to investigate the affairs of a company should be less restricted and this recommendation was implemented. But such investigations continued to be extremely rare: presumably, if a company's affairs had reached the stage where such an inquiry seemed necessary the shareholders or creditors usually decided on a winding up.[3]

1. Cox, paras 197/8. An attempt in 1893 to extend the British system to Ireland in the form of the Official Liquidators (Ireland) Bill had also foundered, largely, it would seem, because of the well organised opposition to the proposal in the accountant's profession. See Robinson, pp 115–9.
2. See further paras 34.83 et seq. below.
3. See Chapter 33 below.

2.14 Cox was also concerned with the injustices and inconveniences which had resulted from the strict application by the courts of the rule that a transaction entered into by a company which was not authorised by its constitution (in legal language 'ultra vires') could not be enforced against the company even where the other party did not know that it was ultra vires. Although the committee confined themselves to recommending a simpler and less expensive method of altering the objects of a company as set out in the memorandum of association, the legislature went further. The Principal Act provides that the rule is not to apply where the other contracting party was actually unaware of the ultra vires character of the transaction.[1]

1. For a more detailed discussion of this topic see para 4.13 below.

2.15   The functions of auditors had become of increasing importance since the 1908 Act. As the number of companies increased, so did the desirability of ensuring that their accounts were checked by independent experts. It was not until the Principal Act, however, that, following a recommendation by Cox, a requirement was introduced that such auditors be professionally qualified.

2.16   Another area which also gave rise to concern was the practice of registering nominee shareholdings. Since the 1908 Act expressly prohibited the entry of trusts on the register of shareholders, it was possible for the real owners of shares to be concealed from the public gaze, the registered shareholders being merely their nominees. This was seriously at odds with the great principle of publicity established in the Gladstone legislation, but Cox considered that the only modification of the law which was practicable was the introduction of a requirement that there should be a register of directors' shareholdings. The recommendation was implemented in the Principal Act.

2.17   Between the presentation of the report of the Cox Committee in 1958 and the enactment of the Principal Act in 1963, the report of the Jenkins Committee in Britain was published, and the Principal Act embodies some of their recommendations in addition to Cox's recommednations. A shorter Act in 1959 had also made some useful changes.

The Principal Act, which remains the charter of Irish company law, is one of the largest on the statute book, containing as it does, 399 sections and 13 schedules. Although its structure closely resembles that of the English 1948 Act and many of the sections are taken word for word from that Act or with only the most minor variations, there are also important differences between the two Acts. Some of them, such as the contrasting treatment of private companies, have already been mentioned, and others will be referred to in other parts of this book. The difference between the Acts–and the succeeding English Acts of 1967, 1976, 1980 and 1981–are sufficiently numerous and striking to make it a somewhat hazardous exercise for Irish practitioners and students to rely uncritically on the leading English textbooks.

2.18   The appearance on the statute book of the Principal Act coincided with the beginning of a period of considerable growth in the Irish economy. The industrial expansion of the decade which followed and the increase in agricultural incomes with the country's entry into the EEC in 1973 was accompanied by an unprecedented property boom. This new economic climate also led to the formation of a number of so-called 'secondary banks', a phenomenon which ultimately led to stricter government control of banking with the enactment of the Central Bank Act 1971.

All of this increased economic activity, however, did not alter the predominance of the private company in Irish company law. The number of public companies had remained virtually static between 1925 and 1956, as the following table demonstrates.

As at 31st December	Public Companies	Private Companies
1925	368	1,088
1930	361	1,380
1935	359	2,000
1940	362	2,567
1945	336	3,513
1950	357	5,377
1955	375	7,111
1956	372	7,385[1]

By contrast, as the table demonstrates, there had been a considerable increase in the number of private companies. Far from these trends being reversed during the decades of comparative affluence which followed, they were accentuated.

As at 31st December	Public Companies	Private Companies
1977	338	44,609
1978	339	48,230
1979	339	53,869
1980	338	59,716
1981	339	65,072
1982	337	69,432[2]

1. *Report of the Company Law Reform Committee*, para 41. It should be pointed out, however, that there was a considerable growth in the number of public *industrial* companies during the period. In 1933 there were only 24 such companies whose shares were quoted on the Dublin Stock Exchange with a total issued capital of £4.8 million. By 1957 the number had risen to 80 with a total issued capital of £19.5 million, a reflection of the incentive to development resulting from protectionism. (See Meenan, pp 146–7).
2. *Annual Report of the Department of Trade, Commerce and Tourism 1982* (pl 1784).

2.19 As the economy moved into a deepening recession in the 'eighties, the problems presented by the growing number of insolvencies among companies began to receive more attention. The vast number of private companies limited by shares in a comparatively small economy made the abuse of limited liability a matter of increasing public concern.

Membership of the EEC and Irish Company Law

2.20 The major event in Irish company law, however, since the Principal Act has been the accession of Ireland to the EEC in 1973 and the legislation rendered necessary by that historic step. As a member, Ireland is obliged under the terms of the treaties establishing the community to implement directives of the Council and a number of such directives have been issued in the field of company law. These have as their objective the harmonisation of company law in the member states, thereby facilitating, as it is hoped, the freedom of establishment of commercial enterprises throughout the community.

Although five of the directives have been implemented in Ireland, progress has been generally slow. The Second Directive was only implemented following the institution of proceedings by the Commission against Ireland in the Court of Justice and a finding by that court that Ireland was in default.[1] At the time of writing, four further directives remain to be

S0030625

implemented and, in the case of one of them, implementation is seriously overdue.

1. *EC Commission v Ireland* [1982] ECR 3573.

2.21   The First Directive, which dates from 1968, contained two requirements which were relevant to Ireland. The first which sought protection for third parties dealing with the company so far as ultra vires transactions were concerned had been broadly anticipated by the Principal Act. The second was intended to provide for the publication of certain information concerning the company throughout the community. Both requirements were implemented by the European Communities (Companies) Regulations 1973.[1]

1. SI 1973/163.

2.22   The Second Directive was implemented by the 1983 Act. It introduces the new designation of 'public limited company', and its abbreviation 'plc', for all public companies with limited liability. It contains detailed provisions as to the minimum authorised share capital of such companies, the payment for such share capital, the obligation to offer newly issued shares in such companies to existing shareholders and the maintenance of the capital of such companies.

2.23   Three further directives which are all concerned with coordinating the requirements for the listing of securities on the stock exchanges of the member states and the publication of information by companies whose securities are listed were implemented by the European Communities (Stock Exchange) Regulations 1984.[1]

1. SI 1984/182.

2.24   There are four other directives in force but none of them has so far been implemented in Ireland. The Third (which dates from 1978) is concerned with mergers of public companies. The Fourth, which also dates from 1978, is of much greater significance in the Irish context, containing as it does far reaching requirements as to the publication of company's accounts and their format. The importance of the directive to Ireland is that it is applicable to private companies who have hitherto been exempt from the requirements to file accounts with the Registrar and the consequent exposure of their finances to public scrutiny. While some derogation is permitted from its provisions, any substantial compliance with the directive will have considerable implications for Irish companies. It is believed at the time of writing that the government intends to publish in the near future its proposals for implementing this directive.

Another directive is concerned with the divisions of public companies–or 'scissions' as they are sometimes called on the continent–and in effect complements the Third Directive on mergers. The Seventh Directive deals with the consolidation of accounts but does not require implementation until 1 January 1988.

2.25   In addition to the 1983 Act there have been two other Acts amending the Principal Act in certain relatively minor respects: the Companies (Amendment) Act 1977 and the Companies (Amendment) Act 1982.

Together with the Principal Act, the Stock Transfer Act 1963, the 1983 Act, the Regulations made under the Acts, the relevant Rules of the Superior Courts, The European Communities (Companies) Regulations 1973, the European Communities (Stock Exchange) Regulations 1984 and the decisions of the Superior Courts thereon, they constitute the complete corpus of Irish company law today.

The future of Irish company law

2.26 The future development of Irish company law will be determined to a large extent by developments in the EEC. As we have already seen, four directives have not been complied with and there are further directives in draft form or under consideration, some at least of which may be expected to take mandatory form in the course of the next few years. The controversial draft Fifth Directive which deals with the structures of companies will probably have less effect in Ireland than in other member states, as it is confined to public companies. At the same time, the philosophy which underlies the directive–a desire to make companies accountable to their employeees as well as to their shareholders–is of relevance in Ireland, although there has been singularly little debate on the topic.[1]

As we shall see at a later stage, the responsibility in law of those charged with the management of a company formed under the Acts is to advance the interests of the shareholders. Other laws may impose obligations on the company in relation to its employees, its customers and the public at large; but in any area where such laws are not applicable the company is under no duty in the present state of the law to have any regard to the interests of its employees or to the wider interests of the community as a whole. The proposals in the Fifth Directive to bring a measure of 'industrial democracy' into the field of company law are confined at the time of writing to public limited companies with more than 1,000 employees and would, in that form, have little impact in Ireland. It may be that we shall see an increasing debate in Ireland as to whether the framework of company law should extend some recognition to the principle that all business entities whether they be companies, partnerships or whatever, have wider obligations to society than are encompassed by the making of profits. But it must be said that in the period of deep recession, through which the Irish economy is now passing, it is understandable that the most pressing anxiety for most companies and their employees is the problem of survival.

In one area, at least, the pressure for reform has become so insistent that one can reasonably expect legislative action in the near future. The abuse of the protection of limited liability is causing many problems: in particular, the readiness of some entrepreneurs to put companies into liquidation, leave their creditors to whistle for their money and then form another limited company has understandably caused concern. A number of recent court cases has moreover demonstrated a wholesale disregard on a disquieting scale of the requirements of the law as to the keeping of accounts and the making of returns to the Registrar.

Television and press reports[2] have suggested that new legislation may include the following measures:

(1) the appointment of inspectors to conduct investigations by the court rather than the Minister;

(2) the giving of greater powers to such inspectors as to the obtaining of evidence;

(3) the appointment of inspectors by the Minister to investigate the actual beneficial ownership of shares;

(4) the granting of search warrants by the court to frustrate the removal of books and papers;

(5) provisions enabling auditors of companies to resign but requiring them to state (if it be the case) that there are no circumstances connected with the resignation which should be brought to the attention of the members and the creditors;

(6) requirements that the auditors make such investigations as are necessary during the financial year to satisfy themselves that proper accounts are being kept;

(7) obligations on the auditors in certain circumstances to notify the Director of Public Prosecutions that proper books of account are not being kept;

(8) penalties for 'reckless' reports by auditors;

(9) the imposition of personal liability for the debts of a company on an officer of the company where the court is satisfied that a failure to keep proper books of account contributed to the insolvency of the company;

(10) the imposition of personal liability for the debts of a company on a person who is knowingly party to 'reckless' as well as fraudulent trading;

(11) power for the court to order the payment by one company in a group of a debt due by another company in the group where it is 'just and equitable' for it to do so;

(12) power for the court in a winding up order to order the 'pooling' of all the assets of a group of companies;

(13) restrictions on directors of insolvent companies becoming directors of new companies, including a provision that they may only become directors where the nominal value of the allotted share capital is not less than £500,000;

(14) restrictions, and in some cases prohibitions, on directors or managers who have been found to be reckless, negligent or fraudulent in their management of companies holding similar offices in other companies;

(15) prohibitions on loans to directors, subject to certain exemptions;

(16) limitations on long term service contracts with directors;

(17) a requirement that directors retire at the age of 70;

(18) regulation of 'insider' trading, i.e. the use by persons connected with the company of information acquired because of that connection for their own financial benefit;

(19) compulsory disclosure of the beneficial ownership of the shares in the case of substantial shareholdings, i.e. where an individual holding amounts to not less than 25 per cent of the total share capital carrying voting rights;

(20) measures aimed at 'concert parties', i.e. groups of persons acting together to keep their shareholdings below the 25 per cent level so as to avoid the compulsory disclosure referred to at (19) above;

(21) compulsory disclosure in the directors' report of gifts for political or charitable purposes exceeding a specified limit.

A number of the proposals are clearly influenced by the report in England of the Cork Committee on Insolvency Law and the subsequent White Paper on the same topic.[3] There is no indication as yet, however, that the new legislation will include measures to improve the position of ordinary creditors in windings up of the type recommended by Cork. That report has recommended changes in the position of preferential creditors, most notably the Revenue, and secured creditors, so as to give ordinary creditors greater protection in the event of a winding up. Cork has also made recommendations intended to facilitate the rescuing of companies in financial difficulties by the appointment of an 'administrator' whose primary object would be to restore the company to health, if possible, rather than protect the interests of a particular creditor, the primary duty of the ordinary receiver under the present law.

Clearly a number of proposals referred to above are certain to become law: whether all of them do remains to be seen. Concern is already being expressed in business and accountancy circles as to some of them. Thus, the suggestion that auditors should be obliged to monitor the finances of a company throughout the financial year and not merely at its end has been criticised as virtually unworkable. Again, the sweeping changes hinted at in the case of subsidiaries have created unease: there is the possibility that too drastic surgery in this area may kill reasonably healthy companies simply because of a disease affecting a related company and that this may not be to the ultimate benefit of the wider body of creditors and employees of a group of companies. It is certain that these problems will be the subject of much discussion both inside and outside the Oireachtas before any new measures become law.

1. For a lively discussion of the subject, see Godyer, *The Responsible Company* published in 1961 but remarkably farseeing. See also Gower, pp 66/75 and Keane, *The Corporate Entity: Developments and Possibilities,* Proceedings of Association of Certified Accountants, November 1982.
2. *Irish Independent,* 11 November 1984.
3. *Insolvency Law and Practice: Report of the Review Committee 1982* (Cmnd 8558); *A Revised Framework for Insolvency Law 1984* (Cmnd 9175). Some of the proposals in these two documents have been embodied in the English Insolvency Bill published on 11 December 1984.

2.27   There is no indication at the time of writing that a consolidating Act is in comtemplation. In view of the fact that there has been no major enquiry into Irish company law for over twenty-five years, it seems reasonable to assume that any such proposal would be preceded by a full scale examination of the manner in which the Principal Act has operated over two eventful decades in Irish economic history.

Part two

Formation of a company

Chapter 3

How a company is formed

Distinction between public and private companies

3.01 A distinction of fundamental importance is drawn in the Acts between public and private companies. It is accordingly essential at the outset to understand the nature of the distinction.

A private company to be such must have a share capital and include three provisions in its articles:

(i) the right to transfer shares must be restricted;
(ii) the number of members must not exceed 50; and
(iii) there must be a prohibition on any invitation to the public to subscribe for shares or debentures of the company.[1]

A public company is defined by s 2 of the 1983 Act as being 'a company which is not a private company'. This is the first time that the Acts have defined a public company. The theory which has always been present in companies' legislation is preserved, i.e. that the public company is the basic form of company and that private companies are variants from the norm. In practice, the reverse is the case: there are far more private companies in Ireland than public.

In England, the 1980 Act has brought theory into line with practice: it is now no longer necessary in that jurisdiction for a private company to include the three provisions just referred to in its articles. The basic form of company is now the private company, the public limited company being treated by statute as the exception rather than the rule. It was apparently not thought necessary to go so far in Ireland.

Public companies are almost invariably registered with limited liability. Where they are so registered, they must now be described as 'public limited companies' and the abbreviation 'plc' used instead of the familiar 'Ltd'.

A private company must have at least two members.[2] In the case of a public company the minimum number is seven.[3]

It should be noted that where a private company is in breach of one or more of the relevant provisions in its articles–e.g. where its membership exceeds 50–it does not cease to be a private company. It does, however, forfeit certain of the privileges and exemptions available to a private company.[4]

Where public companies are formed, the company is almost invariably in existence already as a private company. The Acts contain machinery enabling private companies to re-register as public companies.

1. S 33 of the Principal Act. A private company is also now expressly prohibited by s 21 of the 1983 Act from offering its shares or debentures to the public. The company and any officer in default is liable on summary conviction to a fine not exceeding £500 in the event of a breach of the section.
2. S 5 (1) of the Principal Act.
3. Ibid
4. Under s 34 of the Principal Act, the company is treated in such circumstances as though its minimum membership was seven and not two. It also loses the privilege of not having to file its balance sheet and auditor's and directors' reports with its annual return to the Registrar. The court has power under sub-s (2) to relieve the company from such consequences if it is satisfied that the non-compliance with the relevant condition was accidental or due to 'some other sufficient cause'.

3.02 A public company will usually invite the public to subscribe for shares by means of a document called a *prospectus*. This must comply with the strict requirements of the Acts. Moreover, before the company's shares can be quoted or dealt in on the stock exchange, those responsible for the formation of the company must comply with the requirements of that body as set out in the Rules of the Stock Exchange on the *Admission of Securities to Listing*. It is only when those requirements are met that the Council will give permission for the shares to be quoted or dealt in.

3.03 In the case of all companies, public or private, certain steps must be taken before the company comes into being as a legal entity. These are explained in this Chapter. In the case of private companies, the steps to be taken–principally the preparation of the memorandum and articles–are relatively straightforward. But where a private company is re-registered as a public limited company, there are additional requirements to be met. At one time it was sufficient simply to delete the three provisions, already referred to, which are necessary in the case of a private company. Now it is also necessary to ensure that it has the minimum nominal capital required of such companies, that its shares are paid up to a specified extent and that its net assets and share capital are in balance.

It is also possible for a public company to re-register as a private company.

Essential steps in forming a company

3.04 Persons who wish to form a company to be registered under the Acts–the 'promoters'–must first prepare the documents which provide the company with its constitution. These are the *memorandum of association* and the *articles of association*. These documents–together with certain others set out in para 3.06 below–are then lodged with the Registrar with the registration fee.[1] He issues a *certificate of incorporation* when he is satisfied that the documents are in order and that the name chosen for the company is acceptable. The company is thenceforth in existence.

1. The office of the Registrar is in Lower Castle Yard, Dublin Castle.

3.05 The amount of the registration fee is fixed by s 369 of the Principal Act and Part I of the Eighth Schedule to that Act. The Schedule may, however, be altered at any time by the Minister by order[1] and, as so altered, now provides that the fee for the registration of any company is £110.[2]

There must also be paid before the certificate of incorporation is issued the appropriate amount of capital duty. The rate of this duty–which replaced the stamp duty formerly payable on the formation of a company–is fixed by ss 69, 70 and 71 of the Finance Act 1973. Broadly speaking, it is 1% of the actual value of assets of any kind contributed in connection with the subscription for the shares less any liabilities which have been assumed or discharged by the company in consideration of the contribution.

The effect of these provisions is that the minimum amount now payable in respect of fees and duty on the formation of a company limited by shares is £128.50.

1. S 395 (2) of the Principal Act.
2. Companies (Fees) Order 1983 (SI 1983/259).

Documents to be delivered to the Registrar

3.06 Until recently, the only document which had to be delivered to the Registrar when a company was being formed were the memorandum, the articles (if there were any)[1] and a statutory declaration of compliance with the requirements of the Acts as to registration.[2] Since the enactment of the 1982 Act, the Registrar must also be furnished with particulars of the directors' names, addresses, nationalities and occupations, the names and addresses of the secretary or joint secretaries and the location of the registered office of the company.[3]

The documents which must now be delivered when the company is being formed are, accordingly, as follows:

(1)   the memorandum;
(2)   the articles (if any);
(3)   a statutory declaration by the solicitor engaged in the formation of the company or by a person named in the articles as a director or secretary of the company, of compliance with the requirements of the Acts in respect of registration;[4]
(4)   a statement in the prescribed form[5] containing particulars of
    (i)   in the case of the first directors
        (a)   their present and former Christian names and surnames;
        (b)   their usual residential addresses;
        (c)   their nationality, if not Irish;
        (d)   their business occupation, if any; and
        (e)   particulars of any other directorships of bodies incorporated in Ireland held by them.
    (ii)   in the case of the secretary or joint secretaries
        (a)   where he is an individual, his present and former Christian names and surnames and his usual residential address; and
        (b)   where it is a body corporate, the corporate name and registered office.
    (iii)   the situation of the registered office of the company.

1. In the case of companies limited by shares and companies limited by guarantee and not having a share capital, it is not necessary to register articles: see para 3.12 below.
2. S 19 (2) of the Principal Act.
3. S 3 of the 1982 Act.
4. The appropriate form for such a declaration is Form 41A of the Companies (Forms) Order 1983 (SI 1983/289).
5. Form 9B, Companies (Forms) Order 1982 (SI 1982/256).

3.07 The statement must be signed by or on behalf of the subscribers to the memorandum and it must be accompanied by a consent signed by each of the persons named in it as a director, secretary or joint secretary to act in that capacity. If the memorandum is delivered to the Registrar by a person as agent for the subscribers, the statement must so specify and it must also contain the name and address of the person in question.

As soon as the company is incorporated, the persons specified in the statement as directors, secretaries or joint secretaries are deemed to have been appointed to those offices. Any indication in the articles specifying a person as director or secretary is void unless that person is specified as a director or secretary in the statement.[1]

1. S 3 of the 1982 Act.

3.08 The Registrar is expressly precluded from registering a memorandum unless there is delivered with it the statement required by the 1982 Act.[1]

1. S 3 (6) of the 1982 Act.

Official notification

3.09 When a company is incorporated, the company must publish in *Iris Ofigiuil* notice of certain matters. These are specified in Article 4 of the European Communities (Companies) Regulations 1973.[1] These requirements were introduced in compliance with the Second EEC Directive which requires the member states to take steps to ensure that certain essential information concerning companies is easily accessible throughout the community.

The article obliges the company to publish in *Iris Ofigiuil* among other matters notice of the delivery to the Registrar by the company and the issuing by him of the following documents and particulars:

(1) the certificate of incorporation;
(2) the memorandum and articles;
(3) any document making or evidencing an alteration in the memorandum or articles;
(4) every amended text of the memorandum and articles; and
(5) notice of the situation of the registered office and any change therein.

The notice must be published within six weeks of the relevant delivery or issue.

1. SI 1973 163.

3.10 Two important features of this requirement should be noticed. In the first place, the company is not required to publish the *contents* of the various documents in *Iris Ofigiuil:* simply the fact of their having been delivered or issued. In the second place, the failure of the company to publish the relevant notice will not preclude the company from carrying on business. It will, however, mean (under Article 10) that the company will be unable to rely on the relevant documents or particulars as against any other person unless the company proves that the person had knowledge of them.

There is also a curious provision in Article 10 that in the case of transactions taking place within 16 days of the date of publication, the documents and particulars cannot be relied on against a person who proves that it was impossible for him to have knowledge of them. It is far from clear how such a burden of proof could be discharged, since once the publication takes place, it is obviously possible for anyone who reads *Iris Ofigiuil* to have knowledge of the documents. It may be that the provision would only be applicable where the person was abroad at the relevent time or for some other reason unable to obtain a copy of *Iris Ofigiuil*.

It is obviously important for those concerned in the formation of new companies and the alteration of the memorandum and articles of existing companies to ensure that the company has complied with the requirements of Article 4.

Distinction between memorandum and articles

3.11 At one time the constitution of a company was contained in one document, i.e. the deed of settlement. The Joint Stock Companies Act 1856, however, provided for the division of the constitution into two documents, one containing the conditions upon which the company is granted incorporation–the memorandum–and the other setting out the rules under which the company proposes to regulate its affairs (the articles). The distinction has been retained in all subsequent legislation. Because the memorandum contained the fundamental law applicable to the company, the manner in which it could be altered was subject to strict statutory control, which was, however, relaxed with the passage of years, most notably by the Principal Act.[1]

1. See para 4.17 below.

3.12 In the case of a company limited by guarantee and having a share capital and an unlimited company, articles of association must be registered with the memorandum.[1] This is not necessary in the case of a company limited by shares or a company limited by guarantee and not having a share capital; but where no articles are registered in the case of such companies, the model articles contained in Tables A and C of the First Schedule to the Principal Act will be applicable.[2] In practice, articles are almost invariably registered in the case of such companies, although they frequently do no more than adopt the relevant model articles with appropriate amendments. Unlike the memorandum, it has always been possible to amend the articles with comparative ease.[3]

1. S 11 of the Principal Act as amended by s 2 of the 1982 Act.
2. S 13 (2) of the Principal Act as amended by s 14 of the 1982 Act.
3. See para 5.07 below.

Articles are controlled by the memorandum

3.13 As we have seen, the memorandum contains the conditions upon which the company is granted incorporation. It must contain provisions dealing with certain matters–e.g. the name and objects of the company– known as 'the obligatory clauses'.[1] While the company may adopt such articles as it thinks appropriate and amend them from time to time, the articles cannot extend the area of the company's activities as they are defined and circumscribed by the memorandum. The law was thus stated by Carroll J in *Roper v Ward:*[2]

> 'In construing the articles, I am guided by the principle that they are subordinate to and controlled by the memorandum of association which is the dominant instrument. While the articles cannot alter or control the

memorandum or be used to expand the objects of the company, they can
be used to explain it generally or to explain an ambiguity in its terms.'
While, as Carroll J indicated, the articles may be used to explain ambiguities
in the memorandum or to explain it generally, they cannot be used to
interpret any of the obligatory clauses. As Bowen LJ put it in *Guinness v
Land Corpn of Ireland*[3]

'It is ... certain that for anything which the Act of Parliament says shall be
in the memorandum you must look to the memorandum alone. If the
legislature has said that one instrument is to be dominant you cannot turn
to another instrument and read it in order to modify the provisions of the
dominant instrument.'

1. See para 4.01 below.
2. [1981] ILRM 408.
3. (1882) 22 Ch D 349 at 281.

Memorandum and articles are public documents

3.14 The memorandum and articles of association of a company are public
documents. Any person is entitled to inspect them in the Registrar's office
on payment of a small fee.[1] This at one stage could have serious
consequences for persons dealing with the company, since it meant that they
were assumed to be aware of the powers which the company enjoyed and the
objects for which it was created. If the company entered into a contract
which was beyond its powers or outside its objects–in legal terms *ultra
vires*–the company was frequently in a position to repudiate its obligations
because the other party was presumed to be aware of its invalidity. This
principle has, however, been substantially modified in recent times.[2]

1. S 370 of the Principal Act.
2. See Chapter Eleven below.

What kind of company?

3.15 Once it has been decided to form a company, public or private, the
next question for the promoters is whether they will avail of the benefits of
limited liability and, if they do, whether the company should be limited by
shares or guarantee. The advantages of forming a company limited by shares
have already been explained;[1] we now proceed to consider the other types of
company which may be formed.

1. See para 1.03 above.

Companies limited by guarantee

3.16 In the case of a company limited by guarantee, the liability of the
members is limited by the memorandum to the amount which they each
undertake to contribute to the assets of the company in the event of its being
wound up. While the amount which each member undertakes to pay is
normally the same, there is nothing to prevent the memorandum from
stipulating different amounts for different members.[1]

It will be seen that in the case of such companies the members will not be required to provide the company with any cash either on its formation or during the course of its active life. It is accordingly a suitable vehicle for associations which wish to secure the benefits of a separate legal personality and of limited liability but do not require to raise funds from the members. Many charitable and professional bodies find this form of company suitable to their special needs. The management of such companies is normally entrusted by the articles to a council or committee elected by the members rather than a board of directors.

1. Cf Palmer, vol 1 para 3-09.

3.17 A company limited by guarantee may also have a share capital. This, however, is not particularly common. The formation of *public* companies limited by guarantee and having a share capital is now prohibited by s 7 of the 1983 Act.

Unlimited companies

3.18 A company may be formed and registered under the Act which is limited neither by shares nor by guarantee. In such a case, it is known as an unlimited company. Such companies are frequently formed where it is intended that the company will not carry on business. They have proved particularly popular as vehicles for the avoidance of tax, since such schemes frequently involve the transfer of assets from individuals to companies. The company usually holds the property on behalf of the individual whose tax burden is being lightened, with no expectation that it will carry on any business. In such circumstances, the protection of limited liability is not required and is usually not availed of since no capital duty is payable in respect of the formation of such a company.[1]

1. Finance Act 1973 s 67.

Formation of a public limited company

3.19 A public limited company may be formed as an entirely new company. It is, however, far more common for such companies to be formed by converting an existing private company into a public company. At one stage, it was possible to do this by simply passing a special resolution deleting the three provisions which, as we have seen, must be contained in the articles in order to constitute it a private company. The 1983 Act, implementing the Second EEC Directive, now imposes additional requirements intended to ensure that a public limited company has a minimum nominal share capital, that its shares are paid up in money or money's worth to a specified extent and–in the case of a private company being converted into such a company–that its net assets at least equal the total of its called up share capital and undistributable reserves.[1]

Accordingly, where a public limited company is being formed, the amount of the share capital as stated in the memorandum must be not less than the *authorised minimum*. This is fixed by s 19 of the 1983 Act at £30,000, but the Minister has power to increase the amount by order. As we shall see in more detail in Chapter Eight, its allotted share capital must also be paid up in money or money's worth to at least 25 per cent of the nominal value.

1. For the meaning of the expressions 'called up share capital' and 'undistributable reserves' see paras. 13.07 and 31.18 below.

Re-registration of private company as public limited company

3.20 Before a private company can re-register as a public limited company, it must meet the following conditions:
(1) the amount of the nominal share capital must be not less than the authorised minimum;
(2) the allotted share capital must be paid up in money or money's worth to at least 25 per cent of the nominal value; and
(3) its net assets as shown by the balance sheet must at least equal the total of its called up share capital and undistributable reserves.[1]

As we shall also see in more detail in Chapter Eight, while shares may be paid up other than in cash, the 1983 Act requires that such non-cash considerations be properly valued by qualified experts and–where they take the form of undertakings–further requires that the undertaking has been performed or must as a matter of contract be performed within five years. Accordingly, the Act also requires that before a private company is re-registered as a public limited company, such undertakings should have either been performed or their performance be required by contract within five years.

1. S 10(1) and s 9(3)(6) of the 1983 Act.

3.21 We can now consider in detail the steps which must be taken when a private company wishes to re-register as a public limited company.
(1) A special resolution[1] must be passed
  (a) that the company be re-registered as a public limited company;
  (b) that the company's memorandum be altered so that it states that the company is a public limited company and so that it complies with the appropriate form for such a company;[2] and
  (c) that the three provisions in the articles which are necessary to constitute it a private company be deleted.[3]
(2) An application in the prescribed form [4] signed by a director or secretary of the company must be delivered to the Registrar together with the following documents:
  (a) a printed copy of the memorandum and articles as altered in pursuance of the resolution;
  (b) a copy of a written statement by the auditors of the company that in their opinion its balance sheet–which must have been prepared not more than seven months before the date of the application–shows that at its date the amount of the net assets were not less than the aggregate of the called up share capital and undistributable reserves;
  (c) a copy of the balance sheet together with a copy of an unqualified report[5] by the auditors in relation to the balance sheet;
  (d) a statutory declaration in the prescribed form[6] by a director or secretary of the company, stating
    (i) that the special resolution has been passed;
    (ii) that between the balance sheet date and the application there

has been no change in the financial position that has resulted in the net assets becoming less than the aggregate of the called up share capital and the undistributable reserves;

(iii) that the valuation and report mentioned at (3) below have been made and obtained (where they are required) and that the conditions referred to in paragraph 3.20 above have been complied with.[7]

(3) Where shares are allotted by the company between the balance sheet date and the date of the special resolution as fully or partly paid up otherwise than in cash, the consideration must be valued in accordance with s 30 of the 1983 Act,[8] a report with respect to the value must be obtained during the six months preceding the allotment and a copy of the report must accompany the application.[9]

1. For special resolutions see para 25.13 below.
2. Set out in Part I of the Second Schedule to the 1983 Act.
3. S 9 (2) of the 1983 Act.
4. Form 71, Companies (Forms) Order 1983.
5. An unqualified report is one which states 'without material qualification' that the balance sheet complies with the Acts (see Chapter Thirty below) and presents a 'true and fair view' of the company's affairs. A qualification is not 'material' if the auditors state in writing that it is not material for the purpose of determining whether the net assets and share capital are in balance.
6. Form 72, Companies (Forms) Order 1983.
7. S 9(3)(e) of the 1983 Act.
8. See para 8.15 below.
9. S 9 (5) of the 1983 Act.

Formation of unlimited public company

3.22 It is still possible to form an unlimited public company. It is also possible to re-register an unlimited or limited private company as an unlimited public company. If it is already unlimited, this can be achieved by deleting the three provisions in the articles constituting it a private company. If it is limited, the procedure outlined in para 3.26 below for the conversion of limited into unlimited companies must also be followed. In either case, there must be delivered with the application for re-registration a document called *a statement in lieu of a prospectus*.[1]

1. See para 7.18 below.

Re-registration of 'old public limited company'

3.23 A public company limited by shares or guarantee which was in existence prior to the appointed day under the 1983 Act (October 13th 1983) or was incorporated pursuant to an application made before that date (referred to in the Act as 'an old public limited company') may re-register as a public limited company under s 12 of the Act. The procedure is the same as that for the re-registration of a private company. Under sub-s (8), however, an old public limited company is given a period of three years commencing on the appointed day to bring its share capital into conformity with the requirements of the Act. If it does not meet those requirements within that period, re-register as another form of company or wind up voluntarily, it may be wound up by the court.

The 1983 Act also provides (in s 13) that, where an old public limited company fails to re-register as a public limited company within 15 months from the appointed day, the company and any officer who is in default are to be guilty of an offence. The penalty provided is a fine of £250, together with, in the case of a continuing offence, a fine not exceeding £25 per day, but not exceeding £500 in total. No offence is committed where at the expiration of the 15 months period an application under s 12 to be re-registered as another form of company is pending.

It should be noted that failure of the company to re-register within the three year period does not affect its status as a company, so that all transactions entered into by it will remain valid notwithstanding its failure to re-register.

Conversion of public company into private company

3.24 A public company may be converted into a private company by altering its articles so as to add the three restrictions already referred to to the articles. These alterations may be made by special resolution of the company in general meeting. In the case of public limited companies the 1983 Act contains new provisions.

Under s 14 of that Act, the resolution in such a case must alter the memorandum so that it no longer states that the company is to be a public limited company and must make such other alterations in the memorandum as are requisite in the circumstances. There is provision under s 15 for an application to the court for the cancellation of such a resolution. It may be made by the holders of not less than five per cent in nominal value of the company's issued share capital or any class thereof, by not less than five per cent of the members (in the case of a company not limited by shares) or by not less than 50 of the members. No person may make the application who has consented to or voted in favour of the resolution. It must be made to the court within 28 days after the resolution; and the company must give notice of any such application and any order made thereon to the Registrar. The court has power to make an order either cancelling or confirming the resolution and, in addition, may adjourn the proceedings to enable the interests of the dissentient members to be purchased. It may also provide for the purchase by the company of shares of the members, the reduction of the company's capital accordingly and consequential alterations in the memorandum or articles.

Conversion of unlimited company into limited company and vice versa

3.25 An unlimited company may be converted into a company limited by shares or guarantee or both. This is provided for by s 20 of the Principal Act as amended by s 53 of the 1983 Act. A special resolution must first be passed by the company in general meeting that the company should be re-registered as a limited company. The resolution must state

(1) whether the company is to be limited by shares or guarantee; and

(2) if it is to be limited by shares, what the share capital is to be;

and must provide for the making of such alterations in the memorandum and articles as are necessary to bring those documents into conformity with the requirements of the Acts relating to the type of company in question.

An application in writing must then be made to the Registrar,[1] signed by a director or secretary of the company and accompanied by a printed copy of the altered memorandum and articles. The re-registration of a company under the section is not to affect any existing rights or obligations of the company.

Section 54 of the 1983 Act provides that no company is to re-register after October 13th 1983 under s 20 of the Principal Act (which did not contain the requirements as to the passing of a special resolution) except where an application was made before that day.

1. The appropriate form is Form 86, Companies (Forms) Order 1983 (SI 1983/289).

3.26 A limited company may now re-register as an unlimited company, an innovation in our company law which was introduced by s 52 of the 1983 Act. The assent of all the members of the company, is however, required.

The section (which is taken almost word for word from the corresponding s 43 of the English Act of 1967) requires an application in the prescribed form[1] signed by a director or secretary to be made to the Registrar. This must set out such alterations in the memorandum as are required in the case of an unlimited company and the necessary alterations of the articles. It must be accompanied by the following:

(1) An assent in the prescribed form[2] signed by or on behalf of all members;

(2) A statutory declaration by the directors that the persons who have signed the assent constitute the whole membership of the company and that the directors have taken all reasonable steps to satisfy themselves that any person who signed on behalf of a member was empowered to do so;

(3) A printed copy of the altered memorandum; and

(4) A printed copy of the altered articles.

Sub-section (6) provides that past members who are not members at the time of the application for re-registration and who do not become members again are not to be liable to contribute anything more in the event of a winding up than they would have been liable to contribute had the company not been re-registered.

1. Form 85, Companies (Forms) Order 1983.
2. Form 85, Companies (Forms) Order 1983.

3.27 There is no provision in the Acts for the conversion of companies limited by shares into companies limited by guarantee or vice versa; nor for the conversion of companies limited by guarantee and not having a share capital into companies limited by guarantee and having a share capital or vice versa.

Companies incorporated outside Ireland

3.28 The Principal Act also contains certain requirements applicable to companies incorporated outside Ireland which have established places of business within Ireland. All such companies are required to deliver to the Registrar within one month of the establishment of the place of business the following documents:

(1) A certified copy of the charter, statutes or memorandum and articles of the company or other instrument containing its constitution and, if it is not in English or Irish, a certified translation;

(2) A list of directors, containing (in the case of individuals) the Christian names and addresses, nationality (if not Irish), business occupations, particulars of other directorships held in bodies corporate incorporated in Ireland and (in the case of bodies corporate) the corporate name and registered or principal office;

(3) Where an individual is the secretary, his Christian name and surname, any former name or surname and his usual residential address and, where a body corporate is the secretary, its corporate name and registered or principal office;

(4) The names and addresses of one or more persons resident in Ireland authorised to accept service of process on behalf of the company and the address of the company's principal place of business in Ireland.[1]

The Act also requires the delivery within a prescribed time to the Registrar of particulars of alterations in any of the above.[2] There is also provision for the delivery to the Registrar of copies of the balance sheet and profit and loss account and (in the case of a holding company) group accounts in the form in which, if it were a company within the meaning of the Acts, it would have had to lay such documents before the company in general meeting.[3]

Such a company must also state in any prospectus inviting subscriptions for shares and debentures within Ireland the country in which it is incorporated, and must exhibit conspicuously on every place in Ireland where it carries on business and in a legible manner on its various bill heads, letter headings etc. the name of the company and the country in which it is incorporated. If the liability of the members is limited, a statement to that effect must appear in legible characters in any such prospectus, in all such bill heads etc. and on every place where it carries on business.[4]

There is provision for the service of any process or notice on any person whose name has been delivered to the Registrar in compliance with the requirements just mentioned. Where there is no such person in existence or the company has made default in delivering to the Registrar the relevant particulars, any such process or notice may be served by leaving it or sending it by post to any place of business established by the company in Ireland.[5]

There are also provisions in Part XII of the Principal Act setting out certain requirements as to the contents of prospectuses relating to companies incorporated outside Ireland. Chapter Seven below.

1. S 352. As of 31 December 1982 there were 2,387 such companies registered under the Acts. (*Annual Report of the Department of Trade, Commerce and Tourism 1982,* (Pl 1784)).
2. S 353 of the Principal Act.
3. S 354 of the Principal Act.
4. S 355 of the Principal Act.
5. S 356 of the Principal Act.

Companies not formed under the Acts

3.29 Companies formed under the legislation which was replaced by the Principal Act continue to exist despite the repeal of that legislation, and the relevant provisions of the Acts apply to such companies.[1] In addition, the Principal Act enables joint stock companies incorporated before 1862 and companies incorporated under royal charters, letters patent and statute, subject to certain qualifications, to be registered under the Acts[2]

1. Part VIII of the Principal Act.
2. Part IX of the Principal Act.

Chapter 4

The memorandum of association

Essential features of the memorandum

4.01 The memorandum is the fundamental document of the company's constitution and contains the conditions upon which the company is granted incorporation. The name and objects of the company must be stated and, if it is to be a company with limited liability, that fact must also be stated.[1]

The Principal Act provides that in the case of each category of company which may be registered under the Acts the memorandum must be in the form set out in the appropriate table in the First Schedule 'or as near thereto as circumstances admit.' In the case of a company limited by shares, the type most frequently formed, the appropriate form is set out in Table B.[2] (In the case of public limited companies, the appropriate forms are now contained in the Second Schedule to the 1983 Act.) In the case of such a company, the memorandum must contain the following clauses, sometimes referred to as 'the obligatory clauses':

(1) the name clause,
(2) the objects clause,
(3) the limited liability clause,
(4) the capital clause, and
(5) the association clause.

In contrast to English law, there is no requirement that the location of the registered office be stated in the memorandum. But it is now essential to give particulars of its location to the Registrar before the company can be incorporated.[3]

Each of the obligatory clauses is considered in detail below.

1. S 6(1) and (2) of the Principal Act.
2. S 16 of the Principal Act.
3. See para. 3.06 above.

4.02 The memorandum must be subscribed, in the case of a public company, by at least seven persons and, in the case of a private company, by at least two.[1] The signature of each subscriber must be attested by at least one witness. The entire memorandum other than the signatures, must be printed.[2]

1. S 5(1) of the Principal Act.
2. S 7 of the Principal Act.

The name clause

4.03 This clause must state the company's name. In the case of a company limited by shares or by guarantee, the last word of the name must be 'limited' or its Irish equivalent 'teoranta'.[1]

There are important restrictions on the choice of a name for a new company. Under s 21 of the Principal Act, no company may be registered by a name which, in the opinion of the Minister, is undesirable. This will most frequently arise where the name submitted for registration is too like the name of a company already registered.

It should be noted that the power to refuse registration is, in effect, vested in the Minister and not in the Registrar. The latter is not obliged, however, to submit every name proferred for registration to the Minister for approval. It is, accordingly, only where the Registrar himself considers that there is a possibility of the name being undesirable that the Minister's powers come into play. It is therefore important for persons forming a new company to ascertain from the Registrar whether a particular name appears to be available for registration before going through the time-consuming and expensive process of preparing and printing the memorandum and articles.

1. S 6(1) of the Principal Act.

4.04 The Minister has not issued any Practice Note in similar form to the Note formerly published for the guidance of the public in England as to the choice of a name for a company.[1] Clearly registration will not be permitted where the name is too like the name of another company already registered. It is thought, however, that in addition the Minister will usually refuse registration in the following circumstances:

(1) Where the name includes the word 'bank' or cognate words, unless an appropriate licence or exemption has been granted by the Central Bank[2]

(2) Where the name includes the word 'insurance' or cognate words unless an appropriate licence has been granted by the Minister.[3]

(3) Where the name includes the words 'building society'.

It must be remembered that while it is a sensible precaution to ascertain from the Registrar whether a particular name is available for registration, the Registrar cannot give any binding assurance that the company will be registered under the suggested name. It may happen, for example, that by the time the memorandum and articles are prepared and printed, another company will have been registered under the same name or a similar name. To avoid this difficulty, Jenkins recommended that the English legislation should be amended to enable company promoters to reserve a particular name for a short period on payment of a fee.[4] Unfortunately, this practical suggestion has not been adopted here so far.

Section, 21 provides for an appeal to the court against a refusal to register a company by a particular name. This right (which is not conferred by the equivalent English legislation) is rarely availed of in practice, but is a useful safeguard against the use by the Minister of his power in an arbitrary or unreasonable manner.

1. The text of the English Practice Note is in Palmer (22nd edn) Vol. I para 7.12.
2. See para. 1.17 above.
3. See para. 1.18 above.
4. Cmnd 1749, para. 450.

4.05 It may happen that through inadvertence a name may be accepted for registration which is in fact identical with or similar to that of a company already registered. Accordingly, the Principal Act provides that the Minister may within six months after registration compel the company to change its name if the name is too like that by which a company has already been registered. Where a direction is given to this effect by the Minister, the company must comply with it within six weeks from the date of the direction or such longer period as the Minister may allow.[1]

The mere fact that a company has been registered under a particular name without objection from the Minister will not necessarily protect the company if the name in fact closely resembles that of an existing company or business. The company registering under such a name may be liable in proceedings for the tort or civil wrong of 'passing off', i.e. representing a business which is being carried on by another as being carried on by oneself. Similarly, if a company is precluded by contract from using that name, it will in an appropriate case be restrained by injunction from so doing, despite its having been duly registered.

A company may change its name at any time by passing a special resolution to that effect and obtaining the approval in writing of the Minister.[2]

1. S 23(2) of the Principal Act.
2. S 23(1) of the Principal Act.

4.06 A company may carry on business under a name other than its corporate name but must register the name under the Registration of Business Names Act 1963. The following particulars must be registered:

(1) the business name;
(2) the general nature of the business;
(3) the principal place of business;
(4) the name and registered or principal office of the company;
(5) the date of the adoption of the business name.

As in the case of the registration of the company's name, a name cannot be registered which in the opinion of the Minister is undesirable and there is again a right of appeal to the court from the Minister's decision.

4.07 We have seen that the name of a company limited by shares or by guarantee must end with the word 'limited' or 'teoranta'. This reflects a principle of company law which dates from the middle of the nineteenth century that persons who obtain the statutory protection of limited liability must bring the fact that their liability is so limited to the notice of the public. The Principal Act contains provisions intended to ensure that this rule is observed.

In particular the name must be painted up or affixed to the outside of every office or place in which the business of the company is carried on in a conspicuous position in easily legible letters. It must also be engraved in legible characters on the company's seal. It must be mentioned in legible characters in all business letters of the company, all notices and other official publications, all bills of exchange, promissory notes, endorsements, cheques and orders for money or goods purporting to be signed by or on behalf of the company and in all invoices, receipts and letters of credit of the company. In the event of breaches of this requirement, the company and any officer of the company (or any other person acting on its behalf) who is responsible for the breach is liable to fines ranging from £125 to £150.[1]

1. S 114 of the Principal Act as amended by s 15 of the 1982 Act.

4.08 In the case of public limited companies, the 1983 Act contains special provision as to the name. It must end with the words 'public limited company' or 'cuideachta phoibli teoranta' or with their respective abbreviations 'p.l.c' or 'c.p.t'. Neither the words nor the abbreviations may be preceded by the word 'limited' or 'teoranta' or their respective abbreviations 'ltd' or 'teo'.[1]

Section 56 of the Act makes it an offence for any person who is not a public limited company to carry on any trade, profession or business under a name which includes as its last part, the words 'public limited company' or their Irish equivalent or the respective abbreviations. This applies also to an old public limited company, but not until the end of the transitional period of three years within which such companies must either comply with the requirements of the Act as to public limited companies or re-register as private companies:[2] It is also an offence for a public limited company to use a name which may reasonably be expected to give the impression that it is a company other than a public limited company, in circumstances in which the fact that it is a public limited company is likely to be material to any person. This provision does not apply to old public limited companies.

A person guilty of an offence under the section and in the case of a company any officer in default, is liable on summary conviction to a fine not exceeding £500 and, in the case of a continuing offence a fine not exceeding £50 for every day on which the offence is committed, and not exceeding £1,000 in total.

1. S 4 of the 1983 Act.
2. See para 3.23 above.

4.09 In addition to exposing the company and its directors to penalties, the use of the company's name in an incorrect form may also render the director or officer concerned personally liable for a debt of the company.

Section 114(4) of the Principal Act provides that any officer of a company or other person acting on its behalf who signs, or authorises to be signed, on behalf of the company any bill of exchange, promissory note, endorsement, cheque or order for money or goods in which the name of the company is not mentioned as required by the Acts is personally liable to the holder of the bill or cheque or whatever it may be for the amount involved, unless it is paid by the company. The effect of the provision is to make the officer concerned liable as a surety, i.e. he has to pay only if the company defaults.

It is clear that the officer concerned will be liable even though the holder of bill or cheque was not in any way misled by the error. It is also clear that even a minor error may have these consequences. Thus in *Durham Fancy Goods Ltd v. Michael Jackson (Fancy Goods) Ltd.*[1] the plaintiffs in drawing a bill of exchange on the defendant company described it as 'M. Jackson (Fancy Goods) Ltd'. A director of the defendant company accepted the bill on behalf of the company in this form by signing his name to it. It was held that he was prima facie personally liable on the bill under the corresponding English section. Since, however, the plaintiffs had expressly or impliedly represented that they would accept the incorrect form of name, it was also held that they could not rely on the section, an application of the legal doctrine of estoppel.[2]

1. [1968] 2 QB 839.
2. A stricter view has been taken in Scotland of the director's liability: see *Scottish & Newcastle Breweries Ltd v Blair* 1967 SLT 72.

4.10   A private company limited by shares or by guarantee may be granted a licence by the Minister to omit the word 'limited' or 'teoranta' from its name. It must, however, comply with certain requirements before such a licence can be granted i.e.:

(1) its objects must be the promotion of commerce, art, science, religion, charity or any other useful object and the application of its profits or income must be confined to the promotion of its objects;
(2) it must be precluded from distributing any dividend to its members.[1]

Such a licence may be subject to such conditions as the Minister thinks fit. It may also be revoked at any time by the Minister, but he must give notice to the company in advance of his intention to revoke the licence and the company is entitled to be heard in opposition to the revocation.

1. S 24 of the Principal Act as amended by s 58 of the 1983 Act.

The objects clause

4.11   The memorandum must state the objects of the company. The objects are entirely a matter for the promoters: provided they are not unlawful (e.g. the running of illegal lotteries), they may adopt whatever objects they wish.

Once the objects are stated in the memorandum, the company is strictly confined to them. The law confers on the company the power to attain them; but it also restrains the company from travelling beyond them. The statement of objects, in other words, has a positive and a negative effect defined as follows by Lord Cairns LC in the leading case of *Ashbury Railway Carriage and Iron Co Ltd v Riche*:[1]

'It states affirmatively the ambit and extent of vitality and power which by law are given to the corporation, and it states, if it is necessary so to state, negatively, that nothing shall be done beyond that ambit, and that no attempt shall be made to use the corporate life for any other purpose than that which is so specified'

1. (1875) LR 7 HL 653, 670.

4.12   At common law a corporation, unless expressly precluded by its charter or other constitution from doing so, could do any act of which an individual was capable. The reason for confining a company incorporated under the Acts to its stated objects was to protect creditors and investors against the adverse consequences which might result to them from an unauthorised use of the company's assets. The rule caused considerable hardship to persons who dealt with companies, since they were deemed to be aware of the stated objects of the company, the memorandum, as we have seen, being a document open to public inspection. If the transaction was ultra vires – or outside the powers of – a company, the other contracting party was frequently unable to enforce any rights he would otherwise have against the company. Ultimately, the ultra vires rule was modified in its application to such persons by s 8 of the Principal Act and Article 6 of the European Communities (Companies) Regulations 1973.[1] Its effect on such transactions is considered further in Chapter Eleven below.

1. SI 1973/163.

4.13 There is one important qualification to the strict canon of construction referred to in the preceding paragraph. It was held in *Att. Gen. v. Great Eastern Rly*[1] that whatever may fairly be regarded as incidental to or consequential upon those things specified in the memorandum as objects ought not, unless expressly prohibited, to be held by judicial construction to be ultra vires. Thus in the case of companies whose objects entitle them to carry on a particular trade or trades certain powers would normally be implied as incidental or consequential to the stated objects, i.e. power

(1) to employ labour;
(2) to draw and accept bills of exchange (including cheques);
(3) to borrow and give security;
(4) to make contracts for the purchase of supplies;
(5) to open a bank account;
(6) to take and defend legal proceedings and settle them;
(7) to employ agents;
(8) to pay bonuses and pensions to employees.[2]

1. (1880) 5 App Cas 473.
2. Palmer, vol. I, para 9.10.

4.14 While the modification of the strict rule of construction just referred to eased the position of directors and managers of companies, it has nonetheless been standard practice since the rule first evolved for draughtsmen of memoranda to state the objects of the company in huge detail in order to avoid the pitfalls of the rule. Many directors of small newsagency or confectionery businesses would be staggered to find that as a result their solicitors had found it necessary to give them power to construct docks and harbours and promote private acts of parliament.

A further difficulty for the draughtsman was the so-called 'main objects' rule. Where the objects are expressed in a series of numbered paragraphs (as is usually the case) and the first object appears to represent the main object of the company, all the other paragraphs are to be treated as merely ancillary to the main object and as limited and controlled thereby.[1] In order to avoid this rule, it became common practice to insert a paragraph stating that the objects specified in each paragraph of the clause were, except where otherwise expressed in such paragraph, to be 'in nowise limited or restricted by reference to or inference from the terms of any other paragraph or by the name of the company.' It was held by the House of Lords in *Cotman v Brougham*[2] that these words effectively excluded the 'main objects' rule of construction.

It also became common for the objects clause to conclude with the words

'to do all such things as are incidental or conducive to the attainment of the above objects or any of them'.

Such words did no more than declare what the law already was, but a refinement was introduced empowering the company to do anything which 'in the opinion of the directors' could be carried on advantageously in connection with its other objects or incidentally thereto. It has been held in England that these words envisage a subjective test: if the directors honestly believe that a particular act can be advantageously combined with the other objects, it will be authorised by such a clause even if their view proves to be mistaken.[3] Such clauses are now almost invariably used, since they significantly reduce the risk that a transaction will be deemed to be ultra vires.

1. *Re German Date Coffee Co* (1882) 20 Ch D 169 at 188.
2. [1918] AC 514. See also *Anglo-Overseas Agencies v Green* [1961] 1QB 1.
3. *Bell Houses Ltd v City Wall properties Ltd* [1966] 2 QB 656.

Distinction between powers and objects

4.15 The *powers* of a company must be carefully distinguished from its objects. The objects clause, for example, will frequently authorise the company to borrow money; but in the case of most companies this is not an *object* of the company properly speaking but rather a *power* which it requires to achieve its objects. As we have seen, in addition to powers expressly conferred, a company may also enjoy implied powers which it may require to attain its stated objects. But such powers, whether conferred expressly or by implication, may not be used for purposes which are themselves ultra vires or for an object not stated in the memorandum.[1]

1. See further Chapter 11 below.

General principles of law applicable in construing objects clauses

4.16 Whether any act is within the objects and powers of a company is a question of law which depends on the construction to be placed on the relevant clause. In ascertaining the meaning of the clause, the court will seek to discover the intention of the parties, and in so doing will usually be guided by certain well established rules of construction.

These rules may be briefly summarised. The whole document must be read and considered and the court must give effect to the expressed intention. The grammatical and ordinary sense of the words is to be adhered to, unless that would lead to absurdity or inconsistency with the rest of the instrument in which case the grammatical and ordinary sense of the words may be modified so as to avoid that absurdity or inconsistency but no further.[1] Popular words are to be used in their popular sense and technical words in their technical sense, but in each case the prima facie meaning may be modified by the context. The words used must be read with reference to their subject matter. The *ejusdem generis* rule and the maxim *expressio unius est exclusio alterius* may also be applicable.[2]

1. The so-called 'golden rule' of construction laid down in *Grey v Pearson* (1857) 6 HLCas 61 at 106.
2. Palmer, Vol. I, para. 9.29. The *ejusdem generis* rule means that where one has a list of things which can constitute a *genus* or category (i.e. have certain features in common) followed by general words (e.g. 'and other activities'). the general words should normally be construed as referring to other things in the same genus, The *expressio unius* rule means that where the

draughtsman has expressly prescribed a particular mode of dealing with a matter, this excludes any other mode unless it is expressly authorised. See further *Craies on Statute Law*, 7th edn. pp 178/186 and 259/260.

Alteration of objects

4.17 As we have seen, the company's memorandum, unlike its articles, was at one stage, extremely difficult to alter, and prior to the enactment of the Principal Act any alteration invariably required the sanction of the court. Section 10 of the Act, however, enabled a company by special resolution to alter its objects by abandoning, restricting or amending any object or adopting a new object or objects. Unlike the corresponding section in the English Act of 1948, it does not confine the exercise of the power to specific purposes stated in the section.

4.18 There is provision in the section for a dissenting minority to apply to the court to have any such alteration cancelled. The application must be made by the holders of at least 15 per cent of the issued share capital. It must be made within 21 days of the passing of the special resolution, and no member who voted in favour of the resolution can be counted as part of the 15 per cent. On the hearing of the application (which is made by petition) the court may

(1) confirm the alteration and dismiss the petition;
(2) cancel the alteration;
(3) confirm the alteration, subject to conditions; or
(4) adjourn the petition in order that an arrangement may be made to the satisfaction of the court for the purchase of the interests of the dissenting members.

As amended by the 1983 Act, the section enables the court to make an order permitting the purchase of the dissenting members' shares by the company and the consequent reduction of the company' capital.[1]

1. First Schedule, para 3(b) to the 1983 Act.

4.19 A special resolution for the alteration of the objects must be registered with the Registrar within 36 days of its having been passed by the company. If there is no dissenting minority, the company may deliver a printed copy of the memorandum to the Registrar at once. If there is a dissenting minority of the required size but no application is made within the specified time (21 days), the company must deliver the printed copy as altered within 15 days, making in all 36 days. If there is an application by a dissenting minority, the company must at once give notice of the application to the Registrar. It must deliver to the Registrar an office copy of the court order confirming or cancelling the alteration within 15 days of the date of the order. Where the court confirms the alteration with or without conditions, the company must deliver a printed copy of the memorandum as altered within the same period, i.e. 15 days from the date of the court order. The company and its officers are liable to penalties for failure to give these notices or to deliver these documents.

The limited liability clause

4.20 In the case of a company limited by shares or by guarantee, the memorandum must contain a statement that the liability of the members is limited. The appropriate clause is

'the liability of the members is limited'.

The capital clause

4.21   In the case of a company limited by shares, the memorandum must contain a clause stating the amount of the nominal capital,[1] the number of shares into which it is divided and the amount of each share.

The shares in the capital can be, and frequently are, divided into different classes. The most common divisions are between *preference* and *ordinary* shares and *voting* and *non-voting* shares. These will be discussed in more detail in later chapters: for the moment, it is sufficient to note that preference shares confer on the holders certain rights to be paid dividends in priority to other shareholders and certain rights on the winding up of the company. Voting and non-voting shares are usually distinguished by letters, e.g. 'A Ordinary Shares' and 'B Ordinary Shares.' There are additional categories such as *deferred* shares and *founders'* shares.

It is not necessary to specify the division of the share capital into classes in the memorandum (it can be dealt with in the articles) but it is usual to do so. The rights attached to the classes are, however, usually dealt with in the articles.

1. The nominal capital is the value in money of the shares which the company is authorised to issue. See further Chapter 13 below.

4.22   The amount of the nominal capital in the case of a private company is entirely a matter for the promoters: it can be as large or as small as they wish. In fixing the amount of the capital, they have to bear in mind the funds the company will require and the possible necessity to keep some shares in reserve in case the company requires further capital in the future. In the case of a public limited company, the nominal value of the share capital must be at least the authorised minimum (at present £30,000).[1]

1. S 5(2) of the 1983 Act.

The association clause

4.23   The memorandum concludes with a clause in which the subscribers declare that they desire to be formed into a company and agree to take shares. The names and addresses of the subscribers are appended to this in one column, while a corresponding column states the number of shares taken by each of them.

Each subscriber must sign the memorandum in the presence of at least one witness who must attest the signature. He must write opposite his name the number of shares, which he agrees to take, and he must take at least one. In addition to his address, his occupation should also be stated and if he has none there should be a statement to that effect. The witnesses should also state their addresses and occupations. Subscribers cannot attest each other's signatures, but one witness can attest all the signatures.

Alteration of other clauses

4.24   The memorandum, as we have seen, may contain other clauses in addition to the obligatory clauses. Such clauses may be altered in the same manner as the objects of the company, i.e. by special resolution subject to the right of holders of at least 15 per cent. of the issued share capital or any class thereof to object to the alteration within 21 days from the date of the resolution by applying to the court to have the alteration cancelled. This procedure will not, however be applicable if the memorandum itself prohibits the alteration or provides its own procedure for the alteration. Nor can such an alteration take the form of a variation or abrogation of the special rights of any class of members.

As to the alteration of the *name* of the company, see para. 4.05 above;[1] and as to the alteration of the *capital* clause see Chapter 15 below.

1. S 28 of the Principal Act.

Requirements to be observed when memorandum is altered

4.25 Any alteration of the memorandum, whether of the obligatory or additional clauses, must be embodied in the memorandum and the company and its officers are liable to a fine if they issue a copy which does not contain the alterations.[1] All alterations must be notified to the Registrar, and the company is required by virtue of Clause 4 of the European Communities (Companies) Regulations 1973[2] to publish the alteration in *Iris Ofigiuil*.

1. S 30 of the Principal Act.
2. SI 1973/163.

Effect of the memorandum

4.26 Section 25(1) of the Principal Act provides that the memorandum and articles are to have the same effect as if they had been a deed duly signed and sealed by each member and containing covenants on the part of each member to observe all the provisions of the memorandum and articles. The effect of this section is considered in more detail in Chapter Five.

No member of the company is, however, bound by an alteration in the memorandum or articles after the date on which he becomes a member which requires him to take more shares than the number held by him or increases his liability to contribute to the share capital of, or otherwise to pay money to, the company.[1]

1. S 27 of the Principal Act.

Chapter 5

The articles of association

5.01 The articles of association set out the rules for the management of the company's affairs. They deal with such matters as the appointment and removal of directors, the powers to be exercised by them, the holding of meetings of the members and the transfer and transmission of shares. It is also usual to specify in the articles the rights to be attached to the different classes of shares, e.g. ordinary and preference shares.

5.02 A company limited by shares or limited by guarantee and not having a share capital need not register articles of assocation.[1] Where it does not do so, the model forms set out in Table A or Table C will apply.[2] As we have seen,[3] in the case of a private company limited by shares, the articles must contain certain provisions. These provisions are included in Part II of Table A and accordingly that part of the Table will automatically apply in the case of a private company limited by shares which does not register articles. If a company limited by shares does register articles, the Table A regulations will be applicable, except insofar as they are modified or excluded by the articles. This also applies to a company limited by guarantee and not having a share capital, save that the applicable table is Table C.[4] In practice, it is usual for both types of companies to register articles adopting the relevant table with such amendments as are thought appropriate.

In the case of a company limited by shares whose memorandum is in Irish, the appropriate regulations are set out in that language in Tábla A.[5]

In the case of companies limited by guarantee and having a share capital and unlimited companies, the articles must be in accordance with Tables D and E respectively 'or as near thereto as circumstances admit'.[6]

1. S 11 of the Principal Act as amended by s 2 of the 1982 Act.
2. S 13 (2) of the Principal Act as amended by s 14 of the 1982 Act. Tables A and C are set out in the First Schedule to the Principal Act.
3. See para 3.01 above.
4. S 13 (2) of the Principal Act as amended by s 14 of the 1982 Act.
5. S 13 (3) of the Principal Act.
6. S 16 of the Principal Act.

5.03 The articles must be printed, divided into consecutive numbered paragraphs and stamped as if they were a deed. They must be signed by each subscriber to the memorandum in the presence of at least one attesting witness.[1]

1. S 14 of the Principal Act.

Interpretation and enforcement of articles

5.04 The articles of association are regarded by the courts as commercial documents and are to be construed so as to give them 'reasonable business efficacy'. They are not to be interpreted as meticulously as conveyances and other documents of title to property.[1]

1. *Holmes v Keyes* [1959] Ch 199, 215; *Roper v Ward* [1981] ILRM 408.

5.05 Section 25 (1) of the Principal Act provides that the articles, when registered, are to bind the company and the members to the same extent as if they had been signed and sealed by each member and contained covenants by each member to observe all the provisions which they contain. (The same applies to the memorandum).

The articles, accordingly, constitute a contract between each member and the company. The company is entitled to secure the enforcement of the articles by proceedings against the members and to restrain them from committing breaches of the articles. The members also have a corresponding right to sue the company on foot of the articles.[1]

1. *Imperial Hydropathic Hotel Co. Blackpool v Hampson* [1882] 23 Ch D 1 at 13.

5.06 Section 25 (1) also enables members of the company to enforce the rights conferred by the articles on them, as such members, against other members of the company. The authorities differ as to whether this is because the articles constitute a contract between the individual members, but the entitlement of the members to enforce the rights conferred by the articles *inter se* is beyond doubt, at all events when the company is joined as a party.[1]

It must be borne in mind, however, that the rights and duties which can be enforced by or against the members in this manner are those conferred or imposed on them in their capacity *as members*. Rights and duties conferred or imposed on members in some other capacity–e.g. as directors–cannot be so enforced.

Thus, in the leading case of *Eley v Positive Government Security Life Assurance Co.*,[2] the company's solicitor sought to enforce against the company a clause in the articles which restricted the company's right to terminate his employment as their solicitor. Although he was a member of the company, it was held that the proceedings could not be maintained by him, since the clause relied on by him did not confer any rights on him as a member.

But although the articles cannot constitute a contract in respect of such 'outsider rights', as they are sometimes called, the relevant clauses can be treated as having been incorporated, either expressly or by implication, into some other contract. In this manner, the courts have succeeded in modifying what might seem to be a somewhat harsh rule. Thus, where the articles provide that a director is to receive certain remuneration and a person acts in that capacity without any express contract, he will be regarded as having been employed by the company on the terms set out in the articles, this being the presumed intention of the parties.[3] This will be the case whether or not the director is also a member.[4]

It should also be remembered that any contract which can be spelled out from the articles between the company and its members differs significantly from other contracts, since it is always open to the company unilaterally to alter the terms of the contract by amending the articles in the manner permitted by law.

1. *Wood v Odessa Waterworks Co* (1889) 42 Ch D 636 at 642; *Welton v Saffrey* [1897] AC 299 at 315.
2. (1876) 1 Ex D 20, 28.
3. *Swabey v Port Darwin Gold Mining Co* (1889) 1 Meg 385.
4. *Isaac's Case* [1892] 2 Ch 158.

Alteration of articles

5.07 The articles of association may be altered or added to by means of a special resolution[1] 'subject to the provisions of (the Acts) and to the conditions contained in (the) memorandum.' Any alteration or addition so made is (subject again to the provisions of the Acts) as valid as if it had been contained in the articles and is subject to alteration in the same way.[2]

1. A special resolution must be carried by a majority of three fourths of the members entitled to vote who vote at a meeting. At least twenty one days' notice of the intention to propose it must be given. See para 25.13 below.
2. S 15 of the Principal Act.

5.08 Accordingly, provided the alteration or addition is not rendered invalid by some provision in the Acts or in its own memorandum, the company is at liberty to alter or add to its articles as it thinks fit by means of a special resolution. But this general principle is subject to one important qualification: the power thus given must be exercised by the members *in good faith for the benefit of the company as a whole*.[1]

While the words italicised represent the law on this matter, some difficulty has been encountered by the courts in defining the criteria by which the validity of an impugned alteration should be determined. The words 'in good faith' indicate that the test is a subjective one: in other words, if a sufficient majority of the members honestly believe that a particular alteration is in the interests of the company as a whole, it does not matter whether the court takes the same view. In the words of Scrutton LJ in *Shuttleworth v Cox Bros & Co*. 'it is not the business of the court to manage the affairs of the company. That is a matter for the shareholders and directors'.[2] If, however, there is no reasonable ground for deciding that the proposed alteration is for the benefit of the company, this of itself may be sufficient evidence of a lack of good faith.[3]

Applying these principles, alterations of articles have been upheld although their effect was detrimental to individual members of the company. Thus in *Greenehalgh v Arderne Cinemas Ltd*[4] a minority shareholder claimed that an alteration which enabled the majority to sell their shares to outsiders without first offering them to existing shareholders (which they were obliged to do under the original articles) was invalid. The interests of the minority were, it was said, being sacrificed to those of the majority. The Court of Appeal agreed with the trial judge that the plaintiff's case could not succeed. However, Lord Evershed MR seems to have regarded the test as more in the nature of an objective one. Observing that the phrase 'for the benefit of the company as a whole' did not refer to the company 'as a commercial entity' but to the members as a general body, he went on:

'the case may be taken of an individual hypothetical member and it may be asked whether what is proposed is, in the honest opinion of those who voted in its favour, for that person's benefit.'[5]

Applying that test, it was held that the alteration was valid.

Lord Evershed's test may be criticised as begging the question. Whether the alteration is seen as being for the benefit of the 'individual hypothetical member' may depend on whether that member is one of the majority who approve the alteration and presumably see it as for their benefit or the minority who see it as to their detriment. The position has been rendered even less clear in England by the decision in *Clemens v Clemens Bros Ltd.*[6] That case appears to suggest that a decision of the majority may be set aside where it is detrimental to the interest of the minority if such a result would be 'equitable'; and that although the decision was taken in good faith in what were thought by the majority to be the interests of the company as a whole, including the minority.

It is thought that the latter decision goes too far and would not be followed in Ireland. If, however, the effect of the alteration is to *discriminate* between the majority supporting the alteration and a dissenting minority so as to give the former an advantage of which the latter are deprived, it seems clear that it will be invalid.[7] Moreover, if it is oppressive or a fraud on the minority, this of itself will be evidence of bad faith which will render the alteration invalid.[8]

1. *Allen v Gold Reefs of West Africa Ltd* [1900] 1 Ch 656 at 671.
2. [1927] 2 KB 9 at 23.
3. Ibid.
4. [1951] Ch 286.
5. Ibid at 291.
6. [1976] 2 All ER 268.
7. Cf Gore-Brown, 4–8; Gower, p 627.
8. *Shuttleworth v Cox Bros Ltd,* per Bankes LJ at p 18.

5.09 It must also be remembered that a proposal by the majority to alter the articles, although valid in law, may nonetheless enable the minority to obtain relief from the courts under s 205 of the Principal Act on the ground that the affairs of the company are being conducted in disregard of their interests.[1] In addition, when the alteration involves the variation of rights attached to classes of shares, an application may be made to the court under s 78 of the Principal Act by not less than 10 per cent of the holders of the issued shares in that class for the variation to be cancelled.[2]

1. See para 26.11 et seq below.
2. See para 16.10 below.

Company cannot bind itself not to alter articles

5.10 Subject to the principles explained in the preceding paragraphs, a company has an unfettered right to alter its articles conferred by statute, and it cannot deprive itself by contract of that right.[1] If by altering its articles it commits a breach of contract, that will clearly render the company liable to damages. It is thought, however, that the company cannot be restrained by injunction from committing a breach of contract by altering its articles and that the remedy of the injured party is in damages only. The decision to the contrary in *British Murac Syndicate Ltd v Alperton Rubber Co Ltd*[2] proceeds on the assumption that an earlier decision of *Punt v Symons & Co Ltd*[3] (where it was held that no action for a declaration lay in such circumstances) had been overruled by the Court of Appeal in *Bailey v British Equitable Assurance* Co.[4] That assumption, however, may not be correct.[5] But it would seem that the company may be restrained from *acting on foot of* the articles as so altered, if to do so would constitute a breach of contract. An *obiter dictum* to the contrary of Lord Porter in *Southern Foundries (1926) Ltd v Shirlaw*[6] is not supported by authority.[7]

1. *Allen v Gold Reefs of West Africa* [1900] 1 Ch 656 at 673.
2. [1915] 2 Ch 186.
3. [1903] 2 Ch 506.
4. [1904] 1 Ch 374.
5. Cf Buckley, vol 1, pp 47–8.
6. [1940] AC 701 at 740.
7. See also Gower, pp 558/9.

Other features of alterations

5.11 An alteration may be lawful, although it affects members' rights retrospectively, e.g. by giving the company a lien on the shares of members for debts incurred before the alteration.[1]

The articles may include a provision that they can only be altered or added to with the consent of a named person. This is a somewhat meaningless provision, however, since the article giving such a veto can itself be removed by means of a special resolution.

Allen v Gold Reefs of West Africa above.

Chapter 6

The promoters

6.01 Those who bring about the formation of a company are known as 'the promoters'. It is important to appreciate that the expression has this wide significance for lawyers, because to the layman the expression 'company promoter' probably suggests a professional financier of some sort (not infrequently with unsavoury overtones). But although it applies to those who organise a massive public flotation, it equally applies to the small shopkeeper who decides to convert his business into a limited liability company. The relatively wide meaning given by the law to the expression must be stressed, because the law treats promoters as having certain obligations to the companies which they bring into being and gives corresponding rights to the companies.

6.02 A promoter is, therefore,
> 'one who undertakes to form a company with reference to a given project, and to set it going and who takes the necessary steps to accomplish that purpose'.[1]

Thus, to take the commonest form of company promotion in Ireland, a person running a business may decide at some stage to convert it into a limited liability company. With this in mind he will normally instruct an accountant or solicitor to take the steps set out in the succeeding chapters. One of the objects of the company, as set out in the memorandum, will be
> 'to acquire the business now being carried on by A B as a going concern and for that purpose to enter into an agreement in the terms of a draft already prepared and for the purpose of identification signed by the said A B'.

A B is the promoter of the company and so also is any person who assists him in the operation. But it should be noted that the accountant or solicitor will not be treated as a promoter simply because he has prepared the necessary documents or valuations.[2] If, however, he goes further than this as, for example, by finding someone else to invest in the company, he may well be treated as a promoter.[3]

1. Per Cockburn CJ in *Twycross v Grant* (1877) 2 CPD 469 at 541.
2. *Re Great Wheel Polgooth Ltd* (1883) 53 LJ Ch 42.
3. *Bagnall v Carlton* (1877) 6 Ch D 371.

Duties of promoters

6.03 Where the company is formed as a 'one man company', i.e. where virtually all the shares are owned by the promoter and he also nominates the directors, the duties owed by the promoter are of little importance. Where there are other investors–and most importantly of all where the public is invited to subscribe–his duties are of more significance. It cannot be said that in Ireland the topic is of great practical importance, however, and its treatment here is correspondingly abridged.

6.04 The promoters of the company stand in a *fiduciary* position towards the company.[1] This means that the law regards promoters as being bound by certain obligations of trust which are not applicable to persons engaged in ordinary commercial dealings. It means that they may have to *disclose* certain matters which in an ordinary business context they would be free to keep secret; and it also means that they may have to *account* to the company for certain profits which in such a context they would be free to retain.[2]

One of the most obvious examples of this fiduciary position of promoters arises in the purchase and sale of property by a promoter. The promoter may buy a property expressly as a trustee for the company which he is forming or helping to form: in that case, he must disclose any profit he is making on the sale to the company and, if required, pay over the profit to the company. Even where the purchase is not made expressly as trustee for the company, he will still be under a duty to disclose any profit on the resale, if he originally bought the property with the formation of the company in mind.[3] It would seem however, that he cannot be required to *pay over* the profit to the company unless his intention was to buy *on behalf of* the company, rather than on his own behalf with the object of reselling to the company.[4]

1. *Erlanger v New Sombrero Phosphate Co* (1878) 3 App Cas 1218 at 1236 per Lord Cairns LC.
2. *Emma Silver Mining Co v Grant* (1879) 11 Ch D 918.
3. *Gluckstein v Barnes* [1900] AC 240.
4. *Omnium Electric Co v Barnes* [1914] 1 Ch 332 at 347.

6.05 The duty of disclosure is not fulfilled by telling the facts to people who are in theory in positions of control in the company, such as directors, but who are merely the instruments of the promoters. The disclosure must be made either to a board of directors which is genuinely independent or to all the members of the company.

This principle was laid down by the House of Lords in the well known case of *Gluckstein v Barnes*.[1] There the promoters had formed a syndicate for the purpose of buying and reselling Olympia, the exhibition centre in London. They bought the freehold of the property for £140,000 and then promoted a company to whom they agreed to sell the freehold for £180,000. They disclosed the profit of £40,000 to the public who were invited to subscribe: what they did not disclose was that they had also bought debentures in the company which originally owned the property at prices below par and that these were being paid off by the liquidator of that company at par out of the £140,000. As a result they were making an additional profit of £20,000 but this was disclosed only to the initial members of the company who were all part of the original syndicate. It was held that this could not possibly be regarded as a genuine disclosure to the company.

The case also illustrates another proposition: that a partial disclosure of the facts can sometimes be worse than no disclosure.

1. [1900] AC 240. It had been previously held in *Erlanger's case* that the disclosure had to be to an independent board of directors. *Gluckstein's case* made it clear, however, that disclosure to all the members of the company would suffice.

Remedies for breach of duty by promoters

6.06 Where the breach of duty on the part of the promoters has resulted in a secret profit, the remedy of the company will normally be an action for damages. In some circumstances, however, the company will be entitled to *rescission* of the contract. This is the remedy provided by the law to put the parties to the contract back in the same position as they would have been in if no contract had been entered into. But a contract will not be rescinded by the court unless the parties can be restored to that position. In the words of Lord Blackburn in *Erlanger v New Sombrero Phosphate Co.*

'It is, I think, clear on principles of general justice, that as a condition of a rescission there must be a *restitutio in integrum*. The parties must be put in *statu quo* ...'[1]

Even where the parties cannot be restored precisely to the state they were in before the contract, however, rescission may be possible if the result can be regarded as 'practically just'.[2] For example, rescission may require the return of the property by one contracting party to another and the fact that the property has deteriorated in value may not be an obstacle to rescission where the result could be regarded as equitable in the circumstances. This will be particularly the case where the party who will suffer the consequences of the depreciation in value has been guilty of fraud.

The principle is well illustrated by the decision in *Armstrong v Jackson,*[3] which was not a case involving company promoters, but indicates the approach the courts have tended to adopt in such cases. The plaintiff engaged the defendant stockbroker to buy 600 shares in a company. The defendant fraudulently concealed from the plaintiff the fact that he was the owner of the shares.[4] Even though the shares had dropped substantially in value, rescission was ordered of the contract.

But such a result will not be possible where the rights of innocent third parties will be affected or where no 'practically just' result can be achieved by rescission. The difficulties which may flow from rescission, even in the case of fraud, are clearly illustrated by a celebrated Irish case in recent times.

In *Northerm Bank Finance Corporation v Charlton and Ors*[5] the defendants, GC, HC and GS and two parties who were not defendants, PQ and VD, wished to acquire control of a public company named J. & G. Mooney & Co. Ltd, which owned a well known chain of public houses. The plaintiff bank, who were their advisers, recommended that for this purpose they should form a holding company, PQ Holdings Ltd. The bank agreed to act as the agents of the promoters and to advance the major portion of the money required for the purchase of the shares. They stipulated, however, that the promoters were to provide £500,000 which was to be used before the money advanced by the bank was used. The sum to be provided by each promoter was agreed and it was also agreed that each contribution was to be deposited in the bank and maintained at the agreed figure until the bid for the shares in Mooneys either succeeded or failed.

The promoters duly formed PQ Holdings Ltd and its issued share capital was allotted to them. The bank advanced £1.3 million to PQ Holdings Ltd on security provided by the promoters and the company. The defendants deposited their agreed contribution with the bank and the purchase of the Mooney shares began. Unknown to the defendants, however, PQ had withdrawn three-quarters of his contribution. During the course of the acquisition the other promoters and the bank decided that it would be desirable that PQ should cease to be associated with PQ Holdings Ltd and the defendants purchased his share with the aid of £50,000 advanced by the bank. The trial judge (Finlay P.) found as a fact that the defendants were informed, by one of the bank's officials before this advance was made, that PQ was not substantially indebted to the bank, contrary to the fact. The whole venture collapsed when the stock exchange refused a requotation of the Mooney shares; and the bank ultimately sued the defendants for interest on the money advanced. The defendants, who had become aware for the first time that PQ had withdrawn threequarters of his contribution without their having been informed, counter-claimed for fraudulent misrepresentation and this was treated as a claim for rescission.

In the High Court, Finlay P, held that the bank had been guilty of fraudulent misrepresentation through one of their officials and ordered the rescission of the agreement between the bank and the defendants by the repayment to the defendants of the various sums deposited with the bank and the transfer to the bank of the shares in Mooneys and PQ Holdings Ltd. On an appeal to the Supreme Court, that court declined to interfere with the trial judge's findings of fact in judgments which now provide the *locus classicus* for the appellate jurisdiction of the Supreme Court in relation to findings of fact. By a majority of three to two, however, they also decided that rescission should not have been granted, since *restitutio in integrum* was not possible, and ordered a retrial on the issue of damages. The majority took the view that the transfer of the shares in Mooneys and PQ Holdings to the bank, far from effecting *restitutio in integrum*, radically altered the *status quo ante*, since the bank had never owned the shares.

The defendants relied on the decision in *Armstrong v Jackson* but this was distinguished by Henchy J. on the ground that in that case the broker had been the owner of the shares and accordingly *restitutio in integrum* was possible. In Charlton's case the bank had never been the owner of the shares and had never acted other than as agent for the promoters. Accordingly, the only remedy available to the defendants was damages for fraudulent misrepresentation by the bank as agent-advisers.

Charlton's case was, of course, a case in which the fraud relied on was not that of the promoters, but of agents and advisers on whom the promoters relied. But it is thought that the principles referred to by the majority, which are derived from the law of contract generally and are not peculiar to company law, would also apply in a case where the fraud was that of the promoters.

1. (1878) 3 App Cas 1218 at 1278.
2. *Ibid: Spence v Crawford* [1939] 3 All ER 271.
3. [1917] 2 KB 822.
4. Fraudulently, because as the plaintiff's agent he owed him a duty to disclose any interest he had in the shares.
5. (1979) IR 149.

Remuneration of promoters: pre-incorporation contracts

6.07 A company cannot enter into a contract before it is formed. Accordingly, a promoter who expects to obtain a reward for his services has to take the risk that the company will not pay him when it does come into existence.

It was also the law at one time that a company could not even *ratify* a contract entered into on its behalf before it was formed. Thus, even if the promoter could obtain the assent of the company to the agreement to pay him for his services, the agreement was still unenforceable. The law was, however, amended in Ireland by s 37 of the Principal Act, which implemented a recommendation to that effect by Jenkins. (The recommendation has never been implemented in England). The section provides

'(1) Any contract or other transaction purporting to be entered into by a company prior to its formation or by any person on behalf of the company prior to its formation may be ratified by the company after its formation and thereupon the company shall become bound by it and entitled to the benefit thereof as if it had been in existence at the date of such contract or other transaction and had been a party thereto.

(2) Prior to ratification by the company, the person or persons who purported to act in the name or on behalf of the company shall in the absence of express agreement to the contrary be personally bound by the contract or other transaction and entitled to the benefit thereof.

(3) This section shall not apply to a company incorporated before [1 April 1964]'.

It will be seen that in addition to enabling the company to ratify contracts entered into before its formation (sometimes called 'pre-incorporation contracts') the section also makes it clear that unless and until such a contract is so ratified, the contracting parties remain personally liable. It is, accordingly, open to the promoter to sue the person who promised him remuneration where that person has acted on behalf of the company and has not expressly stipulated that he is not to be personally liable.

6.08 The remuneration of the promoter may take various forms. He may simply sell on a business or a particular property to the company at a profit. Or the business or property may be sold directly by its owners to the new company and the promoter may receive a commission from the owners. Another method is for the promoters to ensure that part of the share capital takes the form of *founders' shares* entitling the holders to be paid dividends in priority to other shareholders. The promoters may also be relieved of their liability to pay for such shares in cash: they can be credited as having been fully paid up in consideration of the rendering of services by the promoter to the company. Lastly, the promoters may be given an option to subscribe for unissued shares at par, i.e. at their nominal value, within a specified time, such as a year, from the formation of the company. Since the shares may well rise in value during that time, this will often represent a valuable option to a promoter.

Chapter 7

Flotation of a company

7.01 A company is said to be 'floated' when its shares are offered for sale either to the public at large or to clients of an 'issuing house', i.e. a merchant bank or similar financial institution specialising in this business. The operation is described as the 'flotation' of the company. As we have seen, a private company cannot invite the public to subscribe for shares or debentures in the company. Accordingly, a flotation will usually take place only when a company is formed as a public company or an existing private company is re-registered as a public company.

7.02 As has been frequently stressed in this book, the majority of companies formed in Ireland are private companies. The total number of public companies on the register has never exceeded 375,[1] a miniscule figure compared to the number of public companies in the United Kingdom at the corresponding times. Such businesses as have been floated as public companies have tended on the whole to start life as family concerns. They are generally formed as private companies, and the decision to float the company is normally taken when the family is no longer able to provide the capital needed for expansion from their own resources or are advised that it would be imprudent to do so for tax reasons.

Although flotations in Ireland are relatively infrequent, a knowledge of the basic legal requirements is essential for both the student and the practitioner. Both should remember, however, that because of the lesser significance of the topic in Ireland, the treatment of it in this book is substantially less detailed than in the leading English text books. As the requirements in English law are broadly similar, those works may be consulted without any serious risk of confusion.

1. See para 2.18 above.

Types of flotation

7.03 A company can be floated in a number of different ways:

(1) The company may make a *direct offer* to the public, i.e. the public may be invited to subscribe for shares directly by the publication of a prospectus. This method is not often employed today.

(2) The company may make an *offer for sale*. In this case, the entire issue is sold to an issuing house who then offer the shares to the public by the publication of a prospectus. The major advantage of this procedure, as contrasted with a direct offer, is that the issuing house agrees to take the

whole issue even though it may not be fully subscribed: in other words they underwrite the issue.

(3) The company may decide not to offer the shares for sale to the public at large either directly or by an offer for sale through an issuing house. Instead they may allot the shares to an issuing house who *place* them with their clients. The placing is usually done in large blocks and the issuing house may either purchase the shares themselves and then sell them to individual clients or simply arrange beforehand to place the shares with the clients. Placing of shares in this manner has become particularly common in modern conditions, where potential sources of new capital will often be 'institutional investors' such as insurance companies, pension funds etc. A company wishing to raise new capital other than by borrowing may be advised to seek the necessary finance from such large investors rather than adopt the more hazardous procedure of inviting the public at large to subscribe.

(4) The company may decide to offer the shares by *tender*. If any of the methods already mentioned are employed, the shares will all be offered at the same price. This may enable speculators to make an easy profit by 'stagging', i.e. applying for shares and disposing of them immediately if they rise in value. To avoid this, shares are sometimes offered by tender: a minimum price is fixed below which the shares will not be allotted and bids are invited. The shares will then normally be allotted to the highest bidders.

(5) The company may make a *rights issue*. This only arises where there has already been a flotation. The company may wish to raise fresh capital and rather than make a new offer of shares, either to the public at large or by means of a placing, it may decide to raise the necessary funds by allotting shares to the existing shareholders. They are given the right to apply for a given number of new shares in proportion to their existing holdings.

A rights issue should be carefully distinguished from an issue of *bonus shares* which is essentially a method of distributing profits which have hitherto been undistributed by increasing the nominal amount of the issued share captial. In the case of an issue of bonus shares, no new funds are raised for the company. By contrast, the whole purpose of a rights issue is to raise new funds. In order to make the issue more attractive to the shareholders, the shares are offered to them on better terms than would be case if they were being offered to the public, and there is consequently an element of 'bonus' in a rights issue, which leads to the shares being sometimes rather misleadingly described as bonus shares.

Legal controls on flotations

7.04 Although one of the major objects of the new companies' legislation in mid-nineteenth century England was to protect the public against unscrupulous promoters. it soon became apparent that it was not adequate for that purpose. The celebrated and much criticised decision of the House of Lords in *Derry v Peek*[1] that directors were not liable for misleading statements in company prospectuses unless they were shown to be fraudulent seemed to place a premium on careless and irresponsible publicity. It led to the enactment of the Directors' Liability Act 1890 which was ultimately replaced by s 49 of the Principal Act. This entitles persons who have suffered loss and damage as a result of any untrue statement in a prospectus to recover compensation from persons connected with the issue, such as the directors at the time the prospectus is issued and the promoters.

1. (1889) 14 App Cas 337.

7.05 The Principal Act also contains detailed provisions designed to ensure that prospectuses of companies offering shares for subscription by the public contain adequate information about the company's business and are not misleading. In particular, there are requirements as to the publication of information relating to the company's financial commitments, 'material' contracts entered into by the company within the period of five years before the issue of the prospectus and reports by the company's auditors. There are also requirements as to statements by experts–such as geologists in the case of a mining company or valuers in the case of property–which may be included in the prospectus. These provisions are contained in ss 44 to 52 inclusive and in the Third Schedule.

7.06 Traditionally the marketing of shares and debentures in public companies has been done by securing a 'quotation' for them on a recognised stock exchange. The largest and most celebrated such exchange in these islands is, of course, the London Stock Exchange, but stock exchanges were also established in Dublin, Cork and Belfast. That in Dublin was established in 1799 by 39 Geo. III c.40 ('An Act for the Better Regulation of Stockbrokers') which remains on the statute book to this day. In 1965, a federation of stock exchanges in the United Kingdom and the Republic of Ireland was formed, and ultimately all the stock exchanges in the two islands were merged in 1973 in the Stock Exchange of the United Kingdom and the Republic of Ireland.

In addition to complying with the requirements of the Acts, a flotation must also comply in practice with the requirements of the stock exchange. It is in theory possible to invite the public to subscribe for shares or debentures without seeking stock exchange approval, but in practice this is not feasible. Unless the shares are admitted to that body's list of securities and quoted on the exchange they will have little attraction for the investor. Moreover, where an offer is made or a placing effected with the assistance of an issuing house, they will insist on the exchange's requirements being met so far as they are applicable. These requirements have become progressively more stringent in recent years: and more recently still the stock exchange's minimum requirements have been given the force of law by the European Communities (Stock Exchange) Regulations 1984.[1] which implement in Ireland three of the EEC Directives.[2]

1. SI 1984/282. The Regulations, which were made by the Minister under s 3 of the European
    Communities Act 1972, came into force on January 1 1985.
2. See para 2.23 above.

7.07 The first of the three directives (The *Admissions Directive*) sets out the conditions which must be met before shares or debentures may be admitted to the official stock exchange listing. The Committee of the Irish Unit of the Stock Exchange (referred to in the Regulations as 'the Irish Stock Exchange') is established as the 'competent authority' for deciding on the admission of securities to listing.

The second directive (the *Listing Particulars Directive*) requires the member states to ensure that the admission of shares or debentures to the official listing is conditional upon the publication of an information sheet, called in the directive and the Regulations the *Listing Particulars*. The Directive sets out detailed requirements as to the information which must be given in the listing particulars and again the Irish Stock Exchange is designated as the competent authority for ensuring that these requirements are met and for permitting exemptions from the requirements in certain areas.

The third directive (the *Interim Reports Directive*) requires information to be published on a regular basis by companies the shares of which have been admitted to an official stock exchange listing. Again the competent authority for ensuring that these requirements are met or for adapting them to the circumstances of particular companies is the Irish Stock Exchange.

7.08 Article 12(3) of the Regulations provides that where the applicaton form for shares in or debentures of a company contains the listing particulars approved of by the stock exchange or indicates where they can be obtained or inspected, most of the provisions of the Principal Act already referred to as to the information which must be contained in a prospectus are not to apply.

7.09 The Admissions Directive stipulates that companies must be of a specified minimum size before they are admitted to official listing. It also permits the member states, however, to provide for admission to listing when that condition is not fulfilled, if the competent authorities are satisfied that there will be an adequate market for the shares concerned. In Ireland, the relevant regulations–the *Regulations of the Stock Exchange for the Admission of Securities to Listing*–include requirements that the company should have a minimum market value of £700,000 and that at least 25 per cent. of the equity capital should already be in the hands of the public.

7.10 Article 4.1 of the Listing Particulars Directive requires the particulars to contain

'the information which, according to the particular nature of the issuer and of the securities for the admission of which application is being made, is necessary to enable investors and their investment advisers to make an informed assessment of the assets and liabilities, financial position, profits and losses, and prospects of the issuer and of the rights attaching to such securities.'

By virtue of Article 4(1) of the 1984 Regulations, this obligation is imposed on the persons responsible for preparing the particulars and their solicitors. In addition to this general requirement, there are detailed provisions (contained in the Schedules to the Directive) as to the specific information which the particulars must give. Apart from full details as to the issue of shares and the manner in which it is being financed or underwritten, information must also be given as to the ownership of the company, its borrowings and the activities which it carries on.

It should also be noted that under Article 5.1 of the Admissions Directive, the Irish Stock Exchange may make the admission of securities to official listing subject to more stringent conditions than those set out in the Directive. Accordingly, the current regulations of the stock exchange for the admission of securities to listing must always be consulted when a flotation is being contemplated.

7.11 It will be seen that the Listing Particulars Directive and the stock exchange regulations are now the instruments which must be referred to when a company is being floated, rather than the Third Schedule to the Principal Act. One provision of the Act, however, remains applicable: where the listing particulars contain a statement by an expert–e.g. a geologist's report in the case of a mining company–the particulars must not be issued unless the expert has given his consent to their issue with the statement included in the form and context in which it is included. The expert must not have withdrawn his consent before a copy of the particulars is delivered for registration.

7.12 A copy of the listing particulars must be delivered for registration with the Registrar before the date of publication. The issuer and every person who is knowingly party to their publication without their having been so registered is guilty of an offence and liable on summary conviction to a fine not exceeding £1,000.

7.13 The 1984 Regulations provide for an appeal to the High Court from a decision by the Irish Stock Exchange to reject an application for admission to official listing or the discontinuance by the exchange of a listing. The High Court may set aside the decision of the stock exchange where it is satisfied that the procedures laid down by the Regulations and the directives have not been complied with in any material respect. The matter is then remitted to the stock exchange for reconsideration.

The unlisted securities market

7.14 With a view to encouraging small businesses to seek capital from the public, the stock exchange has in recent years created a special market in unlisted securities known as the *Unlisted Securities Market*, or USM for short. This has several advantages for a company whose capital requirements are small when compared with those which normally seek a stock exchange quotation and hence has proved particularly attractive to some Irish entrepeneurs. The USM is not subject to the requirements of the 1984 Regulations and the Directives, but is subject to the relevant provisions of the stock exchange regulations governing the USM.

Civil liability for misleading statements made in connection with flotations

7.15 As we have seen, s 49 of the Principal Act entitled persons who suffer loss and damage as result of any untrue statement in a prospectus to recover compensation from persons connected with the issue. This section remains in force and applies to untrue statements in listing particulars (which are deemed to be a prospectus by Article 12 of the 1984 Regulations) made by the following:

(a) the directors at the time the particulars were issued;
(b) any person who has authorised himself to be named and who is named in the particulars as a director or as having agreed to become a director;
(c) the promoters and
(d) anyone who has authorised the issue of the particulars.

They are relieved of liability in certain specified circumstances. If the person concerned can prove that he

(a) has withdrawn his consent to becoming a director before the particulars are issued and has not authorised their issue;
(b) has given reasonable notice that they were issued without his knowledge or consent where that is the case; or
(c) withdraws his consent after the issue of the particulars on becoming aware of any untrue statement in them and gives reasonable public notice of the withdrawal and of the reason thereafter

he will not be liable in damages.

The person concerned will also be relieved of liability where he can prove that he had reasonable grounds for believing the statement to be true and did in fact believe it to be true up to the time of allotment. In the case of a statement by an expert or a copy or extract from a report or valuation of an expert,[1] he must be able to prove that what was in the particulars fairly represented the statement or was a correct and fair copy of an extract from the report or valuation; and that he had reasonable grounds for believing and did in fact believe up to the issue of the particulars that the person making the statement was competent to make it. He must also be able to prove that the expert had given the consent required by the Act and had not withdrawn it before delivery of the particulars for registration or (to his knowledge) before allotment. Where the statement purports to be a statement made by an official person or contained in what purports to be a copy or extract from a public official document, he must prove that the statement was a correct and fair representation of the statement or copy or extract from the document.

1. See para 7.11 above.

7.16 It will be seen that the section places the onus of proof on the directors or promoters where the statement is shown to be untrue. In general terms, they must be able to establish that they did not authorise the misstatement or that they had reasonable grounds for believing it to be true.

The measure of compensation is the difference between the actual value of the shares (not exceeding the price paid) and the value they would have had if the statement in question had been true. The limitation period for issuing proceedings making a claim under the section is six years from the date on which the cause of action arises, i.e. the date on which the shares were allotted to the plaintiff.[1] In the case of fraud the period begins to run from the time when the fraud was, or might with reasonable diligence, have been discovered.[2]

1. Statute of Limitations 1957, s 11.
2. Ibid, s 71(1).

7.17 In addition to the statutory remedy under s 49, an action for damages for a negligent misstatement in a prospectus has been maintainable since the decision of the House of Lords in *Hedley Byrne & Co. Ltd v Heller & Partners Ltd* in 1964.[1] which has also been applied in Ireland.[2]

A person entitled to compensation under the Principal Act or damages at common law in respect of untrue statements in listing particulars is not necessarily entitled to *rescission* of the contract of allotment, i.e. he may not be entitled to have his name removed from the register and be repaid the money which he had subscribed for his shares. Where the misstatement is not material and is not made negligently, he will not be entitled to rescission.[3] Moreover, even in the case of a negligent misstatement, the remedy of rescission will only be available to the original subscriber for the shares and not to a subsequent purchaser.[4] The right of rescission, where it is applicable, may be lost if the allottee of the shares fails to repudiate the allotment as soon as he discovers that the statement on the faith of which he subscribed is untrue.[5] He may also lose the right to rescind where he takes some step which in effect ratifies the contract, e.g. endeavouring to sell the shares to someone else, accepting dividends or attending meetings of the company.[6]

1. [1964] AC 465.
2. *Securities Trust Ltd v Hugh Moore & Alexander Ltd* [1964] IR 417.
3. *Re Wimbledon Olympia Ltd* [1910] 1 Ch 630.
4. *Peek v Gurney* (1873) LR 6 HL 377.
5. See para 24.10 below.
6. *Hop and Malt Exchange and Warehouse Co, ex parte Briggs* (1866) LR 1 Eq 483.

Criminal liability in respect of misstatements in connection with flotations

7.18 The Principal Act also imposes criminal liability in respect to misstatements in a prospectus. Section 50 provides that where a prospectus includes an untrue statement any person who authorised the issue of the prospectus is liable on conviction on indictment to imprisonment for a term not exceeding two years or a fine not exceeding £2500 or both.[1] The section also provides, however, that the person is not to be liable if he proves either that the statement was immaterial or that he had reasonable grounds to believe and did in fact believe up to the time of publication that the statement was untrue.

1. As amended by s 15 of the 1982 Act.

Statement in lieu of a prospectus

7.19 Where a private company applies to be re-registered as an unlimited public company the company must deliver to the Registrar with its application a document called a *statement in lieu of a prospectus*. This must comply with certain requirements set out in the Second Schedule to the Principal Act. Such a document is also required in the case of an unlimited public company which does not issue a prospectus.

The requirements as to delivering a statement in lieu of a prospectus were first introduced in England when shares could be allotted by means of offers for sale and placings without complying with the requirements of the Acts as to prospectuses. All such issues are now subject to the requirements of the 1984 Regulations and the stock exchange regulations. Even before the enactment of the 1984 Regulations, the statement in lieu of a prospectus had ceased to be of practical significance and it was dispensed with in the English 1980 Act, following a recommendation to that effect by Jenkins. It is not easy to understand why it has been thought fit to retain it in Ireland in the case of public unlimited companies, an extremely rare breed.

Chapter 8

Application for and allotment of shares

8.01 One of the first steps to be taken in the formation of a company limited by shares is the giving of the shares to the members of the company. This process is known as the *allotment* of shares and is effectively set in train as soon as the memorandum is signed by the two subscribers required by the Principal Act. These persons agree to take a specified number of shares in the company and, when the company is incorporated, it proceeds to allot that number of shares to the subscribers and to allot further shares to other persons who may apply.

The procedure of allotment is governed by a number of rules which are somewhat similar to the rules relating to the formation of contracts: understandably so, because an allotment of shares in response to an application is a form of contract. In addition, however, there are a number of statutory restrictions to be observed, some of them applicable only in the case of public companies.

8.02 In the case of a company limited by shares, every shareholder is normally a member of the company. In addition to the allotment of shares to him, however, there is another step which must be taken before he becomes in law a member: his name must be placed on the register of members. But in the case of the subscribers to the memorandum, this is not necessary: s 31 (1) of the Principal Act provides that

'the subscribers of the memorandum of a company shall be deemed to have agreed to become members of the company, and, on its registration, shall be entered as members in the register of members.'

It has been held in England that the effect of the corresponding section is that a subscriber automatically becomes a member and a shareholder as soon as he signs the memorandum, even though the company fails to allot the shares to him.[1]

1. *Evans' Case* (1867) 2 Ch App 427.

The application

8.03 The application for shares may be made orally or in writing. Like any other *offer,* it may, under the general law of contract, be revoked before *acceptance.*[1] (Under that law, to constitute a valid contract there must be an offer which has been accepted.) The application may also be *conditional,* in which case an allotment which does not comply with the condition may be repudiated.[2]

66

1. For statutory restrictions on the revocability of an application in the case of an allotment in a public company, see para 8.22 below.
2. *Ex parte Wood, Sunken Vessel Recovery Co* (1859) 3 de G & J 85.

The allotment

8.04 The allotment of the shares in response to the application does not constitute the acceptance of an offer. The acceptance only takes place when the applicant is notified that he has been allotted the shares for which he applied. At that stage, a valid and enforceable contract comes into being. As we have seen, however, the applicant does not become a member of the company until his name has been placed on the register. But where there is such a valid contract, both parties, the company and the allottee, are entitled to secure its performance by a decree of specific performance.[1]

1. *New Brunswick etc. Land Co. v Muggeridge* (1860) 1 Dr & Sn 363.

8.05 The notification to the applicant, which is necessary to constitute a valid contract of allotment, may be in writing, verbal or by conduct.[1] Notice may be given either to the applicant or his agent duly authorised to receive such notice.[2] The notice must be given within a reasonable time from the application. The applicant is entitled to revoke his application at any time before the notice of the allotment (subject to certain statutory restrictions in the case of an allotment of a public company), but the revocation must also be made within a reasonable time.[3]

It was held in *Household Fire Insurance Co. v Grant*[4] that the notice of allotment was given to the allottee as soon as the notice was posted. This has repeatedly been stated to be the law in the leading English text books. The learned editors of Palmer, however, suggest that it may need reconsideration in the light of the decision of the Court of Appeal in *Holwell Securities v Hughes*.[5] It was held in that case that, where notice of acceptance of an offer is communicated by post, the notice must actually *reach* the offeror before a contract comes into existence, save in exceptional circumstances where it is clear that the parties intended that the *posting* of the notice was sufficient to make the acceptance effective. However, that was a case of an option which had to be exercised by 'notice in writing to the intended vendor' and it is thought that the reasoning would not necessarily be applicable to a notice of allotment of shares in a company.

1. *Gunn's Case* (1867) 3 Ch App 40.
2. *Levita's Case* (1870) 5 Ch App 489.
3. *Crawley's Case* (1869) 4 Ch App 322.
4. (1879) 4 Ex D 216.
5. [1974] 1 All ER 161; Palmer, vol I, para 22.13.

Renounceable letters of allotment

8.06 As we have seen, a person to whom shares have been allotted does not by virtue of that fact alone become a member. For this to happen, his name must be entered on the register of members. Sometimes, however, the letter of allotment is 'renounceable', i.e. the allottee is entitled to renounce his rights to become a member in favour of another person. Where such *renounceable letters of allotment* are issued, they incorporate two forms: a form of renunciation to be signed by the original allottee and a form of acceptance to be signed by the acceptor of the renunciation.

Where the letters are renounceable, any person in effect may become a shareholder in whose favour the letters are renounced. Accordingly, the issue of such letters may result in an issue being construed to be an offer of shares to the public which will be governed by the rules relating to such offers. In the case of a private company, letters of allotment as such are usually not required at all: it is sufficient to issue the allottee with a share certificate which both indicates that his offer has been accepted and constitutes his title to the shares.

Authority required for allotment of shares by directors

8.07 The articles normally provided that the allotment of shares was entirely a matter for the directors (article 5). Now, by virtue of s 20 of the 1983 Act, the directors must be authorised to make the particular allotment by

(a) the company in general meeting, or
(b) the articles of association.

It is also provided, however, that the authority to allot shares may be general and not limited to a particular allotment. It may also be unconditional or subject to conditions. Presumably, draughtsmen of articles will take care to include a general authority which is unconditional and amendments to the same effect may be expected to existing articles. The authority must state the maximum amount of shares which may be allotted and the date on which the authority will expire, which cannot be more than five years from the date of incorporation (where the authority is contained in the articles of the company on its incorporation) or from the date of the resolution (in any other case). The authority may be revoked or varied by the company in general meeting, whether or not it is contained in the articles.

The authority may be given, varied, revoked or renewed by an ordinary resolution of the company, even where an alteration of the articles is involved. (Normally a special resolution is required for the alteration of the articles.[1]) Notice of the delivery of a copy of the resolution to the Registrar must be published in *Iris Ofigiuil* by the company, if it is a public limited company, within six weeks of its delivery.[1a]

The authority may be renewed for a further period not exceeding five years, whether or not it has already been renewed. This must be done, however, by the company in general meeting and must again specify the amount of shares which may be allotted and the date on which the authority will expire. The directors are allowed to allot shares even though the authority has expired, where the allotment is in pursuance of an offer or agreement by the company before the authority expired and the authority allowed it to make such an offer or agreement which might require shares to be allotted after the expiration of the authority.

There is also a provision relieving companies during a transitional period of three years[2] from complying with the section where they re-register as public limited companies and the allotment is made in pursuance of an offer or agreement made before the first general meeting of the company after its re-registration as a public limited company.

The section does not apply to shares taken by the subscribers to the memorandum or to shares allotted in pursuance of an employees' share scheme. Nor does it apply to a right to subscribe for, or to convert any security into, shares other than the allotted shares.

An allotment of shares made in contravention of the section remains valid. But a director who knowingly and wilfully contravenes or authorises or permits a contravention of the relevant provisions is guilty of an offence and liable on conviction to a fine not exceeding £2,500.

1. For special resolutions, see para 25.13 below.
1a. S 55 (1) (b) of the 1983 Act.
2. Beginning on 13 October 1983, the date on which the Act came into force.

8.08   It is thought that these provisions (which implement requirements of the Second EEC Directive and are virtually the same as corresponding provisions of the English 1980 Act) will make little difference in practice to the operations of most companies. The articles of new companies will probably include a provision authorising the directors to allot shares up to the limit of the nominal share capital of the company. In the case of existing companies, the articles will doubtless be amended to give such an authority in respect of unallotted share capital. It is true that the authority cannot be for longer than five years and can then be renewed only by the company in general meeting. But this would be of importance only where a majority of the company was unwilling to extend the authority of the directors any further; and since the majority in any event has power to remove the directors (except life directors) the change is not of any great practical significance.

Rights of pre-emption in the allotment of shares

8.09   A 'right of pre-emption' might be broadly described as a right of 'first refusal'. We have seen that articles of a private company must include provisons restricting the right of the members to transfer their shares;[1] and it has long been common in such articles to provide that a member wishing to dispose of his shares must first offer them to the other members of the company. The 1983 Act (again implementing the relevant requirements of the Second Directive in language virtually indistinguishable from the English 1980 Act) has now given members of all companies, public and private, such a right on the allotment of new shares in the company. This in effect obliges the company, when making a new issue of shares, to give an existing shareholder a right of first refusal in respect of shares in the new issue equal in proportion to his existing holding. In the case of a private company, however, the right of pre-emption may be excluded by a provision to that effect in the memorandum or articles.

This right of pre-emption is not given to the holders of preference shares. Moreover, where the new issue takes the form of shares allotted, or to be allotted, under an employees' shares scheme, the general body of shareholders has no right of pre-emption in respect of such an issue. But the holders of employees' shares themselves enjoy the right of pre-emption in respect of any new issue of shares to the general body.

In addition to being generally authorised to allot shares under s 20, the directors may also be authorised to allot shares pursuant to the authority as if the statutory pre-emption rights did not apply to the allotment or applied only in a modified manner. Such a power must be given either by the articles or by a special resolution of the company. The company is also given power (where the directors have a general authority to allot) to exclude the application of the right of pre-emption to a specified allotment where such a course is recommended by the directors. The notice of the meeting at which the necessary resolution is to be proposed must be accompanied by a written statement from the directors giving their reasons for the recommendation, the amount to be paid to the company in respect of the shares allotted and the directors' justification of that amount.

1. See para 3.01 above.

8.10   Section 23 confers the pre-emption right. It precludes the company from allotting 'equity securities' unless it has made an offer to the holders of 'relevant shares', or 'relevant employee shares' to allot to them on the same–or more favourable–terms a proportion of the securities as nearly as practicable equal to the proportion in nominal value held by them of the aggregate of relevant shares and relevant employee shares.

'Equity securities' are defined by sub-s (13). They do not include shares taken by the subscribers, or bonus shares. With these exceptions they include all relevant shares and the right to subscribe for, or convert securities into, relevant shares. 'Relevant shares' are defined as meaning all shares other than

(a) shares giving a right to participate as to dividend or capital only up to a specified amount (which, generally speaking, would mean preference shares); and

(b) shares held or allotted in pursuance of an employees' share scheme.

The offer must be open for a period of at least 21 days and must not be withdrawn before the end of that period.

The statutory right of pre-emption does not apply where the allotment of equity securities is made in accordance with a provision in the memorandum or articles which confers a right equivalent to the statutory right. It is also excluded where the shares to be allotted are to be wholly or partly paid up otherwise than in cash.

By virtue of sub-s (12), the definition of shareholders entitled to pre-emption rights is extended to include those who held appropriate shares at any time during the period of 28 days ending on the day before the date of the offer.

8.11   While these complex provisions will be of importance in the case of public limited companies, obliging such companies to turn to their existing shareholders first if they wish to raise fresh capital, their practical significance is much reduced in Ireland by the fact that private companies may exclude the pre-emption rights by amending the memorandum or articles. It will not even be necessary to effect such an amendment where the memorandum or articles already contain a requirement or authority inconsistent with the statutory pre-emption rights. As we have seen, however, the form of pre-emption right most frequently to be found in memoranda and articles is one which obliges the shareholders to offer the shares to the existing shareholders before selling to an outsider, and such a provision would not appear to be inconsistent with s 23.

Directors' duty of good faith in relation to allotments

8.12 In exercising powers to allot shares, the directors are bound to act in good faith in the best interests of the company.[1] It is important to bear in mind that this limitation on their powers may invalidate an allotment even where the new and complex requirements of the 1983 Act as to allotments have all been observed or where they have succeeded in derogating from those requirements by procuring the necessary alterations of the memorandum or articles.

1. *Nash v Lancegaye (Ireland) Ltd* (1958) 92 ILTR 11; para 27.17 below.

Paying for shares

8.13 Shares may be issued either for cash or some other consideration equivalent to cash, such as the rendering of services or the transfer of property. Where the issue is for cash, the allottee becomes laible to pay the full nominal value of the shares allotted to him either upon allotment or at some time in the future. Any person who subsequently becomes the owner of the shares is liable to pay the full amount remaining unpaid on the shares. The person whose name appears on the register as the owner of the shares is liable to pay the unpaid amount, even where he holds the shares in trust for someone else: under s 123 of the Principal Act no notice of any trust may be entered on the register or be receivable by the Registrar.

The principle that shares could be issued for a consideration other than cash has been accepted since the last century. It was implicitly acknowledged by the legislature when it required, in the case of such an allotment, the registration of the contract under which the shares were allotted. It was given express statutory recognition for the first time, however, in s 26 of the 1983 Act which provides that

'shares allotted by a company and any premium payable on them may be paid up in money or money's worth (including goodwill and expertise'.[1]

That Act, however, also contains elaborate provisions, applicable only to public limited companies, as to the valuation of such 'non-cash consideration'.

Where shares are allotted for a consideration other than cash, the company must under s 58 (1) (b) of the Principal Act deliver to the Registrar for registration, within one month of the allotment, the contract in writing constituting the title of the allottee to the shares. (If the contract is not in writing, particulars of it must be registered.)

Where shares are allotted on foot of such a contract, the court cannot enquire into the adequacy of the consideration.[2] But, in the case of a public limited company, there is now a statutory requirement that the non-cash consideration be valued by an independent expert; and since a company may not issue shares at a discount,[3] the creditors and investors may reasonably assume that the capital described as 'paid up' is, in real terms, paid up.

These provisions do not apply to private companies, and in the case of such companies the rule that the adequacy of the consideration cannot be enquired into represents a significant erosion of the supposed protection afforded to creditors by the existence of a paid up capital. The only exceptions to the rule are where the contract itself can be set aside–as in the case of fraud–or where the consideration, on the face of the transaction itself, is clearly inadequate or illusory.[4] There must be, of course, what the law regards as consideration and thus shares allotted by way of gift or in consideration of services freely rendered in the past cannot be regarded as paid up.[5]

Where the shares are allotted in considation of the release of a debt due by the company to the allottee, this is treated as an issue for cash and no contract need be registered.[6] But where the shares are allotted by way of accord and satisfaction, i.e. as part of a compromise or settlement, they are not treated as having been paid for in cash and a contract must be registered.[7]

1. The draughtsman has rightly avoided the ugly expression employed by the draughtsman of the English 1980 Act, 'know how'.
2. *Pell's Case* (1869) 5 Ch App 11.
3. See para 8.25 below.
4. *Re Wragg Ltd* (1897) 1 Ch 796, 836; *Hong Kong & China Gas Co v Glen* [1914] 1 Ch 527.
5. *Re Eddystone Marine Insurance Co* [1893] 3 Ch 9.
6. *Re Harmony and Montaque Tin and Copper Mining Co, Spargo's Case* (1873) 8 Ch App 407; *Larocque v Beauchemin* [1897] AC 358.
7. *Re Johannesburg Hotel Co* [1891] 1 Ch 119.

8.14 In the case of a public limited company, s 26 (2) of the 1983 Act prohibits the company from accepting in payment for its shares or any premium payable on them an undertaking to do work or perform services for the company or any other person. If the company allots shares in consideration of such an undertaking, the shareholder becomes liable to pay the company their nominal value and the whole of any premium, or a proportionate part where the shares are treated as partly paid up, together with interest at the appropriate rate. A subsequent purchaser is similarly liable unless he is a purchaser for value who did not know of the contravention of the section.

A public limited liability company is also prohibited from allotting shares as fully or partly paid up otherwise than in cash if the consideration is, or includes, an undertaking which is to be or may be performed more than five years after the date of the allotment. This would apply to a case where, for example, the company accepted an undertaking to transfer property to the company in payment of shares at some date in the future. Such a deferred payment is permissible but only if it is to be made within the five year period. There are similar provisions rendering the allottee liable for the amount involved in the event of a contravention of the section or where the undertaking is not performed.

8.15 In the case of a public limited company, where shares are allotted as fully or partly paid up otherwise than in cash, the consideration must be valued in accordance with s 30 of the 1983 Act, a report obtained from the valuer and a copy of the report sent to the proposed allottee. The report must be made within the period of six months immediately preceding the allotment.

The valuation and report must be made by an independent person, who is defined as a person qualified at the time to be appointed as auditor of the company. That would normally be a qualified accountant; but the section also enables him to obtain a further report from another expert, e.g. a valuer in the case of property, where he thinks it reasonable to do so. That expert must not himself be an officer or servant of the company or an associated company.

The report must state the nominal value of the shares and any premium, describe the consideration and the date and method of valuation and state the extent to which the shares are to be treated as paid up. It must include, or be accompanied by, a note to the effect that the consideration as valued (together with any cash paid) is not less than the nominal value of the capital to be treated as paid up and any premium. The note must also state, where another expert has been employed, that it appeared reasonable to employ such an expert, that any method of valuation employed was reasonable and that there appears to have been no material change in the value of the consideration since the valuation.

The section provides that, where the allottee has not received the report or there has been some other contravention of the section of which he knows or ought to have known, he is to be personally liable to the company for so much of the nominal capital as was to be treated as paid up by the consideration together with interest. There are also supplementary provisions in s 31

(a) enabling the person making a report or valuation for the purposes of s 31 to obtain information necessary for the report or valuation from any officer of the company;
(b) requiring the company to deliver a copy of any such report with the return of allotments; and
(c) making it an offence to make a false or misleading statement to a person making a report or valuation.

Arrangements involving an allotment in consideration of the transfer of shares in another company, and mergers which involve an allotment, are exempted from the requirements of s 30. This exemption applies to an arrangement only where it is open to all the shareholders in the other company or to all the shareholders in the class affected.

There are similar provisions requiring the obtaining of an expert's valuation and report where the company acquires non-cash assets from the subscribers for a consideration equal in value to one-tenth of the nominal capital within two years from the date when it is issued with a certificate that it is entitled to do business.[1]

1. S 32.

Minimum payment for shares in public limited company

8.16 In the case of a public limited company, a share may not be allotted unless it is paid up as to at least 25 per cent of the nominal value of the shares together with the whole of any premium on it. The proportion which had to be paid up on allotment was 5 per cent under the Principal Act but was increased to 25 per cent by s 28 of the 1983 Act. That section also renders the allottee liable to the company for so much of the 25 per cent as is not paid, together with interest. This does not apply, however, to the allotment of a bonus share in contravention of the section, unless the allottee knew or ought to have known that the allotment was a contravention.

The section does not apply to shares allotted in pursuance of an employees' share scheme.

Additional statutory restrictions on allotments by public companies

8.17 In addition to the restrictions already referred to, there are three specific limitations on the power of a public company to make an allotment.

In the first place, there must have been a minimum response to the invitation to the public to subscribe. In the second place, the company must allow a short period to elapse from the issuing of the prospectus before it makes an allotment. In the third place, if it has been stated that a stock exchange quotation will be sought, that quotation must be obtained.

8.18 The first restriction is imposed by s 53 of the Principal Act. It prohibits the making of an allotment of any share capital offered to the public for subscription unless an amount described in the section as the *minimum subscription* has been subscribed. This is defined as the amount which, in the opinion of the directors, must be raised by the issue of share capital in order to provide for certain specified matters, such as working capital, the purchase of property, the payment of preliminary expenses, etc. These requirements–which must be carefully disntinguished from the obligation to fix the nominal share capital at not less than the *authorised minimum*[1]–are intended to ensure that the company does not proceed with the flotation until the funds and assets which it has told the public it will require have in fact been provided.

If the minimum subscription is not raised at the expiration of 40 days from the issue of the prospectus, any money received from applicants for shares must be repaid forthwith. If it is not repaid within 48 days after the issue of the prospectus, the directors are jointly and severally liable to repay it with interest at the rate of 5 per cent per annum from the expiration of the 48th day. A director is not liable, however, if he proves that the default was not due to any misconduct or negligence on his part.

This restriction is supplemented by s 22 of the 1983 Act. It prohibits a public limited company from making any allotment of any share capital offered for subscription unless

(a) the capital is subscribed in full; or
(b) the offer states that even if it is not subscribed in full, the amount of the capital subscribed may be allotted in any event or in the event of specified conditions being satisfied.

Where conditions are specified, they must be satisfied before any allotment is made. In the event of an allotment being made contrary to the provisions of the section, the same consequences follow as in the case of a contravention of s 53 of the Principal Act.

1. See para 3.19 above.

8.19 The second restriction is imposed by s 56 of the Principal Act. It provides that no allotment may be made of any shares in pursuance of a prospectus issued generally, i.e. to persons who are not existing members, until the beginning of the fourth day after the date of issue of the prospectus. This is to enable prospective investors to consider the flotation carefully before committing themselves. The prospectus may fix a longer period; and whichever day is chosen, whether the statutory minimum of the fourth day or some later day, is known as 'the time of the opening of the subscription lists'.

8.20 The third restriction is imposed by s 57 of the Principal Act. This provides that where a prospectus, whether issued generally or not, states that application has been made or will be made for permission for the shares to be dealt in on any stock exchange, any allotment of the shares will be void if the permission is not applied for before the third day after the issue of the prospectus or, if the permission has not been granted, within six weeks of the closing of the subscription lists. There is provision for the repayment forthwith by the company without interest of all money received from applicants where the permission has not been so applied for or has been refused. If the money is not repaid within eight days, the directors are liable to repay it with interest at 5 per cent from the expiration of the eighth day, except where a director proves that the default in repayment was not due to any misconduct or neglect on his part.

Consequences of irregular allotments

8.21   An allotment made in contravention of the statutory requirement set out in para 8.19 above, i.e. before the fourth day, is valid, but the company and its officers are liable to a fine not exceeding £500. Where the statutory requirement as to the minimum subscription is not complied with, the allotment is voidable, i.e. may be set aside at the instance of the applicant for shares. There is a time limit, however: the allotment may only be set aside within one month of the allotment. Any director who knowingly contravenes or permits the contravention of the requirement is liable to compensate the company and the allottees for any loss, damages and costs which they may have sustained as a result. The claim must be made, however, within two years of the date of the allotment.

Revocability of application for shares in public company

8.22   An application for shares is, as we have seen, unusually revocable by the applicant until the shares have been allotted to him. In order to discourage 'stagging'–applications for shares by speculators hoping to make a quick profit instead of a long term investment–the Principal Act imposes a restriction on this power of revocation in the case of an application made in pursuance of a prospectus issued generally. Such an application is irrevocable until after the expiration of nine days after the day on which the prospectus is issued.[1] (The period is longer than the period provided for in the English 1948 Act and than the period recommended by Jenkins, which was seven days.) The effect of the statutory restriction is that 'stags' can no longer apply for shares and withdraw their application as soon as it becomes apparent that the shares are not going to rise significantly.

There is an exception to the restriction on revocability: the application is revocable within the statutory period where a promoter, director or other person who has authorised the issue of the prospectus gives public notice under s 49 which relieves him of responsibility for mis-statements in the prospectus.

1. S 56 (5) of the Principal Act.

Return of allotments

8.23   Whenever a company limited by shares or a company limited by guarantee and having a share capital makes any allotment of its shares, the company must, within one month thereafter, deliver to the Registrar for registration a return of the allotments stating

(a) the number and nominal value of the shares allotted;
(b) the names, addresses and occupations of the allottees; and
(c) the amount, if any, paid or due and payable on each share.

If the return is not made in accordance with these requirements (or if the contract referred to in para 8.13 is not delivered for registration) every officer of the company who is default is liable to a fine not exceeding £500. Where the court is satisfied that the failure to comply with any of these requirements was accidental or due to inadvertence or that it is just and equitable to do so, it may extend the time for delivering the document in question for such period as it thinks proper.[1]

1. S 58 of the Principal Act as amended by s 15 of the 1982 Act.

Issue of shares at a premium

8.24 There is nothing to prevent the company from issuing shares at a premium, i.e. at a nominal value which is lower than the cash or its equivalent which it receives for them. This frequently happens in the case of private companies, because in that case, as we have seen, the company very often begins life when a person operating a business decides to convert it into a limited company. Since he will own virtually all the shares himself, there will be little point–and some additional expense–in allotting shares which are equivalent in nominal value to the value of the business which he is transferring to the company. The shares allotted to him in such a case will frequently be substantially less in nominal value than the actual value of the business transferred to the company and consequently will be regarded as having been issued at a premium.

But, while the company is perfectly entitled to get more from the shareholders in cash or kind than the nominal value of the shares on allotment, such a premium is not part of the trading profits of the company and may not be treated as such. It must accordingly be transferred to a separate account known as the *share premium account*.[1] The provisions of the Principal Act which ensure that a company's capital can only be reduced in specified circumstances apply equally to the share premium account.[2] It may, however, be applied for the following purposes:

(1) paying up unissued shares (other than redeemable preference shares[3]) as fully paid bonus shares to the members;
(2) writing off the preliminary expenses of the company;
(3) writing off the expenses of, or the commission paid on, any issue of shares or debentures in the company;
(4) providing for the payment of the premium payable by the company on the redemption of redeemable preference shares or debentures.

It was held in England that the corresponding section in the 1948 Act applied in a takeover where the company making the allotment was a newly formed company which had no assets other than those which it acquired from the company being taken over as consideration for the allotment of its shares.[4] It accordingly received substantially more than the nominal value of the shares allotted and this sum had to be transferred to the share premium account, although in fact it represented pre-acquisition profits made by the company being taken over. Such sums should normally have been available for distribution to the shareholders in the form of a dividend, but the section

76

did not make any provision for this. The law has now been altered in England[5] to provide for an exemption in these circumstances from the obligation to transfer the premium on such an issue to capital account, but the law has not been changed in Ireland.

1. S 62 of the Principal Act.
2. See para 13.11 below.
3. See para 17.10 below.
4. *Henry Head & Co v Ropner Holdings Ltd* [1952] Ch 124; *Shearer v Bercain Ltd* [1980] 3 All ER 295.
5. Section 37 of the 1981 Act.

Issue of shares at a discount

8.25   A company may not issue shares at a discount, i.e. at a price which is lower than the nominal value of the shares. This rule was laid down almost a century ago by the House of Lords in *Ooregum Gold Mining Co. of India v Roper*[1] and has now been given statutory force by s 27 of the 1983 Act. This also provides that where shares are allotted at a discount, the allottee is liable to pay the amount of the discount to the company together with interest. The same liability attaches to a subsequent purchaser of the shares, unless he purchases for value without notice of the contravention.

It had been possible to issue shares at a discount with the sanction of the court but this provision in the Principal Act was repealed by the 1983 Act. It is still lawful, however, to pay a commission not exceeding 10 per cent of the price at which the shares were issued to any person in consideration of his agreeing to take shares or procure others to take shares. This exception, which is provided for by s 59 of the Principal Act, is intended to facilitate the payment of commission for underwriting or other services. The wording of the section is sufficiently wide to cover a commission for simply subscribing for the shares; but such an arrangement will usually be viewed with suspicion by the courts.

The rule is simply one against issuing shares at a discount; there is no obligation on a company, as we have seen, to issue shares for cash.[2]

1. [1892] AC 125.
2. Para 8.13 above.

Chapter 9

Commencement of business

9.01 The company comes into being when the Registrar issues a certificate to the effect that it has been incorporated. In the case of a private company, it may thereupon commence business and exercise any power it may have to borrow money. In the case of a public company, however, there are certain requirements which must be met before the company commences business or exercises its borrowing powers. And in every case, the company must have a registered office in Ireland.

Certificate of incorporation

9.02 When the memorandum of a company is delivered to the Registrar for registration, he must first satisfy himself that all the requirements of the Acts in respect to the registration and connected matters have been met. He then certifies under his hand that the company is incorporated; in the case of a limited company, that the company is limited; and in the case of a public limited company, that it is such a company. This document is called the *certificate of incorporation.*

From the date mentioned in the certificate as the date of incorporation the subscribers to the memorandum become in law a body corporate with the name mentioned in the memorandum.[1] Usually the date of incorporation specified in the memorandum is the date on which the Registrar actually signs the certificate, but if the Registrar specifies an earlier date as the date of incorporation, it is from that date and not the date of actual signature that the legal existence of the company dates.

1. S 18 (2) of the Principal Act.

9.03 The certificate is conclusive evidence that

(1) all the requirements of the Acts in respect of registration and of matters precedent and incidental thereto have been complied with;
(2) the association is a company entitled to be registered and duly registered under the Principal Act; and
(3) the company is a public limited company, if the certificate contains a statement to that effect.[1]

It follows that in no circumstances may the courts look behind the certificate to ascertain whether the company has in fact been lawfully incorporated, e.g. by having the requisite number of subscribers (seven) in the case of a public company.[2]

1. S 19 of the Principal Act; s 5 (4) of the 1983 Act.
2. *Oakes v Turquand* (1867) 2 HL Cas 325.

Restrictions on the commencement of business

9.04 A private company is entitled to commence business as soon as the certificate of incorporation is issued. Public companies are, however, precluded from commencing business or exercising borrowing powers until a number of requirements imposed by the Acts have been met. In the case of public limited companies formed as such, these requirements are set out in s 6 of the 1983 Act.

Such a company may not commence business or exercise any of its borrowing powers until the Registrar has issued it with a certificate under the section or the company is registered as another form of company. The Registrar must issue the certificate where

(a) an application is made in the prescribed form;[1]
(b) he is satisfied that the nominal value of the allotted share capital is not less than the authorised minimum;[2] and
(c) there is delivered to him a statutory declaration complying with the section.

The statutory declaration must be in the prescribed form[3] and must state:

(a) that the nominal value of the allotted share capital is not less than the authorised minimum:
(b) the amount paid up, at the time of the application, on the allotted share capital;
(c) the amount, or estimated amount, of the preliminary expenses of the company and the persons by whom any of those expenses have been paid or are payable; and
(d) the amount or benefit paid or given or intended to be paid or given to any promoter of the company, and the consideration for the payment or benefit.[4]

The section applies only to public limited companies which are formed as such. A private company or old public company which re-registers as a public limited company does not require such a certificate.

A certificate under the section is conclusive evidence that the company is entitled to do business and exercise any of its borrowing powers.

Where a public limited company does business or exercises any borrowing powers in contravention of s 6, the company and any officer in default are guilty of an offence and liable on summary conviction to a fine not exceeding £500. A transaction entered into by a public limited company which has not complied with the section remains valid, but if the company fails to comply with its obligations under the transaction, the directors are jointly and severally liable to indemnify the other party for any resulting loss or damage.

1. Companies (Forms) Order, 1983 (SI 1983/289) Form 70.
2. See para 3.19 above.
3. No form appears to have been prescribed at the time of writing.
4. The company must publish notice in *Iris Ofigiuil* of the delivery of the declaration within six weeks of its delivery.

9.05 The restrictions on public companies commencing to carry on business were formerly contained in s 115 of the Principal Act. That section remains in force, but since it is confined in its application to public unlimited companies, its significance is greatly reduced. Companies affected by the section who have a share capital and issue a prospectus inviting the public to subscribe for their shares may not commence business or exercise any borrowing powers until the requirements set out in sub-s (1) have been met. These include a requirement that shares to the amount of the 'minimum subscription'[1] have been allotted, being shares subject to the payment of the whole amount thereof in cash. This requirement need not be met where the company does not issue a prospectus, but in that case the company must deliver to the Registrar for registration a statement in lieu of a prospectus.[2]

1. For the meaning of the 'minimum subscription' see para 8.18 above.
2. See para 7.18 above.

The registered office of the company

9.06 Every company registered under the Acts must at all times have a registered office in Ireland to which communications and notices may be addressed. Notice of its situation must be given to the Registrar prior to incorporation.[1] The situation of the office need not be stated, however, in the memorandum. A company and every officer in default which carries on business without having such an office or omits to notify the Registrar of its situation is liable on summary conviction to a fine not exceeding £500.[2]

The situation of the office within Ireland can be altered from time to time. Notice of any such change must be given to the Registrar within fourteen days from the change. It is not sufficient to include the change in the annual return.[3]

1. Section 113 of the Principal Act as substituted by s 4 of the 1982 Act.
2. Ibid.
3. Ibid.

9.07 The fact that the registered office of every company registered under the Acts must be in Ireland means that all such companies are Irish in nationality and have an Irish domicile. It does not necessarily follow, however, that such companies *reside* in Ireland. Whether a company is properly regarded as resident in Ireland can be important when questions of tax arise and it can also be material in determining whether a company can be served with legal process.

For taxation purposes, a company is normally regarded as residing where the actual management of the company is carried on,[1] even though it ought to be managed elsewhere according to its constitution.[2] The application of this principle may mean that a company is resident in more than one jurisdiction at the same time.[3] Some at least of the superior and directing authority of the company must, however, be present in the jurisdiction in which it is sought to establish such residence.[4]

1. *De Beers Consolidated Mines Ltd v Howe* [1906] AC 455.
2. *Unit Construction Ltd v Bullock* [1960] AC 351.
3. *Swedish Central Rly v Thompson* [1925] AC 495.
4. *Union Corporation Ltd v IRC* [1953] AC 482.

9.08 The following documents must be kept at the registered office:
  (1) The register of members;[1]
  (2) The register of debenture holders (where such a register is kept);[2]
  (3) The register of directors and secretaries;[3]

(4) The register of directors' shareholdings;[4]
(5) Copies of instruments creating charges;[5]
(6) The book containing minutes of general meetings;[6]
(7) The books of account.[7]

1. S 116 (5) of the Principal Act.
2. Ibid, s 91.
3. Ibid, s 195 (1).
4. Ibid, s 190 (6).
5. Ibid, s 109.
6. Ibid, s 146 (1).
7. Ibid, s 147 (3).

Part three

Corporate personality of the company

Chapter 10

Separate legal personality of the company

The rule in Salomon's case

10.01 A company registered under the Acts is an artificial legal entity separate and distinct from the members of which it is composed. This was made clear in the celebrated case of *Salomon v Salomon & Co.*[1]

Aron Salomon was a leather merchant and boot manufacturer carrying on a small but profitable business in Whitechapel. When his sons who worked with him in the business pressed him to give them some sort of stake in it, he went to his solicitors. They advised him to follow the course taken by several businessmen before him and thousands since then: to sell his business lock, stock and barrel to a newly formed company, give his family directorships and nominal shareholdings and take the purchase price in the form of fully paid up shares. The essential control of the business would thus remain in his hands, his family at the same time would be formally recognised as participants and he would in addition, and as a bonus, enjoy the protection of limited liability. He accordingly sold the business to the company for £39,000 and took his payment in the form of 20,000 £1 shares, his wife and five children getting one share each. The payment of the balance of the purchase price was secured by the issue in his favour by the company of a mortgage debenture.

The company encountered unexpected trading problems and, in an effort to keep it afloat, Salomon arranged for a loan to the company secured by a further mortgage. When the mortgage interest fell into arrears, the mortgagee put the company into liquidation and Salomon claimed to be entitled to what little was left in priority to the ordinary creditors on the strength of his mortgage debenture. The liquidator contested his claim and was upheld by Vaughan Williams J at first instance. In the Court of Appeal, Salomon again failed, all three judges treating the formation of the company as a wholly unwarranted perversion of the objects of the companies' legislation.[2] They said that the company was a sham, that Salomon was simply carrying on the same business as before through its agency and that he could and should be made to pay its debts.

The hapless Salomon, by this time literally reduced to being a pauper, appealed to the House of Lords and, in a series of classic judgments, the law lords made it clear that there was nothing whatever in the companies' legislation which prevented the formation of what were in effect 'one man companies'. The courts were not entitled to have regard to the extent of the shares held by individual members or to the degree of influence which one or more might have over the others. The great Irish judge, Lord Macnaghten, who described Salomon feelingly as hard done by, stated the law with incomparable lucidity:

'The company is at law a different person altogether from the subscribers to the memorandum; and though it may be that after incorporation the business is precisely the same as it was before, and the same persons are managers and the same hands receive the profits, the company is not in law the agent for the subscribers or trustee for them. Nor are the subscribers as members liable, in any shape or form, except to the extent and in the manner provided by the Act.'[3]

The decision of the Court of Appeal was unanimously reversed.

1. [1897] AC 22.
2. Reported sub nom *Broderip v Salomon* [1895] 2 Ch 323.
3. At 51.

10.02   The principle laid down in *Salomon v Salomon & Co* has been applied over a wide range of cases in England and Ireland. Thus, in *Lee v Lee's Air Farming*,[1] a pilot in New Zealand had formed a company for the purpose of carrying on his soil spraying business. He was the controlling shareholder and governing director. When he was killed in a flying accident, it was sought to resist a claim by his widow under the relevant workmen's compensation provisions on the basis that he was not a 'worker', i.e. a servant of the company. The court in New Zealand upheld this contention, but it was rejected on appeal by the Judicial Committee of the Privy Council. Since the pilot and the company were separate legal entities, they were capable in law of entering into a contract of service despite the extent of the control exercised by the pilot over the company.

There is a curious feature of the decision, however: Lord Morris of Borthy-Gest, giving the advice of the Judicial Committee, appears to suggest that the result might have been different had the company been 'a sham or a simulacrum'. Whatever about being a sham, the company was clearly a 'simulacrum': no one had any real control over it except the pilot. But the essence of the decision in *Salomon v Salomon & Co.* is that it is entirely immaterial that the company is in effect a 'one man company': it remains a separate legal entity. A company may well be described as the 'alter ego', 'simulacrum', 'puppet', or whatever other expression one may wish to employ, of the person who promotes it, but *of itself* this does not prevent it from being a separate legal entity with all the consequences that follow in law.

The principle worked to the advantage of the shareholder's dependants in *Lee*'s case: in *Tunstall v Steigman*,[2] it operated to the shareholder's detriment. There a landlord of property sought to resist the grant of a new tenancy on the ground that she required the property for the purposes of a business carried on in an adjoining premises. It transpired, however, that the business was in fact being carried on by a company in which the landlord was a majority shareholder. It was held that she could not rely on the company's business requirements to defeat the tenant's claim: it was a different legal entity and was not the landlord.[3] It also defeated a claim by a shareholder in *Roberts v Coventry Corporation*.[4] There the defendants compulsorily acquired premises the freehold of which was vested in the plaintiff. She had granted a yearly tenancy of the premises to a company which carried on business in them and of which she was the majority shareholder. In addition to the value of her freehold interest she claimed a further sum in respect of the loss she would suffer when the defendants terminated the company's yearly tenancy. It was held that this was the company's loss and not hers and that she could not recover compensation in respect of it.

1. [1961] AC 12.
2. [1962] 2 QB 593.
3. The reverse situation occurred in *Pegler v Craven* [1952] 2 QB 69, where the tenant failed to obtain a new tenancy, when the premises had been occupied by a company in which he was the majority shareholder.
4. [1947] 1 A11 ER 308.

10.03 In Ireland, the principle also worked to the shareholder's disadvantage in *Battle v Irish Art Promotion Centre Ltd,*[1] where the majority shareholder in, and managing director of, a company was refused leave by the High Court and the Supreme Court to conduct the defence of an action against the company. The company had not enough money to retain solicitor and counsel and the applicant wished to defend the case so as to protect his own business reputation. He was, of course, entitled to appear for himself, but the company was a separate legal entity and accordingly could only be represented by solicitor or counsel.

The principle was also applied more recently by Barrington J. in *Irish Permanent Building Society v Registrar of Building Societies and Irish Life Building Society.*[2] In that case, the plaintiffs sought to prevent the registration of the second defendants, the Irish Life Building Society, as a building society on the grounds *inter alia* that it was not an autonomous body but was the subsidiary of another, i.e. the Irish Life Assurance Company. It was accepted by Barrington J. that that building society was the 'creature' (in no pejorative sense) of the insurance company: its directors were all nominees of the latter which had also provided all its funds. He held, however, applying the principle in Salomon's case, that this did not mean that the society was not a separate legal entity: it was such an entity and was accordingly registrable.

Again, in *Gresham's Industries Ltd (in liquidation) v Cannon,*[3] the liquidator of the plaintiff company brought proceedings against the majority shareholder claiming the repayment of sums said to have been lent by the company to him. The defendant, while admitting that the payments had been made, claimed that they were intended for, and used for, the purposes of other companies of which he was also the majority shareholder and that in effect the money was being used for the benefit of a group of companies of which he was the owner. Rejecting the contention that this afforded any defence, Finlay P. said

'It seems to be a fundamental principle of the law that if a person decides to obtain and use the benefit of trading through limited liability companies and if for any purposes, whether the limitation of his liability, tax purposes or otherwise he transfers assets from one company to another or makes drawings from one company and invests them in his own name in another company he cannot subsequently be heard to ignore the existence of the legal entities consisting of the different companies and to look upon the entire transaction as a personal one.'

1. [1968] IR 252.
2. [1981] ILRM 242.
3. Unreported; judgement delivered 2 July 1980.

10.04 It also follows logically from Salomon's case that a shareholder cannot sue, or be sued, on foot of contracts entered into by the company. Similarly, he can neither sue nor be sued in respect of torts committed against or by the company.[1] It also follows that a shareholder does not have an insurable interest in the assets or business of the company.[2] By contrast, a debenture holder has such an interest because, unlike a shareholder, he has an interest in the property and business of the company.

1. *British Thomson-Houston Co v Sterling Accessories Ltd* [1924] 2 Ch 33.
2. *Macaura v Northern Assurance Co* [1925] AC 619.

10.05 The legislature has provided that, in certain circumstances, the normal consequences of the rule in Salomon's case are not to follow. That case established that a company is not in law the agent of a shareholder simply because of the degree of control enjoyed by that shareholder. It follows that such a shareholder, whatever the extent of his shareholding or of the control exercised by him over the board of directors, cannot normally be made liable for the debts of the company. In two instances, however, considered in detail below, the legislature has provided that shareholders or directors may be liable for the debts of the company despite the fact that the company is not their agent.

Salomon's case also established the general principle that control of a company, however extensive, cannot justify the inference that the company and the shareholder are to be treated as one legal entity. Again the legislature has modified the principle in certain circumstances. In the case of a company which is a shareholder, where the extent of the control by that company is sufficient to render one or more companies the *subsidiary* or *subsidiaries* of that company, the latter–the parent or *holding* company–may be required to present its own shareholders with *group accounts*, showing the state of affairs in the group of companies as a whole. This result should not logically follow if each of the companies in the group is to be treated for all purposes as separate and distinct legal entities. Similarly, the legislature has provided that the extent of a shareholder's control may be taken into account in order to prevent the avoidance of tax by the formation of companies having no real independent existence from the shareholder.

There have also been a number of cases in which the courts in England and Ireland have refused to apply the fundamental principle established by Salomon's case or have at least declined to apply it in its full rigour. Commentators have wrestled bravely with the task of extracting general rules underlying these cases, but have usually found it an impossible one. There is substance in Gower's waspish comment that the cases where the principle has been relaxed represent haphazard refusals by the courts to apply logic where it is too flagrantly opposed to 'justice, convenience or (especially) the interests of the Revenue'.[1]

1. At 112.

10.06 These modifications in special circumstances by the legislature and the courts of the principle in Salomon's case have been frequently described as occasions on which 'the veil of corporate personality is lifted': so frequently, indeed, that it is almost impossible to dislodge the phrase in any discussion of the topic. Yet it is a singularly unhelpful and confusing metaphor: there is no veil, as Gower points out, which prevents the law from seeing who owns a company.[1] On the contrary, the great principle underlying all modern companies' legislation is the requirement that the identity of those who control the company should be ascertainable by the public.[2] There is nothing to prevent a court in any case from ascertaining who the persons in control of a company are, if that is relevant to any issue which the court has to resolve. What it cannot do (without modifying the rule in Salomon's case) is draw the inference from the mere fact of that control that the company is the agent or trustee of the shareholder or treat the controlling shareholders and the company as one legal entity.

We now examine in detail the cases in which the legislature and the courts have modified the rule in Salomon's case.

1. At 112.
2. Subject to the qualification that the shares may be held by nominees whose identity is not ascertainable from an inspection of the register. See para 24.11 below.

Modifications of the rule in Salomon's case: (1) the legislature

10.07 A reduction in the number of members of a company below the legal minimum–two in the case of a private company and seven in the case of a public company–may expose the surviving member or members to liability for the debts of the company. In such a case the company continues to exist as a legal entity. To that extent, the principle in Salomon's case is respected, but it is modified so as to render the surviving member or members liable for the company's debts. They are, however, given a breathing space of six months. Where the company carries on business for more than that period while the number of members is below the minimum, every person who is a member during that time and is aware that it is so operating is to be liable for the debts of the company contracted during that time.[1] In practice the provision is rarely used.

1. S 36 of the Principal Act.

10.08 Section 297 of the Principal Act provides that where a company's business has been carried on by the company with intent to defraud creditors or for any fraudulent purpose, the court may declare that any of the directors who were knowingly parties to the fraud and any other person who was knowingly party to carrying on the fraudulent trading shall be personally responsible for all or any of the debts of the company.

This section, while again it does not affect the separate legal existence of the company, is a far more important erosion of the rule established in Salomon's case that control of a company's affairs does not make the controller responsible for its debts. It is, however, subject to one important proviso: it is only applicable where the company is being wound up. It is discussed in more detail in paras 34.83 et seq below.

10.09 Where a company is a 'subsidiary' of another–i.e. where a majority of its shares are held by that company or it is effectively controlled by it–it remains in law a separate legal entity and again the central principle established by Salomon's case is preserved. The legislature has, however, significantly modified one of the consequences that would otherwise flow from the separate personalities of the companies. Before the Principal Act a public company which carried on its business through private subsidiaries was in effect freed from its statutory obligation to let its shareholders know its real financial situation. Since the private companies were separate legal entities, the shareholders in the holding company had no right to see their accounts. Nor could they ascertain the true position by examining the accounts annexed to the company's annual return and filed with the Registrar since private companies, as we have seen, were never required in Ireland to file their accounts with the Registrar.[1] The Oireachtas, following the example established in England by the 1929 and 1948 Acts, provided in the Principal Act that a public company which is a 'holding company'–i.e. one which effectively owns or controls one or more subsidiaries–must present its members with group accounts relating to the company and all its subsidiaries. These requirements are considered in more detail in Chapter Thirty.

1. See para 2.08 above.

10.10 The concept of the separate legal personality of the company has obvious possibilities for people seeking to reduce the burden of taxation. This led the legislature in England to introduce further modifications of the Salomon principle by permitting tax liability to depend on the degree of actual control exercised by people over the affairs of companies. For that purpose, it developed the concept of the 'close company' and thus sought to ensure that individuals do not ease the burden of taxation on their business profits by retaining them in such companies and obtaining the benefit of them without taxation through such stratagems as loans and interest payments from the companies. The Oireachtas has again followed the English example. The relevant provisions, which will be found in Part X of the Corporation Tax Act 1976 are of great complexity and lie outside the scope of this book. It is sufficient to note that 'close companies' are, generally speaking, companies under the control of five or fewer 'participators' and that the Act brings within the taxation net various 'distributions' of their profits made, or deemed to be made, by such companies to the participators. Similar provisions are to be found in the Capital Gains Tax Act 1975.

10.11 The Oireachtas has also had regard to the extent of the control enjoyed by shareholders in order to regulate mergers and takeovers. For the purposes of the relevant legislation–the Mergers, Takeovers and Monopolies (Control) Act 1978–a merger or takeover is defined as existing when two or more enterprises come under 'common control'. In the case of a company common control is deemed to exist when the right to appoint a majority of the board of directors or a specified proportion of voting shares is acquired by another enterprise. These provisions are considered further in Chapter Thirty-Two below.

10.12 The foregoing are all cases where the legislature has modified the consequences of Salomon's case in clear and unequivocal language. It has been recently held by the House of Lords that such language must be used before the courts will treat the principle of the case as having been dislodged. Lord Diplock acknowledged, however, the possibility that even in the absence of express words, a purposive construction of a statute might lead inexorably to the conclusion that it must have been the intention of parliament to modify the rule[1]

1. *Dimbleby & Sons Ltd v NUJ* [1984] 1 All ER 751.

Modifications of the rule in Salomon's case: (2) the courts

10.13 As we have noted, while there have been a number of cases in which the courts have modified the rule in Salomon's case, it is not easy to extract any general principle underlying such cases. One qualification is clearly established beyond doubt, however: the courts will not permit the statutory privilege of incorporation to be used for a fraudulent purpose. This is entirely consistent with the general approach adopted by the House of Lords in Salomon's case: in that court the view which found favour with the Court of Appeal that the Act was being used for a fraudulent object was emphatically rejected. Had the law lords been dealing with a case in which a company was formed with a fraudulent object, the result might have been different. In at least two cases, however, there has been a further refinement of this qualification: it has been held in England that the court will not allow the Acts to be used for the purpose of evading contractual or other legal obligations.

Thus in *Gilford Motor Co v Horne*,[1] the defendant had entered into an agreement with the company which employed him not to canvass their customers for business in the event of his leaving. He sought to evade this agreement on leaving the company by forming a company and using it as a vehicle for such canvassing. It was held that he could be restrained from so doing. Similarly, in *Jones v Lipman*,[2] the defendant who had contracted to sell his house to the plaintiff tried to avoid a decree of specific performance of his contract being given against him by conveying the house to a company formed by him. Russell J rejected a defence based on the company being a separate legal entity, describing the company as

'the creation of the defendant, a device and a sham, a mask which he holds before his face in an attempt to avoid recognition by the eye of equity.'[3]

Applying the same form of reasoning, the Court of Appeal in *Re Bugle Press Ltd*[4] made it clear that the privilege of incorporation could not be used for an improper purpose, such as the obtaining of a particular statutory remedy in circumstances where it was never intended to apply. In that case, the holders of 90 per cent of the shares wished to buy out the holder of the remaining ten per cent. For that purpose, they formed a company and transferred their shares to it. They then attempted to acquire the remaining ten per cent under the statutory procedure provided for buying out compulsorily a minority shareholding when a takeover of a company is being effected.[5] There had, of course, been no real takeover of a company: the new company which held the 90 per cent shareholding had been formed solely with a view to expropriating the minority. It was held that the majority could not avail of the particular remedy in such circumstances.

In these cases, the company was variously described as 'a cloak', 'a sham', 'a device' and 'a mask'. One should not be misled, however, by the use of such metaphors. The more pejorative their overtones, the more seductive is the conclusion that the court is justified in ignoring the separate personality of the company. An interesting example of this process at work is the following passage from the judgment of Lord Denning in *Wallersteiner v Moir*[6] where he described the relationship between the plaintiff and certain companies in these terms:

'He controlled their every movement. Each danced to his bidding. He pulled the strings ... I am of the opinion that the court should pull aside the corporate veil and treat these concerns as being his creatures, for whose doings he should be, and is, responsible ...'[7]

All these expressions could have been applied with equal force to the relationship between Salomon and the company (or between the insurance company and the building society in the Irish Permanent case). Not surprisingly, Lord Denning's brethren on the Court of Appeal in *Wallersteiner v Moir* declined to go as far as he did. it is submitted that such a relationship *of itself* does not justify the court in disregarding the separate personality of the company. But if in addition the company has been formed for some fraudulent, illegal or improper purpose, the court is clearly entitled to do so and, in such circumstances, the company may no doubt be properly, if unhelpfully, described as 'a sham', 'a facade to conceal the true facts' or whatever.

1. [1933] Ch 935.
2. [1962] 1 A11 ER 442.
3. At 445.
4. [1961] Ch 270.
5. See para 32.12 below.
6. [1974] 3 A11 ER 217.
7. At 238.

10.14   The cases mentioned in the previous paragraph are readily enough reconcilable with a general legal principle that the courts will not permit statutory privileges to be used for fraudulent purposes, using the word 'fraudulent' in its more generous equitable sense as including attempts to evade contractual or other legal obligations or the use of such statutory privileges for improper purposes. We next come to a series of cases in which the courts have been prepared, in apparent conflict with Salomon's case, to infer the existence of an *agency* or *trust* and which are less easy to explain on the basis of any general principle.

In *Smith Stone & Knight v Birmingham Corporation*,[1] a holding company was the owner of property in which one of its subsidiaries was carrying on business. When it was compulsorily acquired by the defendants, the holding company was held entitled to compensation for disturbance arising from the relocation of the business, Atkinson J. taking the view that the subsidiary was carrying on the business as the agent of the holding company. This decision suggested a number of criteria for determining whether such an agency should be inferred, i.e.

(1) were the profits of the subsidiary treated as the profits of the holding company?
(2) were the persons running the business of the subsidiary appointed by the holding company?
(3) was the holding company the 'head and brain' of the trading venture?
(4) did the holding company govern the adventure, decide what should be done and what capital should be employed in it?
(5) were the profits from the business the result of the 'skill and direction' of the holding company?
(6) was the holding company in 'effectual and constant control'?

It is doubtful whether these criteria are capable of general application: if an agency were to be inferred in every case where they were met, a significant number of subsidiaries would have to be treated as the agents of their holding companies. It would then be difficult to avoid the logical corollary that the holding company was in each case liable for the debts of the subsidiary, opening up a huge breach, not merely in the principle of separate corporate existence, but in the principle of limited liability as well.

It can safely be said that the courts have been more willing to draw an inference of agency where the controlling shareholder is another company (as in *Smith Stone & Knight v Birmingham Corporation*) and particularly where there is no other shareholder. There has also been a tendency to draw this inference with greater readiness in cases where any other result might lead to avoidance of tax liability. Thus in *Firestone Tyre & Public Co v Llewellin*,[2] an American company formed a wholly owned subsidiary in England for the purpose of manufacturing tyres and supplying them to the European market. The English company received the payments for the tyres and, after deducting the costs of manufacture and a figure of 5 per cent, transmitted the balance to the American company. Although the English company was independent in its day-to-day operations and only one of the directors was a director of the American company as well, it was held to be carrying on the business as the agent of the American company and the latter was accordingly liable to pay tax in respect of the profits of the business. It is virtually impossible to reconcile this decision with the earlier decision of *Ebbw Vale UDC v South Wales Traffic Area Licencing Authority*[3] where the Court of Appeal refused to treat the plaintiff transport company as the agent of the British Transport Commission, although that body held all the shares except two in the company. The defendants had argued that they had no jurisdiction to deal with an application by the plaintiff company to increase their fares, since the service was being 'provided' in effect by the commission and hence, under the relevant legislation, a fare increase had to be approved by another body. The court held on the authority of Salomon's case that as the company was a separate legal entity it was providing the service itself and not as the agent of the commission.

1. [1939] 4 A11 ER 116.
2. [1957] 1 A11 ER 561.
3. [1951] 2 KB 366.

10.15   The desire to avoid apparent injustice or illogicality or to frustrate the ingenuity of tax lawyers has also led the courts to flirt on occasions with the heresy of treating the company as a trustee for its shareholders. As we have seen, one of the fundamental differences between the company and other forms of business organisations, such as partnerships, is that the property of the business is vested in the company and not in its proprietors. For that reason a shareholder has no insurable interest in the assets of the company and the suggestion that he had was rejected by Devlin J. in one case as being 'beyond the reach of sustained argument'.[1] Yet in *Littlewood Mail Order Stores Ltd v IRC*,[2] the Court of Appeal was not deterred by these well-established principles from treating property vested in a subsidiary as being held on behalf of the parent company where a contrary conclusion would have enabled the parent company to avoid tax liability.

This decision is in stark contrast to *Wm Cory & Son Ltd v Dorman Long & Co Ltd*,[3] where a parent company claimed that barges registered in the name of a subsidiary were held in trust for them. Had this argument proved successful, they would have been entitled as owners to the benefit of a statutory limit on their liability for the negligence of the master of one of the barges. It was held that the barges were not held in trust for them and that they were not the owners within the meaning of the relevant section.

1. *Bank voor Handel en Scheepvaart NV v Slatford* [1953] 1 QB 248 at 269.
2. [1969] 3 A11 ER 855.
3. [1936] 2 A11 ER 386.

10.16   A similar inconsistency can be seen in what may be called the 'club' cases. Many clubs formed for social reasons find it convenient to incorporate themselves as companies, usually limited by guarantee. Such clubs are frequently registered under the Registration of Clubs (Ireland) Act 1904 in order to avail of the provisions of that Act enabling clubs to supply their members with drink without a licence. In the case of an unincorporated body, no difficulty arises: the assets of the club, including the stock of drink, are vested in trustees or a committee on behalf of the members and a sale of drink to a member is clearly a distribution of the members' common property to an individual member which under the Act does not require a licence. But where it is vested in a company, it cannot be said to be held in trust for or on behalf of the members, if the principles stated already are applicable. Accordingly a sale to an individual member would seem to be a transaction between two legal entities–the company and a member–rather than a distribution of the common stock of the association among the members. This was the view taken in *Wurzwel v Houghton Main Home Service Ltd*,[1] disapproving of an earlier decision to the contrary of *Newell v Hemingway*.[2] Yet in a later case of *Trebanog Working Men's Club v Macdonald*,[3] where the same view was taken as in *Newell v Hemingway*, Lord Hewart CJ swept aside the argument based on Salomon's case as applied to such clubs, saying

> 'once it is conceded that a members' club does not necessarily require a licence to serve its members with intoxicating liquor because the legal property in the liquor is not in the members themselves, it is difficult to draw any legal distinction between the various legal entities which may be entrusted with the duty of holding the property on behalf of the members, be it an individual, or a body of trustees, or a company formed for the purpose, so long as the real interest in the liquor remains, as in this case it clearly does, in the members of the club. In this connection, there is no magic in the expression 'trustee' or 'agent'. What is essential is that a holding of the property by the agent or trustee must be a holding for and on behalf of, and not a holding antagonistic to, the members of the club.'[4]

This passage was cited by McWilliam J in *Re Parnell GAA Club Ltd*,[5] where he rejected as not well founded an objection to the renewal of a company's registration under the 1904 Act on the ground that the assets, including the drink, were vested in the company.

Accordingly, in this area also, the courts have declined to apply in its full rigour the principle in Salomon's case and it would seem to be the law in both Ireland and England that a members' club is not debarred from selling drinks to the members merely by reason of the fact that it is a company.

1. [1937] 1 KB 380.
2. [1888] 60 LT 544.
3. [1940] 1 KB 576.
4. At 582.
5. [1984] ILRM 246.

10.17 A number of cases in England prompted Gower to the conclusion that there was evidence of

> 'a general tendency to ignore the separate legal entities of various companies within a group and to look instead at the economic entity of the whole group. The courts are here following the lead of the legislature ...'[1]

Of these, he thought the leading example to be *Holdsworth & Co v Caddies*.[2] Mr. Caddies was employed by the company as its managing director under a written contract. He claimed damages for breach of contract on the ground that the company had confined him to performing duties as managing director of one of their subsidiaries. The company relied successfully on a clause in the contract which provided that 'as such managing director he shall perform the duties and exercise the powers in relation to the business of the company and the businesses ... of its existing subsidiary companies ...which may from time to time be assigned to or vested in him by the board ...'

One of the arguments advanced on Mr Caddies' behalf was that the subsidiaries were separate legal entities under the control of their own boards. But even applying Salomon's case in its full rigour, this fact did not seem to assist his case, since the clause expressly envisaged that the company could assign him duties in relation to the subsidiaries. It appeared to follow that if the parent company could procure the assignment to him of such duties by virtue of their control of the subsidiaries, they would not be in breach of their contract. This scarcely involved any watering down of the Salomon principle and the opinions of the law lords appear for the most part to be based on the actual words of the clause itself. Lord Reid did, however, observe that the argument based on the separate legal personalities was 'too technical' since 'an agreement *in re mercatoria* ... must be construed in the light of the facts and realities of the situation ...'[3]

A somewhat similar observation was made by Viscount Simonds in *Scottish Co-operative Wholesale Society Ltd v Meyer*,[4] where a number of minority shareholders in a company claimed relief under the relevant section of the companies' legislation which entitles the court to grant relief where shareholders are being treated oppressively.[5] The oppressive conduct in that case was passive rather than active: the majority shareholding was held by another company which was prepared to let the subsidiary go to the wall since that suited their interests. Again the law lords were in general content to decide the case on the ground that culpable inaction of this nature on the part of the majority could constitute oppression just as much as active oppression. Viscount Simonds, however, thought that the court could have regard to the positively detrimental actions of the parent company, remarking that

'the section warrants the courts in looking at the business realities of a situation and does not confine them to a narrow legalistic view.'[6]

The passage quoted from Gower was cited with approval by Lord Denning in *DHN Food Distributors Ltd v Tower Hamlets London Borough Council*.[7] As in some of the earlier decisions, this case arose out of a compulsory acquisition of property. The acquiring authority sought to resist a claim for compensation for disturbance on the ground that the company which owned the property had not carried on any business there. The evidence established that the company which owned the property was one of a group of three companies in common ownership, one of which carried on business in the property. Lord Denning held that the court could look to the economic entity of the whole group and treat the business as being carried on by that group. It is a noteworthy feature of the decision, however, that his brethren, Goff LJ. and Shaw LJ, were of the view that the case could, in any event, have been decided against the acquiring authority on two other grounds, i.e. that the company actually in occupation and carrying on the business was the owner in equity of the property and was further entitled to occupy the property in perpetuity under an irrevocable licence. On either basis, they said, the company could be regarded as entitled to be compensated as the true owner.

1. At 131.
2. [1955] 1 All ER 725.
3. At 738.
4. [1959] AC 324.

5. See para 26.10 below.
6. At 343.
7. [1976] 3 All ER 462.

10.18 Reservations as to the correctness of Lord Denning's view were expressed in the House of Lords in *Woolfson v Strathclyde Regional Council* where Lord Keith of Krinkel said:

'I have some doubts ... whether the Court of Appeal properly applied the principle that it is appropriate to pierce the corporate veil only where special circumstances exist indicating that (it) is a mere facade concealing the true facts.'[1]

It was, however, applied in Ireland by Costello J in *Power Supermarkets Ltd v Crumlin Investments Ltd and Another*.[2] This is the most important recent Irish decision in this area and the facts must be set out in some detail.

The first defendants entered into an agreement with the plaintiffs, who controlled the Quinnsworth chain of supermarkets, to grant them a lease of a large unit in a shopping centre. In the agreement, the first defendants covenanted

'not during the term to grant a lease for or to sell or permit or suffer the sale by any of its tenants or so far as within (the first defendant's) control any sub or under tenants of groceries or food products in or over an area exceeding 3000 square feet in any one unit ... forming part of the shopping centre...'

The shopping centre was not initially a financial success and was sold to a company called Cornelscourt Shopping Centre Ltd, the sale being carried out by way of a transfer of the shares in the first named defendants. This company was one of the Dunnes Stores group of companies who operated a rival chain of supermarkets. It was important, indeed essential, from their point of view that they themselves should have a retail outlet in the shopping centre. Since it was the policy of the group that each of its retail units should be operated by a separate company, a new company–Dunnes Stores (Crumlin) Ltd–was formed and the freehold in one of the units conveyed to it by the first named defendants. When the company began to trade, the plaintiffs sought to restrain them from so doing.

It was established in evidence that the individual companies–approximately 150–which made up the Dunnes Stores group were only notionally separate companies. All the affairs of the group were managed by members of the Dunne family and, in the case of Dunnes Stores (Crumlin) Ltd there had been no further meetings of its directors after the first meeting. In the case of the first named defendants, similarly, there were no further meetings after the purchase of shares. The unit was conveyed by the first named defendants to Dunnes Stores (Crumlin) Ltd for a nominal consideration and without any of the covenants which would normally have accompanied such a transaction if carried out at arms' length.

Costello J held that Dunnes Stores (Crumlin) Ltd were bound by the covenant, although not a party to it. Having cited the views of Lord Denning and Shaw LJ in *DHN Ltd v Tower Hamlets London Borough Council*, he went on:

'It seems to me to be well established from these as well as from other authorities (see *Holdworth & Co v Caddies; Scottish Co-operative Wholesale Society Ltd v Meyer*) that a Court may, if the justice of the case so requires, treat two or more related companies as a single entity so that the business notionally carried on by one will be regarded as the business of the group, if this conforms to the economic and commercial realities of the situation.. It would, in my view, be very hard to find a clearer case than the present one for the application of this principle.'[3]

While this passage appears to have been approved of by the Supreme Court[4] and undoubtedly represents the law in Ireland, it is respectfully suggested that it is open to criticism as stating the law too widely. The 'justice of the case' is a somewhat elusive concept and it is extremely difficult to predict with anything approaching certainty how it might or should be applied in specific cases. Thus in the case under discussion it was perhaps open to question whether justice required the reading of the covenant in the sense favoured by Costello J. It was after all a stipulation which restricted the covenantor's freedom to trade and as such hardly merited any particularly benevolent or purposive construction. It is an important feature of the case that Dunnes Stores (Crumlin) Ltd, although a company without any real independent existence, was *not* formed with a view to evading the covenant but simply in pursuance of the general policy of the group to have their outlets operated by separate companies. Hence there was no room for the application of the principles underlying cases such as *Gilford Motor Co v Horne* that the courts will not countenance the formation of companies for illegal or improper purposes.

The decision does, however, reflect another important tendency in this field: the courts will be more inclined to disregard the separate corporate personalities of the companies in a group if to do so will avert the possibility of injustice to outside parties. It will be less inclined to do so, where the companies themselves seek to avoid the disadvantages of incorporation while clinging to the advantages.[5]

This approach was to a limited extent endorsed by Carroll J in *The State (Thomas McInerney & Co Ltd) v Dublin County Council*.[6] In that case, a subsidiary company served a purchase notice under s 29 of the Local Government (Planning and Development) Act 1963 in respect of land of which its holding company was the registered owner. The local authority on whom the notice was served disputed its validity on the ground that the subsidiary was not the 'owner' within the meaning of the section. The subsidiary relied on both *Smith Stone & Knight* and *DHN Ltd*, but the court rejected the contention that on the basis of these decisions the subsidiary could be treated as the owner. Carroll J said

'In my opinion, the corporate veil is not a device to be raised and lowered at the option of the parent company or group. The arm which lifts the corporate veil must always be that of justice. If justice requires (as it did in the DHN case) the courts will not be slow to treat a group of subsidiary companies and their parent company as one. But can it be said that justice requires it in this case?'

She went on to answer that question in the negative.

---

1. 1978 SC (HL) 90.
2. Unreported; judgement delivered 22 June 1981.
3. He also decided in favour of the plaintiffs on another ground, i.e. that the covenant in question was a restrictive covenant which ran with the land.
4. *Re Bray Travel Ltd and Bray Travel (Holdings) Ltd*, unreported; judgments delivered 13 July 1981. There were no written judgments in this case and I am indebted to my colleague Mr Justice Murphy for the note of the judgments delivered which appears in the Appendix.
5. A point made in an interesting article on this topic by Mr Gerard McCormack, *Judicial Application of Salomon's Case in Ireland*, Incorporated Law Society of Ireland Gazette, May 1984.
6. Unreported; judgement delivered, 12 December 1984.

10.19 A company, being an artificial personality, can only act through human agency. For certain purposes, it is accordingly necessary to ascertain the conduct and status of those who control its activities, whether they be the shareholders, the directors or the managers. We have already seen that it is only in this manner that the residence of the company can be ascertained: a company which is wholly owned by French shareholders and carries on its activities in France through a staff resident in that country does not reside in Ireland, simply because its registered office is in Ireland.[1] Similarly, as we shall see in Chapter 12 a company is capable of committing crimes, but can only do so through the agency of human beings. In order to determine whether the company had the criminal intent necessary in the case of serious crime, it may be necessary to examine the conduct of those who control the company.

While these are sometimes referred to as instances of 'lifting the veil', it is thought that this is not an accurate statement of the true legal position. These cases do not involve any modification of the rule in Salomon's case, since they do not erode in any sense the separate legal personality of the company. This was made clear by the House of Lords in the leading case of *Daimler Co Ltd v Continental Tyre (Great Britain) Co Ltd*[2] where the issue was whether the famous motor car company should be treated as an enemy alien during the First World War because it was owned by German shareholders and controlled from Germany, although its registered office was in England. In a powerful speech, Lord Parker disposed of the fallacy that Salomon's case prevented the courts from looking at the individual members in order to determine the *character* of the company. The company was held to be an enemy alien. It is thought that this also justifies the later decision of Danckwerts J in *The Abbey Malvern Wells Ltd v Minister of Local Government and Planning*.[3] In that case, the plaintiff company claimed to be a charitable body and hence exempt from certain development charges. The plaintiff company managed a school on a profit making basis, but the shares themselves were all held on charitable trusts so that the proprietors made no private profits. It was held that the court was entitled to take this into account in determining whether the company was a charitable body and their claim succeeded on this basis.

1. See para 9.07 above.
2. [1916] 2 AC 307.
3. [1951] Ch 728.

10.20 From this welter of conflicting decisions, the following principles may be extracted with some hesitation:

(1) The rule in Salomon's case is still the law. The company and its shareholders are separate legal entities and the courts normally cannot infer from the degree of control exercised by the shareholders a relationship of principal and agent or beneficiary and trustee between the shareholders and the company.

(2) The courts, however, will not permit the statutory privilege of incorporation to be used for any *fraudulent, illegal or improper purpose*. Where it is so misused, the courts may treat a company thus incorporated as identical with its promoters.

(3) In certain cases, where no actual misuse of the privilege of incorporation is involved, the courts may nonetheless infer the existence of an *agency* or a *trust*, if to do otherwise would lead to injustice or facilitate the avoidance of tax liability.

(4) In the case of *a group of companies*, the court may sometimes treat the group as one entity, particularly where to do otherwise would have unjust consequences for outsiders dealing with companies in the group.

(5) The rule in Salomon's case does not prevent the court from looking at the individual members of the company in order to determine its *character* and *status* and where it legally resides.

Chapter 11

Contracts

11.01 A company, being a legal entity, can enter into contracts as an individual can. It is, however, subject to one major limitation from which the individual is free: it cannot enter into a contract which is *ultra vires*, i.e. beyond its powers. As we have seen, any act which is not authorised, either expressly or by implication, by the memorandum is *ultra vires* the company. This rule renders such contracts void, not merely as between the company and its members, but also as between the company and the other party to the contract (referred to in this chapter as 'the outsider'). Coupled with the principle that persons dealing with the company are presumed to be aware of the contents of its public documents, including the memorandum, (an application of the legal doctrine known as *constructive notice*) this rule was capable of causing serious injustice and has been significantly modified by the Oireachtas in favour of outsiders dealing with the company.[1]

1. Para 11.04 below.

Pre-incorporation contracts

11.02 A company cannot enter into any contract until it has been incorporated, since until that time it does not exist in law. Nor until the enactment of the Principal Act of 1963 could the company ratify the contract *after* its incorporation. Section 37 of the Act, however, provides that
> 'Any contract or other transaction purporting to be entered into by a company prior to its formation or by any person on behalf of the company prior to its formation may be ratified by the company after its formation and thereupon the company shall become bound by it and entitled to the benefit thereof as if it had been in existence at the date of such contract or other transaction and had been a party thereto.'[1]

If the company does not ratify the pre-incorporation contract, it can neither sue nor be sued on foot of it. But if the other party to the contract can prove that the company has benefited under the contract–if, for example, it has received goods and refused to pay for them–he may be entitled to recover the money in a quasi-contractual action. And, even without ratification, the contract is binding on those who purported to contract on the company's behalf.

1. This was one of the Irish innovations in the Act. The English Acts contain no such provision.

Form of contracts

11.03 Provided the contract is not *ultra vires*, it can be entered into by the company in the same form as a similar contract entered into by an individual. Section 38 of the Principal Act provides that a contract which if made between private persons would be required to be in writing and under seal may be made on behalf of the company in writing under the common seal of the company. Where if made between private persons, it would have to be in writing and signed by the parties to be charged therewith, it may be made on behalf of the company in writing, signed by any person acting under its authority, express or implied. It may be varied or discharged in the same manner in which it is authorised to be made. (It should be noted that this last provision of the Principal Act is permissive and not mandatory. Consequently, where a contract can be validly varied or discharged in some other manner under the general law, it can be so varied or discharged in the case of a company. Thus, a contract under seal can lawfully be varied or discharged by a simple contract and this also applies to contracts executed under the seal of a company.)[1]

The number of instances in which a company must contract under seal are rare. A conveyance or assignment of freehold or leasehold land must, however, be by deed, and an agreement made without consideration will not normally be enforceable unless it is under seal. In both of these cases, accordingly, the document must be under the common seal of the company.

The most important examples of contracts which must be evidenced in writing to be enforceable are those specified in the Irish Statute of Frauds and, of such contracts, the most important in practice are contracts for the sale of land. Where a company is party to such a contract, it will accordingly not be enforceable against the company unless it is evidenced in writing signed by a person acting under the authority of the company, express or implied.

1. Palmer, vol 1, 27.09.

The ultra vires rule and the doctrine of constructive notice

11.04 The rule that a company had no power to enter into a contract which was not expressly or impliedly authorised by its consititution–the 'ultra vires' rule–was firmly established in the early days of the Companies' Acts in England. Moreover, persons dealing with the company were presumed to be aware of the contents of the company's public documents, including the memorandum. This latter principle–an application of the doctrine of 'constructive notice'–meant that a trader who entered into a contract with a company which was *ultra vires* the company's memorandum could not seek to uphold the contract by pleading that he was unaware of the company's incapacity.

The injustice which the rule was capable of producing was vividly illustrated in *Re Jon Beauforte (London) Ltd.*[1] In that case, the company was engaged in mnaufacturing veneer panels, an object which was not authorised by the memorandum. They ordered coke from a fuel merchant for use in the factory where the panels were being manufactured. Since the company's notepaper indicated that they were in the business of manufacturing veneer panels, the fuel merchant was held to be actually aware that the coke would be used for that purpose; and although he was wholly unaware that the company was not entitled to carry on that business, he was assumed to be so aware under the doctrine of constructive notice. In the event, he was unable to recover the price of the coke.

The doctrine was modified in Ireland by s 8 (1) of the Principal Act which provides that

'Any act or thing done by a company which if the company had been empowered to do the same would have been lawfully and effectively done, shall, notwithstanding that the company had no power to do such act or thing, be effective in favour of any person relying on such act or thing who is not shown to have been *actually aware*, at the time when he so relied thereon, that such act or thing was not within the powers of the company, but any director or officer of the company who was responsible for the doing by the company of such act or thing shall be liable to the company for any loss or damage suffered by the company in consequence thereof.'

Accordingly, an outsider who entered into a transaction unaware of the contents of the memorandum and articles was now able to enforce the transaction against the company, even though it was *ultra vires*. To that extent, the section implemented the recommendations of Jenkins in this area. Jenkins had also recommended, however, that the transaction should be enforceable even where the memorandum and articles had been read, provided that the person reading them had 'honestly and reasonably failed to appreciate that they had the effect of precluding the company from entering into the transaction.' It appeared that the draughtsman of the Principal Act had refrained from following this recommendation and this was so decided in *Northern Bank Finance Corporation v Quinn and Achates Investment Company*.[2]

In that case, Q borrowed £145,000 from the plaintiff bank. The loan was secured by a guarantee of the defendant company supported by a mortgage of certain property. When Q defaulted on the repayment instalments, the plaintiff bank issued proceedings against Q and the company. The evidence established that the memorandum and articles of the company had been furnished to and read by the solicitor for the plaintiff bank. Keane J held that the transaction was *ultra vires* since it was not authorised by the memorandum and articles and s 8 (1) of the Principal Act did not assist the plaintiff bank since their solicitor had read the memorandum and articles, although he failed to appreciate that they precluded the company from entering into the transaction.

1. [1953] Ch 131.
2. Unreported; judgement delivered 8 November 1979.

11.05 The First EEC Companies Directive required the abolition of the *ultra vires* rule as it affected outsiders. But in an important proviso, it permitted member states to maintain the rule, where the company proved that the outsider knew that the act was beyond the objects of the company 'or could not, in view of the circumstances, have been unaware of it'. Disclosure of the statutes (i.e. the memorandum and articles) was not to be sufficient for this purpose.

The Directive was implemented in Ireland by the European Communities (Companies) Regulations 1973,[1] article 6 of which provides that:

'(1) In favour of a person dealing with a company in good faith, any transaction entered into by any organ of the company, being its board of directors or any person registered under these regulations as a person authorised to bind the company, shall be deemed to be within the capacity of the company and any limitation of the powers of that board or person whether imposed by the memorandum or articles of association or otherwise may not be relied upon as against any person so dealing with the company.

(2) Any such person shall be presumed to have acted in good faith unless the contrary is proved.

(3) For the purposes of this Regulation, the registration of a person authorised to bind the company shall be effected by delivering to the Registrar of Companies a notice giving the name and designation of the person concerned.'

The scope of this regulation and its relationship to s 8 of the Principal Act is not clear. It is certainly more limited in its application than s 8, since it is confined to contracts entered into by the board of directors and registered agents and does not apply to unlimited companies. Such contracts are enforceable by outsiders under the terms of article 6 even though *ultra vires*, provided the outsiders entered into them in 'good faith'. Where the person is not aware of the lack of capacity of the company–as in the case where he has not read the memorandum and articles–it seems clear that he should be treated as having acted in good faith. Insofar as the directive can be used as a guide to the construction of the Regulations, its terms would appear to confirm this, stating as it does that disclosure of the statutes is not to be treated as putting the outsider on notice of the company's lack of capacity. To that extent, the Article goes no further than s 8 of the Principal Act. It is thought, however, that it would also protect the outsider who read the memorandum and articles but–to use again the language of Jenkins– 'honestly and reasonably failed to appreciate that they had the effect of precluding the company from entering into the transaction'.[2]

1. SI 1973/163.
2. The article was not relied on in *Northern Bank Finance Corporation Ltd v Quinn and Achates Investment Company*, presumably because the company was not a limited company.

11.06 We have seen that the *powers* of a company cannot be used for purposes which are *ultra vires*. We shall also see at a later stage that the directors must use their powers in good faith for the benefit of the company as a whole.[1] If, for example, the company borrows money for an object not stated in the memorandum, the act of borrowing, while within the capacity of the company, is nonetheless unlawful. Similarly, if the directors enter into a contract which is authorised by the memorandum but is solely for their own financial advantage, their action is unlawful. In either of these cases, the transaction, although not *ultra vires*, may be set aside as an improper use of the company's powers.

Where, however, an outsider is not aware of the fact that the transaction is an improper exercise of the company's powers and there are no circumstances which should have caused him to inquire whether it was improper, it will be binding on the company. There are a number of English decision which make it clear that an outsider will be able to enforce such a contract, unless he has actual or constructive notice of its unlawful nature, and it is thought that these decisions would be applied in Ireland.[2]

1. See para 22.14 below.
2. *Re David Payne 86 Young v David Payne 86* [1904] 2 Ch 608; *Rolled Steel Products (Holdings) Ltd v British Steel Corporation and Co Ltd* [1984] BCLC 466.

11.07 Such transactions, it should be emphasised, are within the powers of the company. They must be distinguished from transactions affected by s 8 of the Principal Act. The latter are unenforceable by the outsider only when he has *actual* notice of their *ultra vires* character, i.e. when he has read the memorandum and articles. Even though he has constructive notice of the memorandum and articles, in the sense that he is deemed to be aware of their existence and could ascertain their contents if he wished, he will not be precluded by such constructive notice from enforcing the contract. As we have seen, it would seem that the same considerations apply to a transaction within the scope of Article 6 of the 1973 Regulations.

11.08 It would seem logical that an *ultra vires* contract, being a legal nullity, should be incapable of enforcement by the company. This was so held at first instance in *Bell Houses Ltd v City Wall Properties Ltd*[1]: the decision was reversed in the Court of Appeal, but on the ground that the contract was not *ultra vires*. While doubts have been expressed as to the correctness of this view,[2] it would seem a logical corollary to the general *ultra vires* rule which remains the law notwithstanding its statutory modification in favour of outsiders seeking to enforce such contracts.

1. [1966] 1 QB 207; [1966] 2 QB 656.
2. See Gower, p 172.

Liability of company in respect of unauthorised or irregular transactions

11.09 A contract may be fully within the capacity of a company and hence not affected by the *ultra vires* rule. But the outsider may still be unable to enforce the contract against the company because the person who entered into it on behalf of the company was not authorised to do so. Again a contract may be within the capacity of the company and yet be unenforceable because some condition as to its validity has not been complied with. Thus it may be fully within the powers of the company to borrow money but only with the sanction of a resolution of the members. If such a resolution is not passed, the contract may be unenforceable.

It must be emphasised that these two categories of contract are not instances of contracts which are *ultra vires*: they are within the capacity of the company but are either *unauthorised*, or *irregular* because of non-compliance with some legal requirement whether contained in the memorandum and articles or elsewhere.

11.10 In the case of each of these categories, however, the contract may still be enforceable. In the case of the unauthorised contract, it may be enforceable because the person who entered into it was acting under an *apparent* or *ostensible* authority as an agent of the company. In the case of an irregular contract, it may be enforceable because the outsider did not know of the irregularity and cannot be presumed to have been aware of it. He may be actually aware, to take the example already given, that the memorandum and articles require the sanction of a resolution to borrowing, because he has read these documents, but he is not presumed to be aware whether the resolution has actually been passed or not. In the case of such matters of 'indoor management', as they are called, the rule in the leading case of *Royal*

British Bank Ltd v Turquand[1] applies and the outsider is not affected by an irregularlity of which he has no notice.

Although these two categories of contract are different, they may on occasions overlap. Thus the articles of association may require certain formalities to be complied with when the company appoints a managing director. The company may permit someone to act as managing director without complying with those formalities. If he then enters into a contract of a type normally within the authority of a managing director, it will be binding on the company, although never authorised by them, in favour of an outsider who was unaware of the irregularity. It will be so binding for two reasons: first, because it was within the person's ostensible authority and secondly because under the rule in *Turquand*'s case the outsider is not affected by a non-compliance with the articles of which he had no knowledge.

Each of the categories will now be considered in turn.

1. (1856) 6 E & B 327.

Unauthorised contracts: the doctrine of ostensible or apparent authority

11.11 There is a general principle of law which may be stated as follows. Where one person (known as an agent) enters into a transaction purportedly on behalf of another (known as a principal) the transaction will be binding on the principal only if the agent acts *either* within the scope of an authority conferred on him prior to the transaction or subsequently by ratification *or* within the scope of an *ostensible or apparent* authority not actually conferred on him.[1]

1. Bowstead on Agency, 14th edn. 16, 235.

11.12 As applied to companies, cases of *actual* authority present no difficulty. If a person is expressly authorised by one of the 'organs' of the company–the board of directors or the members in general meeting–to enter into a contract which is within the powers of the company, it will be binding on the company. Similarly, if a person duly appointed to a particular office in the company enters into a contract which is normally within the scope of the relevant officer's authority, it will also be binding on the company.

The majority of trading companies employs a managing director whose function it is to carry on the business of the company in the usual way and do all acts necessary for that purpose. Such acts normally include signing cheques, borrowing money, giving security for the company's indebtedness, receiving the payment of debts on behalf of the company and giving guarantees. A managing director, accordingly, has *actual* authority to bind the company in the case of such transactions.[1] But his authority is generally limited to commercial transactions: he would not normally be entitled, for example, to approve a transfer of shares or to sell the property of the company. Again, it must be emphasised that there is nothing to prevent the company from expressly authorising the managing director to enter into such a transaction, in which event it will be binding on the company. In the case of ordinary commercial transactions, however, express authorisation is not required: the managing director has authority by virtue of his appointment to enter into such transactions and this is an example of actual authority.[2] His authority may, of course, be limited by the terms of his contract with the company or the articles, but unless the outsider is actually aware of the limitation, he will not be affected by it. In this case, the authority is ostensible rather than actual.

The position of the chairman of a company may be contrasted with that of the managing director. The former will not usually be regarded as having authority to enter into everyday commercial contracts in the same manner as the managing director: his functions are limited, as his title suggests, to presiding at meetings of the board of directors and the members.

1. *Hely-Hutchinson v Brayhead Ltd* [1968] 1 QB 549.
2. Ibid.

11.13   In most cases, of course, an outsider dealing with the company will not know whether the agent was in fact actually authorised to carry out the transaction in question or whether he was actually appointed to the office in question. He may still be protected in such cases, however, even if it should transpire that the agent was not so authorised or was not actually appointed to the particular office. This will arise when the agent is acting under an *ostensible or apparent* authority.

In the leading modern case on the topic, *Freeman and Lockyer v Buckhurst Park Properties (Mangal) Ltd*[1] Diplock LJ. laid down four conditions which must be satisfied before the doctrine can be successfully invoked.

(1) *There must be a representation made to the outsider that the agent had authority to enter on behalf of the company into a contract of the kind sought to be enforced.* Such a representation can be either positive or tacit. If the company have acquiesced in the agent's entering into such contracts on previous occasions, they may be regarded as having tacitly represented that he had authority to do so.

(2) *Such a representation must be made by a person or persons who themselves had actual authority to manage the business of the company either generally or in respect of the matters to which the contract relates.*

(3) *The outsider must have been induced by the representation to enter into the contract, i.e. he must have actually relied on it.*

(4) *The memorandum or articles of association must not deprive the company of the capacity to enter into the kind of contract sought to be enforced or to delegate the authority to enter into a contract of that kind to the agent.*

In that case, the plaintiffs were a firm of architects who sued the defendant company for fees due to them in respect of plans prepared by them at the request of one of the directors. The evidence established that, although the director in question had never been formally appointed managing director of the company, he had acted for some time as if he were managing director without objection from the only other director. It was held that the company was bound by the contract entered into by him, since they tacitly represented that he was entitled to act as managing director and such a contract was within the normal scope of the authority of such an agent. There was no question of the company being unable to delegate that authority, since the appointment of a managing director was expressly authorised by the articles.

1. [1964] 2 QB 480.

11.14   The doctrine of ostensible authority was also applied by Hamilton J in *Kilgobbin Mink and Stud Farms Ltd v National Credit Company Limited*.[1] In that case, the plaintiff company was the lessee of premises in Suffolk

Street, Dublin. When the rent fell into arrears, they came to an arrangement with the lessors, the defendant company, under which they agreed to surrender the premises in consideration of being forgiven the arrears and being paid a sum of £8,500. The plaintiff company passed a resolution authorising the chairman, BL, to surrender the premises. BL (who owned all except one of the shares in the plaintiff company) wrote to the lessors requesting them to pay the sum of £8,500 by direct debit into the bank account of another company of which he was the controlling shareholder, which they did. The plaintiff company having got into financial difficulties, a receiver was appointed and he instituted proceedings in their name claiming the sum of £8,500 from the lessors. Hamilton J. dismissed the claim, holding that BL in requesting the payment to be made into the bank account of another company (which was trading in the same premises) was acting with the ostensible authority of the plaintiff company and that the lessors were entitled to rely on that authority.

It is thought that the decision is not free from difficulty. This was not a case of actual authority: the resolution did no more than authorise BL to surrender the premises and did not entitle him to divert the £8,500 to another company. The transaction was not within the normal scope of a chairman's authority. There are moreover clearly difficulties in treating it as a case of ostensible authority. There was no express representation that BL was entitled to write the letter in question and there had been no tacit acceptance by the company of his acting in a similar manner in the past and hence no 'holding out' of BL as having authority. The transaction was obviously a somewhat unusual one and the facts were wholly unlike those in *Freeman and Lockyer's case*. It is, of course, the case that in strict logic the position in law should have been the same if no receiver had been appointed and, as Hamilton J pointed out, it is inconceivable that the plaintiff company could have recovered the £8,500 if the receiver had not been appointed. But if the plaintiff company had had the temerity to sue for the £8,500 at the instance of BL rather than the receiver, the court might have been able to dismiss the claim on the basis that the recovery of the money by BL. when it had already been paid, would be a fraudulent misuse of corporate personality and hence within one of the established exceptions to the rule in Salomon's case.[2]

It is respectfully submitted that *Kilgobbin Mink and Stud Farms Ltd v National Credit Company Ltd* is not a sufficient authority for extending the doctrine of ostensible authority as laid down in earlier decisions and may properly be regarded as capable of distinction having regard to the unusual nature of the facts.

1. Unreported; judgement delivered 16 February 1978.
18. See para 10.12 above.

The rule in Royal British Bank v Turquand

11.15 The rule in its original form may be stated as follows. While persons dealing with a company are assumed to have read the *public documents* of the company (i.e. the memorandum and articles) and to have ascertained that the proposed transaction is not inconsistent therewith, they are not required to do more: they need not inquire into the regularity of the internal proceedings–the 'indoor management' of the company–and may assume that all is being done regularly.

11.16 A characteristic example of the rule in operation relates to meetings of the board of directors of a company. The articles may stipulate that certain acts may only be done with the authority of the board. A person dealing with the company may be aware of the provision because the articles are sent to him or someone acting on his behalf such as a solicitor. He may also be aware that the articles contain requirements as to a quorum for such meetings. But he may not know–and cannot be presumed to know–whether a quorum was present when the particular act was authorised or indeed whether the board ever authorised the act at all.

Since the abolition of the doctrine of constructive notice in relation to ultra vires acts by s 8 of the Principal Act, the rule in Turquand's case is not of such significance as before. An outsider who has not actually read the memorandum and articles need not rely on the rule: he is protected by s8. But where the company establish that the outsider was aware of the relevant provisions, the rule can still be of importance. In *Ulster Investment Bank Ltd v Euro Estates Ltd and Another*,[1] for example, the liquidator of the first defendant company challenged the validity of a mortagage executed by the company in favour of the plaintiff bank on the ground *inter alia* that a quorum was not present at a meeting of the directors which authorised the affixing of the seal to the deed. The memorandum and articles had been furnished to the bank and s 8 was not relied on; but Carroll J rejected the liquidator's claim, holding that the rule in Turquand's case applied.

1. [1982] ILRM 57.

11.17 The exceptions to the rule in Turquand's case should be noted. Clearly it can have no application where the outsider is shown to have been aware of the irregularity. Equally it does not apply where the circumstances were such as to put the outsider on enquiry as to whether the transaction was irregular. Thus in *Underwood v Bank of Liverpool*,[1] it was held that the fact that a director was lodging company cheques to his own personal account was sufficiently unusual to have put the outsider on enquiry; and accordingly that he was not entitled to rely on his lack of knowledge as bringing him within the rule.

The rule applies only to outsiders. Consequently, a director of the company who enters into a particular transaction in his capacity as a director will not be able to make the case that he was unaware of the internal management of the company which rendered the transaction irregular. But this is only so where he enters into the transaction as a director: if he contracts as an outsider, the fact that he happens to be a director of the company with whom he is contracting is not necessarily a ground for attributing to him knowledge of the 'indoor management' of that company which he does not actually possess.[2]

It should, however, be borne in mind that even directors who contract as outsiders are not in the same position as complete outsiders: they have, for example, means of knowledge denied to the latter, such as access to the minutes and accounts of the company. In an appropriate case, this may be a relevant factor in determining whether knowledge of an irregularity should be attributed to them.

1. [1924] 1 KB 775.
2. *Hely-Hutchinson v Brayhead Ltd,* above.

11.18 It is usually said that the rule does not apply where a document is forged so as to purport to be the company's document. This view has, however, been strongly challenged by one leading English commentator.[1] It is based upon a dictum by Lord Loreburn LC. in *Ruben v Great Fingall Consolidated*.[2] In that case, the forged document–a share certificate–was both forged and issued by the company secretary in return for an advance of money. Quite clearly, such a transaction was not merely unauthorised: it was also incapable of attracting the protection either of the rule in Turquand's case or of the doctrine of ostensible authority. Even if the document had been genuine, it would still have been a patently irregular transaction, since a secretary would not normally be empowered to enter into such a transaction; and the case could have been decided on that basis without regard to the forgery. It is thought that even in the case of a forged document, the rule should still apply where

(a) the transaction was within the ostensible authority of the company's agent and was not *patently* irregular,
(b) the outsider was unaware of the forgery, and
(c) there were no circumstances to excite suspicion.

1. Gower, pp 203/5.
2. [1906] AC 439 at 443.

11.19 Finally, it should be borne in mind that the rule is for the protection of outsiders and not of the company. The outsider who enters into a transaction which he subsequently discovers to be invalid because of some defect in indoor management is entitled to rely on the invalidity if sued on foot of the transaction, unless he can be shown to have waived the invalidity.[1]

1. Gower, p 192.

Chapter 12

Tort and crime

Capacity to sue in tort and liability for torts

12.01 A tort is a wrongful act, other than a breach of contract, in respect of which the remedy in law is an action for unliquidated damages.[1] Although historically the specific tort or wrong of negligence was of limited importance only, it has in modern times become by far the most common of torts. A wide range of other torts, however, still comes before the courts, such as defamation, assault, trespass, passing off of goods and false imprisonment.

1. *Salmond on Tort*, 18th edn, p 7.

12.02 A company is entitled to sue in respect of torts committed against it. Clearly, however, there are some torts which, of their nature, cannot be committed against a company, such as assault and false imprisonment. It has been held, however, that a trading company can sue for defamation where its business reputation–as distinct from the individual reputation of a shareholder, director or employee–has been damaged.[1]

1. Halsbury's *Laws of England,* 4th edn, vol 28, para 25.

12.03 A company may also be sued in respect of torts committed by it. As we have seen, a company, being an artificial entity, can only act through its organs and agents and accordingly is liable in tort only where the tort in question is committed by one of its organs or agents.

It follows that if one of the organs of the company, such as the board of directors or the members in general meeting, authorise the commission of a tort, the company will be liable. Similarly, if the company expressly authorises an agent to commit a tort on its behalf, the company will be liable.

It is submitted that the company will be so liable even where the tort is committed in the course of pursuing an object which is *ultra vires* the company.[1] But, while agents of the company have on occasions an implied authority to commit acts on behalf of the company without being expressly authorised to do so, it is submitted that they can never enjoy an implied authority to commit a tort in pursuance of an *ultra vires* object. Thus an employee of the company has implied authority to do any act which is necessary for the performance of the work he is employed to do; and this implied authority may render the company liable for a tort, such as a negligent act committed in the course of his work. But this does not extend to such an act where it is *ultra vires* the company.[2]

1. *Campbell v Paddington Corporation* [1911] 1 KB 869. It has been suggested that the case is not an entirely satisfactory authority for the statement in the text, since the act in

110

question–the erection of stands in the street by the defendant local authority–may have been within their powers. (See A.I. Goodhart, 'Corporate Liability in Tort and the Doctrine of Ultra Vires', *Essays in Jurisprudence and the Common Law*, 1931, and an essay under the same title by Dafydd Jenkins in *Irish Jurist* (New Series) vol 5, p 11.) The view of the law in the text is, however, also supported by *National Telephone Co Ltd v Constables of St Peter's Port* [1900] AC 317 and *Batson v School Board for London* (1903) 67 JP 457.

2. *Poulson v London & SW Rly* (1867) LR 2 QB 534.

Criminal liability

12.04 A company is capable in law of committing a crime and of suffering the punishment prescribed by law for the crime in question. To this general rule, however, there are certain exceptions which again flow from the fact that the company is an artificial legal entity different in its nature from a human being.

12.05 Certain crimes, i.e. bigamy and perjury, can only be committed by the person actually charged with them: they cannot be committed by someone else acting on the accused's behalf. Accordingly, a company is incapable of committing such crimes. Moreover, there are certain punishments which can be inflicted only on human beings, i.e. capital punishment and imprisonment. (The celebrated question asked by counsel in the reign of James II, 'can you hang its common seal?'[1] retains its validity in the era of the limited liability company.) A company can, of course, suffer other punishments, such as a fine and sequestration of its assets.

1. In *R v City of London* 8 State Trials, 1087 at 1138.

12.06 In general, a person cannot be found guilty of a criminal offence unless he intended–or can be presumed to have intended–to commit that offence. In the language of the criminal law, there must not only be *actus reus*, i.e. the actual commission of the offence, there must also be *mens rea*, i.e. an intention to commit the offence.

In the case of a company, proof of the *mens rea* presents no difficulty where an organ of the company–such as the board of directors or the company in general meeting–has authorised the commission of the offence. Equally there is no difficulty where the company expressly authorises the commission of an offence by one of its agents, e.g. an employee. While there is no authority on the point, it seems clear in principle that the fact that the act in question is *ultra vires* the company or committed in the course of pursuing an *ultra vires* object is no defence to a criminal charge.[1]

Where the company has not expressly authorised the commission of a crime but it is committed by one of its agents, such as an employee acting in the course of his employment by the company, the company may still be criminally liable. It will undoubtedly be so liable where the statute creating the offence makes a company liable for the offence when it is committed by one of its officers or employees. Whether the statute imposes such a liability will depend on the language used.[2] In the absence of express language to that effect, however, the statute will normally be construed as imposing criminal liability on the company only where there is active participation in the commission of the crime by those who are managing the affairs of the company.[3]

1. Gower, pp 169–170.
2. Pennington, pp 111–112.
3. *Tesco Supermarkets v Nattrass* [1972] AC 153.

Part four

The capital of the company

Chapter 13

Types of capital

Meaning of 'capital'

13.01   The word 'capital' suggest to the layman that part of an enterprise, be it commercial, social or even domestic, which is permanent in its nature and not used up in the day-to-day operations. In this sense, when one thinks of the capital of a business, one usually has in mind the factory or office premises, the machinery and furniture, its investments etc. By contrast, the actual cash receipts from its trading operations one thinks of as its 'income' to be applied in paying day-to-day debts, with any surplus going to the owners as representing the profits. Similarly, a family may regard their house and furniture, together with any savings and investments they may have, as their 'capital'.

13.02   This is not, however, what the term 'capital' necessarily means to lawyers and accountants. For them it may have a different significance which it is important to appreciate.

It is normal in the case of a well run business of any size to prepare at regular intervals a statement of all the property of the business–its *assets*–and what it owes–its *liabilities*. This document–the balance sheet– is one with which every student of company law should be familiar. In its traditional form, it shows on the right hand side of the page, the assets, i.e. the buildings, plant, machinery, stock in trade, debts owing to the business, cash in the bank, etc. On the left hand side are shown the liabilities. Where the assets are not cash, such non-cash assets in modern accountancy are carried at certain valuations, the basis of the valuations being shown either on the face of the balance sheet or indicated by accounting policies. The total of the liabilities will appear on the left in cash and the balance, where they are less than the assets, is the value in money terms of the business to its owners *as it appears from the balance sheet*. (As we shall see, when we come to deal with company accounts in more detail, because of the valuation methods employed it is not necessarily an accurate guide to that value at the time when the balance sheet is available for scrutiny.) This balance in the case of a company is referred to by accountants as 'the shareholders' equity'.

13.03   The description just given of the essential features of a balance sheet is deliberately simplified. A moment's consideration will show that even the simplest balance sheet will have further refinements. Thus some assets, of

115

their nature, will not be disposed of in the day-to-day operations. These assets, which include buildings, machinery, etc., are called *fixed assets* to distinguish them from those assets which are regularly disposed of, such as the stock in trade. The latter are called *current assets* or *working capital*.

13.04   We now come to the meaning of the word 'capital' in company law. Here again it has a precise significance and one that is different from the meanings we have been discussing. Generally speaking, it refers to the *share capital* of the company.

We have seen that in the case of a company limited by shares the company is owned by its members–the shareholders–in shares having a specified money value. The shareholders either pay for their shares in money or by means of some other consideration or agree to pay for them when called upon to do so. The individual shares will generally have the same cash value–£1, £5, £10 or as the case may be–and a shareholder will be allotted one or more such shares. The value of the units is set, in the case of a public company, at a level which will create the most attractive market for the shares by making them more easily traded in on the stock exchange. The total value of the shares thus issued and allotted is usually called the *issued share capital* of the company and it is this that is normally meant when the 'capital' of the company is referred to. It must be distinguished from the *nominal share capital*, i.e. the amount of the capital as stated in the memorandum which represents the limit of the capital which the company is authorised to issue. (The latter is also sometimes referred to as the *authorised share capital*).

13.05   We can now return to our balance sheet: and we find that, in the case of a company having a share capital, an item appears on the liabilities side which is unique to such enterprises. This is the *issued share capital* of the company. It is not in the strict sense a liability of the company: the members will have no legal grievance if it is all lost in the course of the company's operations. But, as the fund contributed by the members, it appears logically along with the liabilities in order, again, to give an indication of the worth of the company to the people who own it, i.e. the members. If the assets on the right hand side exceed the total liabilities including the share capital, the surplus represents that value as it appears from the balance sheet. It might seem logical that where the balance sheet shows such a surplus the issued share capital should simply be increased to bring the two sides into balance, but this is not the way a company's accounts are treated. Instead, the balancing figure is separately shown, usually with the description *reserves*.

13.06   We have seen that the issued share capital must never exceed the nominal share capital. Both figures should always appear in the balance sheet; and with this in mind, we can now construct a typical balance sheet of a company limited by shares.

We will use the modern vertical layout rather than the old fashioned right/left layout.

116

LEINSTER INDUSTRIAL PROCESSES LTD
BALANCE SHEET
AS AT
31ST DECEMBER 1984

	Notes	1984 £	1983 £
FIXED ASSETS	1	170,000	160,000
CURRENT ASSETS			
Stocks		20,000	18,000
Debtors		12,000	15,000
Cash		8,000	5,000
		40,000	38,000
CURRENT LIABILITIES			
Creditors		15,000	17,000
Overdraft (secured)	2	6,000	7,000
		21,000	24,000
NET CURRENT ASSETS		19,000	14,000
		189,000	174,000
Financed by:			
Share Capital	3	100,000	100,000
Reserves		65,000	44,000
Shareholders' Funds		165,000	144,000
Loans (secured)		224,000	30,000
		189,000	174,000

NOTES:

1. A separate note will be attached showing fixed assets and depreciation analysed over major categories of assets.
2. That part of the loans payable within twelve months of the balance sheet date will be shown as a current liability. The balance will be included as a long term loan.
3. A separate note will be given showing the authorised, issued and paid up position for each class of capital.

13.07 One further feature of the balance sheet should be noted. As we have seen, the issued share capital of the company consists of the shares which have been allotted to the shareholders and for which they have paid *or agreed to pay*. The issued share capital must accordingly be divided in the balance sheet between the amount which has actually been paid–the *paid up capital*–and the amount which shareholders have agreed to pay if called upon to do so–the *uncalled capital*. Accountants treat the paid up share capital as part of 'the shareholders' equity' and it appears in the balance sheet proper. The amount unpaid appears by way of a note, because accountants treat it as more in the nature of a contingent asset.

13.08 Clearly the actual value of the shares will fluctuate with the fortunes of the company; and one of the major factors in determining their value will

117

be the net asset value of the company. Whatever their *actual* value may be, however, the *nominal* value of the shares–£1, £5, £10–will remain the same. In the case of a public limited company, the shares may rise and fall in value on the stock exchange from day to day, but the nominal value is always the same.

It is obviously somewhat anomalous that the nominal value of the shares should bear no relationship to their actual value in the market and this has led to calls from time to time for the introduction of 'no par value' shares. Such shares have been permitted in some states in the USA since 1912 and in Canada since 1918. Their introduction was recommended by Cox and there have been frequent suggestions to the same effect in England. As yet, however, no attempt has been made in either jurisdiction to give statutory effect to these proposals.

Reserve capital

13.09   A company may resolve by special resolution that a specified portion of its uncalled capital is not to be capable of being called up, except in the event, and for the purposes of, its being wound up. The amount in question is called the *reserve capital* of the company. Where this power is availed of, the company is in a position not unlike that of a company limited by guarantee and having share capital. The members may each have to contribute in the event of a winding up; but it differs from the case of a company limited by guarantee, since in the latter case each member, or class of members, normally undertakes to pay the same amount in the event of a winding up. In the case of a company with a share capital, the amount which each member has to pay in respect of the reserve capital will vary depending on the number of shares which he owns.

Importance of capital

13.10   The courts have from the earliest days of modern company law attached great importance to the capital of the company; and they have been particularly concerned to see that it is not *reduced* save with proper safeguards and subject to specified conditions. The limitations on a company's power to reduce its capital will be considered in detail in the next two chapters, but it is sufficient to note at this point that the courts' concern springs from an anxiety to see that creditors of the company are not prejudiced by an unwarranted reduction of the capital on the faith of which they may have extended credit to the company.

It must be said, however, that in many instances the protection supposedly afforded to creditors by the maintenance of this legal principle is largely illusory. As we have seen, the huge preponderance of companies formed under the Acts are private companies. The amount of the paid up capital of such a company can be as small as the promoters wish. (In this context, its position is markedly different from that of a public limited company.) Moreover, even where the paid up capital is substantial, it may still be no real guide to the financial strength of the company. That can only be ascertained from the balance sheet (and even that is not a wholly reliable guide) which is not available to the public in the case of a private company.

Share premium account

13.11   Because of the importance of the principle referred to in the preceding paragraph, the law requires certain items which are not strictly part of the capital of the company to be dealt with as though they were.

The first of these items arises when the company issues shares at a *premium*, i.e. receives more in cash or kind than the nominal value of the shares. The amount by which the cash or other consideration exceeds the nominal value must be transferred to a separate account known as the *share premium account*. It would not be regarded as a proper business practice to pay any part of this as a dividend, since it is not really a profit. It may, however, be paid out in the form of *bonus shares*[1] because no reduction in the capital in real terms is thereby effected.[2]

1. See para 7.03 above.
2. For other circumstances in which the company may apply the share premiums account, see para 8.24 above.

Capital redemption reserve fund

13.12   As we shall see in Chapter Seventeen, a company limited by shares has in one instance the right to *redeem* shares, i.e. repay to the shareholder the amount paid up on the shares and wipe them out of existence, as it were, thereby reducing the capital of the company. This arises where the company has power under its memorandum or articles to issue *redeemable preference shares*. One of the ways in which the shares may be redeemed is out of profits; but, since it is not regarded as good commercial practice to utilise profits for the reduction of capital, the company is required in that event to form a *capital redemption reserve fund*, which appears as a liability in the balance sheet. The company may, if it wishes, use this fund to issue bonus shares which are treated as fully paid up. Thus the shareholders get the profits, but the capital of the company remains the same in real terms, since the capital redemption reserve fund is simply replaced by the bonus shares.

Equity share capital

13.13   The phrase 'equity capital' is sometimes used by accountants to describe the net asset value of a company limited by shares. In company law, however, it has a different meaning: it refers to the total issued share capital of the company, excluding only those shares which do not confer on the holders participating rights or which limit the rights of the holders in relation to dividends or capital.

Loan capital

13.14   Many companies raise money for their operations in other ways besides the issuing of shares. The money thus borrowed will normally be secured by a *debenture* or series of debentures or debenture stock. While, generally speaking, any document issued by the company which acknowledges a debt due by it may be called a debenture, in modern usage it invariably refers to such an acknowledgement when supported by a security of some sort. That security may take the form of a *fixed charge* of one of the company's assets or a *floating charge* over the assets and undertakings of the company or of both. Debentures are frequently referred to as *loan capital*; but it will readily be seen that it is not an appropriate description, since a debenture does not confer on its holder the status of a shareholder. Nor has the debenture holder any of the rights of a shareholder in relation to such matters as dividends, the right to attend at meetings and vote, etc.

Chapter 14

The maintenance of capital

14.01 The law has always attached great importance to the maintenance by a company of its issued share capital. It is regarded as a basic protection to creditors since, whether it is paid up in whole or in part, it constitutes a fund to which the creditors may have recourse in the event of the company being unable to pay its debts as they fall due.

This protection is, as we have seen, somewhat illusory, since there is nothing to prevent a company from fixing its share capital at a token figure of £10; and many people deal with limited companies on a day-to-day basis without troubling to enquire what the issued share capital of the company is. Moreover, the requirement that a company should maintain its capital intact is subject to the important qualification that losses of capital suffered in the ordinary course of business are recognised as legitimate.

14.02 In the case of public limited companies, however, the requirements of the law in this area are more stringent. We have already seen that, under the 1983 Act, such a company cannot commence business until the Registrar has certified that the nominal value of its allotted share capital is not less than the authorised minimum, i.e. £30,000.[1] That Act, which implemented in Ireland the Second EEC Directive, also contains provisions, which must now be examined in detail, designed to ensure the maintenance of a company's capital. Some of these are confined in their application to public limited companies: others, including s 40 which imposes on companies the obligation to convene an extraordinary meeting in the event of a serious loss of capital, are of general application.

1. Para 9.04 above.

Meeting to consider serious loss of capital

14.03 Paid up capital may be diminished or lost in the course of the company's trading; that is a result which no legislation can prevent ...' This observation of Lord Watson in *Trevor v Whitworth*[1] reflects the acknowledgement by the law that losses of capital suffered in the ordinary course of business are legitimate. The object of s 40 of the 1983 Act is to ensure that the directors and shareholders are given an opportunity of at least considering what steps, if any, should be taken in the event of the capital falling below a defined level.

1. (1887) 12 App Cas 409 at 423.

14.04 The section, which applies to all companies having a share capital, provides that where the net assets of the company are half or less of the amount of the company's called-up share capital[1] the directors must convene an extraordinary general meeting of the company for the purpose of considering whether any, and if so what, measures should be taken to deal with the situation. The meeting must be convened not later than 28 days from the earliest day on which the fact of the loss becomes known to any director and must be for a date not later than 56 days from that day.

1. For the meaning of these expressions see paras 13.02, 13.03, 13.04, 13.07 above.

14.05 The Act provides for stringent penalties where there is a failure to convene a meeting in accordance with s 40.[1] Each of the directors who knowingly and wilfully authorises or permits that failure to continue, is guilty of an offence. He is liable on indictment to a fine not exceeding £2,500 or, at the discretion of the court, to imprisonment for a term not exceeding two years or to both the fine and the imprisonment. The District Court is given jurisdiction to try these offences summarily, where the justice is of opinion that the facts proved or alleged against the director constitute a minor offence fit to be tried summarily, the Director of Public Prosecutions consents and the defendant, having had his right to be tried by jury explained to him, does not object. In that event, the defendant is liable on conviction to a fine not exceeding £500 or, at the discretion of the court, to a term of imprisonment not exceeding six months or to both.

1. S 57 (2).

14.06 The section is intended to provide some sort of safeguard for shareholders in a company in the event of a serious worsening in the net asset position of the company. It may be of some limited benefit to creditors, since directing the minds of the shareholders to the company's real financial position may also alert them to the dangers of becoming involved in fraudulent trading. There is, however, no obligation on the shareholders to take any steps to bring the company's net assets into line with the paid up capital. It would appear, moreover, that the section, although not expressly so confined, will in practice be of most relevance to public limited companies. There is still nothing to prevent private companies from having token share capitals only and accordingly being outside the ambit of the section.

Acquisition by a company of its own shares

14.07 One of the oldest principles of company law is that a company cannot buy its own shares. This rule–first laid down by the House of Lords in *Trevor v Whitworth*–is a further recognition by the law of the importance of not permitting the company's capital to be reduced to the detriment of the creditors.[1] Apart from that general consideration, it has in any event been regarded as undesirable for the company to deal in its own shares: there is always the danger that the price paid for the shares may be artificially high or low, enabling the directors (where they have shareholdings of their own) to manipulate the value of their shares to their own advantage and to the detriment of the other shareholders. Accordingly, such transactions have always been outlawed, even where expressly permitted by the memorandum. The only exceptions permitted were the redemption of preference shares under s 64 of the Principal Act[2] and the purchase of shares in pursuance of an order of the court under various provisions of that Act.

1. See *Bank of Ireland Finance Limited v Rockfield Ltd* (1979) IR 21.
2. See para 17.10 below.

14.08   The law has now been given statutory form in s 41 of the 1983 Act. This provides that, subject to certain specified provisions, no company having a share capital shall acquire its own shares, whether by purchase, subscription or otherwise. A company limited by shares may, however, acquire any of its own fully paid shares otherwise than for valuable consideration. (This exception is probably intended to provide for cases in which the company is acting as an executor or trustee.)

Four express exemptions are permitted by sub-s (4) viz:

(1) the redemption of preference shares in pursuance of the articles;[1]
(2) the acquisition of any shares in a reduction of capital duly made;[2]
(3) the purchase of any shares in pursuance of orders of the court under s 15 of the 1983 Act and ss 10 and 205 of the Principal Act;[3]
(4) the forfeiture of any shares, or the acceptance of any shares surrendered in lieu, in pursuance of the articles for failure to pay any sum payable in respect of those shares.[4]

Where a company purports to act in contravention of the section, the acquisition is rendered void and the company and every officer of the company who is in default are guilty of an offence. The company is liable on indictment to a fine not exceeding £2,000. Any officer found guilty is liable to a fine not exceeding £2,500 or imprisonment for a term not exceeding two years or to both. The offences may be tried in the District Court if the justice is of opinion that the facts proved or alleged against the defendant constitute a minor offence fit to be tried summarily, the Director of Public Prosecutions consents and the defendant, having been informed by the justice of his right to a trial by jury, does not object.[5]

1. Ibid.
2. See para 15.08 below.
3. For s 15 of the 1983 Act, see para 3.24 above. For s 10 of the Principal Act see para 4.18 above. For s 205 of the Principal Act, see Chapter 26 below.
4. See para 18.06 below.
5. S 57 (2) of the 1983 Act.

14.09   The Second EEC Directive, under which these provisions were introduced, provided that the general rule might be relaxed; and in England the opportunity has been taken to give companies a much wider power[1] to acquire their own shares, virtually repealing the decision in *Trevor v Whitworth*. No corresponding legislation has, however, been introduced in Ireland.

1. S 46 of the English 1981 Act. The section distinguishes between 'on market' and 'off market' transactions. It is only in the former case–when the shares are sold on a recognised stock exchange–that the restrictions may be lifted generally. It should also be remembered that in England there are now far more severe restrictions than in Ireland on 'insider' dealings by directors in shares, so that one of the main reasons for retaining the rule has ceased to be of importance.

14.10   The 1983 Act also contains in s 42 provisions designed to ensure that the requirements of s 41 are not circumvented by means of an acquisition of the company's shares made by a nominee of the company. Where shares in a company affected by s 41 are issued to a nominee of the company, they are to be treated as held by the nominee on his own account and the company are to be regarded as having no beneficial interest in them. The same result follows where they are acquired by the nominee from a third paprty as partly paid up.

The section further provides that if a person who acquired shares or to whom shares were issued as a nominee fails to pay what is due on them within 21 days from being called on to do so, the directors of the company at the time of the issue or acquisition are to be jointly or severally liable to pay that amount. (The same result follows where the shares were issued to him as a subscriber save that in such a case it is the other subscribers who are so liable). If, however, the director or subscriber appears to the court to have acted honestly and reasonably and the court is of the view that, having regard to all the circumstances of the case, he ought fairly to be excused from liability, the court may relieve him either wholly or partly from his liability on such terms as it thinks fit. Where a director or subscriber has reason to apprehend that such a claim will or might be made against him, he may apply to the court for relief and the court has then the same power of granting relief as if the proceedings had been brought.

The section does not apply where the company has no beneficial interest in the shares or to shares issued in consequence of an application before 13 October 1983 or transferred in pursuance of an agreement made before that day.

14.11   The undesirable practice of a company trafficking in its own shares could be carried on if a subsidiary were permitted to own shares in its parent company. Section 32 of the Principal Act accordingly provides that, with certain exceptions, a body corporate cannot be a member of a company which is its holding company and any allotment or transfer of shares in a company to its subsidiary is accordingly void.

Financing by a company of an acquisition of its shares

14.12   The belief that the financing by a company of a purchase of its own shares was open to the same objections as the direct purchase of its shares by the company prompted the enactment of s 60 of the Principal Act. This prohibits the giving of financial assistance by a company for the purchase of its shares. It is, however, subject to a most important proviso: such a trans-action is valid if it has been authorised by a special resolution of the company passed within the preceding 12 months and certain other conditions are fulfilled. A modification of the strict prohibition on such transactions contained in the English Act of 1948 was recommended by Jenkins, but not implemented until 1981 in that jurisdiction.[1]

1. Ss 42, 43, and 44 of the English Act of 1981.

14.13   In addition to the passing of the special resolution just referred to, a statutory declaration of a specified nature must also be made if the proviso is being availed of. The declaration must be made by two directors of the company (or, where there are more than two, by the majority of them) and must state

(a) the form such assistance is to take;
(b) the persons to whom it is to be given;

(c) the purpose for which it is intended to be used; and
(d) that the declarants have made a full enquiry into the affairs of the company and have formed the opinion that the company, having carried out the transaction in question, will be able to pay its debts as they fall due.

The declaration must be made at a meeting of the directors held not more than 24 days before the meeting of the company at which the resolution is to be considered. Copies of the declaration must be forwarded with each notice of the meeting and must be delivered on the same day as the notices are issued to the Registrar.

Any director who makes such a declaration without having reasonable grounds for his opinion as to the capacity of the company to pay its debts is liable to imprisonment for a term not exceeding six months or a fine not exceeding £500 or to both.[1] Where the company is wound up within the period of 12 months after the making of the statutory declaration and its debts are not paid in full within the period of 12 months after the commencement of the winding up, there is a presumption until the contrary is shown that the director did not have reasonable grounds for his opinion.

Every member of the company has the right to receive notice of and attend the meeting at which the resolution is to be proposed and any provision to the contrary in the articles is of no effect.

1. S 60 (5) as amended by s 15 of the 1982 Act.

14.14   Unless all the members of the company entitled to vote at general meetings of the company vote in favour of the resolution, the transaction authorised by the resolution cannot be carried out until a period of 30 days has elapsed after the passing of the resolution. During that period, an application may be made to the court by the holders of not less in the aggregate than 10 per cent of the nominal value of the issued share capital or any class thereof for the cancellation of the resolution. If such an application is made, the resolution is of no effect except to the extent that it is confirmed by the court. The application must be made within 28 days after the date on which the resolution is passed; and once made the transaction cannot be carried out until the application has been disposed of by the court. The application cannot be made by anyone who has consented to, or voted in favour of, the resolution.

14.15   Where no such resolution is passed, the prohibition will apply except in five specified cases dealt with below. It is in extremely wide terms: it is unlawful for a company

'to give, where directly or indirectly, and whether by means of a loan, guarantee, the provision of security or otherwise, any financial assistance for the purpose of or in connection with a purchase or subscription ... of or for any shares in the company.'
It has been held in England that this invalidates a purchase by the company where the purposes of the transaction is to put the vendor in funds and thereby enable him to buy shares in the company.[1]

1. *Belmont Finance v Williams Furniture Ltd (No 2)* [1980] 1 All ER 393.

14.16   Where a company acts in contravention of the section, every officer who is in default is liable on conviction on indictment to imprisonment for a term not exceeding two years or a fine not exceeding £2,500 or to both; or, on summary conviction, to imprisonment for a term not exceeding six months or to a fine not exceeding £500 or to both.[1] The section also provides that any transaction which is in breach of it is to be voidable at the instance of the company against any person (whether a party to the transaction or not) who had notice of the facts which constitute the breach.

A security given by the company (such as a mortgage) which assists the purchase of its shares is also voidable in such circumstances. There is no corresponding provision in the English legislation and this led to divergent judicial views as to whether such a security was valid.[2] There is no room for such doubts in Ireland, however, having regard to the plain wording of the section.

It will be noted that a transaction in breach of the section is only voidable as against another party where that party had notice of the facts constituting such a breach. It was held by the Supreme Court in *Bank of Ireland Finance Ltd v Rockfield Ltd*[3] that 'notice' in the section means *actual* as distinct from *constructive* notice. The fact that if appropriate enquiries had been made the illegality would have come to light will not be sufficient to invalidate the transaction. In that case the plaintiffs had advanced money to a company on the security of a mortgage of the company's property. The advance was in fact being used to finance the acquisition by a third party of shares in the company, but the plaintiffs were not aware of this, although had enquiries been made it would have come to light. When the plaintiffs sought to enforce their security against the company, their claim was resisted on the ground *inter alia* that s 60 of the Principal Act had not been complied with. This defence succeeded in the High Court but on appeal the Supreme Court held that as the plaintiffs had taken the security without actual notice of the irregularity it should not be set aside as against them.

1. S 60 (15) as amended by s 15 of the 1982 Act.
2. See Palmer, vol I, 38.10-11.
3. [1979] IR 21.

14.17 There are five exceptions to the prohibition in the section (apart from cases where the transaction is authorised by a resolution). They are:

(a) the payment of a dividend properly declared by a company;
(b) the discharge of a liability lawfully incurred by the company;
(c) the lending of money by the company in the ordinary course of its business, where the lending of money is part of its ordinary business;
(d) the provision by the company of money in accordance with a scheme intended to assist employees or former employees (including directors holding salaried offices) to acquire shares in the company;
(e) the making of loans to persons other than directors *bona fide* in the employment of the company with a view to enabling them to acquire shares in the company.

14.18 The power to validate a transaction prohibited by s 60 of the Principal Act is no longer available to public limited companies since the 1983 Act. Such a company may only provide financial assistance for the purchase of its own shares where the case falls within one of the permitted exceptions set out in the preceding paragraph. Moreover, even in such cases, the company may only give such assistance if

(a) the company's net assets are not thereby reduced *or*
(b) to the extent that they are so reduced, the assistance is provided out of profits available for dividend.

The prohibition extends to companies registered or re-registered under the 1983 Act as public limited companies in addition to public limited companies formed as such. In the case of the former, there is a saver for transactions in breach of the section which were authorised by a special resolution passed before the application for registration or re-registration.[1]

1. 1983 Act, First Schedule, para 10.

Other provisions

14.19   Another general principle which reflected the law's concern that capital should be maintained intact was the prohibition on paying dividends out of capital. This is dealt with in detail in Chapter Thirty-One below.

14.20   The law does permit the reduction of a company's capital where the reduction is sanctioned by the court. The circumstances in which this may be done are discussed in the next chapter.

Chapter 15

Alteration (including reduction) of capital

15.01 A company may wish to alter its capital for a variety of reasons. Before considering the various alterations that it may wish to make and how such alterations may be lawfully made, it is as well to remind ourselves of the different types of capital. There is first the *nominal capital*, i.e. the amount of the share capital which the company is authorised to issue. There is secondly the *issued share capital*, i.e. the shares which the company has allotted or agreed to allot to the members or shareholders for cash or some other valuable consideration.[1]

1. There is, technically, a difference between the issued and allotted share capital. A company making a new issue must first issue the capital and then proceed to allot it. In practice, the issued and allotted share capital are invariably the same.

15.02 If a company wishes to raise more money by increasing its issued share capital, there is no difficulty in doing so even where the increase will exceed the nominal capital. By simply passing a resolution, the company may increase its nominal capital to the required amount and the new shares can then be issued, provided only that this machinery is authorised by the articles of association. By contrast, where a company wishes to *reduce* its issued share capital, the procedure is more complex. In particular, the reduction must be confirmed by the court before it becomes effective. This again reflects the concern of the law with ensuring that the company's capital remains intact.[1] Where, however, the company simply wishes to reduce the nominal capital by cancelling shares which have not been taken or agreed to be taken by anyone, it may do so by a resolution. This is called a 'diminution' of the capital and is deemed by the Principal Act not to be a reduction.[2]

Finally, the company may wish to consolidate shares (e.g. convert every block of five £1 shares into one £5 share) or sub-divide shares (the reverse operation) or convert shares into stock or *vice versa*. The difference between shares and stock is that (a) shares may have to be numbered while stock need not be and (b) stock need not be divided into equal parts.

The various ways in which a company's capital may be altered are now considered in greater detail.

1. See para 14.01 above.
2. S 68 (1) (e) and (2).

Increase in capital

15.03 When a company wishes to increase its share capital and for that purpose to alter its memorandum, it can do so by a resolution passed at a

127

general meeting of the company, provided it is authorised to do so by the articles of association. This is provided for by s 68 of the Principal Act and s 70 requires notice of the increase to be given to the Registrar within 15 days after the passing of the necessary resolution. If such notice is not given, the company and every officer who is in default is liable to a fine not exceeding £250.[1]

If the articles do not authorise an increase, it is, of course, possible to amend the articles so as to confer such a power on the company. Where the Table A regulations apply, the increase may be effected under Article 44 by an ordinary resolution of the company.

1. S 70 (3) as amended by s 15 of the 1982 Act.

Consolidation and sub-division of shares

15.04 Section 68 of the Principal Act also empowers a company by a resolution passed at a general meeting to consolidate and divide all or any of its share capital into shares of larger amount than the existing shares; and to sub-divide its shares, or any of them, into shares of smaller amount than is fixed by the memorandum. Where a sub-division is effected, the proportion between the amount paid and the amount, if any, unpaid on each share is to be the same in the case of the reduced share as it was in the case of the original share. Notice must be given to the Registrar within one month of the consolidation or sub-division; and again there is provision for a fine not exceeding £250 on the company and every officer in default.[1]

If the articles do not authorise consolidation or sub-division, they can be altered to give the necessary power. Where the Table A regulations apply, the consolidation or sub-division may be effected under Article 45 by an ordinary resolution of the company. The articles may properly contain a provision enabling the company on a sub-division to attach a preference to some of the shares resulting from the sub-division.[2]

1. S 69 (2) as amended by s 15 of the 1982 Act.
2. *Andrews v Gas Meter Co* [1897] 1 Ch 361.

Conversion of shares into stock and reconversion of stock into shares

15.05 Section 68 of the Principal Act also empowers a company by resolution passed at a general meeting to convert all or any of its paid up shares into stock and reconvert that stock into paid up shares of any denomination, provided it is authorised by its articles so to do.

15.06 At one time shares had to be numbered. This was not necessary, however, in the case of stock. It was, accordingly, possible to transfer, say, £25,000 of stock in a company: if shares to the equivalent amount were being transferred, it was necessary to transfer, say, 25,000 shares of £1 each numbered 1 to 25,000. The advantages of converting shares into stock were therefore significantly reduced when it became possible to have shares without numbers. Section 80 (2) of the Principal Act provides that if at any time all the issued shares in a company (or all the issued shares of a particular class) are fully paid up and rank *pari passu* for all purposes (i.e. are on the same footing with regard to rights to dividends, etc.), they need not have a distinguishing number, so long as those conditions still obtain.

15.07 As in the case of the other powers conferred by s 68, it is always possible to amend the articles so as to confer the power to convert shares into stock and vice versa if the articles do not contain such a power. If the Table A regulations apply to the company, the conversion or reconversion may be effected under Article 40 by an ordinary resolution of the company. Under Article 41, the directors have power to fix the minimum amount of stock transferable. This must not exceed the nominal value of the share from which the stock arose. Thus if the shares are £5 each in nominal value, the directors can fix the minimum amount of stock transferable at £5 or less. The units thus created are called *stock units*.

Stock cannot be issued directly by the company.

Reduction of capital

15.08 Where a company proposes to reduce its share capital, it can usually do so only with the confirmation of the court. As we have seen, importance has always been attached to the maintenance intact by the company of its capital, but there are circumstances where it has been thought legitimate for a reduction to be effected.

A reduction of capital can take two forms. First, the amount involved may be returned to the shareholders in the form either of cash or assets or their liability for the uncalled capital reduced or extinguished. Secondly, there may be no actual return of cash or assets, the reduction in this case taking the form of an adjustment to the balance sheet to bring the capital into line with the assets.

15.09 A reduction of the first type may be considered desirable because the company is over-capitalised, i.e. has more capital than it requires, or because it is paying too much interest on its capital and wishes to raise alternative capital more cheaply. Section 72 (2) of the Principal Act provides that, subject to confirmation by the court, a company may by special resolution reduce its share capital by

(a) extinguishing or reducing the liability of the shareholders in respect of uncalled capital, or
(b) paying off any paid up capital which is in excess of the wants of the company.

Where (b) is adopted, the company may pay off capital on the basis that it may be called up again in whole or in part.

15.10 A reduction of the second type is appropriate where the company has lost a significant part of its capital. The original capital may have been used to purchase assets to be used in the course of the company's business. In time, because of trading losses, the assets may be significantly reduced. A reduction of the capital to allow for such losses will mean that the balance sheet accurately reflects the true situation of the company. Moreover, one of the items on the assets side in such circumstances–the profit and loss account–will probably be in debit, thereby precluding the company from distributing dividends until the losses have been cleared off out of subsequent profits. By writing down its capital, the company can write off this debit balance and put itself in a position to distribute future profits in the form of dividends.

Section 72 (2), accordingly, further provides that a company may, subject to confirmation by the court, by special resolution cancel any paid up share capital which is lost or unrepresented by available assets.

Reduction must be fair and equitable

15.11 The reduction of capital must be fair and equitable. The same percentage must be paid off or cancelled or reduced in respect of each share.[1] Moreover, where the share capital is divided into different classes, any reduction must treat shareholders in accordance with any rights that may be attached to their shares, unless those rights have first been varied.[2] However, provided these requirements are met and the conditions imposed by s 72 are observed, the court will usually confirm the reduction. Thus a rateable reduction has been permitted on both ordinary and preference shares, where the latter have no priority as to capital, even though the dividend payable on the preference shares which must be paid in priority to the dividend on other shares will inevitably be reduced as being paid on a smaller amount.[3]

1. *Bannatyne v Direct Spanish Telegraph Co* (1886) 34 Ch D 287; *Re John Power & Son Ltd* (1934) IR 412.
2. *Re Floating Dock Co of St Thomas* [1895] 1 Ch 691. As to the procedure necessary where a variation of rights is involved, see para 16.10 et seq below.
3. *Re McKenzie & Co* [1916] 2 Ch 450.

Procedure on a reduction of capital

15.12 As in the case of any other alteration of the share capital, a reduction must be authorised by the articles before any reduction can be effected. Once the alteration is authorised by the articles–which can always be amended if necessary for this purpose–a special resolution can then be passed. The application for confirmation to the court is then made by petition,[1] which states that the company is incorporated, its business, its subsequent history, the facts on which the application for a reduction is grounded and the passing of the special resolution.[2]

1. Rules of the Superior Courts, Ord. 75, r 3.
2. Form No 1, Appendix N.

15.13 The subsequent procedure depends on whether the reduction is being effected simply because the capital has been lost or is not represented by assets; or because the company is over capitalised and it is desired to pay off capital or reduce the liability of the shareholders. In the former case, the procedure is relatively straightforward: the court fixes a day for the hearing of the petition and directs the publication of advertisements in Iris Ofigiuil. Creditors are usually not entitled to be heard.[1]

In the latter case, the rights of creditors are carefully protected by s 73 of the Principal Act. Any creditor who is entitled to any debts which would be admissible against the company in a winding up is entitled to object to the reduction.[2] A list of creditors must be settled by the court; and the court may only dispense with the consent of the creditor in any particular case if the company secures the payment of the debt by appropriating the full amount of the debt. Where the company is disputing the amount of the debt or it is not ascertained, it must secure or appropriate so much of it as the court fixes after an inquiry and adjudication similar to that in a winding up.[3]

1. *Re Meux's Brewery Ltd* [1919] 1 Ch 28.
2. S 73 (2) (a).
3. S 73 (2) (c).

Forfeiture of shares not a reduction requiring confirmation

15.14   As we shall see in Chapter Eighteen, shares in a company can always be forfeited for non-payment of calls or failure to pay an instalment due in respect of a call.[1] This does not constitute a reduction of capital requiring confirmation by the court.[2] Where, however, the shares are surrendered, different considerations will apply, even though they are surrendered by the shareholder in anticipation of their being forfeited. Generally speaking, a surrender of shares is regarded as a reduction of capital requiring confirmation by the court before it can be effective.[3]

1. See para 18.06 et seq. below.
2. It is expressly envisaged by Articles 33 to 39 of Table A. See also *Bellerby v Rowland and Marwoods' SS Co* [1902] 2 Ch 14 at 32.
3. *Trevor v Whitworth* (1887) 12 App Cas 409 at 438; *Bellerby v Rowland and Marwoods's SS Co. Ltd* [1922] 2 Ch 14 at 22.

Chapter 16

Shares: (1) General

Nature of a share

16.01 Where a company has a share capital, each of the members owns at least one *share* of that capital and is consequently a *shareholder* in the company. This does not mean that he is the owner of any part of the company's assets or that he owns them jointly with his fellow shareholders. But he is along with them the owner of the company itself and the controller of its destinies.

While there has been much debate as to the precise nature of a share, it is clear that its most important practical feature is that it confers certain *rights* on the shareholder. These rights are essentially *contractual* since, as we have seen, the articles of association constitute a contract between the share-holders and the company.[1] But a share is also more than a mere contractual right: its ownership gives the shareholder an interest recognised by the law in the company itself. The importance of this interest of the shareholder in the company is reflected by the opinion of the Supreme Court in *Private Motorists' Provident Society and Another v Attorney General*[2] that it constitutes a right of property protected by Article 43 of the Constitution.

Since the shareholders are in effect the owners of the company, and not merely persons with contractual rights against the company, they are clearly distinguishable in law from debenture holders. The latter have no proprie-tary interest in the company itself, although they normally have an interest in its assets.

1. Para 5.05 above.
2. [1984] ILRM 88.

Rights of the shareholder

16.02 The principal rights of the shareholder are threefold:

  (i) to receive a share of the company's distributable income in the form of a *dividend;*
  (ii) to attend at and (normally) to vote at meetings of the company, and
  (iii) to participate in the distribution of the assets of the company when it is wound up and its creditors have been paid.

Any of these rights may, however, be abridged, or excluded completely, by the memorandum and articles. In addition, the shareholders have other rights conferred on them by the Acts (such as rights in relation to seeing the accounts of the company, inspecting its books, petitioning the court in

132

relation to its affairs, etc.) which are dealt with in the appropriate sections of this book.

Duties of the shareholder

16.03 The shareholder's principal duty is to pay the amount which he has agreed to pay for his shares in the company. Sometimes that amount is payable in full when the shares are allotted to him. Alternatively, part or the whole of the amount may only become payable when a *call* is made by the company on the shareholder; or the terms of the allotment may provide for the payment of the amount by instalments at fixed times. In the case of a public limited company, one-quarter at least of the agreed amount must be paid on allotment.[1]

1. S 28 of the 1983 Act.

Amount and numbering of shares

16.04 An essential feature of a share is that the extent of the shareholder's interest in the company is measured by a money sum. Accordingly, each share has a specific monetary value, known as its nominal value. This is provided for by s 6 (4) (a) of the Principal Act which requires the memorandum in the case of a company having a share capital to state 'the division thereof into shares of a fixed amount'. Thus the memorandum may provide that
'the capital of the company is £250,000 divided into 50,000 shares of £5 each.'
Since the coming into force of the Decimal Currency Act 1969, it has been necessary to state the value of the share in terms of decimal currency. Although companies have been registered with share capitals expressed in foreign currency, the better view appears to be that the capital must be expressed in terms of Irish pounds or pence.

16.05 Section 80 of the Pirncipal Act requires each share in a company having a share capital to be distinguished by its appropriate number. This requirement may, however, be dispensed with where all the issued shares (or all the issued shares of a particular class) are fully paid up and rank *pari passu* (i.e. stand on the same footing) for all purposes, so long as those conditions continue to exist.
Shares–or any other interest of a member in a company–are personal estate. They are not of the nature of real estate. This distinction was formerly of importance in determining succession to property on death, but has ceased to be of any significance since the abolition of the different rules governing the devolution of real and personal property which was initiated by the Administration of Estates Act 1959 and completed by the Succession Act 1965.

Different classes of shares

16.06 *Prima facie* all shares are presumed to be of equal status. The rights of all the shareholders are the same in regard to the payment of dividends, voting at meetings and participation in the assets on a winding up.

Obviously, the amount of cash to which each shareholder is entitled by way of dividends or on a winding up will depend on the number of shares held by him; but the shares themselves all stand on an equal footing.

At an early stage in the development of modern company law, however, it became common for the constitution of companies to provide for the division of the shares into different classes and for the giving of *preferential rights*, as they were called, to classes of shares. The shares to which such rights were attached were known as *preference shares*.

The provision for the division of the shares is usually contained in the memorandum. If, however, the memorandum expressly provides that all the shares are to be equal, that provision cannot be modified by the articles. And if the memorandum provides for the division of the shares into classes and the rights to be attached to such classes, the articles cannot be subsequently altered by special resolution so as to alter those provisions.[1] In practice, the rights attached to the different classes are usually dealt with in the articles.

A preference share normally gave its holder the right to a dividend of a fixed amount–5%, 10% or as the case might be–in priority to the holders of other shares. It could also give its holder the right to participate in the capital available for distribution on a winding up in priority to other shareholders. Or it could give the preference shareholder both rights. It became an accepted method of giving someone prepared to fund the operations of the company a form of security; but the advantages from the investor's point of view of taking a debenture led to the latter replacing the preference share as the more attractive security. (As we have seen, a debenture holder, unlike a shareholder, almost invariably has an interest in the assets of the company.) Preference shares are, however, still frequently encountered in practice in Ireland in both private and public companies. They are dealt with in detail in the next chapter.

1. *Campbell v Rofe* [1933] AC 91 at 98.

16.07 Another division of shares sometimes encountered is between voting and non-voting shares. It is permissible for a company to divide its shares into such categories (usually distinguished by letters, e.g. 'A' shares and 'B' shares) but the practice is not approved of by the Stock Exchange, since it can mean in practice that those who own the company–the shareholders–do not necessarily control its activities.

16.08 A category of shares which has virtually ceased to exist today is *founders'* or *deferred* shares. These entitled their holders to various rights, such as the right to a fixed percentage of the profits in any year after a specified dividend–also expresssed in percentage terms–had been paid on the other shares. They were usually allotted to the persons with whom the enterprise had begun, e.g. the vendors of a business sold to the company on its formation.

16.09 Any shares which do not have preferential rights attached to them are known as *ordinary* shares. Their holders reap the principal benefit when the company is doing well, since they will receive all the distributed profits that remain after the payment of any fixed preferential dividend. Similarly, when the company is doing badly, they will be the principal victims, since the preference shareholders will cream off what profit there is. It is for this reason that in the case of a company whose shares are dealt in on the Stock Exchange it is the value of the ordinary shares which really reflect the value placed by the market on the company itself. The holders of the ordinary shares are regarded as the owners of the equitable interest in the company as contrasted with the secured lenders, whether they be debenture holders or preference shareholders; and hence the reference frequently encountered to the ordinary shares of such companies as 'equities'.

Variations of rights of classes of shareholders

16.10 As we have seen, the rights attached to the different classes of shares are usually specified in the articles. We have also seen that the articles can be amended at any time by a special resolution of the company. Can the company alter the special rights attached to a particular class of shares, e.g. the right of the preference shareholder to a fixed dividend in priority to the other shareholders?

Section 78 of the Principal Act made it clear that where the memorandum or articles themselves contained a procedure for the variation of such special rights with the consent of a specified proportion of that class or the sanction of a resolution passed at a separate meeting of the class, the rights could be lawfully varied by complying with the procedure. This, however, was subject to the right of a dissenting minority of the class to apply to the court for an order cancelling the variation. What was not clear was whether the rights could be varied if no such procedure was contained in the memorandum or articles. The position has now been clarified by s 38 of the 1983 Act.

16.11 Where the rights are attached to the class otherwise than by the memorandum (e.g. by the articles) and the articles do not contain any procedure for the variation of the rights, they may be varied, but only where the following requirements are met:

(a) the holders of three-quarters in nominal value of the issued shares of the class consent in writing, or
(b) the variation is sanctioned by a special resolution passed at a separate general meeting of the holders of that class.

Any other requirements imposed by the articles or otherwise must also be met.

Where the rights are so varied, the holders of not less in the aggregate than 10 per cent of the issued shares of that class (not being persons who consented or voted in favour) may apply to the court to have the variation cancelled. Where such an application is made, the variation is not to have effect unless and until it is confirmed by the court.

The application must be made within 28 days after the consent has been given or the resolution passed. It may be made by such one or more of the dissenting shareholders on behalf of them all as they may appoint in writing for that purpose. The court, after hearing the applicant and any other person who applies to be heard and appears to the court to be interested, may disallow the variation if it is satisfied that, having regard to all the circumstances of the case, the variation would unfairly prejudice the affected shareholders. If it is not so satisfied, it must confirm the variation.

The decision of the court is final, but there is provision for an appeal to the Supreme Court on a question of law.

The company must forward a copy of the court's order to the Registrar within 21 days after it has been made. If default is made in complying with this provision, the company and every officer in default is liable to a fine not exceeding £250.

16.12 Where the rights are attached to the class by the memorandum or otherwise and the memorandum or articles contain a procedure for the variation of the rights, they may be varied in accordance with that procedure. But if the variation of the rights is connected with

(a) the giving, variation, revocation or renewal of an authority to the directors to allot shares,[1] or
(b) a reduction of capital under s 72 of the Principal Act,

the two requirements mentioned in the preceding paragraph must also be met, i.e. the variation must receive the consent of the holders of three-quarters in nominal value of the issued shares of the class or the sanction of a special resolution passed at a general meeting of the class.

Where the procedure for the variation provides for obtaining the consent of a specified proportion of the holders of the issued share capital or the sanction of a special resolution passed at a general meeting of the class, the holders of not less than 10 per cent of the issued shares of the class who do not consent or vote in favour may apply to the court for an order cancelling the variation under the procedure explained in the preceding paragraph.

1. See para 8.07 above and s 20, 1983 Act.

16.13 Where the rights are attached to the shares by the memorandum and the memorandum and articles do not contain any procedure for their variation, they may be varied if all the members agree to the variation. The rights may also be varied if this is required by an order of the court made under ss 10, 203, or 205 of the Principal Act or s 15 of the 1983 Act.

16.14 The English courts have adopted a somewhat restrictive approach in defining what constitutes a variation or abrogation of a special right attached to a class of shares. It might be thought, for example, that to make a new issue of shares ranking *pari passu* (i.e. on an equal footing so far as rights to dividends, capital on winding up, etc. are concerned) with existing shares would be to vary the rights of the existing shareholders. Article 4 of Table A, indeed, expressly provides that the rights conferred upon the holders of any shares are *not* to be deemed to be varied by the issue of new shares ranking *pari passu* with them. But even without such a provision in the articles, it would appear that such an issue does not constitute a variation of the rights of existing shareholders.[1]

Again, in *Greenhalgh Cinemas v Arderne Cinemas (No 2)*,[2] the Court of Appeal held that a subdivision of ordinary shares of 10s each into shares of 2s each did not constitute a variation of the rights of the holders of another class of ordinary shares of 2s each, although the result was to change the control of the company. Even more surprisingly in *White v Bristol Aeroplane Co. Ltd*,[3] where the articles provided that the rights attached to any class of shares might be *affected* in any manner with the sanction of a resolution at a separate meeting, it was held that the rights of existing preference shareholders were not 'affected' within the meaning of the articles by the issue of new preference stock to the ordinary shareholders giving them a majority over the existing preference stock. Lord Evershed MR drew a distinction between being 'affected as a matter of business' (which the rights clearly were) and 'varied as a matter of law' (which they were not). It was the enjoyment of the rights, and not the rights themselves, which in the view of the court was affected.

There must be some doubt as to whether the last two decisions, which have been criticised by English commentators,[4] will be followed in Ireland.

1. *Re Scwheppes Ltd* [1914] 1 Ch 322.
2. [1945] 2 All ER 719, [1946] 1 All ER 512.
3. [1953] Ch 65.
4. Palmer, vol. I, 33-33.

Shares certificates

16.15 Each shareholder in a company is furnished with a document called a *share certificate*. This is the evidence of the shareholder's title to the shares. It is issued under the common seal of the company and s 87 (1) of the Principal Act provides that as so issued it is to be *prima facie* evidence of the member's title to the shares. It enables dealings with the shares to be accomplished more expeditiously, since it can be produced on any sale or mortgage of the shares by the owner and may be safely accepted by the purchaser or mortgagee as evidence of his title.

The articles of association sometimes provide (Article 8) for the issue by the company of *split certificates*. Persons or bodies who hold shares on trust for a number of people avail of split certificates in order to enable the different holdings to be disposed of individually.

16.16 The fact that the share certificate is *prima facie* evidence of the title of the shareholder to the shares may mean that the company will be liable to those who suffer damages as a result of an incorrect share certificate being issued. This may happen in two ways: first, the certificate may be issued in the name of a person who was not entitled to be a member and, second, the certificate may incorrectly state the amount paid up on the shares.

In each case, the company may be liable to a person who suffers damage as a result of the issue of the incorrect certificate because of the legal doctrine of *estoppel*. In the first case, if the company issues a certificate to a person who was not entitled to be registered as a member–because, for example, he had lodged a forged transfer of the share–the company will be liable to a person who purchases the shares on the faith of the certificate.[1] The purchaser will not be entitled to be registered as a member in such circumstances–the original shareholder whose name was forged on the transfer will remain the member–but he will be entitled to damages. Although the company cannot register him as a member they must compensate him for the damage he thereby suffers: they are precluded or estopped from asserting that the facts set out in the certificate are incorrect. In the second case, where the certificate wrongly states that the shares are fully paid up, the company cannot make a call upon the shareholder for the amount unpaid: again, they are estopped from asserting that the certificate is incorrect.[2]

The company will not be liable where the certificate itself is forged by a person who had no authority to issue such a certificate.[3] Nor will the company be liable where the transferee is aware of the incorrect nature of the certificate.[4] But where the shares have been transferred to a purchaser who takes them in good faith without notice of the irregularity, a subsequent purchaser who takes them with notice will get a good title. The application of the estoppel principle would be frustrated if the purchaser in whose favour it operates could not freely transfer the shares without regard to the state of knowledge of subsequent transferees.[5]

Normally the estoppel operates only in favour of a purchaser of the shares: it is seldom available to the person to whom the certificate was issued. But there are exceptional cases where the person to whom the certificate was issued may hold the company liable. Thus where the company issued a certificate to a person who was lending money to the company on the security of an allotment of shares and the certificate incorrectly stated that the shares were fully paid up, the company were held to be estopped from asserting the contrary.[6]

1. *Re Bahia and San Francisco Railway Co* (1868) LR 3 QB 584.
2. *Burkinshaw v Nicholls* (1878) 3 App Cas 1004.
3. *Ruben v Great Fingall Consolidated Co* [1906] AC 439.
4. *Re Caribbean Co Crickmer's Case* (1875) 10 Ch App 614.
5. *Barrow's Case* (1880) 14 Ch D 432.
6. *Bloomenthal v Ford* [1897] AC 156.

Share warrants

16.17 A company may issue a document called a *share warrant* instead of a certificate. This entitles the bearer of the warrant to the shares, with the result that they can be transferred to another person simply by delivery of the warrant. They are treated in the result in the same manner as other negotiable instruments, such as cheques, which do not require the execution of an instrument of transfer. Section 88 of the Principal Act entitles a company to issue such share warrants where it is authorised so to do by its articles.

Private companies may not issue share warrants. They are, in fact, extremely rare in practice today in the case of public companies.

Chapter 17

Shares: (2) preference shares

17.01 As its name indicates, a preference share is one that gives the shareholder certain preferential rights not enjoyed by the other shareholders. Invariably it confers on the holder the right to the payment of a dividend representing a fixed percentage of the distributable profits in priority to the payment of the dividend to the other shareholders. In addition, it may confer on him the right to be repaid his capital in priority to the other shareholders in the event of a winding up.

Cumulative and non-cumulative preference shares

17.02 No problem arises if the distributable profits of the company are sufficient to pay the fixed dividend (of 5% or whatever it may be) on the preference shares. But what if the profits are insufficient? Is the shareholder then entitled to be paid the arrears for the following year or whenever the profits are sufficient to pay him? This depends on whether the shares are *cumulative* or *non-cumulative*. Where they are cumulative, the arrears[1] must be paid off as soon as the profits permit. Where they are non-cumulative, the preference shareholder is not entitled to be paid arrears of dividend. If the clause defining the rights simply declares that the preference shareholders are to be entitled to a preferential dividend of a specified percentage, that is enough to make the share cumulative. Where it is desired to make them non-cumulative, this must be made clear in the relevant clause. The clause should state that the dividend is to be paid 'out of the profits made by the company in each year' or words to the same effect. Such words will be enough to make the shares non-cumulative preference shares.[2]

1. 'Arrears' is a convenient but imprecise description. Where the profits are not sufficient to pay a preferential dividend, the company need not pay it and hence does not owe any arrears.
2. *Staples v Eastman Photographic Materials Co* [1896] 2 Ch 303.

Preferential dividends payable only out of profits

17.03 As can be gathered from the last paragraph, and as common sense would suggest, a preferential dividend can only be paid where distributable profits are available from which it can be paid. Moreover, even where such profits are available, the terms on which the shares were issued may make it plain that the preferential dividend is only to be paid when it is *declared;* and this is indeed usually the position. The terms of issue sometimes, however, provide that the profits shall be distributed by way of preferential dividend where the *directors* declare a dividend, in contrast to the usual position where such a dividend is declared by the *company* in general meeting. But even in such a case, the directors will retain a discretion as to whether the dividend should be declared or not.[1]

1. *Bond v Barrow Haematite Steel Co* [1902] 1 Ch 353 at 362.

17.04 It follows from the foregoing that, unless the articles otherwise provide, a preferential dividend can normally only be paid when the company or directors declare a dividend. There is nothing to prevent the company continuing to put profits to reserve and declining to pay any dividend. Moreover, even where the articles expressly confer a right to a preferential dividend in the event of sufficient profits being earned, a question may still arise as to the fund out of which it is to be paid. Thus, where the directors were authorised by the articles to set aside sums to reserve before recommending any dividend, and the preferential dividend was payable out of 'profits available for dividend' it was held that any sums transferred by the directors to reserve had to be deducted before the profits available for dividend could be ascertained.[1]

If there are arrears of preferential dividend, must they be paid out of the reserves (assuming that there are distributable reserves) in priority to the ordinary dividend? As always when the rights of shareholders are being considered, the answer will ultimately depend on the wording of the particular articles or the terms of issue of the shares. Unless the articles or the terms of issue indicate otherwise, however, it would seem that arrears of preferential dividend should be paid out of reserves, where the reserves are created by transferring profits to reserve which would otherwise have been available for the preferential dividend.

In *Re Lafeyettex Ltd, Lafeyette v Nolan and Another*,[2] the relevant article provided that

'such dividend shall be cumulative and arrears thereof shall be a first charge on the *subsequent profits* of the company.'

Kingsmill Moore J held that the effect of this article was that a preferential dividend in arrears could not be paid out of profits which had been earned before the dividend was payable and placed to reserves: such a dividend could only be paid out of profits earned subsequently. This is an example of how the general principle referred to may be displaced by the actual wording used in the articles. It should be said, however, that the authority of the decision is somewhat weakened by the fact that the point appears to have been conceded in argument by counsel for the preference shareholders. It has been criticised by Pennington as being unduly restrictive in its construction of the rights of preference shareholders.[3] It does, however, illustrate the important general principle that the undoubted right of the preference shareholders to be paid arrears of dividend out of profits placed to reserves which would otherwise have been available to pay their dividend may be excluded by the articles or the terms of issue.

1. *Fisher v Black & White Publishing Co* [1901] 1 Ch 174.
2. [1950] IR 100.
3. 4th edn, p 187.

Preferential rights as to capital

17.05   Where a preference share confers a preferential right to a dividend, it does not follow that the shareholder is also entitled to the return of his capital in priority to the other shareholders in the event of a winding up. On the contrary, it is clear that, unless such a right is expressly conferred by the articles all shareholders stand on the same footing so far as their right to repayment of capital is concerned, because the presumption of equality between shareholders has not been displaced.[1]

1. *Re Driffield Gas Light Co* [1898] 1 Ch 451; *Birch v Cropper, Re, Bridgewater Navigation Co Ltd* (1889) 14 App Cas 525.

Right to participate further in profits and capital

17.06   Once the preference shareholder has been paid his fixed dividend, he is not entitled to participate further in the division of the profits, unless an express right to do so is conferred on him by the memorandum or articles. So much was made clear by the decision of the House of Lords in *Will v United Lankat Plantations*.[1] It also appeared from the earlier House of Lords decision in *Birch v Cropper*,[2] however, that the preference shareholder *was* entitled to participate in the distribution of the surplus assets of the company on winding up after the debts had been paid and the capital returned. It also appeared that this result followed whether or not the preference shareholder was entitled to the return of his capital in priority to the ordinary shareholders. If the preference shareholder was entitled to the return of his capital in priority to the other shareholders, this did not necessarily exhaust his rights.

This is still the law in Ireland, as is made clear by the decision of the former Supreme Court in *Cork Electric Supply Co Ltd v Concannon and Another*.[3] That case (which arose out of the establishment of the Electricity Supply Board and the consequent compulsory acquisition of the Cork company's assets and undertakings by the Board) came before the High Court in the form of a construction summons in which the company sought the directions of the court as to whether, in the event of the company being wound up, the rights of the preferences shareholders should be treated as exhausted by the existence of a clause in the articles entitling them to a fixed cumulative preferential dividend of 5% per annum and also the right in a winding up to the return of their capital in priority to the ordinary shareholders. If they were to be treated as exhausted, it followed that the preference shareholders would not be entitled to participate in the distribution of the surplus assets which were expected to be available as a result of the anticipated winding up. Johnson J was of the opinion that the rights were exhausted by the existence of such a clause, but his decision was unanimously reversed on appeal. Kennedy CJ, having referred to a number of English decisions, went on as follows:

'Out of all these cases, after consideration, what we derive is only this, that the right to participate in a distribution of surplus assets on a winding up will be taken from preference shareholders by a clause in the Articles of Association delimiting their rights exhaustively to the exclusion of any other rights and that the question whether a particular clause does so exhaust the rights attached to the preference shares exhaustively and exclusively is a question of the construction of the particular Articles of Association in each case ... '[4]

He went on to hold, in common with the other members of the court (Fitzgibbon and Murnaghan JJ) that the particular clause in that case did not exhaust the rights.

It does not appear that the question was ever reopened in the Irish courts. In England the Court of Appeal came to a similar conclusion not long afterwards in *Re William Metcalf & Son Ltd.*[5] But in a series of later decisions in the House of Lords and the Court of Appeal, the view of the law which had found favour in *Concannon's* case and *Re William Metcalf & Son Ltd* was rejected. It is now clear from *Scottish Insurance Corpn v Wilsons and Clyde Coal Company*,[6] *Prudential Assurance Co. v Chatterly-Whitfield Collieries Co Ltd*[7] and *Re Isle of Thanet Electricity Supply Co Ltd*[8] that in that jurisdiction the law now is that where the articles set out the rights attached to a class of shares to participate in the profits while the company is a going concern or to share in the property of the company in liquidation, *prima facie* the rights so set out in each case are exhaustive.

Concannon's case remains the law in Ireland unless and until it is over-ruled by the Supreme Court, which is not, of course, bound rigidly by *stare decisis.*[9] The later English decisions reflect the growing tendency among businessmen to treat preference shares as more in the nature of securities akin to debentures rather than as shares in the ordinary sense. It would follow logically from such a view that, in the absence of an express provision in the articles indicating an agreement to the contrary, a preference shareholder should not normally expect to receive more than the preferential rights actually given to him.

1. [1914] AC 11.
2. (1889) 14 App Cas 525.
3. [1932] IR 314.
4. p 328.
5. [1933] Ch 142.
6. [1949] AC 462.
7. [1949] AC 512.
8. [1950] Ch 161.
9. *Attorney General and Another v Ryan's Car Hire Ltd* [1965] IR 642.

17.07 It has also been held in England that where the preference shareholder is not entitled to share in the profits remaining after the payment of the fixed dividend, this does not exclude his right to share in profits which remain undistributed when the company is wound up. This is because the profits at that stage cease to be profits and become assets of the company.[1]

1. *Dimbula Valley (Ceylon) Tea Co v Laurie* [1961] Ch 353.

Arrears of preference dividends in a winding up

17.08 We have seen that in the case of cumulative preference shares, the shareholder will normally be entitled to be paid his dividend out of the profits of succeeding years where the particular year's profits are insufficient. This right to be paid arrears of dividend does not necessarily apply in a winding up, however; whether such arrears are payable in those circumstances will depend on the wording of the articles. If the article makes it clear that the priority afforded to dividends extends to a winding up, the shareholder will be entitled to such arrears. Where the articles are silent, the courts have in some cases been able from the words used to infer such an intention.[1] But if the dividends are not merely in arrears, but are actually *owed* by the company (as where they have been declared), they are payable as a preferential debt.[2]

1. *Re de Jong (F) & Co Ltd* [1946] Ch 211; *Re E W Savory Ltd* [1951] 2 All ER 1036.
2. *Re Imperial Hotel (Cork) Ltd* [1950] IR 115.

Redeemable preference shares

17.09   It has already been pointed out that preference shares are more closely akin to debentures than to ordinary shares. It follows that the higher the proportion of such shares in a company's capital, the greater will appear the dependence of that company on loan capital as contrasted with purely investment capital. It is obviously desirable for a company to be in a position to pay off such indebtedness, provided its financial position permits it to do so. Since, however, paying off– or 'redeeming'–shares clearly reduces the capital of the company, contrary to the fundamental rule against such reductions, it was not possible at one time for a company to issue preference shares on the basis that they could be redeemed subsequently by the company.

17.10   The power to issue redeemable preference shares was first conferred on Irish companies in 1959 and then only to a limited extent. A more comprehensive power is given by s 64 of the Principal Act which is closely modelled on s 58 of the English Act of 1948. Such shares may be issued by the company provided the following conditions are observed:

(1) The shares may only be redeemed out of profits which would otherwise be available for dividend or out of the proceeds of a fresh issue of shares made for the purposes of the redemption;

(2) the shares cannot be redeemed unless they are fully paid;

(3) if the company pays a premium on redemption, it must be provided for out of the profits or out of the share premium account[1] before the shares are redeemed;

(4) where the shares are redeemed otherwise than out of the proceeds of a fresh issue, the company must transfer to the capital redemption reserve fund[2] out of the profits which would otherwise have been available for dividend a sum equal to the nominal value of the shares redeemed.

Condition (4) is intended to ensure that the company's balance sheet continues accurately to reflect the true state of the company's assets and liabilities: it ensures that a book profit does not come into existence as a result of the cancellation of the shares which could subsequently be distributed by the company if its liquid position so permitted.

1. See para 8.24 above.
2. See para 13.12 above.

17.11   The section expressly provides that the redemption of the shares is not to be taken as reducing the authorised share capital of the company. Hence no sanction of the court is required. The redemption of the shares may, subject to compliance with the conditions of the section, be effected on such terms and in such manner as may be provided by the articles. The articles normally provide that the board of directors may effect the redemption without seeking the approval of the company in general meeting.

Chapter 18

Shares: (3) calls, liens, forfeiture and surrender

Nature of a call

18.01 When the entire amount due to be paid by a shareholder for his shares is not paid on allotment, the company is generally entitled to require the unpaid balance to be paid at any time thereafter. The liability continues until the company is dissolved or struck off the register, so that in the event of the company being wound up each shareholder remains liable including those who have ceased to be shareholders. The process of collecting the unpaid balance is known as a *call;* and hence the totality of the balances unpaid on the shares is known as the *uncalled capital*.

The amount due may also be payable by fixed instalments payable at specified times: strictly speaking, a demand for the payment of such an instalment is not a call. In the case of public limited companies, the terms of issue very rarely, if ever, leave any part of the capital to be called. The normal provision is to require the payment of the entire amount by instalments within a relatively short time.

How a call is enforced

18.02 The articles usually contain a procedure for the making of calls. That contained in Table A is to be found in Articles 15 to 21 inclusive. They provide that the directors may from time to time make calls, provided that no call exceeds one-fourth of the nominal value of the share and that at least one month elapses between successive calls. They also provide that the shareholder is to receive at least 14 days' notice of the making of a call. The directors are also given power to revoke or postpone calls.

18.03 Where a call is properly made in accordance with the articles and the amount is not paid by the shareholder, the necessary proceedings should be by way of summary summons. The articles usually contain a provision providing for the payment of interest at a rate to be determined by the directors but not to exceed a specified sum.

18.04 While the directors have a discretion as to when they will exercise a power to make calls, it is a discretion that must be exercised in good faith and for the benefit of the company. The calls should be made *pari passu* unless the articles otherwise provide: i.e. each of the shareholders should be asked to pay the same amount and the call should be made at the same time on each of them. The articles sometimes provide (Article 20) that the directors may, on the issue of shares, differentiate between holders as to the amount of the calls to be paid and the times of payment. While the articles may be amended to include such a provision, the amendment cannot impose liability on shareholders who were allotted shares before the amendment. Even where the articles permit such a differentiation between shareholders, it would require special grounds to justify it.[1]

1. *Galloway v Halle Concerts Society Ltd* [1915] 2 Ch 233.

Payment in advance of calls

18.05 The articles sometimes include a provision enabling the directors, if they think fit, to receive from shareholders money uncalled and unpaid on any shares. Where they exercise this power, they may pay interest at such rate not exceeding a specified sum as may be agreed between themselves and the shareholders in question on the money advanced until such time as the money would have become payable. Clearly, this is a power capable of being abused by the directors and it has been held that it must be exercised by them in good faith and for the benefit of the company.[1] The rate of interest must not be excessive.

1. *Sykes' Case* (1872) LR 13 Eq 255. In that case, the directors made a call in advance when the company was insolvent and used the amount collected to pay their own fees. It was held that this was an improper use of the power.

Forfeiture of shares

18.06 The articles almost invariably contain a provision enabling the company to forfeit the shares in the event of the failure of a member to pay any call or instalment of a call on the day appointed for payment (Articles 33 to 39 inclusive). In the Table A form, they empower the directors in such an event to serve a notice on the defaulting shareholder requiring payment of so much of the call or instalment as remains unpaid together with interest on or before the expiration of 14 days from the date of service of the notice. The notice must state that, in the event of the amount not being paid on or before that date, the shares will be liable to be forfeited. If the requirements of the notice are not complied with, the shares may then be forfeited by resolution of the directors.

18.07 The forfeiture of a share means, of course, that the capital of the company is to that extent reduced. Where the forfeiture is in respect of non-payment of a call, however, it is a valid reduction of the capital which does not require the sanction of the court under s 72 of the Principal Act. Forfeiture of shares for any other cause constitutes a reduction of capital and is accordingly not lawful.[1]

1. See Chapter Fifteen.

18.08 Where shares in a public limited company are forfeited, the result may be to bring the nominal value of allotted shares of the company below the authorised minimum under s 19 of the 1983 Act. Section 43 of the Act, accordingly, provides that, where shares in such a company are forfeited and not disposed of by the company within three years of the date of forfeiture, the company must cancel the shares and reduce the amount of its share capital by the nominal value of the shares. If this has the effect of bringing the nominal value of the company's allotted share capital below the authorised minimum, the company must apply for re-registration as another form of company, stating the effect of the cancellation. The directors are then dispensed from complying with ss 72 and 73 of the Principal Act– dealing with reduction of capital with the confirmation of the court–but must pass a resolution altering the company's memorandum so that it no longer states the company is a public limited company and making any other alterations in the memorandum and articles as are requisite in the circumstances. The application for re-registration must be in the prescribed form[1] and signed by a director and secretary of the company. It must be delivered to the registrar together with a printed copy of the memorandum and articles as altered by the resolution.

If a company required to register under the section fails to do so, s 21 of the 1983 Act is to apply to it as if it were a private company, i.e. the company or its officers commit an offence if they offer its shares or debentures to the public either directly or through an offer for sale or placing. Except for that purpose, however, the company in the event of failure to re-register continues to be a public limited company. If the company fails to cancel any share or to re-register when required to do so by the section, the company and any officer in default is guilty of an offence and liable on summary conviction to a fine not exceeding £25 for every day on which the offence continues, but not exceeding £500 in total.[2]

If the Registrar is satisfied that a company may be re-registered in accordance with s 43 he is required to retain the application and other documents delivered to him and issue the company with an appropriate certificate of incorporation. The company by virtue of its issue becomes the form of company stated in the certificate and the alteration in the memorandum and articles takes effect accordingly. Such a certificate is to be conclusive evidence that the requirements of s 43 in respect of re-registration and matters precedent and incidental thereto have been complied with.

1. Companies (Forms) Order 1983 (SI 1983/259). Form 83.
2. Sub-s (8).

18.09 The procedure described in the immediately preceding paragraph is also applicable in the following circumstances:
　(1) where shares in the company are surrendered in lieu of forfeiture;
　(2) where a company acquires its own shares in a manner not permitted by s 41 of the 1983 Act;
　(3) where a person acquires shares in a company with financial assistance from the company and the company has a beneficial interest in the shares; and
　(4) where a nominee of the company acquires the shares from a third party without financial assistance from the company and the company has a beneficial interest in the shares.
If in any of these instances the shares (or the company's interest in them) are not disposed of by the company within the period of three years from their surrender or acquisition, they must be cancelled and, if the cancellation brings the nominal value of the allotted share capital below the authorised minimum, there must be an application for re-registration.

Cessation of membership on forfeiture

18.10 Article 37 provides that a person whose shares have been forfeited ceases to be a member of the company. It should follow from this that he would also cease to be liable for calls, including calls made while he was a member. However, the article goes on to provide that he is to remain liable to pay all moneys which were payable by him to the company at the date of the forfeiture.

Relief against forfeiture

18.11 Since a court applying principles of equity 'leans against' forfeiture, it will be essential for a company seeking to rely on a forfeiture of shares to be in a position to establish that it has complied strictly with all the relevant requirements of the Articles. Provided, however, those requirements have been met in full, there is no room for the application of the equitable doctrine of relief against forfeiture such as would be available, for example, if a lease of land were being forfeited.

Article 36 empowers the directors to sell the forfeited shares or otherwise dispose of them on such terms and in such manner as the directors think fit. The share certificate will still be in the possession of the shareholder and since he may not return it to the company upon his shares being forfeited, Article 38 provides that a statutory declaration that the declarant is a director or secretary and that a share in the company has been duly forfeited on a date stated is to be conclusive evidence of the facts therein stated against all persons claiming to be entitled to the shares.

Surrender of shares

18.12 Shares in a company may be surrendered in order to avoid all the formalities of a forfeiture, provided that the articles authorise such a procedure. They cannot be validly surrendered, however, unless circumstances justifying their forfeiture have arisen. A surrender in any other circumstances would constitute an unlawful reduction of the company's capital.[1]

Where a valid surrender of shares in a public limited company brings the allotted share capital below the authorised minimum fixed under s 19 of the 1983 Act, the requirements of s 43 of the same Act which oblige the company to re-register as another form of company in such circumstances, must be complied with.

1. *Bellerby v Rowland & Marwood's SS Co Ltd* [1902] 2 Ch 14.

Lien on shares

18.13 A *lien* is, in essence, the legal right of a person to keep possession of another's property until a claim he has against that person has been met. A lien can also arise, however, where the claimant is not in possession of the property in question: it is then known as a *non-possessory lien*.

A company has no lien over its shares either for amounts outstanding in respect of the shares themselves or for any other debts owing to the company by the shareholders, unless such a lien is expressly conferred by the articles. In practice the articles invariably confer such a lien, usually described as 'a first and paramount lien on every share (not being a fully paid share) for all moneys (whether immediately payable or not) called or payable at a fixed time in respect of that share ... and a first and paramount lien on all shares (other than fully paid shares) standing in the name of a single person for all moneys immediately payable by him or his estate to the company ... ' (Article 11)

18.14   A lien of this nature is of no practical significance so far as money unpaid on the shares is concerned, since the company will normally have available to it the far more effective remedy of forfeiture. Where it is sought to enforce the lien in respect of other debts owing by the shareholder to the company, questions may arise as to the priority of the lien over other charges to which the shares may be subject. It is clear that the company's lien will be enforceable where it has no notice of such other charges. Where the company has notice, however, the other charges will normally prevail. It is true that under s 123 of the Principal Act no notice of any trust is to be entered on the register or is receivable by the company, but it was decided by the House of Lords in *Bradford Banking Co. v Briggs*[1] that this did not mean that the company was entitled to disregard notice of other charges or interests and that they retained their priority. The principle of the decision was applied by the Irish Court of Appeal in *Rearden v Provincial Bank of Ireland*.[2]

It would appear that the same considerations apply even where the articles provide, as they frequently do, that the company is not to be bound to recognise any equitable claim to or interest in the shares. But where the company has no notice of the equitable interest or charge, it will be able to rely on a clause of this nature. It was held in *New London and Brazilian Bank v Brocklebank*[3] that a person who acquired an equitable interest in shares could not assert his title to the shares and at the same time repudiate the terms upon which the shares were allotted, including such a clause.

1. (1886) 12 App Cas 29.
2. [1896] 1 IR 532, 571.
3. (1882) 21 Ch D 302.

18.15   Article 12 provides that the company may enforce a lien conferred by the articles by a sale of the shares. The sale cannot be effected, however, until after the expiration of 14 days after notice in writing has been given to the registered holder demanding payment of the amount then due. To provide for the possibility that the registered holder will not execute a transfer of the shares, article 13 empowers the directors to authorise some person to transfer the shares to the purchaser. The purchaser is not bound to see to the application of the purchase money and his title to the shares is not to be affected by any irregularity in the proceedings in reference to the sale.

Public limited company cannot create charges over its own shares

18.16   A public limited company is precluded by s 44 of the 1983 Act from creating a lien or other charge over its own shares, except in respect of amounts unpaid on the shares. The section makes void all other charges over its own shares except

(a) charges entered into by banking and hire purchase companies in connection with transactions entered into by them in the ordinary course of their business;

(b) charges which were in existence before the registration or re-registration of the company as a public limited company; and

(c) charges by a public company which did not apply to be re-registered in the period prescribed by s 12 of the Act which were in existence during that period.

Chapter 19

Transfer and transmission of shares

19.01 A share is a chose in action, i.e. a thing recoverable only by action and not by taking possession of it. The most obvious example of a chose in action is a debt: a person who claims to be owed money by another can only enforce such a claim by recovering judgment for the amount owed and then executing the judgment. By contrast, if he claims to be entitled to land, for example, he can bring proceedings claiming recovery of the land itself. A share is in essence a bundle of rights and duties to which the shareholder is entitled or subject; and the rights, as in the case of a debt, can only be enforced by action against the company.

A share, like any other chose in action, can be assigned to a third party. It has, however, one peculiar feature which is of importance when one is considering the requirements for an effective assignment. In order to make the person to whom the share is being assigned the successor to all the rights and duties of the original shareholder, a transfer of the share itself is not enough; the transferee must also be entered on the register as a member of the company.

An assignment of shares can be of two kinds: voluntary or involuntary. A *voluntary assignment* occurs when the shareholder transfers his shares to another either by way of a sale or gift. An *involuntary assignment* occurs when the shares are vested in another person because of the insolvency or death of the shareholder. A vesting of the shares on the insolvency or death of the shareholder is usually referred to as a *transmission*.

Transferability of shares

19.02 It is an essential feature of a share that it is freely transferable, unless the articles provide otherwise. In this it differs, as we have seen, from an interest in a partnership: the succession of one partner by another requires the consent of the ongoing partners. But we have also seen that in the case of a private company, the right to transfer shares must be restricted by the articles. Such a restriction can take a variety of forms, but the most common are provisions

(a) giving the directors a discretion to refuse to register the transfer of a share to a person of whom they do not approve;

(b) requiring the shareholder to offer any shares which he proposes to sell to the existing shareholders first, i.e. what is sometimes called a right of pre-emption.

A provision of the first type is to be found in Article 24 and is invariable in private companies in Ireland. A provision of the second type is also extremely common. In both instances, the objective (apart from ensuring that the company is a private company and, accordingly, enjoys the various privileges accorded to such companies) is to preserve the relatively closed nature of the enterprise. In some cases, this will mean confining it to members of the family originally associated with the enterprise or their friends and business connections.

19.03 Where the directors are given an unqualified discretion as to registering transfers, the court will not interefere with the exercise of that discretion, provided they exercise it in good faith and for the benefit of the company.[1] As in the case of other such powers conferred on them by the Acts or the articles, it is for them, and not the court, to decide what is in the best interests of the company.[2] Sometimes the articles provide that the directors may only decline registration on prescribed grounds, and in that event the court can enquire as to whether they did in fact decline on one of the specified grounds.[3] Thus, in the case of the article which entitles the directors to refuse to register a transfer to any person of whom they do not approve, the court can enquire as to whether the refusal was on grounds personal to the proposed transferee. In one case, it was held that such an article gave no power to the directors to decline registration of a transferee to whom they had no personal objection but who was the nominee of a person of whom they disapproved.[4]

Again, the articles may provide that the directors may decline to assign without assigning any reasons for their refusal. If, however, they elect to give reasons, the court may consider whether they were legitimate or not, i.e. whether they have applied the correct principles in exercising their discretion.[5]

1. *Re Smith & Fawcett Ltd* [1942] Ch 304.
2. See para 27.15 below.
3. *Re Bede Steam Shipping Co Ltd* [1917] 1 Ch 123.
4. Ibid.
5. *Re Bell Bros ex parte Hodgson* (1891) 65 LT 245.

19.04 As we have just seen, where the articles empower the directors to decline to register a transfer and no grounds are specified on which the refusal to register must be based, their decision will only be set aside on proof of lack of good faith; and the burden of proof rests on the person who alleges bad faith.[1] It is not an easy onus to discharge since the directors may simply decline without specifying reasons; but an example of a case in which the onus was discharged is *Re Hafner, Olhausen v Powderly*.[2] In that case, the plaintiff's uncle left him by his will 500 shares in a private company which carried on a long established and highly regarded business as pork butchers. The personal representatives having transferred the shares to the plaintiff, the directors refused to register the transfers. The articles entitled them to decline to register

'in their absolute and uncontrolled discretion without assigning any reasons.'

The plaintiff claimed that the directors had refused to register the transfers because they had voted themselves excessive remuneration which would have the effect of starving the shareholders of dividends and they realised that, if the plaintiff became a shareholder, he would be in a position to challenge this behaviour. The directors had in fact adamantly refused to give any reasons for their refusal to register the transfers. Black J held that, while the directors were within their legal rights in not giving any reasons, he was also entitled to infer from their refusal that the plaintiff's apprehensions were well founded. It followed that the plaintiff had discharged the onus of proving that the directors were not exercising their discretion in good faith for the benefit of the company as a whole. The Supreme Court on appeal held that he was entitled to come to this conclusion on the evidence.

1. *Re Smith & Fawcett Ltd* [1942] Ch 304.
2. [1943] IR 426.

19.05 The company must have ready for delivery to the transferee the certificate of any shares transferred within two months after the lodgment of the transfers for registration. This is provided in s 86 of the Principal Act which also provides that if the company fails to issue the certificate within 10 days after the service on it of a notice requiring its issue, it can be directed to do so by the court. Where the directors refuse to register a transfer, the company must notify the transferee of their refusal before the expiration of the two months' period.

19.06 An article giving a right of pre-emption usually takes the form of a provision that a share shall not be transferred to any person who is not a member of the company so long as any member is willing to buy the share at a fair price. Where the articles contain such a provision, there is no restriction on transfers of shares between members; but should the member wish to sell his shares to an outisder, the pre-emption clause comes into effect. The articles usually provide that the 'fair price' is to be determined in the absence of agreement by the auditor of the company. While the articles must be phrased in clear and unambiguous language in order to give such a right of pre-emption to the existing shareholders, the courts will not allow the obvious purpose of such a provision to be defeated by too literal a construction of the articles. This was made clear by the House of Lords in *Lyle & Scott Ltd v Scotts' Trustees*,[1] where the articles provided that the existing shareholders were entitled to a right of pre-emption where any of their number was 'desirous of transferring his ordinary shares'. A takeover bid was made for the company and the shareholders who were in favour of accepting the offer were paid the full price without executing any transfers of the shares. They gave the purchaser irrevocable proxies to vote on their behalf, thus avoiding any necessity for the purchaser to be registered as a shareholder. When the transaction was challenged on behalf of the company, the shareholders in question argued that it was not invalidated by the articles: they were not obliged to offer the shares to the other shareholders, since they were no longer 'desirous' of transferring their shares, they having been paid their money and the purchaser being in effective control. Not surprisingly, this bold argument was rejected, the House of Lords holding that it was not open to shareholders who had agreed to transfer shares and had been paid for them to contend that they were not 'desirous' of transferring their shares.

1. [1959] AC 763.

19.07 It was said by Denning L J in *Dean v Prince*[1] that the auditor of the company in determining the fair price of the shares for the purpose of a pre-emption clause is acting as an expert and not as an arbitrator. The practical consequence is that he may be liable to a party who suffers loss as a result of a negligent valuation carried out by him. while *Dean v Prince* is accepted in both England and Ireland as correctly stating the law, it is usual to provide expressly in articles that the auditor in carrying out such a valuation shall be deemed to be acting as an expert and not as an arbitrator.

1. [1954] Ch 409 at 426.

Form of transfer

19.08 At one time, the formalities for transferring shares were regulated by the articles. Since the Stock Transfer Act 1963, however, the procedure has been simplified in the case of fully paid shares. They can now be validly transferred by an instrument under hand in the form set out in Schedule I of the Act. In the case of unpaid shares, the mode of transfer is still in theory regulated by the articles; but these usually require no more than that the transfer should be in 'the usual or common form'. It is thought that in the case of partly paid shares this requirement would be met by a transfer complying with the Stock Transfer Act 1963.

Section 81 of the Principal Act provides that, notwithstanding anything in the articles of a company, it shall not be lawful for the company to register a transfer of shares or debentures unless a proper instrument of transfer has been delivered to the company. This ensures that the stamp duty payable on the transfer is not avoided by the company's dispensing with a transfer when the parties have agreed to the transfer and the price has been paid. In the case of a fully paid share, this requirement is met by an instrument which complies with the Stock Transfer Act 1963; and, as has been pointed out above, such an instrument will also usually be sufficient in the case of a partly paid up share.

It should be noted that in the case of fully paid shares the transfer need not specify the name of the transferee, having regard to the provisions of the Stock Transfer Act 1963. It is thought, however, that in a case to which the Act does not apply, e.g. a partly paid share, the name of the transferee must still be specified to render the instrument a 'proper instrument of transfer' for the purpose of s 81 of the Principal Act.

Certification of transfers

19.09 We have seen that it is an essential feature of a transfer of shares that the transferee should become registered as a shareholder in succession to the transferor. No difficulty arises where the transferor is parting with all his shares in the company: on completion of the transaction, he hands over his share certificate to the transferee who can thereupon be registered. Where, however, the transferor is retaining some of his shares or where he is selling the shares to a number of transferees, such a course is not practicable. In such circumstances the appropriate procedure is for the company to *certificate* the transfer of shares. The company should not do this unless the transferor lodges the certificate with the company. Where the company certificates the transfer of shares, section 85 of the Principal Act provides that the certification shall be taken as a representation by the company to any person acting on the faith of the certification that there has been produced to the company such documents as on the face of them show a *prima facie* title to the shares in the transferor.

Capacity to transfer

19.10 An infant is capable of transferring his shares in the company. In the case of a person of unsound mind so found, the transfer must be authorised by the President of the High Court.

Exchange control requirements

19.11 A transfer of shares to a person may require the consent of the Minister for Finance to be valid under the provisions of the Exchange Control Acts 1954 to 1982. This arises where the transfer is to a person resident outside what are called in the Acts 'the scheduled territories'. The scheduled territories initially meant in effect the countries in the sterling area. Since Ireland left the sterling area in 1979, the scheduled territories have in effect been confined to Ireland itself and any transfer to a person resident outside Ireland, including persons resident in the United Kingdom, requires the Minister's consent.

Transmission of shares

19.12 When a shareholder dies, his shares in common with his other property vest in his personal representatives, i.e. his executors or administrators. This takes place automatically by operation of law: no transfer will have been executed in favour of the personal representative. We have seen that the company cannot in general register a transfer of shares unless a proper instrument of transfer has been delivered to the company. This does not mean, however, that the personal representative cannot be registered as a member: s 81 (2) of the Principal Act provides that the company may have power to register as shareholder or debenture holder any person to whom the right to any shares in or debentures of the company has been transmitted by operation of law.

The articles usually contain a provision (Article 30) enabling the personal representative to elect either to be registered himself as shareholder or to have his nominee registered as shareholder. Where he elects to be registered himself, he must notify the company in writing to that effect. Where he elects to have his nominee registered, he must execute a transfer to the nominee. Any restrictions imposed by the articles on the transfer of the shares, such as a power vested in the directors to refuse to register a transfer or a right of pre-emption given to the other shareholders, are usually made applicable to such a notice of transfer (Article 31). The article also usually enables the directors to require the personal representative to elect either to be registered himself or transfer the shares within 90 days and, until he so elects, to withhold the payment of dividends, bonuses or other moneys payable in respect of the shares. (Article 32).

19.13 Although the company can, accordingly, register a personal representative as a member, he cannot be placed upon the register without his consent. If he is lawfully registered as a member, he may become personally liable for the amounts unpaid (if any) on the shares. Section 82, however, enables the personal representative to transfer the shares *before* he is registered as a member of the company. Moreover, s 87 provides that the production of the grant of probate or letters of administration must be accepted by the company as sufficient evidence of the personal representative's title. The appropriate procedure for a personal representative to adopt who does not wish to be registered as a member is to transfer the shares to the persons beneficially entitled or to sell them in exercise of his powers as personal representative.

19.14 As in the case of the death of the shareholder, so also on his bankruptcy there may be a transmission of shares by operation of law, in this case to the official assignee in bankruptcy. There is no automatic vesting of the shares in the official assignee upon the adjudication of the shareholder as a bankrupt, however: he is entitled to elect whether he will take the shares or not. In this respect the law in Ireland differs from that of England where there is an automatic vesting in the trustee in bankruptcy on adjudication. Articles 30, 31 and 32 referred to above apply to a vesting of shares in the official assignee in the same manner as in the case of a transmission on death.

If the shares are onerous, the official assignee may, within 12 months of the vesting of the shares in him, disclaim the shares.[1] Such a disclaimer does not affect the rights of any third parties in respect of the shares: it simply relieves the estate of the bankrupt from the obligation of membership, such as the liability to pay uncalled capital.

1. Bankruptcy (Ireland) (Amendment) Act 1872, ss 97 and 98.

Part five

Borrowing by the company

Chapter 20

Borrowing powers of companies

20.01 The memorandum almost invariably authorises the company to borrow money. But even where such a power is not given in express terms, the company may still be entitled to borrow, if the borrowing can fairly be regarded incidental to the objects of the company.[1] In the case of non-trading companies, however, it will only be implied if there is something in the memorandum or articles to indicate, either expressly or inferentially, that it was intended to give such a power.[2] If the memorandum or articles do not confer such a power, either expressly or by implication, they can be altered by special resolution to provide the company with the necessary powers.[3]

If the memorandum or articles restrict the amount which the company may borrow, such a limitation must be observed or the necessary amendment effected. It is, however, most unusual for a modern memorandum or articles to contain such a restriction. In the case of a public unlimited company, the borrowing powers cannot be exercised until a certificate has been issued by the Registrar under s 115 of the Principal Act;[4] and in the case of a public limited company, until a certificate has been issued by him under s 6 of the 1983 Act.[5]

1. See para 4.13 above.
2. *R. v Reed* (1880) 5 QBD 483 at 488, 489.
3. See para 4.24 and para 5.07 above.
4. See para 9.04 and para 9.05 above.
5. See para 9.04 above.

Security for borrowing

20.02 A company has, as incidental to a power of borrowing, the power to give such security as is necessary for the purpose of obtaining the required advance.[1] In the case of a company which has borrowing powers, accordingly, it is not necessary to confer such a power in express terms, but again it is usual to do so. Such a power includes a power to mortgage the uncalled capital of the company.[2]

The advance may be secured by a mortgage of the company's real or leasehold property, which can be either legal or equitable. In the former case, the morgage will be by deed, in the latter by deposit of title deeds. Or it may be secured by an issue of debentures or debenture stock, secured in turn by a floating charge over the company's assets and undertaking or a fixed charge or both. The nature of debentures and the meaning of a floating charge are fully discussed in the following chapter.

1. *Australian, etc, Company v Mounsey* (1858) 4 K & J 733.
2. *Re Phoenix Bessemer Co* (1875) 44 LJ Ch 683.

Ultra vires borrowing

20.03   If the company borrows money without having power to do so, the transaction is *ultra vires* and void. Where, however, the borrower can show that he was not aware that the transaction was *ultra vires* the company, it may be enforceable by him against the company. This modification of the *ultra vires* rule has been fully discussed in Chapter Eleven.

Chapter 21

Debentures and floating charges

21.01 The simplest definition of a debenture is that it is a document which provides evidence of a debt. In practice, however, for businessmen, lawyers and accountants it has assumed a more complex significance. It is now normally taken as meaning an instrument by which a company acknowledges its indebtedness and which is secured by a charge on the company's assets and/or undertaking. The charge can be either a fixed or specific charge of a particular asset– e.g. a mortgage of land– or a 'floating' charge over the assets and undertakings which is not attached to any specific asset.

A debenture can be either one instrument standing by itself and entered into between the company and a single lender or it can be one of a series of similar instruments issued to a number of lenders. The person to whom the debenture is issued–the *debenture holder*–does not become a member of the company and therefore is legally in a category distinct from a shareholder. He might be regarded as being in a position inferior to the shareholder in that he cannot attend meetings of the company or vote or inspect the company's accounts. He is in a position superior to the shareholder, however, in that he has the right to payment of a fixed rate of interest on his investment which is payable irrespective of whether the company has made profits or not. In addition, where the debenture is secured by a charge, he has a direct interest in the company's assets which a shareholder has not.

21.02 When a company issues debentures to the public, it can do so by issuing a series of debentures in identical terms but for different amounts to individual lenders. In practice, however, it is more common to issue *debenture stock*. Where this is done, the company creates a loan fund and issues stock certificates to each of the debenture holders stating the share of the fund to which he is entitled. The advantage of so doing is that the debenture holder can then sell as much of his investment as he pleases, whereas otherwise he would have to sell the whole debenture or nothing at all. The debenture stock certificate will declare him entitled to, for example, £500 debenture stock divided into £1 units. He may then transfer, say, 100 stock units and go through the same process of transfer and certification as if he were selling 100 £1 shares in the company.[1]

1. See para 19.09 above.

21.03 Where a debenture is secured by a charge on specific property of the company, the charge thus created has the characteristics of an ordinary mortgage of property, with one important exception. It is a fundamental principle of the law applicable to mortgages generally that the person whose property is mortgaged must have the right to get it back upon repayment of the advance, and whatever interest is due, either at any time or at a specified time. This right of the mortgagor–the 'equity of redemption'–may not be curtailed: there cannot be a 'clog' upon the equity of redemption, as the courts of equity put it. In the case of a debenture, however, it may be redeemable at a fixed time or at the option of the company; or it may be irredeemable. The creation of irredeemable debentures–or 'perpetual debentures' as they are sometimes called–is expressly authorised by s 94 of the Principal Act. This provides that a condition in a debenture or any deed securing a debenture is not to be invalid by reason only that the debentures are thereby made irredeemable or redeemable only on the happening of a contingency, however remote, or on the expiration of a period, however long.

21.04 Where a debenture is secured by a fixed or a floating charge, and the borrower defaults, the lender has the normal remedies available to a mortgage including an order for sale. Usually, however, the first remedy invoked by a debenture holder in the event of a default is the appointment of a *receiver,* who takes possession of the company's assets and normally has power to sell them.

21.05 Debentures issued by public companies are not unknown in Ireland and, in addition, semi-state bodies, such as the ESB, from time to time make issues of 'loan stock' which in its essential features is not very different from debenture stock. But by far the most common form of debenture in Ireland is the single debenture secured by a floating charge (and frequently by a fixed charge as well) issued by a private company to a bank or other lending institution to obtain the finance necessary for the company's operations which cannot be provided by the promoters.

Debenture stock

21.06 Where debenture stock is issued by a company, it is usual for a trust deed to be executed by the company. When trustees are appointed, the company covenants with the trustees (who are expressly appointed to represent the interests of the debenture holders) to pay the capital sum secured by the debenture either at a fixed date or in the event of a particular contingency, such as the winding up of the company, and to pay the agreed interest on the advance. The deed usually provides for the securing of the repayment of the capital by a fixed and floating charge.

The trustees are expected to protect the interest of the debenture holders. To that end, s 93 of the Principal Act provides that any provision in the trust deed or any contract with the debenture holders secured by such a deed which relieves the trustees of liability for breach of trust where they fail to show the 'degree of care and diligence' required of them as trustees is to be void.

Series of debentures

21.07 Where a series of debentures is issued by the company, they incorporate standard conditions indorsed on the back of each debenture. One of the standard conditions provides that each debenture is to rank *pari* *passu*, i.e. on an equal footing, in point of time without priority or preference one over another. This is necessary because all the debentures are not issued at the same time and it would affect their marketability as securities if one debenture holder were to secure priority over another simply by the accident of his debenture being issued first.

The 'pari passu' condition referred to in the preceding paragraph also incorporates a prohibition on the company's creating any mortgage or charge on its assets so as to rank *pari passu* with the series of debentures. There is generally an exception for specific charges for securing temporary loans or bank overdrafts in the ordinary course of business. The standard conditions also include provisions for the immediate repayment of the monies advanced in the following circumstances:

(1) if the company makes default in the payment of interest for a period of six months and the debenture holder calls in the principal;

(2) if a winding up order is made or a valid winding up resolution passed;

(3) if a distress or execution is levied against any of the chattels or property of the company and not discharged within five days;

(4) if a receiver is appointed over the undertaking and/or assets of the company; or

(5) if the company ceases or threatens to cease to carry on business.

Similar conditions are also invariably included in a single debenture. In addition, the conditions indorsed on a series of debentures include provisions requiring a register of debenture holders to be kept by the company and enabling the company to regard the registered debenture holders as entitled to the benefit of the debenture to the exclusion of persons equitably entitled.

Transferability of debentures

21.08 A debenture is transferable in the manner provided by the debenture itself. Section 81 of the Principal Act is applicable, however, and the company accordingly may not register a transfer of debentures unless a proper instrument of transfer has been delivered to the company. But it is possible to issue *bearer debentures* which can be transferred by delivery in the same manner as share warrants.[1] Such bearer debentures are in law negotiable instruments.

The transferee of a debenture takes it subject to the same equitable rights of the company as the debenture holder, even where he acquired the interest of the debenture holder in good faith for valuable consideration and without notice of any such equitable rights. However, in the case of a series of debentures the standard conditions usually provide that the capital and interest are to be payable by the company without regard to any such equities.

1. See para 16.17 above.

Requirements as to prospectus, allotment etc. in the case of debentures

21.09 The requirements of the Acts in the case of public companies as to the prospectus or statement in lieu thereof are generally speaking the same in the case of debentures as in the case of shares. Similarly, where the debentures are listed on a stock exchange, the regulations of that exchange will be applicable.

Convertible debentures

21.10 A company may issue convertible debentures, i.e. debentures which may be converted into shares in the company at a stated rate of exchange.

Remedies of debenture holders

21.11 Where there is a default in the payment of capital or interest by the company, the debenture holder may in every case bring proceedings for the recovery of the money which he is owed and prosecute them to judgment and execution in the ordinary way. He may also petition for the winding up of the company in such circumstances. Indeed where the debenture is unsecured–an extremely rare circumstance in Ireland today–these are his only remedies.

Where, however, the debenture is secured by a fixed charge, a floating charge or both, the debenture holder has a remedy which is frequently more attractive to him and, in many instances, the company itself. This is the appointment of a *receiver*. He can be appointed either by the debenture holder in exercise of a power granted for that purpose by the debenture or by the court on the application of the debenture holder. On his appointment the powers of the company and the directors' authority in relation to the property charged are suspended and may only be exercised with the consent of the receiver. Moreover, since he is usually appointed as a *manager* in addition to being a receiver, he can conduct the business of the company for as long as he deems appropriate in the interests of the debenture holder.

Action by individual debenture holders where series issued

21.12 Where a series of debentures is issued, an individual debenture holder can bring an action to enforce his debenture against the company. Such an action can be grounded either on an actual default by the company or on the fact that the company is in jeopardy. The debenture holder brings the proceedings on behalf of all the debenture holders[1] and the terms of the debenture usually require him to obtain the consent of a specified majority of his fellow debenture holders before proceedings are issued. Normally, the first step taken in such an action is the appointment of a receiver. Where a number of different actions is brought by the debenture holders, the court has power to consolidate them.[2]

1. Rules of the Superior Courts, Ord 15, r 9.
2. Ibid, Ord 49, r 6.

Proof by debenture holders in winding up

21.13 A debenture holder who wants to prove for his debt in the winding up of an insolvent company may either realise his security or value it and in either case prove for the balance. For the purpose of ascertaining the balance for which he can prove, the debenture holder must apply the proceeds of his security in the payment of interest accrued due up to the commencement of the winding up. He may then prove as an unsecured creditor for the balance of the principal and interest due at the commencement of the winding up after deducting the amount realised from the security.[1]

1. See para 34.74 below.

Floating charges in general

21.14 A *floating* charge is a form of charge particularly associated with companies. The conventional *fixed* or *specific* charge invariably involves the vesting of the legal interest in the property in the lender at the time of the transaction. Thereupon the lender has all the usual remedies in the event of the borrower's default, such as sale, possession, a receiver, etc. The charge, in other words, attaches immediately to the specific property being offered as security.

By contrast the floating charge does not attach to any specific asset at the time of its creation. There is no vesting of the legal estate in any property at that point: the charge floats above the entire assembly of assets to which it relates and which frequently consists of all the assets and undertaking of the company. It does not descend, as it were, and attach itself to any specific asset until certain specified events occur. At that stage, the floating charge is said to *crystallise*.

Floating charges became a popular form of security with joint stock companies at an early stage.[1] Such companies often wished to raise finance on the strength of assets other than real or leasehold property, such as their stock-in-trade, book debts, etc. It was difficult, however, to create fixed charges over such items, since they were constantly being disposed of in the course of the company's business, and it might have been necessary in theory to create a fresh security every time a new item was acquired by the company while releasing the charge on those which were being disposed of. The floating charge, which enabled the borrower to go on using the charged assets in the ordinary course of his business, provided a solution to this problem.

1. Their validity was first recognised in *Re Panama, New Zealand and Australian Royal Mail Co* (1870) 5 Ch 318. It should be remembered, incidentally, that while they are normally created by companies rather than individuals, there is nothing to prevent an individual creating one: see Gough, *Company Charges* Part II.

21.15 Floating charges also created their own problems. Precisely because they were attached to no specific asset and were usually taken by banks and similar institutions to secure both present and future borrowing, it was peculiarly difficult for an unsecured creditor of the company to estimate the availability of assets to meet the debt owing to him by the company. If the company was wound up, such a creditor could find that all the assets had been captured by a floating charge. Quite often such charges were created by the company in the knowledge that the company was in serious financial straits and in response to pressure from one of its creditors. Sometimes directors of the company, who would be in the best position to know that the company was tottering, tried to protect their own position by taking floating charges to secure advances previously made by them.

To deal with such problems, the 1908 Act provided that such charges were to be invalid if created within three months from the commencement of the winding up except in relation to any money paid to the company at the time of or subsequently to the creation of the charge, together with interest thereon. Cox recommended the extension of the period to 12 months in the case of a floating charge in favour of a director and six months in any other case. In the event, the draughtsman of the Principal Act provided that the charge was to be invalid if made within the 12 months's period, without distinguishing between charges in favour of directors and others, thus following the example of the English 1948 Act. Section 288 provides that a floating charge created within 12 months before the winding up shall, unless it is proved that the company immediately after the creation of the charge was solvent, be invalid, except to the amount of any cash paid to the company at the time of or subsequently to the charge, together with interest at the rate of five per cent, per annum.[1]

The Principal Act also provides that a receiver appointed under a floating charge must pay preferential creditors (such as the Revenue) out of assets coming into his hands before paying over any sums due to the holder of the charge.[2]

Where a receiver is appointed under a floating charge, it is frequently the case that the property is already subject to a fixed charge. In that event, the floating charge, which usually crystallises only upon the receiver's appointment, must yield priority to the fixed charge and, as a result, the receiver will be unable to sell the property without the consent and co-operation of the holder of the fixed charge.

1. See para 21.29 below.
2. S 98.

21.16 It may accordingly be important to ascertain whether a particular charge is properly described as a 'floating charge'. It was defined as follows by Lord Macnaghten in *Illingworth v Houldsworth*:[1]

'I should have thought there was not much difficulty in defining what a floating charge is in contrast to what is called a specific charge. A specific charge, I think, is one that without more fastens on ascertained and definite property or property capable of being ascertained and defined; a floating charge, on the other hand, is ambulatory and shifting in its nature, hovering over and so to speak floating with the property which it is intended to affect until some event occurs or some act is done which causes it to settle and fasten on the subject of the charge within its grasp and reach.'

In another frequently quoted passage, Romer LJ in *Re Yorkshire Woolcombers' Association*[2] said that if a floating charge had three characteristics, it was a floating charge viz:

'(1) If it is a charge on a class of assets of a company present and future;
(2) if that class is one which, in the ordinary course of the business of the company, would be changing from time to time; and
(3) if you find that by the charge it is contemplated that, until some future step is taken by or on behalf of those interested in the charge, the company may carry on its business in the ordinary way so far as concerns the particular class of assets I am dealing with.'

It is important to note, however, that Romer LJ also made it clear that a charge could still be a floating charge without having all three of these characteristics. An interesting example is afforded by the Supreme Court decision in *Welch v Bowmaker (Ireland) Ltd and the Bank of Ireland*.[3]

In that case the company had issued a debenture in favour of the first defendant, clause 3 of which charged the undertaking and assets of the company, present and future, with the payment of moneys owed to that defendant and also charged 'as a specific charge' the lands 'specified in the schedule hereto'. The schedule described three of the four parcels of land owned by the company. The first condition endorsed on the debenture stated that the charge thereby effected was to be 'as regards the company's lands and premises for the time being' a specific charge and as regards the other assets of the company a floating charge and stated that the company was not at liberty to create any mortgage or charge on its property for the time being in priority to the debenture.

One month after the execution of the debenture, the company deposited with the defendant bank the title deeds of the fourth parcel of land by way of equitable mortgage to secure the repayment of moneys owed by the company to the bank. At the time of the deposit, the bank was aware of the existence of the debenture but not of its terms. The company became insolvent and its assets were insufficient to pay both defendants. In the course of the winding up of the company, the first defendant claimed that a specific charge had been created over the fourth parcel which took priority over the bank's equitable mortgage. The bank claimed that a floating charge only had been created over which its mortgage took priority. (The floating charge, if it were one, did not crystallise until the commencement of the winding up and consequently would be postponed to any legal or equitable mortgage created before the winding up.) The High Court upheld the first defendant's claim, but the Supreme Court (Henchy and Parke JJ, Kenny J *dissentiente*) allowed the bank's appeal, holding that the terms of the first condition indorsed on the debenture when read with clause 3 made it clear that the intention of the parties was to create a floating charge only. It seems a reasonable inference from the judgments that the majority, although accepting that the asset in dispute was not of a class which in the ordinary course of business would change from time to time, did not consider that fact sufficient to prevent the charge from being a floating charge.

1. [1904] AC 355 at 358.
2. [1903] 2 Ch 284 at 295. *Illingworth v Houldsworth* (above) is in fact the same case, as decided on appeal in the House of Lords.
3. [1980] IR 251.

21.17 There has been considerable discussion as to whether the floating charge is a form of security which takes immediate effect but allows the borrower to continue using the assets captured by it until crystallisation; or whether it is a mortgage of future assets which is of no legal effect until crystallisation. The comments in the earlier English decisions tended to favour the first view, but in more recent times the preference appears to have been for the second.[1]

1. This is the view taken by Pennington in an essay entitled *Genesis of the Floating Charge*, (1960) 23 MLR 630, 644/6. However, Gough in *Company Charges* questions whether the earlier decisions when analysed support the proposition that a floating charge takes immediate effect: see pp 135–137.

21.18 It was clear from an early stage that there was no difficulty in creating a floating charge over the book debts of the company. The subject matter presented the three characteristics referred to by Romer LJ, and even prior to his judgment in the *Yorkshire Woolcombers' Case*, it had been held by the

House of Lords in *Tailby v Official Receiver*[1] that a floating charge could be created over book debts, even though the debts had not yet come into existence.

A *fixed* charge over book debts had, of course, the attraction for the lender that it would retain its validity even if the winding up took place within twelve months, and would not be postponed to any preferential debts. In *Siebe Gorman v Barclays Bank Ltd*,[2] Slade J held that it was possible to create such a fixed charge and that its existence was not negatived but was reinforced by a requirement that the debts when collected were to be paid into a special account out of which payments could only be made if approved by the lender. In *Re Armagh Shoes Ltd*,[3] Hutton J held that a charge over present and future book debts was a floating charge although described as a fixed charge. In that case, the decision in *Siebe Gorman v Barclays Bank Ltd* was distinguished, there being no clause in the debenture requiring the payment of the book debts into a special account. Such clauses were contained in the debenture and deed of charge which were considered in *Re Keenan Brothers Ltd*,[4] where the charge was also described as a fixed charge. Keane J held, however, that it was a floating charge: he declined to follow *Siebe Gorman v Barclays Bank Ltd*, stating that the requirement that the debts be collected by the borrower and paid into a special account was more consistent with the existence of a floating charge than a fixed charge. Both Hutton J and Keane J expressed the view that the description of the charge as a fixed charge in the deed creating the charge was not conclusive. Whether the charge was a fixed or floating charge had to be determined by considering the deed as a whole.

1. (1888) 13 App Cas 523.
2. [1977] 2 Lloyds' Reports 142.
3. [1982] NI 59.
4. Unreported; judgment delivered 5 October 1984. This decision is under appeal to the Supreme Court at the time of writing.

Effect of a floating charge

21.19   A floating charge usually takes the form of a charge by the company over

'its undertaking, and all its property, present and future, including its uncalled capital for the time being.'

This will capture all the assets of the company, both in its ownership at the time of the debenture and which it subsequently acquires. It is, however, not necessary that the charge should extend so far: it may be confined to a class of assets, such as book debts.[1]

1. *In Re Yorkshire Woolcombers' Association*, above.

21.20   It is a usual feature of a floating charge that the company remains free to deal with its property in the ordinary course of business, despite the existence of the charge, until the charge crystallises. In particular, it may sell, let, mortgage, or otherwise deal with its assets and may pay dividends out of profits as if a floating charge had not been created.

Thus, in the absence of any express prohibition in the debenture, the company may create legal and equitable mortgages prior to the crystallisation of the floating charge and, if created, they will have priority over the floating charge.[1] This is the case even though the mortgagees have notice of the existence of the floating charge.[2] As we shall see, however, it is standard practice to provide for such a prohibition.[3]

But although in the absence of such a prohibition, there is nothing to prevent the company from creating legal and equitable mortgages, it cannot create a second or subsequent floating charges to rank in priority to or *pari passu* with the existing floating charge. Such a charge would require to be authorised by the debenture.[4]

1. *Re Florence Land Co* (1878) 10 Ch D 530; *Re Colonial Trusts Ltd* (1880) 15 Ch D 465.
2. *Wheatley v Silkstone Co* (1885) 29 Ch D 715.
3. See para 21.22 below.
4. *Re Benjamin Cope & Sons*, [1914] 1 Ch 800; *Re Automatic Bottle Makers Ltd*. [1926] Ch 412.

21.21 Debts, as we have seen, are among the assets which can be the subject of a floating charge. But the debenture holder cannot be in any better position in regard to such debts than the company. He becomes entitled to them, accordingly, subject to any right of set off which may arise because of debts incurred by the company in the course of its trading.

Such a right to set off can only be exercised, however, where there is 'mutuality'. If the debts which it is sought to set off are acquired by assignment after the creation of the floating charge, there is no such mutuality and the debts cannot be set off. This was so decided by Budd J in *Lynch and Others v Ardmore Studios*,[1] following the decision of the Court of Appeal in *N.W. Robbie and Co Ltd v Witney Warehouse Ltd*.[2]

1. [1966] IR 133.
2. [1963] 3 All ER 613.

21.22 The flexibility of the floating charge was a source of concern to lending bodies who saw their security in danger of losing its priority to a fixed mortgage created after the floating charge. It has accordingly become standard practice to insert a condition prohibiting the company from creating any mortgage or charge ranking in priority to or *pari passu* with the floating charge. Such a prohibition will be effective, unless the subsequent mortgagee can show that he was not aware of the prohibition in the floating charge.

It is also clear, however, that even if a subsequent mortgagee can be fixed with notice of the existence of the floating charge—as he generally can be because of the requirement that the floating charge be registered[1]—he may still be entitled to priority, since he will usually be able to show that he was not aware of the prohibition. This is clear from a succession of authorities which were considered and approved by the Supreme Court in *Welch v Bowmaker (Ireland) Ltd and Anor* (above). In that case the argument on behalf of the debenture holder was that such prohibitions were common form in modern debentures and that the subsequent mortgagee should be fixed with *constructive* (as distinct from *actual*) notice of the prohibition. (The doctrine of constructive notice means that a person may be deemed in law to be aware of matters of which he does not know but would have known had he made certain inquiries.) Henchy J and Parke J both took the view, however, that the principle referred to was so well settled in law as to be incapable of alteration except by legislation. Parke J warned against the danger of extending the doctrine of constructive notice too far, saying

'the doctrine may be an unruly horse and should be ridden with a firm hand.'[2]

1. Under s 99 of the Principal Act.
2. At p 262.

21.23 As we shall see in Chapter Thirty-Three, certain debts are given a degree of preference in the event of the company's being wound up. Thus the Revenue are entitled to one year's taxes in arrears in priority to the ordinary creditors. A person entitled to a floating charge may rely on his security and not prove for his debt in the event of a winding up, but the preferential creditors will still have to be paid in priority to the debt secured by the floating charge.[1] Similarly, where the charge crystallises by the appointment of a receiver *before* a winding up, the receiver must pay the preferential creditors out of the assets coming into his hands before paying any sums due for principal or interest to the person entitled to the charge.[2]

1. S 285 (7) (b) of the Principal Act.
2. S 98 of the Principal Act.

21.24 When a floating charge crystallises—by the appointment of a receiver, for example—there is an equitable assignment of the company's interest in the property to the person entitled to the floating charge. This does not have the same consequences as a sale of the property, a distinction made clear by Kenny J in *Interview Ltd*.[1] This may be of considerable importance in determining the right of parties to a hire purchase agreement or agreements of a similar nature, where the goods are in the possession of a company in receivership. In the case of such agreements, the goods remain the property of the hire purchase company throughout the currency of the agreement. If a receiver is appointed by the person entitled to the floating charge, the latter does not acquire the interest of the hire purchase company since there has been no sale to him. It follows that the hire purchase company (or supplier of the goods under a similar transaction) will be entitled to retain possession of the goods as against the receiver unless the sums owing in respect of the goods are paid by the receiver. It is also clear that this result will follow whether or not the hire purchase agreement was executed subsequent to the floating charge.[2]

1. [1975] IR 382.
2. See Palmer, vol I, 44–16.

21.25 Where an unsecured creditor recovers judgment against the company but has not executed the judgment, the floating charge will have priority.[1] Where, however, the creditor completely executes the judgment by a seizure or sale of the company's property before the charge crystallises, the floating charge loses its priority.[2] Similarly a landlord can distrain for rent before the appointment of a receiver.[3]

1. *Re Opera* [1891] 3 Ch 260.
2. *Evans v Rival Granite Quarries Ltd* [1910] 2 KB 979.
3. *Re Woundwood Colliery Co* [1897] 1 Ch 373.

21.26 The debenture holder frequently finds today when he comes to realise his security that the suppliers of goods and raw materials to the company who have not been paid claim to be entitled to the ownership of them because of what are known as 'reservation of title' clauses. Such provisions, which have been familiar in continental jurisdictions for a long time but have only been making their appearance here and in England in recent years, also commonly stipulate that the supplier is to be entitled to enforce these rights against the proceeds of sale, where the goods have been resold, or against the finished product into which the raw materials have been converted. While they are usually referred to as *Romalpa* clauses after the English decision[1] which recognised their validity in that jurisdiction, they might be more properly referred to as *Interview* clauses in Ireland, since Kenny J had treated them as enforceable in that case some two years before *Romalpa*. However, to avoid confusion, they will be referred to as *Romalpa* clauses in the ensuing discussion.

Such clauses, if effective, make the suppliers for all practical purposes secured creditors at the expense of ordinary creditors. (A Romalpa clause which is effective as against a receiver appointed under a floating charge will be equally effective as against a liquidator.) It would seem to follow logically that

(a) such clauses to be effective must be in the nature of chattel mortgages and should not be capable of enforcement unless the clause imposes on the company which buys the goods an obligation to hold the goods, any goods into which they are converted or the proceeds of sale of the goods in trust for the supplier;

(b) the mortgage or charge thus created by the company to be enforeable must be registered under s 99 of the Principal Act.[2]

Unfortunately, these aspects of the clauses were not analysed in any depth in the *Interview* and *Romalpa* decisions; and confusion has been increased by the fact that the decisions on such clauses in both jurisdictions in subsequent years have naturally been addressed to the actual wording of the clauses in issue and the particular facts of the relevant cases. It is clear that intervention by the legislature is required to introduce a reasonable degree of certainty into the present law but recommendations by Cork to that effect have not been implemented by the recent English Insolvency Bill. It remains to be seen whether the Oireachtas will adopt a different course.

The crucial difficulty that such a clause presents is that in such transactions both parties—the supplier and the company–envisage that the goods will be either sold on to a third party or used in the manufacture of some product. In either case, Irish and English law as it now exists requires that there be some sort of fiduciary obligation on the company to account for the proceeds of sale or the end product into which the goods have been converted before it will allow the supplier to recover the price out of the proceeds of sale or the finished product. Where such a fiduciary relationship exists, and where it is possible to identify the property now representing the goods supplied, the law will recognise the rights of the supplier to follow or, in the language of the courts of equity, *trace* his claim into the property. This remedy, which was defined in a celebrated passage in the judgment of Jessell MR in *Re Hallett*,[3] is undoubtedly available to the supplier in such a case. But this may very well mean that the company will have created a charge which to be enforceable must be registered under s 99 of the Principal Act. That is almost certainly the case where the goods have been sold or converted into other goods, but it may also be so where the goods are still in the possession of the company, depending on the language used in the clause in question.

These difficulties inherent in, but not explored by, the judgments in the Romalpa case were illustrated by the subsequent English decisions in *Re Bond Worth Ltd*[4] and *Borden (UK) Ltd v Scottish Timber Products Ltd.*[5] In the first of these, the clause in question purported to reserve to the suppliers of yarn intended to be used by a company in the manufacture of carpets the 'equitable and beneficial ownership' in the yarn until payment. In a lengthy judgment, Slade J held that this clause meant that the suppliers had transferred the *legal*—as distinct from the equitable or beneficial—interest in the yarn to the company. The latter had thereupon created a charge on the yarn to the extent of their indebtedness to the suppliers. But it was in the nature of a floating charge, since the company were still at liberty to sell on the yarn or convert it into carpets. Whatever happened to the yarn, however, the charge crystallised when the company failed to pay in accordance with the terms of supply. It then attached to the yarn, the fibre into which the yarn had been converted or the proceeds of sale as the case might be. But since such a charge required registration under the English equivalent of s 99 of the Principal Act, and had not been registered, it was void.

In *Borden*, the suppliers of resin intended to be used by the company to which it was delivered in the manufacture of chipboard stipulated that 'the ownership of the material' should remain with the suppliers until payment. It was held by the Court of Appeal that once the resin had been converted into chipboard any charge which might have been created over it by the company simply ceased to exist, since the material over which it had been created—the resin—had vanished. Two members of the court—Buckley LJ and Templeman LJ—were also of the view that even if such a charge was still in existence, it would have been void for non-registration. It should be noted that the court in that case did not have to decide whether the language used, differing as it did from the language in *Bond Worth*, was apt to create a charge although Templeman LJ seemed to incline to the view that it was.

More recently still, in *Clough Mill v Martin*,[6] the Court of Appeal dealt with a clause where the rights of the supplier of yarn were spelled out in two distinct provisions. Under the first, the 'ownership of the material' was to remain with the supplier and the right was reserved to it to dispose of the material until payment in full was received or until the company sold the material in a *bona fide* transaction. Under the second, if any of the material was used in manufacture of the other goods, the 'property' in the whole of such goods was to remain in the supplier until payment. It was held that the first provision was not a charge of any sort: it was no more than a contractual term which prevented the property in the goods from passing until they were paid for or sold on by the company and in the meantime entitled the supplier to sell the goods itself if it wished. The capacity of a seller to reserve the property in the goods by such a clause had been expressly recognised by ss 17 and 19 of the Sale of Goods Act 1983. As such a clause, it did not create a charge which had to be registered. The court considered that the second provision, however, did involve the creation of a charge, although it was conceded that this did violence to the language used. In the event, since the defendant, who was a receiver appointed by a debenture holder, had allowed the company to use the yarn in the manufacture of fibre before payment had been made in full, it was held that he was liable in damages for the wrongful conversion of the yarn.

In *Re Interview* an Irish company, EII, had agreed with a German company, AEG, to import their products under a contract governed by German law. Under the contract, AEG retained the property in the goods until they were paid for and EII agreed to assign to AEG any claims they might have against people to whom they sold the goods. Subsequently, it was arranged that another company, Interview Ltd, should acquire EII's stock of AEG products and that they should be supplied directly by AEG with its goods upon the same terms. EII transferred the AEG goods in their possession to Interview Ltd who then became liable to AEG for the price of some of the goods. This debt they purported to discharge by the payment of promissory notes. These promissory notes were dishonoured and a receiver was appointed by a debenture holder over the undertaking and assets of Interview. He applied to the court for directions as to the respective rights of the debenture holder and AEG to the goods still in the possession of Interview, the money representing the sale of such goods since his appointment and the money which was still to be recovered from people to whom the goods had been sold.

Kenny J held that the reservation of title clause was effective and that its enforcement depended on the *lex loci rei sitae*, in this case Irish law. But the question of the necessity for registration under s 99 is not dealt with in the judgment—and presumably was not raised in argument—except in relation to the money still to be recovered. Kenny J held that the relevant term in the AEG contract constituted an assignment by way of security of the book debts of Interview and as such was void for non-registration under s 99.

In *Frigoscandia (Contracting) Ltd v Continental Irish Meat Ltd*,[7] the question of non-registration appears to have been more fully argued. In that case, the facts and the agreement were relatively straightforward: the plaintiff company had delivered and installed an item of plant at the defendant company's factory. The contract provided that until payment the ownership of the plant was to remain with the plaintiff company. When the defendant company failed to pay, the plaintiff company claimed to be entitled to recover possession of the plant against a receiver who had been appointed. McWilliam J held that they were entitled to succeed: the provision was a straightforward contractual term which did not create any charge and accordingly did not require registration. Clearly this decision is to the same effect as the Court of Appeal decision in *Clough Mill Ltd v Martin* on the first provision in the contract.

By contrast, both the facts and the terms of the contract considered in *Kruppstahl AG v Quitmann Products Ltd and Another*[8] were somewhat complicated. In essence, the plaintiff company, a German concern, had supplied steel to the defendant company for use in the manufacture of certain goods such as pedal bins and bread bins. The terms of supply as translated from the German provided that

'all goods supplied remain our property (reserved goods) until all claims are met, particularly also balances due to us on any legal grounds whatsoever. This also applies, if payments are effected in respect of specific claims.'

In addition, however, the contract provided for the possibility that the steel might be used in manufacturing the finished products before it was paid for. It was stated that

'Handling and processing of the reserved goods are performed on our behalf ... The processed goods are deemed to be reserved goods ... In the case of processing, blending and mixing of the reserved goods with other goods by the buyer, (the plaintiff company) acquire a joint title to the new goods in accordance with the ratio of the invoice value of the reserved goods to the invoice value of the other goods used. If (the plaintiff company's) title lapses due to blending or mixing, the buyer assigns to us already at this stage his title to the new goods in accordance with the invoice value of the reserved goods and holds them in trust for (the plaintiff company) without charge. The thus arising joint title is the equivalent of reserved goods ...'

Some of the steel delivered was used by the defendant company in the manufacture of its products. When a receiver was appointed by a debenture holder, the plaintiff company claimed to be entitled to be a secured creditor in priority to the debenture holder in respect of the total indebtedness to them of the defendant company. Gannon J, following Kenny J in *Re Interview*, held that while the contract itself was to be construed in accordance with German law, specific transactions effected in Ireland, such as the delivery of the steel in issue, were regulated by Irish law. Having considered the English authorities already referred to, he concluded that the property in the unworked steel remained in the plaintiff company, but that in the case of the steel used in manufacture, the defendant company were trustees of the finished products and had thereby created a charge which was void for non-registration under s 99. The plaintiff company were accordingly entitled to priority in respect of the unworked steel only.

The most recent Irish decision is that of Carroll J in *Somers v James Allen (Ireland) Ltd.*[9] In that case a company had supplied certain ingredients to a company manufacturing and selling animal feeding compounds. The conditions of sale included a *Romalpa* clause which provided that the 'transfer of title' of the goods should not occur until they had been paid for in full. There was no express provision for what was to happen in the event of the ingredients having been either mixed with other ingredients or used in the manufacture of feeding compounds. A receiver was appointed by the Agricultural Credit Corporation over the property of the company and the supplier who had not been paid claimed to be entitled to the ownership of the ingredients as against the receiver. The ingredients were in fact still identifiable: they had not been mixed with others or used in manufacturing compounds. Carroll J upheld the supplier's claim, saying:

'I do not accept Mr Kelly's submission that the parties intended to split the legal and equitable title to the goods or that such split occurred as a necessary result of their contract. I do not see it as an impossible legal concept that the seller of goods to be used in a manufacturing process can retain title as long as the goods exist in the state in which they were supplied.'

Accordingly, no charge had been created by the company and the clause was not void for non-registration.

Carroll J in the course of her judgment distinguished *Kruppstahl AG* on the ground that a floating charge had been created in that case in respect of the finished steel only and not in respect of the unworked steel. The difficulty remains that in a case such as *Somers v James Allen (Ireland) Ltd* the law is confronted with something of a dilemma: is one to treat the intention of the parties in including such a clause as confined to the unprocessed or unsold goods only? If so, the strange consequence follows that one is attributing to the parties the intention that the title to the goods should pass to the purchaser or to a sub-purchaser when they are used in manufacture or sold on, rather than when they are paid for. This seems wholly at odds with the language used; but the only alternative may be to treat the supplier as reserving his title to the goods until they are paid for, whether they are retained by the purchaser, used in manufacturing or sold on. This appears inevitably to involve the creation of a charge which must be registered under s 99 and raises the further difficulty, in the case of manufactured goods, that the actual subject matter of the supposed charge has ceased to exist.

There is a third possibility: that the intention of the parties is that the legal and equitable title remains in the seller until the sale or manufacture, at which stage for the first time it divides, the legal title passing to the purchaser

174

and the equitable title being retained by the seller. The contract, on this hypothesis, creates a form of springing charge which does not come into existence until the legal estate is vested in the purchaser. The trouble with such a construction is that it appears extremely artificial having regard to the actual language of the clause and again the difficulty posed by *Borden Ltd* remains: how can the charge exist if its subject matter has vanished?

Unless the legislature intervenes, it seems probable that *Romalpa* clauses of this nature will continue to cause problems for receivers and the courts.[10]

1. *Aluminium Industrie Vaasem BV v Romalpa Aluminium Ltd* [1976] 2 All ER 552.
2. See para 22.03 below.
3. (1880) 13 Ch D 696 at 708–711.
4. [1980] Ch 228.
5. [1981] Ch 25.
6. [1984] 1 All ER 721.
7. [1982] ILRM 396.
8. [1982] ILRM 551.
9. [1984] ILRM 437. This decision was affirmed by the Supreme Court on 23 March 1985, but at the time of writing the written judgments are not available.
10. For a discussion of the difficulties created by them for accountants generally, see *Reservation of Title* by Raymond Byrne and Bernard Pierce, ILT (NS) Vol 3, p 26.

21.27 It has also become common practice in recent years for creditors who fear that their debtor intends to remove whatever assets are available to satisfy a judgment out of the jurisdiction to apply to the court for an injunction restraining the debtor from so doing. Such injunctions—known as *Mareva* injunctions[1]—are frequently granted by the courts; but it should be borne in mind that it has been held in England that the debenture holder is entitled in such circumstances to obtain an order discharging the injunction if the persons who obtained the Mareva injunction are unsecured creditors and there appears to be no hope of any surplus becoming available to such creditors.[2]

1. After an English decision in which such relief was granted, *Mareva Compania Naviere SA of Panama v International Bulk Carriers SA* [1980] 1 All ER 213.
2. *Cretanor Maritime Co Ltd v Irish Marine Management Ltd* [1978] 3 All ER 164.

Crystallisation of floating charge

21.28 A floating charge crystallises—i.e. the charge ceases to float and becomes attached to the assets over which it was granted—on the happening of one of two events: (i) the appointment of a receiver[1] or (ii) the winding up of the company.[2] It has also been suggested that the charge may crystallise automatically if there is a default by the company and the debenture so provides. The more generally accepted view has been, however, as stated, i.e. that the crystallisation does not take place until the debenture holder has taken active steps to enforce his security by appointing a receiver or obtaining such an appointment from the court or the company has gone into liquidation.[3]

The proposition that there can be an automatic crystallisation on the default of the company if the debenture is in sufficiently explicit terms to permit of a such a construction rests on some *dicta* in earlier English cases[4] and an express decision to that effect in New Zealand.[5] It is thought, however, that this line of authority is unlikely to be followed in Ireland. The courts here will probably incline to the view that such automatic crystallisation would present problems for other creditors who would have no actual notice of the terms of the debenture and that any such doctrine would need to be the subject of considered legislation and regulation.

1. *Nelson & Co v Faber & Co* [1903] 2KB 367: *Evans v Rival Granite Quarries, Ltd* [1910] 2 KB 979; *N W Robbie & Co v Witney Warehouse Co* [1963] 3 All ER 316.
2. *Wallace v Universal Automatic Machines* [1894] 2 Ch 547.
3. *Nelson & Co v Faber & Co*; *Evans v Rival Granite Quarries Ltd* (above).
4. Summarised in Palmer, Vol I 44–10.
5. *Re Manurowi Transport Ltd* [1971] NZLR 909.

Invalidity of floating charges under ss 288 and 289 of the Principal Act

21.29   A company may sometimes under pressure from one of its creditors execute a floating charge in respect of its existing debts. Or it may do so at the instance of one of its own directors. In order to mitigate the risks to ordinary creditors arising from such transactions, ss 288 and 289 of the Principal Act render invalid floating charges entered into by companies within 12 months of a winding up subject to certain exceptions.

Section 288 provides that such charges are to be invalid unless it is proved that the company, immediately after the charge, was solvent. But the section does not invalidate the charge to the extent that it secures cash paid to the company at the time of or subsequently to the creation of the charge and in consideration of the charge, together with interest on the amount at the rate of five per cent per annum.

21.30   It is to be observed that the burden of proof that the company was solvent immediately after the creation of the charge rests on the lender. In determining whether the company was solvent, the crucial factor is its ability to pay its debts *as they fall due*. Accordingly, where a company carries on its business after the creation of a charge, the value of its fixed and movable assets would have to be ignored in determining whether it was solvent at the critical time, since such assets would not be regarded as available to meet the company's day-to-day liabilities. However, the capacity of the company immediately after the creation of the particular charge, to borrow money on the security of *another* charge must be taken into account. The onus is then on the person claiming that the disputed floating charge is valid to prove that a creditor would in the particular circumstances have been prepared to advance sufficient money on the strength of a further charge to ensure the company's solvency.[1]

1. *Crowley v Northern Bank Finance Co* [1981] IR 353.

21.31   A company which is already running an overdraft frequently approaches its bank with a view to increasing its borrowing and, as it hopes, trading its way out of financial problems. The bank will probably insist on a floating charge in such circumstances; and if the company goes into liquidation within the year, problems may arise as to whether the additional finance was 'cash paid' within the meaning of the proviso to s 288. A further problem may arise if repayments have been made prior to the winding up. Are these to be taken as payments in respect of the money secured by the charge or in respect of the earlier borrowing?

These problems were considered by Kenny J in *Re Daniel Murphy Ltd.*[1] In that case the company had an overdraft of £9,759 with the bank on the security of an equitable mortgage of its premises. They required additional accommodation of up to £15,000 to finance their operations and the bank agreed to give them the facility if they executed a floating charge. The company agreed by letter to this. The preparation of the deed of charge took up some weeks; and about a fortnight after the executed deed was registered with the Registrar, the company went into liquidation. Between the date on which the company wrote its letter agreeing to give the floating charge and the resolution for a winding up, the company lodged £30,887 to its account while cheques amounting to £36,003 were debited.

The first question that arose was whether money advanced by the bank before the charge was executed but after the company had agreed to give it was 'cash paid *at the time of* ... the charge'. Kenny J held that it was, provided that any delay in having the charge completed and registered was not intended to deceive creditors and was not unreasonable and culpable. In that case, he held that there was no intention to deceive nor had there been unreasonable delay.

The next question that arose was whether the money lodged by the company after it had agreed to execute the charge should be regarded as being in repayment exclusively of the £15,000 which the charge was intended to secure or in repayment first of the earlier borrowing.

Kenny J held that the rule in *Clayton's Case*[2]—that payments made on a running account should be appropriated first in discharge of the debtor's earliest liability—was applicable in such circumstances and that accordingly the repayments in question should be treated as having been made first in reduction of the pre-existing overdraft of £9,759. (A similar view as taken in England subsequently in *Re Yeovil Glove Co.*)[3]

The final question that arose was whether the money advanced by the bank after the charge was executed was 'cash paid ... in *consideration* for the charge'. If the word 'consideration' was given its normal meaning in the law of contract, the cash advanced by the bank could not be regarded as having been paid in consideration for the charge, since the charge was consideration in the past, which under that law was not consideration at all. Kenny J took the view that the construction of the section should not be so confined and that accordingly money advanced after the charge could properly be regarded as having been paid in consideration for the charge. Again a similar view was taken in *Re Yeovil Glove Co.*

1. [1964] IR 1.
2. [1816] I Mer 572.
3. [1965] Ch 148.

21.32 Where as a condition of granting accommodation, a lender stipulates for the repayment of an earlier advance out of the new advance or for the discharge of some other liability out of the advance, it appears that the *entire* advance would still be treated as cash paid in consideration for the charge. It is true that in *Revere Trust Ltd v Wellington Handkerchief Co Ltd,*[1] the Court of Appeal in Northern Ireland held that where the lender had stipulated for the immediate repayment of a previous advance of £90 out of an advance purportedly secured by the floating charge, £90 only could be regarded as having been 'cash paid' within the meaning of the section. They came to that conclusion in part at least, however, in reliance on a dictum of Astbury J that the payment of cash had to be 'absolute and uncontrolled'.[2] This dictum was expressly disapproved of by the Court of Appeal in England in *Re Matthew Ellis Ltd*[3] which was decided after the Northern Ireland case. It would appear from that decision that provided the company benefits from the cash advanced and grants the floating charge with that object in view it is immaterial that part of the advance is being utilised to reduce the company's indebtedness to the lender or some third party. It is only where no benefit at all accrues to the company that the cash paid should be disregarded. This would also appear to be consistent with the approach adopted by Kenny J in *Re Daniel Murphy*, although he contented himself with drawing attention to the discrepancy between the two decisions.[4]

1. [1931] NI 55.
2. *Re Hayman Christie & Lilly Ltd* [1917] 1 Ch 545.
3. [1933] Ch 458.
4. At p 15.

Chapter 22

Registration of charges

22.01 It is important for those dealing with a company to be in a position to ascertain what charges the company has created over any of its assets. Section 99 of the Principal Act accordingly requires the registration with the Registrar of certain types of charge specified by the section. It is vital for the lender to ensure that charges governed by the section are in fact registered, since if they are not the Act declares them void against the liquidator and the other creditors.

Unlike the English legislation, however, there is no requirement that the company itself keep a register of charges. It is an important omission, because the list of charges which must be registered under s 99, although wide-ranging, is not exhaustive. Thus, charges by deposit of bills of exchange, dock warrants or other negotiable instruments are not within s 99: nor in Ireland do they require entry in a register by the company.[1] The only obligation on the company, apart from registering charges which require registration under the Acts is to keep copies of every instrument of charge which requires registration at the registered office of the company.[2] The copies may be inspected during business hours by any creditor or member without fee. The company may in general meeting impose reasonable restrictions on this right of inspection, but must allow at least two hours in each day. If inspection is refused, every officer of the company who is in default is liable to a fine not exceeding £500. The court may also by order compel an immediate inspection.

1. On the significance of this omission, see Alexis Fitzgerald, 'A Consideration of the Companies Act 1948 the Companies' Act (Northern Ireland) 1960 and the Companies' Act 1963', Irish Jurist (NS), Vol III, p 47.
2. Ss 109 and 110 of the Principal Act, as amended by s 15 of the 1983 Act.

22.02 A company is also obliged to keep a *register of debenture holders,* but the only entries that need to be made relate to the issue of a series of debentures ranking *pari passu.*[1]

Prior to the enactment of s 91 of the Principal Act, which requires the keeping of this register, it was usual to provide in the standard conditions that such a register should be kept by the company. The section gives statutory effect to this practice; but failure to keep the register does not invalidate the security. There is however a penalty (a fine not exceeding £250) for failure to keep the register. The Registrar must be notified of the place where the register is kept and of any changes in that place and again there is provision for a fine not exceeding £250 if the Registrar is not so notified within 14 days. The register must be kept at the registered office of the company or at the office where it is made up, e.g. the office of the company's auditors.

1. S 91 of the Principal Act.

Charges which must be registered under s 99

22.03 The company must register with the Registrar certain charges which are specified in s 99 of the Principal Act. Failure to comply with this section means that the security is void as against the liquidator and any creditor of the company. It is, accordingly, most important that the requirements of the Act be meticulously observed and its provisions, and the various cases decided in Ireland and England on its ambit, repay careful study.

22.04 The section provides that, in the case of a charge created by the company to which the section applies, the prescribed particulars of the charge verified in the prescribed manner[1] must be delivered to the Registrar for registration within 21 days of its creation. The charges to which the section applies are set out in sub-s (3) as follows:

(1) a charge for the purpose of securing any issue of debentures;
(2) a charge on uncalled share capital of the company;
(3) a charge created or evidenced by an instrument which, if executed by an individual, would require registration as a bill of sale;
(4) a charge on lands wherever situate, or any interest therein, but not including a charge for any rent or other periodical sum issuing out of land;
(5) a charge on book debts of the company;
(6) a floating charge on the undertaking or property of the company;
(7) a charge on calls made but not paid;
(8) a charge on any ship or any share in a ship;
(9) a charge on goodwill, on a patent or a licence under a patent, on a trade mark or on a copyright or a licence under a copyright.[2]

It is made clear by sub-s (10) that a 'charge' in the section includes a mortgage.

Section 100 imposes on the company the duty to send the required particulars to the Registrar within the 21 day period, but also provides that registration of the charge may be effected by any person interested therein, e.g. the person who advanced the money which the charge is intended to secure. The company is also required (by s 101) to register with the Registrar any charge to which property acquired by them is subject, if it is one of the charges specified in s 99. The Registrar for his part is required by s 103 to keep, in relation to each company, a register of charges and, on payment of the prescribed fee, to enter the following particulars in the register:

(1) The date of creation of the charge;
(2) Where the charge is not created by the company, the date of the acquisition of the relevant property;
(3) If the charge is a judgment mortgage, the date of creation of the judgment mortgage;[3]
(4) The amount secured by the charge;
(5) Short particulars of the property charged;
(6) The persons entitled to the charge.[4]

1. Companies (Forms) Order 1964 (SI 1964/45) para 3, Form No. 47. The prescribed particulars are the date and description of the instrument, the amount secured, short particulars of the property charged and the names, addresses and occupations of the owners

of the charge. In the case of a charge securing an issue of debentures, there must also be stated the amount and rate per cent. of any commission, allowance or discount paid to any person in consideration of his subscribing to the issue or procuring subscriptions.
2. It would appear that there is no provision for registering charges on aircraft. In England, such charges must be registered in a Register of Aircraft Mortgages kept by the Civil Aviation Authority and also in the Companies' Registry. See Palmer, vol I, para 45.06.
3. For judgment mortgages, see para 22.13 below.
4. In the case of the issue of a series of debentures, the only particulars that need be delivered are the total amount secured, the dates of the resolutions authorising the issue, a general description of the property charged and the date of the trust deed, if any.

22.05 While the company is required to deliver the necessary particulars of the charge, it is of course of the greatest importance for the person advancing money to the company on the security of the charge to ensure that the necessary particulars are delivered, preferably by delivering them himself as he is entitled to do. While the court has power to extend the time for delivering the particulars if they are not delivered within the 21 day period,[1] the order giving such an extension invariably protects secured creditors who advanced money to the company before the charge was actually registered; and in any event it must not be thought that a person who fails to deliver particulars will automatically be given an extension of time. The surprising number of applications to the court for such extensions indicates that there is a laxity in complying with the time limit which could have disastrous consequences for a lender.

1. See para 22.15 below.

22.06 Some of the charges to which the section applies are considered individually in the succeeding paragraphs, but a few general observations should be made at the outset. First, the failure to register the charge does not affect the company's liability to repay the money which it secures to the lender: on the contrary, under s 99 (1) where the charge is void for non-registration, the money secured thereby becomes immediately payable. Secondly, the section only applies to charges *created* by the company. Charges which come into existence by operation of law are not within its scope. Thus, in *Bank of Ireland Finance Ltd v D.J. Daly Ltd (in liquidation)*,[1] McMahon J held that the lien which an unpaid vendor has over land which he has sold to the company is not a registrable charge, since it comes into existence by operation of law.

Since the word 'charge' includes mortgages, both legal and equitable mortgages of land are registrable. In the case of an equitable mortgage by deposit of title deeds, the mortgage must be registered whether it is accompanied by a memorandum in writing or not.[2] An agreement to deposit title deeds by way of security is also registrable.[3]

The Registrar must give a certificate under his hand of the registration of any charge registered in pursuance of Part IV of the Principal Act (including charges registered under s 99) stating the amount secured by the charge. The certificate is conclusive evidence that the requirements of Part IV as to registration have been complied with. Consequently, such a certificate can be relied on by the person entitled to the charge, even though incomplete or inaccurate particuars of the charge have been delivered.

1. [1978] IR 79.
2. *Re Wallis & Simmonds (Builders) Ltd* [1974] 1 All ER 561. This is so even though the debt secured by the deposit is owed not by the depositor but by a third party: ibid.

3. *Re Jackson & Bassford Ltd* [1906] 2 Ch 467. Cf *Re Farm Fresh Frozen Foods Ltd,* unreported, Keane J, judgment delivered 23 June 1980.

Charges requiring registration under s 99 of the Principal Act

22.07 *Charge for the purpose of securing any issue of debentures* It has been held in New Zealand that this only applies to a charge securing a series of debentures and not to one securing a single debenture.[1] Where the debenture incorporates a floating charge that charge will of course be registrable under s 99 (3) (f).

1. *Automobile Association (Canterbury) Inc v Australasian Secured Deposits Ltd.* [1973] 1 NZLR 417.

22.08 *Charges created or evidenced by an instrument which if executed by an individual would be registrable as a bill of sale.* The relevant Irish legislation on bills of sale is to be found in the Bills of Sale (Ireland) Acts, 1879 and 1883. Those Acts permit the registration of all assurances of personal chattels with certain exceptions. It has been held in England, however, that s 95 of the English 1948 Act (corresponding to our s 99) applies only to charges securing the repayment of money,[1] It would follow that not every transaction entered into by a company which if entered into by an individual would require registration as a bill of sale need be registered under s 99.

Moreover, since charges only are within the scope of the section, sale and hiring transactions (including hire purchase agreements) are not registrable as bills of sale.[2] They must, however, be genuine sale and hiring transactions: if what was intended was an assignment by way of charge of the goods concerned rather than an absolute assignment, the transaction will require registration. In every case, the court looks to the whole substance of the transaction in order to see whether the parties intended to create an absolute assignment or an assigment by way of charge only.[3]

In *Borden (UK) Ltd v Scottish Timber Products Ltd*[4] Buckley LJ expressed the view *obiter* that the reservation of title clause in that case, if effective, would have required registration as a bill of sale. In *Kruppstahl AG v Quitmann Products Ltd,*[5] where the point arose directly, Gannon J held that the reservation of title machinery applicable to the worked steel was within s 99 (3) (c).

1. *Stoneleigh Finance Ltd v Phillips* [1965] 2 QB 537.
2. *Manchester Rly Co v North Central Wagon Co* (1888) 13 App Cas 554.
3. *Stoneleigh Finance Ltd v Phillips* (above). per Russell LJ at p 574.
4. [1981] Ch 35 at 46.
5. [1983] ILRM 551.

22.09 *Charges on land.* As we have seen, the word 'charges' includes mortgages, both legal and equitable.

In the case of charges on land, registration may also be necessary under two other systems of registration.

(a) *Registered land.* In the case of land the title to which is registered under the Registration of Title Act 1964, s 80 of that Act provides as follows:
    '(1) Where a company registered under (the Principal Act) is regis-
    tered as owner of land registered under this Act or as owner of a
    registered charge, the Registrar shall not be concerned with, and a

person claiming under a registered disposition for valuable consideration shall not be affected by, any mortgage, charge, debenture,
debenture stock, trust deed or other incumbrance created or issued by
the company, unless such incumbrance is registered as a burden or
protected by caution or inhibition under this Act.
(2) No compensation shall be payable under s 120 by reason of a
purchaser's acquiring any interest under a registered transfer from the
company free of any such incumbrance not so registered or protected.'

A legal charge of land, such as a mortgage, created by a company must
accordingly be registered as a burden on the folio in the Land Registry if
priority is to be successfully claimed. In the case of a floating charge, it is
thought that registration as a burden is not possible: in this case, a caution or
inhibition should be entered on the folio.[1] This effectively warns any person
dealing with the lands comprised in the folio that no dealing should be
completed without notice to the owner of the floating charge.[2]

Unless the registrar of titles is furnished with a certificate from the
Registrar of Companies that the charge has been registered with him within
the statutory period, there is entered on the folio in the Land Registry a note
to the effect that the charge is subject to registration under s 99 of the
Principal Act.[3]

(b) *Unregistered land.* In the case of unregistered land, any charge on the
land may be registered in the Registry of Deeds under the Registry of Deeds
Act 1707.

In the case of both registered and unregistered land, it is possible to create
an equitable mortgage by deposit of the land certificate or the title deeds
without registration in the Land Registry or the Registry of Deeds. Such a
mortgage will generally be entitled to priority over a subsequent incumbrance despite the absence of registration in the relevant registry. Where,
however, the deposit is accompanied by an instrument in writing, it must be
registered to secure priority.

A deed or transfer which is capable of registration either in the Registry of
Deeds or the Land Registry and is not registered will normally be postponed
to a subsequent registered deed or transfer. There is an important
exception, however, in the case of unregistered land, i.e. where the person
taking under the subsequent deed has *actual notice*–either by himself or his
agent–of the earlier deed.[4] *A fortiori* the priority will be lost in the case of
fraud.

There is no such exception in the case of notice where registered land is
concerned. Section 31 of the Registration of Title Act 1964 provides that the
folio in the Land Registry is to be
'conclusive evidence of the title of the owner to the land as appearing on
the register ... '
It goes on to say that
'such title shall not, in the absence of actual fraud, be in any way affected
in consequence of such owner having notice of any deed, document or
matter relating to the land ...'
It is clear that this section excludes the exception for notice which applies in
the case of unregistered land.[5]

It should also be remembered that registration is not the precise
equivalent of notice. As we have seen, where a charge on land is registered
under s 99, a person taking under a subsequent dealing will be fixed with
notice of the statutory particulars which have to be delivered, but not with
the *contents* of the charge.[6] Similarly, where such a charge is registered in the

Land Registry or the Registry of Deeds, a person taking under a subsequent deed or transfer will not be fixed with notice of the contents of the instrument.

1. On the more generally accepted view of the nature of a floating charge, there is no vesting of the legal estate prior to crystallisation and there is consequently nothing in the nature of a 'burden' which can be registered: see para 21.17 above. Cf McAllister, *Registration of Title* p 191.
2. For cautions and inhibitions, see ss 96, 97 and 98 of the Registration of Title Act 1964.
3. Rule 114, Land Registration Rules 1972, SI 1972/330.
4. Wylie, *Land Law*, paras 3.088–3.089.
5. *Re Michael Walsh* [1916] 1 IR 40.
6. Para 21.22 above.

22.10 *Charges on book debts.* This includes both present and future book debts of the company.[1] But where a negotiable instrument, such as a bill of exchange, has been given to secure the payment of a book debt, the deposit of the instrument for the purpose of securing an advance to the company is not a charge which requires registration, this being made clear by s 99 (5). Thus if the bill of exchange is deposited by the company with a bank to secure a loan, this does not constitute a charge on book debts requiring registration.

Where present and future debts due under a hire purchase or credit sales agreement are assigned as security for an advance, the transaction will be registrable as a charge on book debts. In every case, however, the court will look to the substance of the transaction; and if it is clear that an absolute assignment of the debts was intended rather than an assignment by way of security, the transaction will not be registrable.[2]

It has become a common practice for banks advancing bridging finance to purchasers of property to require their solicitors to give an undertaking to lodge the proceeds of sale of a property which they are proposing to sell with the bank in repayment of the bridging finance. It was held by McWilliam J in *Re Kum Tung Restaurant (Dublin) Ltd*[3] that where such an undertaking was given on behalf of a company it was not registrable as a charge under s 99. It was not a charge on land, being a charge on the proceeds of sale and not on the land itself; and it was not a charge on book debts.

1. *Yorkshire Woolcombers' Association* [1903] 2 Ch 384; *Re Lakeglen Construction Ltd, Kelly v James McMahon Ltd* [1980] IR 347.
2. *Stoneleigh Finance Ltd v Phillips*, above.
3. [1978] IR 446.

22.11 *Floating charges.* The nature of a floating charge has been fully explained already.[1] We have also seen that, in the case of registered land, neither the Registrar of Titles nor any person claiming under a registered disposition for valuable consideration is to be concerned with or affected by any mortgage, charge, debenture, debenture stock, trust deed or other incumbrance created or issued by the company unless it is registered as a burden or protected by caution or inhibition under the Act.[2] While a floating charge probably cannot be registered as a burden, it undoubtedly can be protected by a caution or inhibition and this should always be done.[3]

In the case of registered land, a person who has been in adverse possession for twelve years is entitled to be registered as absolute owner on the expiration of that period. It was held in *Halpin v Cremin*[4] that twelve years' adverse possession ousted the rights of the owner of a floating charge even where it crystallised during the twelve year period.

We have already seen that in certain circumstances a 'reservation of title' or *Romalpa* clause may require registration as a floating charge. This view was taken by Slade J in *Re Bond Worth Ltd*[5] and by Templeman LJ *obiter* in *Borden (UK) Ltd*[6] *v Scottish Timber Products Ltd*. In the latter case, Buckley LJ–also speaking *obiter*–took the view that it was more appropriately registrable as a corporate bill of sale[7] and a similar view was taken by Gannon J in *Kruppstahl AG v Quitmann Products Ltd*.[8]

1. Para 21.14 above.
2. Para 22.09 above.
3. Ibid.
4. [1954] IR 19.
5. [1980] Ch 228.
6. [1981] Ch 35 at p 44.
7. At p 46.
8. [1982] ILRM 551.

22.12 (a) *Charges on calls made but not paid*. These do not require elaboration.

(b) *Charges on ships*. Where such charges take the form of legal mortgages, the requirements of the Mercantile Marine Act 1955 must be observed.

It was held by McWilliam J in *Re South Coast Boatyard, Barbour v Burke and Ors*[1] and by the Supreme Court on appeal that a yacht was not a 'ship' within the meaning of the section.

(c) *Charges on goodwill, patents, trademarks and copyrights*. Charges over patents and registered trademarks must also be notified to the Patents Office.

1. Unreported; judgment in High Court delivered 20 November 1978; in Supreme Court, 31 July 1980.

Judgment mortgages

22.13 The judgment mortgage is a form of security peculiar to Ireland. A creditor who has recovered judgment for a sum of money may convert the judgment into a mortgage affecting any lands owned by the debtor. He then has the same rights, powers and remedies as if the land had been mortgaged to him by deed. He converts the judgment into a judgment mortgage by filing an affidavit containing the matters prescribed by the relevant statutes in the court in which he obtained the judgment.[1] He must register an office copy of this affidavit in the Registry of Deeds or, where it affects registered land, in the Land Registry. Prior to the Principal Act, such a form of security did not require registration under the 1908 Act, since it was not a charge created by the company. Cox recommended that the law should be altered by requiring the judgment creditor to send a copy of the affidavit to the Registrar within a specified time.

The recommendation was partly implemented by s 102, which requires the creditor to cause two copies of the affidavit (certified to be correct copies by the appropriate registry) to be delivered to the *company* (not the Registrar as Cox had recommended) within 21 days after the date of registration as a judgment mortgage. The company must within three days of receipt of the copies deliver one to the Registrar for registration. The appropriate registry is also required to deliver a copy of the affidavit to the Registrar 'as soon as may be'.

Cox did not make any recommendation as to what effect non-compliance with the requirement should have. The Principal Act did no more than impose a penalty on the judgment creditor and the company not exceeding £100 (now increased to £500 by the 1982 Act). There seems no reason why failure to register the charge should not have as its consequence the invalidity of the charge: whether a mortgage is created by deed or by the conversion of a judgment mortgage would seem to be irrelevant from the point of view of the other creditors of the company.[2]

1. Judgment Mortgage (Ireland) Acts 1850 and 1858.
2. This point was made by Deputy Gerard Sweetman in the debate on the committee stage, but seems to have been lost sight of. See also Fitzgerald, 'A Consideration of the Companies' Act 1948' etc (above). Irish Jurist (NS) Vol III 262.

Charges by overseas companies

22.14 The provisions of s 99 as to registration of charges extend to charges created on property in Ireland by companies incorporated outside Ireland which have established places of business in Ireland and to judgment mortgages against such companies.

Extension of time and rectification of errors

22.15 The court has jurisdiction under s 106 of the Principal Act to extend the time for registration of a charge under s 99 and to rectify any omission or misstatement in the particulars delivered.

The court must be satisfied that the omission to register the charge within the required time or the omission or misstatement in the particulars was
'accidental or due to inadvertence or some other sufficient cause or is not of a nature to prejudice the position of creditors or shareholder or the company or that on other grounds it is just and equitable to grant relief.'
The court accordingly has a wide discretion under the section, but it is not empowered to delete an entry in its entirety.[1] Nor can the time for registration be extended when the charge has already been registered out of time because of a mistake as to the date on which it was created.[2]

The order extending the time is invariably made subject to a proviso that it is to be without prejudice to the rights of creditors acquired prior to the registration. Unsecured creditors are not protected by the proviso: it only applies to creditors who have acquired some form of proprietary interest in the property the subject of the charge. But once the company is wound up, the position is different: all the creditors of the company have an interest at that stage in the property, whether secured or not. The proviso would in such circumstances have to extend to all the creditors and this would render the making of the order a futile exercise. It has accordingly been held in England in *Re Resinoid & Mica Products Ltd*[3] and *Victoria Housing Estates Ltd v Ashpurton Estates Ltd*[4] that an order extending the time cannot be made once the company has been wound up, save in the most exceptional circumstances.[5]

While the position is clear once a winding up has begun, differing views have been expressed as to whether the court is concerned on an application to extend the time for registration with the *imminence* of a winding up. Although it was the practice in England for the affidavit grounding the application to include averments to the effect that the company was carrying on business normally and was solvent, Romer LJ said in *Re MIG Trust Ltd*[6] that this was not necessary and that the court was not concerned with the imminence of a winding up. A different view was taken, however, by Clauson J in *Re L.H. Charles & Co Ltd*[7] where he required the holder of the charge to give an undertaking that in case the company should be wound up within a month and the liquidator should apply to the court within 21 days to discharge the order, he would submit to the jurisdiction of the court and abide by any order the court might make for the rectification of the register by the removal of any registration effected under the order.

A similar order was made by Hamilton J in *Re Telford Motors Ltd.*[8] The debenture holder in that case had omitted to register his charge and was only alerted to his position when he received a notice that the company was convening a meeting with a view to passing a winding up resolution and that a creditors' meeting was being held. He thereupon applied to the court for an extension of time and this was granted by Hamilton J subject to the undertaking. The relevant particulars were duly delivered to the Registrar the morning after the Court's order. The company passed a winding up resolution that afternoon; and the liquidator in due course applied to the court for an order setting aside the registration of the charge. Hamilton J acceded to the application, pointing out that the unsecured creditors had acquired rights once the winding up order was made and were entitled to the benefit of the proviso.

More recently, the Court of Appeal in England in *Re Resinoid & Mica Products Ltd* and *Victoria Housing Estates Ltd v Ashpurton Estates Ltd* have made it clear that the court is concerned on such an application with the imminence of a winding up and have disapproved of the observations of Romer LJ in *RE MIG Trust Ltd.* In the latter case, Lord Brightman cited with approval the following passages from the majority judgment in the Australian case of *Re Flinders Trading Co Pty Ltd:*[9]

'If at the date of the hearing of the application for enlargement of time for registration of a charge, there is insufficient evidence of the company's solvency or if it be made to appear that the company is unable to pay its debts as they fall due and that a winding up order is imminent and inescapable, the court ought not ... extend the time for registration of the charge.'

It is accordingly, clear that where a winding up is imminent the court should refuse the application for extension of the time or, at least, require the giving of an undertaking in the form used in *Re Telford Motors Ltd.* It would also seem to follow that in any other case the order should only be made where there is evidence that the company is solvent and able to pay its debts as they fall due.

As we have seen the order extending the time for registration invariably included a proviso that the order is to be without prejudice to the rights of parties acquired prior to the registration of the charge. It appears from decisions in England that a proviso in this form simply protected rights acquired *after* the expiration of the 21 day period. Rights acquired during the 31 day period were not protected. The reason for this was that the charge was treated as being validated *ab initio* when the time was extended.[10] According to Palmer,[11] a new form of proviso received the approval of the Companies, Court judges in England as a result of the decision in *Watson v Duff Morgan and Vermont Holdings Ltd*[12] viz:

'That the time for registering the charge be extended until the day of   ; and this order is to be without prejudice to the rights of the parties acquired during the period between the creation of the said charge and the date of its actual registration.'

This form of proviso avoids the somewhat anomalous consequence which followed from the old version, i.e. that whether charges were protected by the proviso depended on their having been created after the 21 day period rather than before. This form of proviso is also now in use in Ireland.

1. Re *C L Nye Ltd* [1971] Ch 443.
2. Ibid at p 474 per Russell LJ.
3. [1983] Ch 132.
4. [1983] Ch 110.
5. For a case in which the order was made although the winding up had probably already commenced, see *Re R.M. Arnold & Co Ltd* [1984] BCLC 535.
6. [1933] Ch 542.
7. [1935] WN 15.
8. Unreported; judgment delivered 27 January 1978.
9. [1978] 3 ACLR 318.
10. *Re Ehrmann Bros* [1906] 2 Ch 697.
11. Vol I, 45.10.
12. [1974] I All ER 794.

Chapter 23

Receivers

23.01 The remedy most usually availed of by debenture holders is the appointment of a *receiver*. As his titled indicates, his main function is to receive or get in all the assets of the company on behalf of the debenture holder and dispose of them in due course in order to pay off the principal and interest due. In addition, he is also frequently appointed the *manager* of the company's affairs with power to carry on its business for as long as is necessary. The receiver may be appointed either by the debenture holder himself or by the court on the application of the debenture holder. In practice, the debenture invariably contains a provision entitling the debenture holder to appoint a receiver without recourse to the court in defined circumstances.

The debenture usually provides that the debenture holder may appoint a receiver 'at any time after the principal moneys hereby secured become payable'. The usual form of the clause providing for the latter event is as follows:

'The principal moneys hereby secured shall immediately become payable:
(a) if the company makes default for the period of six months in the payment of any interest hereby secured and the (debenture holder) before such interest is paid, by notice in writing to the company, calls in such principal moneys; or
(b) if an order is made or an effective resolution is passed for the winding up of the company; or
(c) if a distress or execution is levied or enforced upon or against any of the chattels or property of the company, and is not paid or discharged within five days; or
(d) if a receiver is appointed of the undertaking of the company or of any of its property or assets; or
(e) if the company ceases or threatens to cease to carry on its business.'[1]

The debenture holder must ensure that one or more of the specified causes has arisen before taking the serious step of appointing a receiver. Sometimes his position is simplified because the company itself requests the appointment of a receiver and that request will usually be accompanied by an express warning that, if a receiver is not appointed, the company will be forced to cease trading, thereby bringing ground (e) into operation. The company may adopt this attitude because to continue trading at a stage when the company appears to be insolvent may expose the directors to personal liability for the debts of the company.[2] The debenture holder has, of course, the option–frequently availed of in practice–to decline to appoint a receiver. In that event, he will simply await the inevitable winding up and rely on his fixed charge to defeat the unsecured creditors.

1. Palmer, vol I, 43.25.
2. See para 34.83 below.

23.02 The following consequences flow immediately from the appointment of a receiver by the debenture holder:

(1) A floating charge crystallises[1] and becomes a fixed charge on the assets and/or undertakings over which it was created.

(2) The powers of the company and the directors' authority are suspended in relation to the assets covered by the receivership and may only be exercised with the consent of the receiver.[2]

(3) Where the receiver is appointed manager, he is entitled to carry on the business of the company.

(4) The receiver may, if he considers that the interests of the debenture holder so require, dispose of any asset of the company, including its entire undertaking.

Existing contracts remain binding on the company, but the receiver is under no personal liability in respect of them.[3]

1. See para 21.28 above.
2. But note that the directors do not cease to be directors and are still bound by their duties to the company. See para 27.15 below.
3. *Re Newdigate Colliery Co Ltd* [1912] 1 Ch 468; *Ardmore Studios (Ireland) Ltd v Lynch* [1965] IR 1. The receiver may ensure that such contracts are performed, however, if he thinks that this is in the interest of the debenture holder. This will not render him personally liable, unless there is a novation, i.e. an express acceptance by the receiver of personal responsibility. See para 23.04 below.

Receiver usually the agent of the company

23.03 If there is no provision to the contrary in the debenture, the receiver on his appointment will be regarded as the agent of the debenture holder who appoints him. In practice the debenture invariably provides that the receiver is to be deemed to be solely the agent of the company and that the company is to be solely responsible for his acts or defaults and for his remuneration.

Where the debenture provides that the receiver is to be deemed to be the agent of the company, the agency thus created will be terminated on a winding up.[1] In an effort to prevent this happening, the debenture sometimes confers a purportedly irrevocable power of attorney on the receiver. There is some doubt, however, as to whether such a power of attorney can be irrevocable. It appears that it can be irrevocable only when coupled with an interest; and the receiver, as distinct from the debenture holder, rarely has any interest in the property charged.[2]

Prior to a winding up, however, there is no doubt as to the effectiveness of such a power of attorney. In *Industrial Development Authority v Moran,*[3] the Supreme Court rejected an argument that the effect of s 40 of the Principal Act–which recognises the validity of deeds executed abroad under an Irish power of attorney but is silent as to the validity of such deeds when executed in Ireland–was to invalidate deeds executed by a receiver in Ireland under a power of attorney.[4]

1. *Gosling v Gaskell* [1897] AC 575.
2. Palmer, vol I, 46.06.
3. (1978) IR 159.
4. Reversing the decision of the High Court, which is not reported.

Liability of receiver on contracts

23.04 We have seen that one of the consequences of the appointment of the receiver is that existing contracts (including contracts of employment) remain binding on the company. The receiver is not, however, personally liable in respect of such contracts, unless there is a novation, i.e. an agreement between the company, the receiver and the other contracting party that the receiver will assume the rights and obligations of the company under the contract.[1]

1. *Parsons v Sovereign bank of Canada* [1913] AC 160.

23.05 In the case of a contract entered into by the receiver after his appointment the position is quite different. Section 316(2) of the Principal Act provides that he is to be personally liable on any contract entered into by him in the performance of his functions, unless the contract provides that he is not to be so liable. This is so whether the contract is entered into by him in the name of the company, in his own name or otherwise. He is, however, entitled to be indemnified out of the assets of the company in respect of his personal liability.

A supplier to the company may, of course, insist on payment of his outstanding account before he deals with the receiver. It was held by Costello J in *W & L Crowe Ltd and Another v ESB; Ionos Ltd and Another v ESB*[1] that the ESB are entitled to refuse to enter into a new supply contract with the receiver until the company's existing account is paid, even though the receiver is prepared to accept personal responsibility for future electricity charges. He held that there was no statutory entitlement to a new supply of electricity in such circumstances.

The possibility that this might turn out to be the position in law was adverted to at the committee stage of the Principal Act and the Minister was pressed by one deputy to ensure that semi-state utilities such as the ESB were not made, in effect, preferential creditors.[2] There was, however, no provision made in the Principal Act for the position which has now emerged as a result of Crowe's case.

1. Unreported; judgment delivered 9 May 1984.
2. *Official Report (Unrevised) of Parliamentary Debates: Special Committee on Companies Bill 1962*, Column 491.

Duty of receiver to act in good faith and liability for negligence or fraud

23.06 Although a receiver is usually deemed to be the agent of the company by virtue of the terms of his appointment, his primary duty is towards the debenture holder, who has appointed him to protect his interest and who is ultimately responsible for his remuneration. It follows that the receiver's relationship with the debenture holder is a fiduciary one, i.e. one of trust, and that he must show good faith towards the debenture holder in his conduct of the receivership. In one case, it was said that he is obliged to discharge his duties with 'punctilious rectitude'.[1] Plainly he will also be liable to the debenture holder in damages if his conduct of the receivership is negligent, i.e. if he is guilty of any lack of reasonable care as a result of which the debenture holder suffers loss.

1. *Re Magadi Soda company Ltd* (1925) 41 TLR 297 at 300.

23.07 While the receiver's primary duty is towards the debenture holder, it is also clear that he owes certain duties to the company. Opinions have differed, however, as to the extent of such duties. On one view, the duty of the receiver is simply to act in good faith and strictly within the terms of his appointment. On this view, which was expressed in the Australian case of *Expo International Property Ltd v Chant*,[1] the receiver is not liable for negligence in the conduct of the receivership, provided he has acted in good faith. The alternative view is that the receiver may be liable for negligence, even though he has acted in good faith.

It is thought that the latter view represents the law in Ireland, supported as it is by *dicta* both here and in England. The question usually arises where the receiver is alleged to have parted–or to be about to part–with the property of the company at an undervalue. In *Holohan v Friends' Provident and Century Life Office*,[2] a mortgagee in possession was restrained by injunction by the Supreme Court from disposing of property at an undervalue, and *Casey v Intercontinental Bank*[3] also appears to recognise a duty on the mortgagee to secure the best price possible for the mortgaged property. In England, the Court of Appeal in *Cuckmere brick Co Ltd v Mutual Finance Ltd*[4] held that a mortgagee exercising his power of sale owes a duty to the mortgagor to obtain 'the true market value'. In *Standard Chartered Bank v Walker*,[5] it was held that this duty extended to the guarantor of the company's debt. In that case, Lord Denning said

> 'if it should appear that the mortgagee or the receiver have not used reasonable care to realise the assets to the best advantage, then the mortgagor, the company and the guarantor are entitled in equity to an allowance. They should be given credit for the amount which the sale should have realised if reasonable care had been used.'[6]

This passage was cited with approval by Carroll J in *McGowan and Ors v Gannon*.[7] In that case, she also posed the question as to whether a receiver who has tested the market and found it very bad is entitled to sell at a bargain price or is obliged to wait in the hope that there will be an upswing in the market. As the question was not argued, she left it unanswered. In England, however, in *Bank of Cyprus (London) Ltd v Gill*,[8] it was held that while a mortgagee in possession was not obliged to wait for the market to rise, and could sell at any time, he was nevertheless obliged to take proper steps to secure the best available price at the time he sold. This would presumably apply also to a receiver. It would seem to follow that, while every case should be judged on its own facts, there is no general obligation on a receiver to wait for the market to rise. If he makes a reasonably prudent assessment of the market at the relevant time, he will not be held liable simply because it appears subsequently that by waiting he might have got a better price. If the amounts are substantial and he is in serious doubt, he should not hesitate to apply to the court for directions.[9]

1. [1980] ACLC 34 at 43. It was also said in that case that the receiver was under a duty to account for his conduct of the receivership when it was over and this would also appear to be the position in Irish and English law: see para 23.09 below.
2. [1966] IR1.
3. [1979] IR 364.
4. [1971] Ch 949.
5. [1982] 3 All ER 938.
6. P 942 j.

7. [1983] ILRM 516. A similar view was taken by O'Hanlon J in *Lambert v Donnelly*, unreported; judgment delivered 5 November 1982.
8. [1980] 2 Lloyds' Reports, 51.
9. See para 23.18 below.

23.08 The question has been raised as to whether the receiver's liability to the company can be excluded by the terms of the debenture. It was held in *Expo International Property Ltd v Chant* that such a condition is ineffectual, partly on the ground that there is no receiver in existence at the time the debenture is executed. It has also been suggested–but the point has yet to be judicially decided–that a condition which purported to relieve him of liability for lack of good faith would be unenforceable as being contrary to public policy.[1]

1. Palmer, vol I, 46.06.

Receiver's duty to account to company

23.09 There is no general duty on a receiver/manager to account to the company whose affairs he is managing. This is clear from the decision of Costello J in *Irish Oil and Cake Mills Ltd and Another v Donnelly*[1] where he refused to grant a mandatory interlocutory injunction to the company to compel the receiver to furnish it with certain information. He also made it clear, however, that a duty to account may arise in a particular case, and instanced the English decision of *Smiths Ltd v Middleton*,[2] where a receiver was ordered to account to the company after the receivership had come to an end.

1. Unreported; judgment delivered 27 March 1983.
2. [1979] 3 All ER 842.

Appointment of receiver by the court

23.10 A receiver can be appointed by the court in an action brought by a debenture holder to enforce his security. The appointment may be made despite the fact that an appointment has already been made by the debenture holder.[1] On the appointment the same consequences ensue as on an out of court appointment[2] with one important addition: an appointment by the court means that the company's employees are automatically dismissed.[3] They may, however, sue the company for damages for wrongful dismissal in such circumstances.[4]

A receiver appointed by the court, unlike one appointed out of court, is an officer of the court. He is an agent of neither the company nor the debenture holder.[5] He does, however, occupy the same fiduciary relationship to the debenture holder[6] and is under the same duty to take reasonable care in the conduct of the receivership.

1. *Re 'Slogger' Automatic Feeder Co* [1915] 1 Ch 478.
2. See para 23.02 above.
3. *Reid v Explosives Co Ltd* (1887) 19 QBD 264.
4. Ibid.
5. *Parsons v Sovereign Bank of Canada*, above.
6. *Re Gent, Gent-Davis v Harris* (1889) 40 Ch D 190.

Set off following the appointment of the receiver.

23.11 The common law recognises the right of a person who owes money to another to set off against the debt money owed by the other contracting party. This principle applies to debts incurred by persons who deal with the receiver. There must, however, be 'mutuality'. Thus set off will not be allowed for debts arising under a pre-receivership contract which has no connection with the receiver's contract.[1]

The crystallisation of the floating charge upon the appointment of the receiver means that debts owing at that stage to the company vest in the debenture holder automatically. He takes them, however, subject to any rights of set off in existence at that date. Thus, in the case of debts incurred in favour of the company before the appointment of the receiver, the debtor will be allowed to set off claims against the company where (a) they arose before the debtor had notice of the crystallisation of the charge or (b) they arose out of the same contract or are closely connected with it.[2]

1. *N W Robbie & Co v Witney Warehouse Co Ltd* [1963] 3 All ER 613, followed by Budd J in *Lynch v Ardmore Studios (Ireland) Ltd* [1966] IR 133.
2. Palmer, vol I, 46.09.

Incapacity to act as receiver

23.12 A body corporate may not act as a receiver. Any body corporate which so acts is liable to a fine not exceeding £500.[1]

Any person who is an undischarged bankrupt who acts as a receiver is liable on conviction on indictment to imprisonment for a term not exceeding two years or on summary conviction to imprisonment for a term not exceeding six months or to a fine not exceeding £500 or both.[2].

1. S 314 of the Principal Act, as amended by s 15 of the 1982 Act.
2. S 315 of the Principal Act, as amended by s 15 of the 1982 Act.

Notification of receiver's appointment, statement of affairs, etc.

23.13 The debenture holder on the appointment of the receiver (whether by the court or under the debenture) must publish notice in the prescribed form[1] of the appointment within seven days in *Iris Ofigiuil* and in at least one daily newspaper circulating in the area where the registered office of the company is situated.[2] He must also deliver to the Registrar a notice in the prescribed form[3] of the appointment. A receiver on ceasing to act as such must also deliver a notice of that fact in the prescribed form[3] to the Registrar.

1. Companies (Forms) Order 1964 (SI 1964/45), para 3, Form 53.
2. S 107 (1) of the Principal Act.
3. Companies (Forms) Order 1964 (above), Form No 57a.

23.14 The receiver on his appointment must give notice of it forthwith to the company. The company must then within 14 days from the receipt of the notice (or such longer period as the court or the receiver may allow) make out and submit to the receiver a *statement of affairs* in the prescribed form.[1] This statement must show as at the date of the receiver's appointment particulars of the company's assets, debts and liabilities, the names and residences of its creditors, the securities held by them respectively and the dates when the securities were respectively given. The statement must be made by the directors and secretary or by such one or more of the following as the receiver may specify:

(1) present and former officers of the company;

(2) those who took part in the formation of the company within the year prior to the receiver's appointment;

(3) employees of the company or those who were employees within the year period and who the receiver thinks may be capable of giving the required information;

(4) persons who are or were within the year period officers of a company which was itself an officer of the company in receivership, e.g. where a company was acting as secretary of the company.

The statement must be verified by affidavit.[2]

Within two months after receipt of the statement, the receiver must send a copy of it, and of any comments he sees fit to make on it, to the Registrar, the company, any trustees for the debenture holders, the debenture holders (so far as he is aware of their addresses) and (where he is appointed by the court) the court.

Within one month after the expiration of the period of six months from the date of his appointment, the receiver must send an abstract in the prescribed form[3] containing the particulars set out in s 319 (2) of the Principal Act to the Registrar. He must send a similar abstract at further intervals of six months and within one month after he ceases to be receiver. The following are the particulars which must be included:

(1) the assets of the company of which he has taken possession since his appointment;

(2) the estimated value of such assets;

(3) the proceeds of sale of any such assets since his appointment;

(4) his receipts and payments during the period of six months, and, where he has ceased to act, during the period from the end of the previous period up to the date of his ceasing to act, together with the aggregate amount of his receipts and payments during all preceding periods since his appointment.

In practice, directors rarely comply with the duty to deliver a statement of affairs. This regrettable tendency has unfortunate consequences in the conduct of receiverships. The receiver has in such circumstances no guidance from those who may be in the best position to give it as to the value of the company's assets. Failure to deliver such a statement will, moreover, render much less informative the abstract which the receiver himself is required to deliver.

1. Companies (Forms) Order 1964 (above), Form No 17.
2. S 319 (1) and 320 of the Principal Act.
3. Companies (Forms) Order 1964, Form No 57.

23.15 Where a receiver has been appointed, every invoice, order for goods or business letter issued by or on behalf of the company or the receiver or the liquidator of the company on which the name of the company appears must contain a statement that a receiver has been appointed. In the event of any default, the company and any officer of the company, liquidator or receiver who knowingly and wilfully authorises or permits the default is liable to a fine of £100.[1]

1. S 317 of the Principal Act, as amended by s 15 of the 1982 Act.

Remuneration of a receiver

23.16 The remuneration of a receiver appointed by the court is fixed by the court.[1] The remuneration of a receiver appointed under a power contained in a debenture may be fixed by agreement between the receiver and the debenture holder. However, the court has power to fix the amount of such remuneration also despite such an agreement.[2] It may do so on the application of a liquidator or any creditor or member of the company. The court's powers extend to fixing the remuneration for a period before the making of the order or the application and are exercisable although the receiver has died or ceased to act before the making of the order or the application. The receiver may also be ordered to account for any amount paid to himself or retained by him in excess of the amount fixed by the court, but this power may only be exercised by the court in special circumstances.

1. Ord 50, r 16 (1) of the Rules of the Superior Courts.
2. S 318 (1) of the Principal Act.

Receiver may be relieved of liability where charge defective

23.17 A receiver who is appointed under a charge which is subsequently discovered to be not effective as a charge on the property or part of it may apply to the court for an order relieving him of general liability. The court, if it thinks fit, may make an order relieving him of liability, but in that event the person who made the appointment is personally liable.[1]

1. S 316 (3) of the Principal Act.

Application by receiver for direction

23.18 A receiver appointed under the powers contained in any instrument may apply to the court under s 316 of the Principal Act for directions in relation to any particular matter arising in connection with the performance of his functions. The court on such an application may give such directions or make such order declaring the rights of persons before the court or otherwise as it thinks just. This is a very useful form of procedure which receivers should not hesitate to avail of if they are in doubt as to any matter arising under the receivership. The application to the court should be made by special summons.

Part six

Membership of the company

Chapter 24

Membership in general

24.01 A member of a company limited by shares must be a shareholder in the company. Conversely, a shareholder in the company must be a member save in one exceptional case. The bearer of a share warrant need not be a member of the company.[1] In the case of a company limited by guarantee and having a share capital, a member need not be a shareholder, since there is nothing to prevent the memorandum and articles from providing for a class of members whose liability will be by way of guarantee only.

All members of a company stand *prima facie* on the same footing. There is, however, nothing to prevent the memorandum and articles, as we have seen, from dividing the shares into different classes some of which carry preferential rights as to dividends or capital or both.[2]

While the shares are therefore of equal status, unless the company's constitution says otherwise, the power and influence of individual members will usually be determined by the number of shares they own in the company. Most importantly, the number of votes to which he is entitled will usually be the same as the number of shares he owns. There can be provision in the memorandum and articles for shares which do not carry voting rights, but this practice is not approved of by the stock exchange representing as it does a divorce between the ownership and control of a company.

1. See para 16.17 above.
2. See para 16.06 above.

Becoming a member

24.02 With one exception, it is essential for a person to be placed on the register of members in order to become a member of the company. The exception is in the case of the subscribers to the memorandum: s 31 (1) of the Principal Act provides that they are deemed to have agreed to become members of the company. As we have seen, it has been held that this means that they become in law members of the company, even if the company fails to place them on the register.[1]

There is another exception which is an apparent exception only. On the death of a member, his personal representative may transfer his shares without being placed on the register.[2] However, it seems clear that if the personal representative elects not to be placed on the register, he never becomes a member and that there is then no member of the company who is entitled to the shares until a transfer has been executed.[3]

1. See para 08.02 above.
2. S 82 of the Principal Act.
3. See Gower, p 466.

24.03 In the case of the subscribers to the memorandum, entry on the register is not necessary to constitute them as members. There is one instance, however, where it may not be possible to treat them as members, namely, where the company allots all the authorised share capital to the others. In that case, it is simply not possible to treat the subscribers as members since the allotment to the others is complete and effective.[1] It would appear, however, that in those circumstances the subscribers would be entitled to recover damages against the company.

1. *Mackley's case* (1875) 1 Ch D 247.

24.04 It will be seen that there are four normal methods of becoming a member: by being a subscriber, by applying for an allotment, by taking a transfer from an existing member and by transmission on death or bankruptcy. In addition, however, a person may become subject to the liability of a member without travelling any of these routes where he holds himself out, or allows himself to be held out, as a member. He may assent to his name appearing on the register of members although he has not in fact become the owner of any shares. Or he may knowingly have permitted his name to remain on the register when he is not the owner of shares. In either case, he may be regarded in law as being subject to the liability of a member, in the first instance because of his express agreement to that effect and in the second instance because he is *estopped* from denying the truth of his own representation.[1] It will follow, of course, that in both cases he will be liable to pay any amount that is unpaid on the shares. But without such assent, express or implied, the mere entry of his name on the register cannot impose laibility on him.

1. *Sewell's case* (1868) 3 Ch App 131 at 138.

Capacity to be a member

24.05 An infant–one under the age of 18 years[1]–may be a member of a company. He may apply for shares and be allotted them, or take a transfer from an existing member. Similarly, he may succeed to shares on the death of a member. But although in any of these cases, he is entitled to be placed on the register and owes a corresponding duty to the company as a member, including an obligation to pay any amount unpaid on the shares, he is also entitled, either during infancy or on reaching his majority, to repudiate his membership of the company. He will then cease to be under any liability in respect of the shares. He may also recover any money he has paid to the company in respect of the shares, provided there has been a total failure of consideration, i.e. where the shares were wholly worthless.[2]

The right which an infant has to repudiate his membership must be exercised with reasonable promptitude when he attains his majority. If he delays unduly or if he performs any act inconsistent with the repudiation, such as attending at a meeting or accepting a dividend, he will be treated as having affirmed his membership.[3] It would also appear that where the company is being wound up he may only repudiate his membership with the consent of the liquidator.

A person of unsound mind can be a member of a company, but again, as in the case of an infant, his membership is voidable. There is nothing to prevent an alien from being a member of a company.[4]

A bankrupt may continue to be a member of a company, although his shares have vested in the official assignee. He may still attend meetings and vote, although the dividends are paid to the assignee.[5]

As we have seen, a company cannot own shares in itself, or in its holding company.[6] Subject to those qualifications, there is nothing to prevent a company from being a member of another company.

1. The Age of Majority Act 1985, which reduced the age from 21 to 18, came into force on 1 March 1985.
2. *Hamilton v Vaughan-Sherrin etc Co* [1894] 3 Ch 589.
3. *Lumsden's case* (1868) 4 Ch App 31 at 34; *Capper's case* (1868) 3 Ch App 458; *Cork & Bandon Rly v Cazenove* (1847) 10 QB 935.
4. *Princess of Reuss v Boss* (1871) LR 5 HL 1761.
5. *Morgan v Gray* [1953] Ch 83.
6. See para 14.11 above.

Register of members

24.06 Every company must keep a register of its members. This must include the following particulars:
   (1) the names and addresses of the members;
   (2) in the case of a company having a share capital, a statement of the shares held by each member, distinguishing each share by its number (so long as it has a number), and the amount paid or agreed to be considered as paid on each share;
   (3) the date at which each person was entered in the register as a member;
   (4) the date at which any person ceased to be a member.[1]
The register is open to inspection by any member of the public on payment of a small fee.[2]

The requirement that every company should keep a register of its members which would be open to public inspection was one of the major innovations of the first modern companies' Act in 1844. Its utility is significantly reduced, however, by a provision that the company may not enter notice of any trust on the register and that no notice of a trust is receivable by the Registrar.[3] There is thus nothing to prevent a person or another company from effectively controlling the company by the use of nominees and concealing this fact from the public. This is subject to one important qualification in the case of the shareholdings of directors, which is explained below.[4]

It has been held in England that the register must indicate the class of shares held by each member.[5]

The entries referred to at (1), (2) and (3) above must be made within 28 days from the date on which the person agreed to become a member, or in the case of the subscribers, within 28 days from the date of registration. The entry referred to at (4) must be made within 28 days from the date when the person ceased to be a member, or if he ceased to be a member other than as a result of action by the company, e.g. by transferring his shares, within 28 days from the date on which evidence satisfactory to the company of the relevant occurrence is produced.[6]

The register at one stage had to be kept in a bound volume or volumes. Section 378 of the Principal Act, however, provides that it may be kept in loose leaf form, subject to precautions against falsification and facilities for discovery.

1. S 116 (1) of the Principal Act as amended by s 20 of the 1982 Act.
2. S 119 of the Principal Act.
3. S 123 of the Principal Act.
4. See para 27.37 below.
5. *Re Performing Rights Society Ltd* [1978] 2 All ER 712.
6. S 116 of the Principal Act.

24.07 In addition to the register, there must in the case of a company having more than 50 members be kept an index of members, unless the register itself is in such a form as to constitute an index. Within 14 days after the making of an alteration in the register, a corresponding alteration must be made in the index.[1]

1. S 117 of the Principal Act.

24.08 Both the register and the index must be kept at the registered office of the company. If, however, the work of making up the register and index is done elsewhere, either by one of the company's officers or someone doing the work on behalf of the company, such as a firm of accountants, both may be kept at that place. It may not be kept outside Ireland. The Registrar must be notified of the place where it is kept and of any change in the place, except where the register has been kept at the registered office at all times since the company was formed.[1]

1. S 116 of the Principal Act.

24.09 The register and index must be open to inspection by members without charge.[1] They are entitled to inspect during business hours, subject to such reasonable restrictions as the company in general meeting may impose, but so that not less than two hours in each day is allowed for inspection. The public have a similar right of inspection, subject in their case to the payment of a small fee. Any member or other person may require a copy of the register or any part of it on payment of a small fee. The copy must be sent by the company within 10 days.[2] The company may close the register for a period not exceeding 30 days in each year but must give notice of the closure by an advertisement in a newpaper circulating in the district in which the registered office is located.[3] This provision means that companies may prevent changes in membership occurring at certain times, e.g. during the period between the giving of notice of the annual general meeting and the meeting itself.

1. S 119 (1) of the Principal Act.
2. S 119 (2) of the Principal Act.
3. S 121 of the Principal Act.

24.10 Section 122 of the Principal Act enables the court in certain circumstances to order the *rectification* of the register. This arises where
(a) the name of a person is entered on, or omitted from, the register without sufficient cause, or
(b) default is made in entering on the register within the 28 day period the fact of a person having ceased to be a member.
The application may be made by a person who is not a member but is

'aggrieved' by the error, by any member or by the company itself. The court may either refuse the application, or order rectification and payment by the company of compensation for any loss sustained by any person aggrieved. The court may decide any question as to entitlement to registration, both as between members or alleged members and as between the company on the one hand and members or alleged members on the other hand. In addition, it may decide any question 'necessary or expedient to be decided for rectification of the register'.

It has been held that the power thus given to the court to order rectification is a discretionary one.[1] Members have succeeded in having their names removed from the register under the equivalent English jurisdiction where the registration was effected as the result of a misrepresentation.[2] In such cases, however, the court will not come to the assistance of the member unless he acts with reasonable expedition. A registration effected as the result of a misrepresentation is voidable only and not void, and will not be set aside at the instance of the member if he delays unreasonably in seeking relief.[3] Moreover, once a winding up has commenced, a registration which is voidable only cannot be set aside.[4] If, however, the registration was void, i.e. a nullity from the begining, it would seem that it may be set aside at any time, whether or not the winding up has begun.

The application for rectification may be made in a summary manner by special summons grounded on an affidavit. If, however, there is a major issue to be determined, the relief should be sought in an action commenced by plenary summons. Any of the parties may be required to make discovery under the Rules of the Superior Courts: thus in *Cory v Cory*[5] a member claimed to have the register rectified on the ground that he had been induced to transfer his shares to a director at an undervalue by a fraudulent misrepresentation as to the company's financial position. The company was required to make discovery on oath of its financial records for a specified period. Where rectification is ordered, notice of the order must be given to the Registrar.[6]

The company may itself, without any application to the court, rectify any error or omission in the register. Such a rectification cannot, however, adversely affect any person without his consent. The company must also give notice to the Registrar of any rectification within 21 days, if the error or omission also occurs in any document forwarded by the company to the Registrar.[7]

1. *Trevor v Whitworth* (1887) 12 App Cas 409 at 440.
2. *Stewart's case* (1866) 1 Ch App 574.
3. *Sewell's case* (above); *Re Scottish Petroleum Co* (1883) 23 Ch D 413 at 434.
4. *Oakes v Turquand* [1867] LR 2 HL 325.
5. [1923] 1 Ch 90.
6. S 122 (4) of the Principal Act.
7. S 122 (5) of the Principal Act.

24.11 Section 123 provides that
'no notice of any trust, express, implied or constructive, shall be entered on the register or be receivable by the Registrar'.
This is one of the most important provisions of the Principal Act: it means that the effective control of the company may be in the hands of persons whose identity cannot be traced and who own the shares through nominees. It is usually supplemented by an article which extends the prohibition on recognising beneficial interest to every conceivable type of such interest which could arise in relation to shares, e.g.

'Except as required by law, no person shall be recognised by the company as holding any share upon any trust, and the company shall not be bound by or be compelled in any way to recognise (even when having notice thereof) any equitable, contingent, future or partial interest in any share or any interest in any fractional part of a share or (except only as by these regulations or by law otherwise provided) any other rights in respect of any share except an absolute right to the entirety thereof in the registered holder ... '
(Article 7)

24.12 This aspect of the legislation is open to serious abuse: directors may have inside knowledge of the affairs of the company denied to some of the shareholders and it is clearly undesirable that, armed with such knowledge, they should be in a position to buy and sell shares in the company without the shareholders knowing that this is happening. The Cohen Committee, on whose report the English 1948 Act was largely based, recommended sweeping changes in this area, including a requirement that there should be compulsory disclosure of those beneficially entitled to 1 per cent or more of the issued share capital. This was rejected by the framers of the 1948 Act as too drastic, but the Act did contain provisions requiring the company to maintain a register of directors' shareholdings and dealings and enabling the Board of Trade to appoint an inspector to investigate the true ownership of the company.

When the Cox Committee considered this matter in 1958, they also rejected the Cohen recommendations as being impractical. They considered that the most serious abuses in the Irish context could be met by a requirement for a register of directors' shareholdings and dealings. In England the Jenkins Committee made less sweeping proposals than those which found favour with Cohen; but they did recommend that compulsory disclosure should be required in the case of shareholdings of 10 per cent and more. They also recommended that certain option dealings by directors should be made a criminal offence. The framers of the Principal Act, however, confined themselves to implementing the recommendation of Cox. In England, the recommendations of Jenkins were implemented by the 1967 Act. The requirements as to disclosure of shareholdings and 'insider' dealings generally were strengthened in that jurisdiction by the 1980 and 1981 Acts.

The position in Ireland, accordingly, is that the only modification of the principle enshrined in s 123 is the requirement that the company maintains a register of directors' shareholdings and dealings. (This provision is considered in more detail in para 27.37 below.) It is believed, however, that new legislation may require the disclosure of beneficial interests in excess of 25 per cent.

There is no equivalent to the English procedure under which the Board of Trade may appoint inspectors to investigate the extent of shareholdings. It is interesting to note that in this area the Principal Act is in step with the Companies' Act (Northern Ireland) 1960 which followed the recommendation of the Patton Committee. They had urged that legislation of this 'oppressive' nature should not be introduced in Northern Ireland.

24.13 The fact that no notice of any trust may be entered on the register does not mean that equitable interests in shares cannot be created: it is perfectly possible for the person appearing on the register to hold the shares in trust for someone else, even though the company cannot be required to recognise anyone but the person named in the register as the owner. The court indeed will intervene by injunction at the instance of the equitable owner to prevent a transaction being completed which would adversely affect his interest in the shares.

Register prima facie evidence of contents

24.14 The register is *prima facie* evidence of any matters directed or authorised to be inserted therein.[1] It is not conclusive evidence and, accordingly, it is always open to a person to adduce evidence that the register does not accurately record a particular matter. Moreover, a person is presumed to be aware that the person whose name appears on the register may not have consented to the registration, and that an allotment or transfer of shares may be voidable because of misrepresentation.[2]

1. S 124 of the Principal Act.
2. See para 24.04 above.

Chapter 25

Meetings

25.01 The principal control exercised by members of a company over its activitites is through meetings of the members which the company holds from time to time. Such meetings are of three kinds:

(a) the annual general meeting;

(b) extraordinary general meetings; and

(c) separate meetings of classes of shareholders.

The *annual general meeting*, as its name indicates, must be held once a year. *Extraordinary general meetings* may be convened when the directors wish, but in addition a defined proportion of the members has the right to require the convening of such a meeting if they wish. *Separate class meetings* are usually required for the purpose of voting on proposals to vary or abrogate the rights attached to the class of shares in question.[1]

There was formerly provision for the holding of a *statutory meeting* within three months from the date on which a company was entitled to commence business. This requirement, which did not apply to private companies, was abolished in the case of all companies by the 1983 Act.[2]

1. See para 16.10 above.
2. S 3 of, and Third Schedule to, 1983 Act.

Annual general meeting

25.02 Every company, public or private, limited or unlimited, and whether having a share capital or not, must hold a general meeting in each year as its annual general meeting in addition to any other meetings in that year; and it must be specified as such in the notices calling it. Not more than 15 months may elapse between the date of the holding of one annual general meeting and the next.[1]

Special provision is made by s 131 (2) of the Principal Act for the first annual general meeting of a company. So long as this meeting is held within 18 months of the incorporation of the company, it need not be held in the year of its incorporation or in the following year.

If the company fails to hold the meetings, the Minister has power, on the application of any member, to call or direct the calling of a general meeting. He may also give such ancillary or consequential directions as he thinks expedient, including directions modifying or supplementing the operation of the articles in relation to the calling, holding or conducting of the meeting. He may also direct that one member of the company present in person or by proxy shall be deemed to constitute a meeting.[2] (This is necessary because of decisions to the effect that a 'meeting' must consist of at least two people.[3])

Where a meeting is held because of the exercise by the Minister of his powers and it is not held in the year in which the default occurred, the meeting is not to be treated as the annual general meeting for the year in which it is held, unless the company so resolve.[4] If they so resolve, a copy of the resolution must be forwarded to the Registrar within 15 days after it has been passed.[5]

1. S 131 (1) of the Principal Act.
2. S 131 (3) of the Principal Act.
3. *Sharp v Dawes* (1876) 2 QBD 26; *Re London Flats Ltd* [1969] 2 All ER 744.
4. S 131 (4) of the Principal Act.
5. S 131 (5) of the Principal Act.

Business at annual general meeting

25.03 The annual general meeting of a company is a most important meeting, since it must be held whether the directors wish it to be held or not. The only matter which must be dealt with at the meeting is the laying before the meeting of the balance sheet, profit and loss account, auditors' report and directors' report on the state of the company's affairs.[1] But this is simply the minimum statutory requirement: the articles may provide in addition that the following matters are to be dealt with at the meeting:
(1) the declaration of a dividend;
(2) the election of directors in the place of those retiring;
(3) the re-appointment of the retiring auditor; and
(4) the fixing of the remuneration of the auditors.
If Article 53 is applicable, items (1) to (4) above and the presentation of the accounts and reports are treated by implication as the 'ordinary business' of the meeting. Any other business transacted at the annual general meeting or at an extraordinary general meeting is treated by Article 53 as 'special business'. But while this means that the items of 'ordinary business' are the matters which will invariably be dealt with at the annual general meeting, it does not preclude the members from raising other matters. A member is perfectly entitled to give notice of his intention to propose a resolution relating to some other matters at the annual general meeting: he does not have to join with other members in convening an extraordinary general meeting for the same day, as is frequently done.

1. S 148 of the Principal Act.

25.04 It should be noted that there is no requirement that the annual general meeting approve or adopt the accounts and reports. Section 148 of the Principal Act does no more than impose on the directors the duty of laying the relevant documents before the meeting.

The profit and loss account must cover the period from the previous accounts to a date not earlier than 9 months before the meeting. (In the case of the first meeting, the period runs from the date of incorporation.) The balance sheet must be as of the date up to which the profit and loss account is made up.

A copy of the balance sheet, profit and loss account, auditors' report and directors' report must be sent to every member of the company (whether or not he is entitled to receive notices of general meetings), every debenture holder (whether or not he is so entitled) and every person, other than a member or debenture holder, who is so entitled at least 21 days before the meeting.[1] In the case of public companies, it is usual to include with the material which must be circulated a review by the chairman of the year's activities.

1. S 159 (1) of the Principal Act.

25.05 The auditors' report must be read at the meeting and must be open to inspection by any of the members.[1] The auditors, if they are qualified, are automatically re-appointed at the meeting, unless
  (1) a resolution is passed at the meeting appointing someone else instead of an auditor or expressly providing that he shall not be re-appointed, or
  (2) an auditor has given the company notice in writing of his unwillingness to be re-appointed.[2]

1. S 163 (2) of the Principal Act.
2. S 160 (2) of the Principal Act.

Extraordinary general meetings

25.06 General meetings other than the annual general meeting are called 'extraordinary general meetings.' They may be convened by the directors of the company, but in addition a most important power is given by s 132 of the Principal Act to the members to require the directors to convene such meetings. The section provides that the directors must convene an extraordinary general meeting on a requisition of members holding at the date of the requisition not less than one-tenth of such of the paid-up capital as carries voting rights at a general meeting. In the case of a company not having a share capital, the number of requisitionists must represent not less than one-tenth of the total voting rights of all the members entitled to vote at general meetings. These provisions cannot be excluded by the articles.

The requisition must state the objects of the meeting, be signed by the requisitionists and be deposited at the registered office of the company. It may consist of several documents in like form each signed by one or more requisitionists.

if the directors do not convene a meeting (to be held within two months) within 21 days from the date of the deposit of the requisition, the requisitionists, or any of them who represent more than one-half of the total voting rights of all of them, may convene the meeting themselves. It may not be held, however, after the expiration of three months from the date of the deposit of the requisition. The requisitionists are entitled to be paid their reasonable expenses of convening the meeting by the company and the company in turn is entitled to retain the amount out of any fees or other remuneration due to the directors in default.

The fact that the requisition contains resolutions which cannot be put before the meeting does not relieve the directors of their obligation to convene the meeting.[1]

1. *Isle of Wight Rly Co v Tahourdin* (1884) 25 Ch D 320.

25.07 The Principal Act also provides (s 134 (b)) that two or more members holding not less than one-tenth of the issued share capital or, if the company has not a share capital, not less than five per cent in number of all the members of the company may call a meeting, unless the articles provide otherwise. Since, however, the articles invariably provide for the convening of meetings, by the directors alone, this is of no practical importance.

Power of court to convene meeting

25.08 The court has a wide power under s 135 of the Principal Act to convene a meeting of the company. It may do so where for any reason it is impractical to call a meeting in any manner in which meetings of the company may be called or to conduct the meeting of the company in the manner prescribed by the articles or the Acts. The court may make the order either on the application of a director or a member who would be entitled to vote at the meeting, or of its own motion. It may order the meeting to be called, held and conducted in such a manner as it thinks fit and may give such ancillary or consequential directions as it thinks expedient. The directions that may be given include a direction that one member present in person or by a proxy shall be deemed to constitute a meeting.[1] Any meeting called, held and conducted in accordance with such an order is to be deemed for all purposes to be a meeting duly called, held and conducted.

1. See para 25.02 above

Notice of meetings

25.09 Not less than 21 days' notice must be given of the annual general meetings of all companies, public and private, and not less than seven days' notice of any other meeting, where the company is a private company or an unlimited company. Not less than 14 days' notice is required in the case of other meetings, where the company is a public limited company.[1] These are the *minimum* periods of notice prescribed by the Principal Act; the articles may provide for longer periods of notice and any such requirement must be observed. If a special resolution is being proposed, 21 days' notice must be given.

The equivalent period in England for meetings other than the annual general meeting is 14 days and no distinction is made between public and private companies. Even this has been criticised as being too short,[2] and in view of the overwhelming preponderance of private companies in Ireland, it would seem reasonable that the period of notice for all companies should be at least 14 days.

If all the members of the company entitled to attend and vote at a meeting and the company's auditors agree, a meeting can be called by shorter notice than is specified in the Acts or the articles.[3]

1. S 133 of the Principal Act.
2. Gower, p 531.
3. S 133 (3) of the Principal Act.

25.10 The articles usually provide that the period of notice given is to be 'clear', i.e. exclusive both of the day of service and the day of the meeting (article 51). If the articles do not so provide, it would appear that clear notice must still be given, according to decisions in England, but a different view has been taken in Scotland.[1] Obviously, it is better to err on the safe side in all circumstances and give the clear period of notice.

1. *Re Hector Whaling Ltd* [1936] Ch 208; *Re Neil McLeod & Sons Ltd, Petitioners* 1967 SLT 46.

25.11 The only persons who must be given notice are those entitled to attend, i.e. the members and the auditors, unless the articles otherwise provide. A member is not entitled to attend accompanied by a solicitor or some other advisor. He is, however, entitled to appoint another person as proxy to attend and vote instead of him; and the proxy need not be a member of the company.[1]

The articles usually provide for a method of service of the notice. Article 133 enables it to be given either personally or by sending it to him by ordinary prepaid post at the address appearing in the register. Notice need not be given to members who are abroad,[2] and in the case of deceased members, their personal representatives need not be notified unless they are on the register.[3] The articles usually provide that proceedings at a meeting are not to be invalidated by accidental omission to give notice or the non-receipt of notice (article 52). It is important to include such a provision, since otherwise a meeting could be rendered ineffective by an accidental failure to give notice. A deliberate failure to give notice will not be excused by article 52, where it is based on an erroneous view that a person is not entitled to notice.[4]

In one case no notice need be given to anyone. This is where all the members of the company and the auditors agree to dispense with notice.[5]

1. Section 136 of the Principal Act.
2. *Re Union Hill Silver Co* (1870) 22 LT 400.
3. *Allen v Gold Reefs of West Africa Ltd* [1900] 1 Ch 656 at 670 per Lindley MR.
4. *Musslewhite v Musselwhite & Co* [1962] Ch 964.
5. *Re Express Engineering Works Ltd* [1920] 1 Ch 466.

25.12 The notice must specify the date, time and place of the meeting. This is usually expressly required by the articles (article 51), but is in any event necessary.[1] In addition, the notice must state the general nature of any *special business* to be transacted at the meeting. This means that a notice convening an annual general meeting need not specify the *ordinary business* of such a meeting such as the presentation of the accounts, declaration of dividend, replacement of the retiring directors, etc. It must, however, specify any other business to be transacted. In the case of an extraordinary general meeting, the notice must specify in general terms the nature of the business to be transacted, since of its nature it will not be ordinary business. The notice must also contain sufficient particulars of the business to be transacted to enable the shareholders to come to an informed decision as to how they will vote. In one Irish case, an injunction was granted to restrain the holding of a meeting where insufficient particulars had been given,[2] and in a number of English cases they have been granted to restrain the directors from implementing resolutions passed at meetings where insufficient particulars had been given.[3]

1. Palmer, vol I, para 54.04; Gower, p 532
2. *Jackson v Munster Bank* 13 LR (Ir.) 118.
3. See cases cited in Palmer, vol I, para 54.04 n 18.

Resolutions

25.13 The decisions of a company must take the form, generally speaking, of *resolutions*, i.e. specific proposals formally advanced by persons entitled to do so and voted upon at duly convened meetings. They are in law of two kinds, *ordinary* and *special* resolutions. Ordinary resolutions may be proposed at the meeting and require only a simple majority of the members present and entitled to vote to be effective. Special resolutions must be passed by not less than three fourths of the votes cast by members who being entitled to vote in person do so (or where proxies are allowed to, do so by proxy). In addition not less than 21 days notice must be given of the intention to propose the resolution.[1] Some of the most important acts which a company may perform may only be done by special resolution.

There are also resolutions of which *extended notice* must be given. They are

(a) resolutions under s 182 of the Principal Act removing a director from office; and

(b) resolutions under s 161 (1) of the Principal Act providing that a returning auditor shall not be re-appointed or that another person shall be appointed in place of a retiring auditor.

These resolutions remain ordinary resolutions, i.e. they can be passed by a simple majority unless the articles otherwise provide. But at least 28 days' notice of the intention to move them must be given to the company. The company must in turn give notice to the members of the resolution at the same time and in the same manner as it gives notice of the meeting at which the resolution is to be proposed. If this is not practicable, it must give notice to the members either by an advertisement in a newspaper circulating in the district in which the registered office is situated or by any other mode allowed by the articles not less than 21 days before the meeting.

If after notice of such a resolution has been given, a meeting is called for a date 28 days or less after the date of the notice, the notice is deemed by s 142 (2) to be in time for the purposes of the section, even though not within the time specified by sub-s (1). This prevents the directors, on receiving such a proposal, from calling a meeting within a period shorter than the 28 days and then arguing that the resolution is invalid because of insufficient notice.

There is nothing to prevent the articles from providing that particular resolutions must be passed by prescribed majorities or that a particular form or length of notice must be given in the case of certain resolutions.

There is no equivalent in Irish law to the *extraordinary resolution* in English law, i.e. a resolution which must be passed by the same majority as is required for a special resolution but of which 21 days' notice need not be given.

1. S 141 (1) of the Principal Act.

No requirement that resolutions be circulated to members

25.14 Where a meeting has been duly convened on a proper notice by the directors, they are not obliged to circulate any resolutions of which the company is given notice to the general body of members. If the members proposing such resolutions wish to ensure that adequate notice is given of their proposals, they must undertake themselves the somewhat expensive and time consuming process of circulating their fellow members. There is no equivalent to s 140 of the English 1948 Act which enables a defined proportion of the members to require the company to give notice of resolutions which they intend to move at the next annual general meeting. In addition, they can require the company to circulate the members with a statement of not more than 1,000 words with respect to the business to be transacted at any meeting. These provisions have been criticised as being somewhat inadequate but it would seem desirable that some provision of this nature should be introduced in Ireland.

Proceedings at meetings

25.15 It has been held that generally speaking to constitute a meeting at least two people must be present. This applies to general meetings of companies, subject to certain exceptions. A meeting of a class of shareholders may take place with only one shareholder attending, if he is the only shareholder of that class. And, as we have already seen,[1] in two instances, the Principal Act provides that one person present in person or by proxy may constitute a meeting, i.e. where a meeting is convened by the Minister or the court and a direction to that effect is given.

1. See paras 25.02 and 25.08 above.

25.16 For a valid meeting to take place, a quorum must be present. Where the articles make no provision for a quorum, two members personally present in the case of a private company and three in the case of a public company constitute a quorum.[1] Article 54 provides for a quorum of three members 'present in person'. Where this wording is used, proxies cannot be taken into account in reckoning whether a quorum is present. Article 5 in Part II (applicable to private companies) provides that 'two members present in person or by proxy' are to be a quorum.

If there is no quorum present, no valid meeting may be held. The articles usually provide in such circumstances that if, after half an hour, there is still no quorum, the meeting is to be adjourned–or in the case of a requisitioned meeting, dissolved–and that at the adjourned meeting the members present shall be a quorum (article 55). This means that at the adjourned meeting, two members only constitute a quorum and one of them may be present by proxy. It has even been suggested that in these circumstances, one person may constitute a quorum, but this can hardly be correct, since there is then no 'meeting'.

1. S 134 (c) of the Principal Act.

25.17 The articles usually provide that the directors may elect a chairman of their meeting (article 104) and that the chairman is also to preside as chairman at every general meeting (article 56). They also usually provide that if the chairman is not present within a specified time at a general meeting or is unwilling to act, the directors present shall choose one of their number to be chairman. If there is no person entitled to act as chairman under such provisions, the first business of the meeting will be to elect one of the members present to be chairman.

The chairman is responsible for the proper conduct of the meeting, for ensuring that order is kept and for deciding any points of order that may arise. It is his duty to ascertain the sense of the meeting with regard to any question before it. He must conduct the meeting fairly and ensure that all persons entitled to speak are given a reasonable opportunity of doing so. At meetings of public companies, he will invariably be flanked by the company's solicitor, and this is also a prudent precaution at meetings of private companies.

Where the articles provide that the chairman 'may' adjourn the meeting, this gives him a discretion as to whether he will adjourn it or not. Where article 58 is applicable, he may only adjourn with the consent of a meeting at which a quorum is present, and must adjourn if directed to do so by the meeting. In *Kinsella v Alliance and Dublin Gas Consumers' Company and Others*[1] (which is discussed in more detail in para 25.22 below), where there does not appear to have been any equivalent to article 58, Barron J held that the chairman had no power to adjourn a meeting contrary to the wishes of the majority. It has been held in England that where a chairman wrongfully purports to adjourn a meeting, the members are entitled to elect another chairman and proceed with the meeting.[2]

1. Unreported; judgment delivered 5 October 1982.
2. *National Dwellings Society v Sykes* [1894] 3 Ch 159.

25.18 Resolutions must be proposed by the chairman or some other member. They need not be seconded. As we have seen, 21 days' notice must be given of special resolutions, and in the case of the removal of directors or auditors extended notice of 28 days must be given. Ordinary resolutions may be proposed at the meeting.

An amendment may be proposed to resolutions other than special resolutions. The latter can only be passed in the terms of which notice was given and accordingly no amendment is permissible, unless it is an amendment which does not affect the substance of the resolution, e.g. an amendment designed to correct clerical errors in the notice.[1] In the case of ordinary resolutions of which notice has been given to the members in the notice convening the meeting, an amendment may only be permitted if it is within the scope of the original resolution.[2] Thus if the notice is of a resolution to increase the remuneration of the directors by £5,000 a year, there could be no objection to an amendment proposing an increase of £3,000 a year. But if the amendment proposed an increase of £10,000 a year, it would be clearly out of order, since members might have stayed away in the belief that the lower remuneration only would be voted to the directors.

The procedure for dealing with amendments is the same as at any other properly conducted meeting, i.e. the amendment should be voted on first. If it is carried, the chairman puts the resolution as amended to the meeting. If it is defeated, the unamended resolution is put.

1. *Re Moorgate Mercantile Holdings* [1980] 1All ER 40.
2. *Re Betts & Co Ltd v McNaghton* [1910] 1 Ch 430.

Voting at meetings

25.19 Unless the articles otherwise provide, all questions arising at a meeting must be decided in the first place by a show of hands.[1] Thus each member present at the meeting and entitled to vote has one vote only; and this is so irrespective of the number of shares which he holds. Not every member present may be entitled to vote, if the shares are divided into voting and non-voting shares. It is the chairman's duty to count the hands and he must in doing so disregard non-members and members without voting rights. A member who holds proxies for other members is entitled to be counted once only.[2] A non-member, however, holding a proxy may be counted.

Clearly a vote on a show of hands is not an entirely satisfactory method of ascertaining the members' wishes since the extent of the members' shareholdings is disregarded. For this reason, s 137 of the Principal Act protects the right (recognised at common law) of members to demand a poll. It provides that any provision contained in a company's articles which excludes the right to demand a poll on any question is to be void. The only exceptions are the election of the chairman and voting on adjournments. A provision in the articles is also void, if it requires a demand for a poll to be made by more than five members having the right to vote at the meeting or a member or members representing not less than one-tenth of all the members having the right to vote at the meeting or holding shares paid up to the extent of at least one-tenth of the total paid up on all the shares conferring the right to vote. It follows that a provision in the articles enabling an effective demand for a poll to be made by a lesser proportion of the members is valid. Thus Article 59 permits a valid demand for a poll to be made by three members present in person or by proxy. That article also permits a valid demand for a poll to be made by the chairman, and he should not hesitate to exercise this power where there is any doubt as to whether a vote on a show of hands truly represents the majority view of the members on a matter of importance.

The articles usually provide that on a poll every member shall have one vote for each share which he holds (article 63). Section 138 of the Principal Act enables a member entitled to more than one vote to use his votes in different ways. He may thus cast some of his votes for a resolution and some against it. This provision enables persons holding shares for a number of different principals to cast them in accordance with the wishes of their principals.

When the poll is demanded, it is a matter for the chairman to fix the time and place at which it will be held. If, however, the articles provide that it is to be taken immediately, it should be taken as soon as practicable in all the circumstances.[3] It is usual and proper for the chairman to appoint scrutineers to examine and count the votes and report the result to him.[4]

If the poll is not completed on the day on which it is begun, it must be continued on another day: the chairman is not entitled to close the poll while there are still members present who wish to vote.[5] The poll may be invalidated if a person entitled to vote is excluded.[6]

1. *Re Horbury etc Co* (1879) 11 Ch D 109.
2. *Ernest v Loma Gold Mines Co Ltd* [1897] 1 Ch 1.
3. *Jackson v Hamlyn* [1953] Ch 577 at 589.
4. *Wandsworth & Co v Wright* (1870) 22 LT 404.
5. *R v St Pancras* (1839) 11 Ad & El 15.
6. *R v Lambeth* (1839) 8 AD & El 356.

25.20 The common law did not recognise any right of a member to appoint a proxy to vote on his behalf at a meeting. It was, however, the usual practice for articles to authorise voting by proxy. Section 136 of the Principal Act gives a member of a company having a share capital who is entitled to attend and vote at meetings the right to appoint a proxy (who need not be a member) to attend and vote instead of him. The proxy so appointed has the same right as the member to speak at the meeting and to vote on a show of hands and on a poll. (It should be noted that this provision is in wider terms than the corresponding provision in the English 1948 Act which gives the proxy the right to speak at a meeting only in the case of a private company.) The restriction of the right to appoint a proxy to companies having a share capital is contrary to the recommendation of Jenkins on this matter and seems difficult to justify. However, sub-s (2) provides that the articles may authorise voting by proxy in a company without a share capital. Sub-section (2) also provides that a member of a company may appoint one proxy only, unless the articles otherwise provide. Again, a difference between the Principal Act and the 1948 Act should be observed: under the latter, there is no such restriction in the case of a public company. The restriction appears unnecessary in the case of any company: it seems unreasonable that a member unable to attend should have his voting power reduced. Moreover, the restriction deprives the nominee shareholder of the ability to give effect to the differing wishes of a number of beneficial owners.

The section also requires the notice convening the meeting of a company having a share capital to include a statement (which must be given 'reasonable prominence') that a member entitled to attend and vote is entitled to appoint a proxy, or, where it is allowed, more than one proxy, to attend, speak and vote instead of him and that a proxy need not be a member. If there is default in complying with this requirement every officer of the company in default is liable to a fine not exceeding £250.[1]

The section also provides that where invitations to appoint proxies are sent to members at the company's expense, and are sent to some members only, every officer of the company who knowingly and wilfully authorises or permits their issue is liable to a fine not exceeding £500. He is not liable, however, if he simply issues a proxy form or a list of persons willing to act as proxies to a member at his request, provided proxy forms or lists are available to all members on request.

The company's articles cannot effectively require the instrument appointing the proxy to be lodged with the company more than 48 hours' in advance of the meeting or adjourned meeting.[2]

In the case of public companies, proxies are invariably 'two way' proxies, i.e. they enable the member to include in the proxy form an instruction to vote for or against the particular proposal. In the absence of any such direction, the proxy may exercise his discretion in deciding which way to exercise the vote. Gower raises the interesting question as to whether they are legally obliged to exercise the authority conferred on them: he suggests that in general there is no such contractual or equitable obligation on a proxy, but that it may arise where, for example, the proxy is remunerated or is present in a professional capacity, e.g. as an accountant or solicitor.[3] Directors, however, must always exercise proxies in accordance with the members' instructions.

The appointment of a proxy can be revoked by the member at any time before the proxy has voted, unless it is made for valuable consideration and is expressed to be irrevocable.[4] In addition, it is automatically revoked by the death of the member before its exercise. The articles usually provide, however, that a vote by proxy is to be valid notwithstanding the previous death or insanity of the member, the revocation of the proxy or the transfer of the shares to which it relates, unless notice in writing of the relevant fact is received by the company at its registered office before the meeting or adjourned meeting begins (article 73).

There are special provisions in the Principal Act for companies which are members of other companies. Section 139 provides that a body corporate may by resolution of its directors or other governing body authorise such a person as it thinks fit to act as its representative at any meeting of the company.

1. S 136 of the Principal Act, as amended by s 15 of the 1983 Act.

2. S 136 (4) of the Principal Act.
3. Pp 540–541.
4. *Spiller v Mayo (Rhodesia) etc Co* [1926] WN 78.

25.21 All the principles relating to the conduct of general meetings of the company—the giving of notice, the election of the chairman, voting, proxies etc.—which have been explained in the preceding paragraphs apply in the same way to separate meetings of classes of shareholders.

25.22 The only persons entitled to vote at meetings are members or their proxies, and some members may of course be precluded from voting because their shares do not carry voting rights. It is also clear that it is entirely a matter for the member as to how he votes. The company has no power to go behind his vote, as it were, and is bound to recognise it even though the member is obviously voting against the interests of the company. Nor can it decline to give effect to it, because the member in voting as he does is in breach of a contractual obligation to someone else[1] or is even defying a court order.[2] But a *majority* of the company cannot by their votes commit a fraud on the minority, a subject which is discussed further in the next chapter.

It is clear from a number of English decisions that the register of members is the only evidence of a member's right to attend and vote,[3] but what is the position if the company fails to register as a member a person who is entitled to be registered? This question arose in *Kinsella v Dublin Gas Consumers' Company and Others*. In that case, a number of members of the defendant company were seeking to gain control of it and remove the board of directors. The company was incorporated under a private Act and the relevant regulations were contained in the Companies Clauses consolidation Act 1845. Under the Act each member had one vote for each share held by him up to ten, one additional vote for every five shares beyond the first ten shares up to one hundred and an additional vote for every ten shares held by him beyond the first hundred shares. The original shares which had a nominal value of £10 had long since been converted into stock and references in the Act to a vote per share or multiples of shares were accordingly references to votes per multiples of stock of £10 denomination.

The plaintiff and his supporters requisitioned an extraordinary general meeting with the object of removing the directors and replacing them with their nominees. Some of the stockholdings were comparatively large, and it was quickly apparent to the plaintiffs camp that they might win the coming trial of strength if their holdings were sub-divided into smaller units. In addition, since the company was a public company, they availed of the time to make purchases of additional stock. In the result, a large number of transfers were received for registration in the month preceding the meeting and the company employed a firm of accountants to cope with the problem of registering them all. This process of registering all the transfers was not completed by the accountants in time for the meeting and it was found as a fact that this was simply because of the amount of paper work involved and was not due to any lack of good faith on the part of the officers of the company or the accountants. Only the registered stockholders were allowed to attend and vote at the crucial meeting and in the event the plaintiffs resolutions were defeated. The plaintiffs then issued proceedings claiming that the proceedings at the meeting were invalid. Barron J dismissed their claim; he considered that he should follow the English decisions which made it clear that only members appearing on the register could vote. He also held that the chairman had no power to adjourn the meeting (so that the process of registration could be completed) in defiance of the wishes of the meeting.

It does not seem satisfactory that a person who has acquired an absolute right to be entered on the register should be deprived of one of his most important rights–the right to attend and vote–because of the company's failure, albeit *bona fide*, to place him on the register. While it is not clear from the judgment whether the chairman actually proposed the adjournment, that would seem to have been an appropriate course for him to have taken in the circumstances. If the proposal for an adjournment was voted down by those present then that would seem to be an improper use of their powers which the court would be entitled to correct in accordance with the principles explained in the next chapter. In the circumstances of Kinsella's case, the course followed might well have been categorised as a fraud on the majority, but absent majorities presumably are also entitled to protection as much as present minorities. If the chairman failed to put any proposal for an adjournment to the meeting, that again would seem to invalidate the proceedings, since a chairman should at least ascertain the sense of the meeting on so important a matter and is hardly entitled to assume that the result was a foregone conclusion. But, as we have seen, it is a fundamental principle of law that membership is not complete until registration, and this was clearly the major factor which influenced the court in applying the earlier authorities.

1. Palmer vol I, para 55/07.
2. *Northern Counties Securities Ltd v Jackson & Steeple Ltd* [1974] 2 All ER 625.
3. E.g. *Pender v Lushington* (1877) 6 Ch D 70; *Wise v Lansdell* [1921] Ch 420 at 430.

Defamatory statements

25.23 Defamatory statements made by members or directors of a company at a general meeting of the company are privileged and are accordingly not actionable in the absence of malice.[1] Fair and accurate reports by the press, radio and television of the proceedings of general meetings of companies are also privileged under s 24 of the Defamation Act 1961. Again the privilege is lost if the statement is published maliciously and, to avail of the defence successfully, a reasonable explanation or contradiction of the defamatory statement must be published.

1. *Pittard v Oliver* [1891] 1 QB 474.

Minutes of meetings

25.24 Section 145 of the Principal Act requires minutes to be made and kept of the proceedings at all general meetings of the company and for penalties in the event of such minutes not being made and kept. As with the register of members, they need not be kept in a bound volume: they may be kept in loose leaf form subject to precautions against falsification and facilities for discovery.

The minutes must be signed by the chairman of the meeting at which the proceedings took place or the chairman of the next succeeding meeting. When so signed they are *prima facie* evidence of what occurred at the meeting. It follows that properly signed minutes may always be adduced as evidence of the proceedings, but also that evidence may in turn be adduced to establish that they are not in some respects a correct record. Nor are they the *only* evidence: if a particular matter is not recorded in the minutes, it may be proved by some other method, such as oral evidence by a person who was present.[1]

Section 145 (3) provides that when the minutes have been properly made and signed, a rebuttable presumption arises that the meeting to which they refer has been duly convened and held, that all proceedings at it have been duly conducted and that all appointments of directors or liquidators made at it are valid.

1. *Re Fireproof Doors Ltd, Umney v Fireproof Doors Ltd* [1916] 1 Ch 142.

25.25 The records containing the minutes must be kept at the registered office of the company. They are open to inspection by members of the company during business hours without charge subject to such reasonable restrictions as the company may by its articles or in general meeting impose, but so that not less than two hours in each day is allowed for inspection. Creditors or members of the public are not entitled to inspect them. A member is also entitled on payment of a small fee to copies of the minutes. Where an inspection or copies are refused by the company, it is liable to a fine not exceeding £125 and the court may also require the immediate production of the minutes or copies in question.[1]

1. S 146 of the Principal Act as amended by s 15 of the 1982 Act.

Chapter 26

Majority and minority rights

26.01 We have seen in the preceding chapter that many of the most important decisions of the company may be taken by a simple majority: some, such as the amendment of the articles, require a three-fourths majority. The Acts thus enshrine the democratic principle of majority rule, which itself was recognised by the common law as applicable to all corporations aggregate.[1] Clearly, a majority in a company may be guilty of behaviour which is detrimental to the interests of a minority and yet strictly within the legal powers of the majority. In this chapter, we examine the somewhat tortuous methods by which the law has sought to protect such minorities, while at the same time recognising the right of the majority to conduct the business of the company in what they see as its best interest.

1. *A-G v Davey* (1741) 2 Atk 212. For an interesting discussion of the evolution of the rule, see G.J. Hand 'The Development of the Common Law Principle of Majority Rule in Arbitration of Matters of Public Concern' Irish Jurist (NS), Vol. IV 74.

The rule in Foss v Harbottle and its exceptions

26.02 In the early days of the companies' legislation, a difficulty arose as to the right of an individual member to sue where he complained that the majority were acting in a manner which was damaging to the company or at least to the minority of which he was a member. In the leading case of *Foss v Harbottle*,[1] it was laid down that only the company could maintain proceedings in respect of wrongs done to it. Neither the individual shareholder nor any group of shareholders had any right of action in such circumstances. The rule was based on the following practical considerations:

(1) If individual members were allowed to bring proceedings to redress wrongs done to the company, the result would be a multiplicity of actions. Accordingly, such actions could only be brought with the authority of a meeting of the company and this effectively meant that only the company could sue.

(2) If the action complained of was one which it was within the powers of the company in general meeting to sanction, then even though it may have been irregular, proceedings would be futile since the company could always ratify it at a general meeting.

In *Foss v Harbottle*, the company in general meeting refused to take any action against directors who were alleged by the minority shareholders to have committed fraudulent acts. The court dismissed an action by the minority shareholders against the directors in which it was sought to compel them to make amends to the company. It was held that only the company could maintain such proceedings.

The principle has been repeatedly applied in cases since then. Thus, in *McDougall v Gardiner*[2] an individual shareholder suing on behalf of himself and all the other shareholders–except the directors–complained that the chairman had ruled that no poll could be demanded and that this was in breach of the articles. His complaint was rejected on the ground that the litigation should have been in the name of the company, since it was for the majority to decide whether they wished to complain or not. This might seem at first sight to be the explanation of the decision in *Kinsella and Others v Alliance and Dublin Gas Consumers Co*[3] which was referred to in the last chapter. There the court declined to intervene when a meeting proceeded to vote on resolutions, although the company had failed to register a substantial body of members who were unable to vote as a result. The court held that the chairman had no power to adjourn the meeting in defiance of the wishes of the majority present in order to allow the process of registration to be completed, but that there was nothing to prevent the aggrieved members from taking steps to have another meeting convened. It does not appear, however, that the point was taken against the plaintiffs that the litigation should have been in the name of the company and neither *Foss v Harbottle* nor *McDougall v Gardiner* is referred to in the judgment.

1. (1843) 2 Hare, 461. The generally accepted statement of the rule in modern case law is by Jenkins LJ in *Edwards v Halliwell* [1950] 2 All ER 1064 at p 1066.
2. (1875) 1 Ch D 13.
3. Unreported; judgment delivered 5 October 1982.

26.03 Four clear exceptions have been established to the rule in *Foss v Harbottle*:

(1) The majority cannot commit an act which is illegal or *ultra vires* the company. An individual shareholder may always bring proceedings in respect of such an act.

(2) There are certain decisions for which more than a simple majority is required. In such cases, if the company purports to act on the strength of a decision by a simple majority, the individual shareholder is again entitled to sue.

(3) Certain actions of the company may purport to abridge or abolish the *individual rights* of a member. In such a case, the member concerned is entitled to sue.

(4) If a majority who are in control of a company commit a *fraud* on the minority, the minority, or an individual member acting on their behalf, may maintain proceedings in respect of the fraud.

The first two of these exceptions are self explanatory and need no elaboration. The second two must be considered in greater detail.

26.04 The majority decisions of the company cannot adversely affect the individual rights of a member. When a person becomes a member of a company, he enters into a contract with the company by virtue of which he becomes entitled to the rights of membership in return for the amount which he pays for his shares or agrees to guarantee. The contract has one unusual feature, namely that the company can unilaterally alter its terms by amending the articles of association. It cannot, however, deprive the member of the right to remain a member of the company with all the rights and privileges of such membership. In addition, the Acts confer certain additional important rights on the individual members, such as the right to receive the accounts and reports, to petition for the winding up of the company etc. None of these individual rights of the members may be taken away or abridged by the company.

These *individual membership rights*, which cannot be interefered with, must be carefully distinguished from the *corporate membership rights* of the members, which can. A consequence of the contract of membership is that the individual member by his contract agrees with respect to some of the rights of membership to accept as binding the decisions of the majority of the members. These rights are known as corporate membership rights. Thus a decision to increase the capital of the company may affect the amount of the dividend, one of the corporate rights of all the members, but a member has no legal grievance if a majority of the members decide on such a course, provided the requirements of the Acts and the articles are observed.

26.05 The rule has no application where the majority in control commit, or attempt to commit, a fraud on the minority. 'Fraud' in this context does not necessarily involve any element of dishonesty, let alone criminality. The word is used more in the sense in which courts of equity were traditionally prone to use it: in such courts, it was usually possible to obtain relief where a person entrusted with powers to be exercised on behalf of others used them for some other purpose. Those courts described conduct of that nature as 'a fraud on the power' and it is in that general sense that it is used here. Within certain limitations, the majority of the members in exercising their control over the company owe a fiduciary duty to the members as a whole to use that control for the benefit of the company as a whole. The major limitation that has to be remembered is that it is for the company, and not for the court, to determine what is in the best interests of the company. If the members by a majority reach a conclusion in good faith that a particular course is in the interests of the company as a whole, their decision will not be interfered with by the court, even though it may have a detrimental effect on the interests of the minority. We have already seen how this principle has been applied in the case of alterations effected by the majority to the articles of the company.[1]

The cases in which the question arose of whether the conduct complained of constituted a fraud on the minority were in the main of a type described in the English textbooks as 'expropriation' cases. Two categories of such cases should be distinguished. In the first, some of the shareholders are compelled to sell their shares to the majority as the result of an amendment effected in the articles by the latters' use of their voting power. These cases have already been fully discussed.[2] In the second, the majority have made use of their controlling position to divert the company's property into their own hands to their profit.

Thus in *Cooks v Deeks*,[3] directors of a railway construction company made use of their privileged position to secure for themselves the benefit of a contract for the building of a railway which should have gone to the company itself. They then used their majority voting position to obtain the passing of a special resolution endorsing their action. The transaction was set aside as being a fraud on the minority.

1. Para 5.08 above.
2. Ibid.
3. [1916] 1 AC 554.

26.06 Cases have also arisen in which the majority have not made a profit for themselves out of the transaction in question, but have simply parted with some property without the company's deriving any material or financial benefit from the transaction. The majority may, for example, decide to make a contribution to charity. Or they may decide to award pensions or gratuities to retiring employees. It is thought that where such an action is expressly authorised by the memorandum or articles, it will not be vulnerable to a challenge by a disgruntled minority.[1] In modern conditions, moreover, tax considerations may also make such donations justifiable as being in the company's interests. It might also be argued that in some cases they are ultimately in the company's interest on the ground that they are desirable because of, for example, good management-labour relations. But where such actions are not expressly authorised by the memorandum or articles, they may undoubtedly be declared unlawful, at all events where they cannot be justified by considerations such as tax advantages or the necessity to preserve the goodwill of employees or trade unions. The often quoted-observations of Bowen LJ that 'charity cannot sit at the boardroom table' and that 'there are to be no cakes and ale except for the benefit of the company'[2] still retain much of their vitality, as the cases show.

In *Parke v Daily News*,[3] for example, the owners of two English newspapers sold their interests in them and then wished to distribute the purchase price among the employees who would become redundant as a result of the sale. They were restrained from so doing at the suit of an individual shareholder on the ground that the directors were obliged to act in the interest of the shareholders alone. It is to be noted that the proposed distribution was not authorised by the memorandum or articles and that it could not be justified as being ultimately in the company's interest on the basis mentioned in the preceding paragraph since the business was about to cease.

A similar conclusion was reached recently by Carroll J in *Roper v Ward and Others*.[4] In that case, a social and recreational club which owned valuable grounds in Dublin sold them and then proceeded to wind itself up voluntarily and appoint the plaintiff as liquidator. (The club was incorporated as a company limited by guarantee not having a share capital). It was obvious that there would be a surplus available for distribution and a meeting of the company decided that certain persons who were not members (although former employees of the business in connection with which the club was established) should be entitled to participate in the distribution. The liquidator having sought the directions of the court on these and other matters, it was held by Carroll J that even a majority of the company present and voting could not give away the company's assets in this manner.

1. *Charterbridge Corpn Ltd v Lloyds' Bank Ltd* [1970] Ch 62. Cf *Northern Bank Finance Corpn Ltd v Quinn and Achates Investment Co,* unreported, Keane J, judgment delivered 8 November 1979.
2. *Hutton v West Cork Rly Co* (1883) 23 Ch D 654 at 673.
3. [1961] 1 All ER 695.
4. [1981] ILRM 408.

26.07 There are passages in some judgments which suggest that there is a fifth exception to the rule in *Foss v Harbottle*, i.e. where it is necessary to permit such an exception 'in the interests of justice'. In *McDougall v Gardiner*, Jones LJ had said that there must be something 'illegal, oppressive or fraudulent' to exclude the application of the rule.[1] In *Burland v Earle*,[2] Lord Davey said that the cases in which the minority could sue were confined to those in which the actions complained of were

'of a fraudulent character or beyond the powers of the company.'
But the principle was stated in somewhat wider terms by Jessell MR in
Russell v Wakefield Waterworks Co.[3] where he said that the rule is not
an inflexible rule and it will be relaxed where necessary in the interest of
justice.

Again in *Heyting v Dupont*,[4] Harman LJ stated that there are cases which
suggest that the rule is not a rigid one and that an exception will be made
where the justice of the case requires it.

The question was considered by Hamilton J in *Moylan v Irish Whiting
Manufacturers Ltd and Others*.[5] In that case, the plaintiff was a director and
chairman of the defendant company. Following a disagreement with his
fellow directors, a resolution was proposed at the annual general meeting of
the company for his replacement as a director and chairman. The resolution
was carried and the plaintiff then issued proceedings claiming that it was
invalid on a number of grounds. Hamilton J found that there had been
irregularities in the notice convening the meeting and the manner in which it
had been conducted, but that the meeting had given its approval to the
course adopted. Having referred to *Foss v Harbottle* and *McDougall v
Gardiner,* he concluded that there had been nothing 'illegal, oppressive or
fraudulent' in the proceedings of the majority and that, accordingly, the
plaintiff was not entitled to relief. More significantly, however, he expressed
his general view as follows:

'Having regard to the provisions of Bunreacht na hEireann, I am satisfied
that an exception to the rule must be made when the justice of the case
demands it.'

There is, accordingly considerable authority for the proposition that the
exceptions to the rule are not confined to the four generally accepted cases.
But it should be noted that in Moylan's case the learned judge was clearly
satisified that the justice of the case did not require the intervention of the
court and it may be that his observations might be regarded as *obiter*. It
would also seem that the remark of Harman LJ quoted above is not a
sufficient basis for allowing further exceptions to the rule: he was content to
say that the facts of the case did not permit of any extension of the exceptions
without laying down any general proposition. Palmer points out[6] that
Buckley LJ–who was a member of the court–in an extrajudicial address to
the Holdsworth Club has said that the passage in question was not intended
to suggest that the court was accepting the proposition. More recently in
Prudential Assurance Co v Newman Industries Ltd.[7] the Court of Appeal
have made it clear that in their view 'the interests of justice' is not a
convincing practical test.

It is thought that the exceptions to the rule are so clearly defined that in
practice the Irish courts would be reluctant to extend them. In support of this
approach, it may be pointed out that, provided the term 'fraud' is given its
wider equitable meaning, the number of cases in which the invocation of the
'justice of the case' formula is necessary must be so few as not to justify the
making of additional exceptions, with the undesirable consequence of
uncertainty as to what the law is.

1. At p 21.
2. [1902] AC 83.
3. [1875] LR 20 Eq 474.
4. [1964] 2 All ER 273.
5. Unreported; judgment delivered 14 April 1980.
6. Vol I para 58.22.
7. [1982] Ch 209.

26.08   While the nature of the rule in *Foss v Harbottle* and its exceptions are clear enough–subject to the possibility just mentioned of a rather vague fifth exception–its application in practice has given rise to procedural problems which must now be considered.

The first problem is well illustrated by *Nash v Lancegaye Safety Glass (Ireland) Ltd and Others.*[1] In that case, the plaintiff was a director and shareholder in the defendant company. He had persuaded the second defendant, JR, to become a director and shareholder, but in subsequent years differences developed between the two and this ultimately resulted in an allotment of shares in the company (which was a public company) being made by the directors (either relations or supporters of JR) to JR of 15,000 preference shares. The allotment was opposed by the plaintiff as not being a *bona fide* exercise by the directors of their powers. The plaintiff requisitioned an extraordinary general meeting of the company to consider and vote upon resolutions removing the other directors from office and appointing new and additional directors. It was clear that if the disputed 15,000 shares were voted, JR and his supporters would have an effective majority at the meeting. The plaintiff accordingly issued proceedings claiming that the allotment was an improper use of the directors' powers and that it should be set aside.

Dixon J found that the allotment was an improper use by the directors of their powers: it had not been made by them in good faith in the interests of the company as a whole but rather to ensure that the company would in future be controlled by JR's family. *Foss v Harbottle* was relied on by the defendants. who contended that the action was premature: the plaintiff should have awaited the outcome of the requisitioned meeting which might well have endorsed the directors' action. This argument was rejected by Dixon J who said that it overlooked the 'fundamental point' that it was precisely the question whether the 15,000 votes could be used at the meeting that was in issue. He accordingly found in favour of the plaintiff.

The difficulty adverted to by Dixon J in allowing the shareholders to decide whether the directors' action should be endorsed was neatly avoided by Buckley J in the subsequent English decision of *Hogg v Cramphorn Ltd.*[2] The facts were not dissimilar: the directors in an effort to ward off an attempt to secure control of the company devised a scheme of allotment which Buckley J found to have been an improper–although not *mala fide*–use of their powers. But since it would have been within the capacity of the company in general meeting to endorse their actions, he allowed the case to stand over until such a meeting was held, subject, however, to an undertaking that the disputed shares would not be voted at the meeting. In the event, the meeting endorsed the directors' actions by a comfortable majority. The distinction between this case and the *Lancegaye* case is that in the latter the battle lines had already been drawn: it was quite clear that without the disputed votes the JR camp would not have won.[3]

1. (1958) 92 ILTR 11.
2. [1967] Ch 254.
3. See also *Bamford v Bamford* [1970] Ch 212.

26.09   The second problem arises where a minority of shareholders wish to bring proceedings, relying on the exception to the rule which permits such an action to be brought where a majority in control of the company are committing a fraud on the minority. Since in such a case the allegation is of damage to the company itself rather than a violation of an individual shareholder's rights, the proceedings should logically be brought by the company itself. Since this, however, is precisely what the majority will not allow, an exception is allowed to the normal legal principle that it is not permissible to institute proceedings based on a wrong done to another party. One or more of the aggrieved minority may in such circumstances bring what has come to be known as a *derivative* action, i.e. one that derives from the injury to the company rather than the injury to individual shareholders.

This gives rise to another problem, however: it may not be possible to determine whether the majority are perpetrating a fraud until the entire action has been heard. If at that stage, it should transpire that there has been no fraud, it would follow logically that the action should never have been allowed to proceed, since it did not come within the permitted exception.

The Court of Appeal in England have recently indicated in *Prudential Insurance Co v Newman Industries Ltd* (above) that the proper course in such circumstances is for the court to determine as a preliminary issue whether the case falls within the exception to the rule. This should be done by requiring the plaintiff to make out a *prima facie* case as to the alleged fraud. If necessary, a meeting should also be convened to decide whether the alleged wrongdoers are in fact in control. If both requirements are met, the action can be allowed to proceed as a derivative action.

While the action is a derivative action taken because of damage to the company, it may also take the form of a representative action as well: there is nothing to prevent the shareholder from taking the action on behalf of a number of shareholders and seeking a representative order under the Rules of the Superior Courts. It has also been held in England that it is open to the court in such an action to order that the company should indemnify the plaintiff against the costs of the action where it was reasonable and prudent in the company's interests to bring the action and he does so in good faith. The court also held that the plaintiff's costs should be paid by the company irrespective of the outcome of the case.[1]

It is also possible for the minority shareholder to sue *in the name of the company* and thus enable the issue of whether the case is truly outside the rule in *Foss v Harbottle* to be decided on an application for a stay of the proceedings. This procedure is rarely availed of nowadays.

1. *Wallersteiner v Moir* (No 2) [1975] QB 373.

26.10 One further point should be noted. The principle of majority rule no doubt justifies the proposition that the majority are entitled to take whatever actions they believe in good faith to be necessary in the interests of the company and precludes a minority from challenging their decision save in the exceptional cases already discussed. But it is submitted that this principle does not absolve the majority from giving a fair hearing to the view of the minority before taking a decision and it may be that a literal adherence to the requirements of the Acts and the articles would not be a defence if in fact there was a want of fairness in the *manner* in which the decision was taken, apart altogether from its intrinsic merits or demerits. As Hamilton J hinted in Moylan's case, the rule in *Foss v Harbottle* must be applied in Irish courts in the light of the Constitution, and artificial bodies such as companies which owe their existence and privileges to Acts enacted after the coming into force of the Constitution must expect to have their activities scrutinised in that context. It is to be presumed under our law that the Oireachtas intended that powers conferred on the majority of the company would be exercised by them in accordance with the principles of natural justice, which in an appropriate case would require giving the minority at least an opportunity to be heard.[1] The observation of Megarry J in *Gaiman v National Association for Mental Health* that

'these duties (of directors towards the corporation) may be inconsistent with the observance of natural justice and accordingly the implication of any term that natural justice should be observed may be excluded'[2]

should be seen in this light.

1. Cf *Glover v BLN Ltd* [1973] IR 388 at 425.
2. [1971] Ch 317 at 335.

Alternative remedy in case of oppression

26.11   Unless the minority shareholder could bring himself within one of the exceptions to the rule in *Foss v Harbottle*, his only remedy until the enactment of s 205 of the Principal Act was to present a petition for the winding up of the company. There was no doubt as to the jurisdiction of the court to order the winding up of the company where it was 'just and equitable' to do so and this could clearly apply to a situation in which a minority were being treated oppressively. But it was frequently not in any one's interests to have a winding up: the assets might have to be sold at less than their real value, the business brought to an end and people thrown out of work. With a view to remedying this situation, the Principal Act, following the recommendations of Cox, provided in s 205 for what has become known as 'alternative remedy' in cases of oppression.

26.12   The section, which is modelled (with one important variation) on s 210 of the English 1948 Act, enables any member of a company who complains that its affairs are being conducted in a manner oppressive to him or any of the members (including himself) or in disregard of his or their interests as members or that the directors' powers are being exercised in a similar fashion to apply to the court for an order designed to remedy the state of affairs complained of without actually winding up the company. A similar application may also be made by the Minister after receiving a report by an inspector appointed by him to investigate the affairs of the company.[1]

If the court is of the opinion that the complaint is well founded, it may make a number of different orders with a view to bringing the state of affairs complained of to an end. In general terms it may prohibit or direct any act, cancel or vary any transaction, and provide for the regulation of the conduct of the company's affairs in the future. Specifically–and this is the remedy most often sought in practice–it may order the purchase of the shares of any member of the company by other members or by the company itself. Where the order provides for the purchase of the shares of any of the members by the company, the court may also order the reduction of the company's capital. The memorandum and articles may also be altered by the order, in which case the company may not make any further alteration or addition inconsistent with the order without the leave of the court.

Although the section is under the cross-heading 'Minorities', it should be noted that it is not confined in its terms to a complaint by a member of an allegedly oppressed minority. In addition to the Minister, the application may be made by any member of a company who complains of oppression. While the section is most frequently availed of by minority shareholders, there is nothing to prevent the majority–or those entitled to 50% of the shares or votes–from applying for relief under the section. It should also be borne in mind that while the more probable outcome of an application for relief which can only be met by an order for the purchase of members' shares is an order requiring the majority to buy out the minority, there is nothing to prevent the court from making an order enabling the minority to buy out the majority.

Under the corresponding section of the English 1948 Act (s 210) the court had to be satisfied that it would be prepared to wind up the company on the 'just and equitable' ground before it could grant the alternative remedy. No such precondition to relief appears in s 205 of the Principal Act and it has now been dispensed with in England by s 75 of the 1980 Act. This is in accordance with the recommendation of Jenkins and the good sense of the draughtsman of the Principal Act in not making it an essential precondition to relief is demonstrated by the experience in England since 1948 which led to a somewhat narrow approach to the granting of relief under s 210.

1. See para 33.07 below.

26.13   The provision of relief of this nature would have seemed peculiarly appropriate in Ireland for two reasons. In the first place, it is a form of relief which is most likely to be invoked by shareholders in small private companies, an extremely prevalent form of business organisation in Ireland. In the second place, the volatile and quarrelsome Irish temperament makes the possibility of internecine warfare between shareholders in such companies more likely than in the neighbouring jurisdiction. It is all the more surprising, therefore, to find that so few decisions have been given by the Irish courts on the section since its enactment. Experience suggests, however, that while recourse to the section is more frequent than the number of decisions would indicate, a great many applications are settled without the court being called upon to adjudicate. The section has in fact proved to be most effective as an *in terrorem* weapon to be brandished at obdurate and unreasonable shareholders.

It is presumably for this reason that the first recorded Irish decision on the section was not given until 1974 when Kenny J gave judgment in *Re Westwinds Holdings Ltd*,[1] and that there have been only two other recorded cases in which relief has been granted under the section, *Re Greenore Trading Co Ltd*[2] and *Re Clubman Shirts Ltd*.[3] In the result, there is a dearth of Irish authority on the section: and English decisions must be treated with caution both because there is a significant difference in the wording of the section and because the Irish courts are unlikely to adopt as restrictive an approach to operating the section as has been the case in England.

1. Unreported; judgement delivered 21 May 1974.
2. Unreported; judgment delivered 28 March 1980.
3. [1983] ILRM 323. There have, of course, been cases in which extemporary judgments were delivered: the comment in the text is confined to cases in which a written judgment survives.

26.14   The first matter to be considered is the category of persons entitled to relief under this section.

As we have seen, to obtain relief under the section, the member has to establish that the company's affairs are being conducted in a manner oppressive *to him or any of the members (including himself)* or in disregard of their interests *as members*. It has been held in England in *Re Bellador Silk Ltd*[1] and *Re Lundie Brothers Ltd*[2] that a petition cannot succeed under the section where the oppression complained of is not oppression of the member in his capacity *as member*, but in some other capacity, e.g. as a director or a creditor. There has been no Irish decision on the point, but there can be little doubt that this narrow construction would have consequences which the legislature can hardly have intended in this jurisdiction. The typical Irish company is the small private company, in which there is frequently only a handful of shareholders. It is quite common to find that all the shareholders are actively involved in the management of the company and that they are also directors. If disputes break out, they frequently come to a head with the attempted exclusion of one of the director/shareholders from further participation in the affairs of the company, beginning with his removal from his office as a director. At that point, the shareholder will have no means of finding out how the company's day-to-day affairs are being conducted, other than by convening an extraordinary general meeting of the company. This may be, and frequently is, part of the strategy by the other shareholders to run the company to their own advantage without regard to the excluded member's interests. It seems wrong that in these circumstances the excluded shareholder should not be able to obtain relief under s 205 and yet this would appear to be the effect of the decisions referred to. On this view it is only where the shareholder can point to some additional course of conduct which can be regarded as oppressive to him as a member that the court will come to his assistance.

Even on a literal reading of the section, it could be argued with some degree of plausibility that this is not a correct construction. It is noteworthy that the draughtsman uses the words *'as members'* only in the second limb of the sub-section dealing with a disregard of the interests of the member. Those words are not used in the first limb dealing with the conduct of the affairs in a manner oppressive to the members. If the draughtsman found it necessary to use those words in the second limb and deliberately omitted them in the first limb, it would seem to follow logically that it is only where a case is being made under the second limb that the offending conduct must relate to the applicant's position as a member. It is true, of course, that there is no obvious reason why such a distinction should have been made by the draughtsman, but that is perhaps a demonstration of the unsatisfactory consequences that flow from too literal a reading of the sub-section. Since in many small private companies, his appointment as a director may have been as much an inducement to him to make his investment as the allotment of shares to him, it would seem reasonable to treat his removal as a director as being capable in certain circumstances of constituting oppressive conduct.

Surprisingly s 75 of the English Act of 1980, which has now replaced s 210 of the English Act of 1948, fails to make it clear that oppression need not be of the member in his capacity as member. Nor has the first decision on the section[3] fulfilled the expectation–perhaps one should say the hope–of Gore-Browne[4] and Gower[5] that the new section would receive a more liberal interpretation than its predecessors.

1. [1965] 1 All ER 667.
2. [1965] 2 All ER 692.
3. *Re a company* [1983] Ch 178.
4. Para 28.13.
5. P 669.

26.15 what constitues 'oppressive' conduct within the meaning of the section? There has been no attempt at a definition of it in the Irish decisions already referred to but in *Greenore Trading Company Limited,* Keane J adopted the definition of Viscount Simonds in *Scottish Co-operative Wholesale Ltd v Meyer*[1] of such conduct as 'burdensome, harsh and wrongful'. It has also been said to denote some lack of probity or fair dealing towards one or more members of the company.[2]

It has been suggested that the conduct complained of must affect some legal right of the applicant, perhaps on the basis that the third of Viscount Simonds' triad of adjectives connotes conduct which is not only wanting in fairness but is also tainted with illegality. It is thought, however, that this is not correct and that the section is designed to assist victims of conduct which, although not unlawful, is unfairly detrimental to their positions as members. It is also clear of course that conduct which is unlawful is within the section, provided that it is properly described as oppressive: the fact that there may be another remedy available to the applicant does not preclude him from obtaining relief under the section.

An interesting example is afforded by *Re Greenore Trading Company Limited.* There the applicant originally owned one-third of the issued share capital which was £24,000. One of the other shareholders, B, who was the manager of the company, agreed to sever his connection with the company. He also owned a third of the shares, and he agreed to transfer them to the third shareholder, V, for £22,500. V, however, only paid £8,000 from his own resources: the balance of the money was provided by the company itself. It was claimed that this was because the balance represented compensation to B for his loss of employment. The transaction was, however, clearly unlawful: if it was compensation for loss of office, it should have been disclosed to the applicant and approved of by the company in general meeting.[3] If it was not, it represented the giving of financial assistance for the purchase of the company's shares contrary to s 60 of the Principal Act. Keane J held that the transaction constituted oppressive conduct and ordered the purchase of the applicant's shares by V. In that case, the applicant might have launched a derivative action under the exception to the rule in *Foss v Harbottle* on the ground that V had been guilty of conduct amounting to fraud and that he was in control of the company. But that could only have resulted in the impugned transaction being set aside. The applicant would have remained a member of a company whose affairs were being conducted in a manner oppressive to him, the very position s 205 is designed to put an end to.

1. [1959] AC 324 at 342.
2. *Re Jermyn Street Turkish Baths Ltd* [1971] 3 All ER 184.
3. S 186 of the principal Act; see para 30.17 below.

26.16 It has also been held by Plowman J in *Re Westbourne Galleries Ltd*[1] that an isolated act of oppression is not sufficient to bring the section into operation. In *Westwinds Holdings Ltd*, however, Kenny J held that a single act could constitute oppression, although it should be noted that *Re Westbourne Galleries Ltd* was not referred to. In *Greenore Trading Company Ltd*, Keane J referred to the decision in *Re Westbourne Galleries Ltd* but did not find it necessary to apply it, since there had been more than one act of oppression. The law is accordingly as stated by Kenny J and in an appropriate case a single act of oppression may be sufficient.

It was held by the Court of Appeal in *Re Jermyn Street Turkish Baths Ltd*[2] that the oppression complained of must be operative at the time when the application is launched, because the section uses the words '*are* being conducted ...' This again seems an unnecessarily narrow construction of the section. The result of the oppressive conduct complained of may be that the company has simply ceased to function. This was the situation in *Scottish Wholesale Society Ltd v Meyer* and yet the House of Lords found no difficulty in upholding the lower courts' finding that there was oppressive conduct within the meaning of the section. similarly in *Re Greenore Trading Co Ltd*, Keane J was satisfied to treat the refusal of the majority to put an end to the state of affairs brought about by the acts of oppression as itself constituting oppression within the meaning of the section.

1. [1970] 3 All ER 374 at 385a.
2. [1971] 3 All ER 184.

26.17 It has been held in England that the section cannot be relied on where the company is insolvent, since in that event the applicant will have no tangible interest in the company.[1] It is thought, however, that this would not apply in Ireland: the English approach is based on the fact that the applicant must be in a position to establish that he would be entitled to an order for the winding up of the company on the 'just and equitable' ground, and that such an order cannot be made on the application of a contributory where there is no possibility of there being any surplus assets available. As we have seen, the Irish section does not contain this requirement.

In *Re Five Minute Car Wash Service Ltd*,[2] the Court of Appeal held that a complaint of unwise, inefficient or careless conduct was not sufficient to justify the granting of relief under the section. Again it must be at least doubtful whether this approach would be adopted in Ireland. If the affairs of the company are being conducted in a manner which has seriously detrimental consequences for the applicant, it would seem reasonable to describe such conduct as oppressive to the applicant even though those in control may have genuinely believed that what they were doing was right. Similarly, it would seem reasonable to treat an unwise or careless handling of the company's affairs as constituting a disregard of the applicant's interests, no matter how good the motives of those in control might be.

1. *Re Bellador Silk Ltd* above.
2. [1966] 1 All ER 242.

26.18 The application is made by petition grounded on an affidavit[1] The petition should make clear the nature of the relief sought, and the affidavit, without being unduly prolix, should depose to the matters on which the petitioner relies in detail. If the respondent files an affidavit in reply which puts the essential facts in issue the next stage will be for the petitioner to bring a motion for directions, and at that stage, if it appears appropriate, the court can direct the trial of issues on oral evidence. The court has jurisdiction to order the hearing, or any part of it, to be *in camera*, if it is of the opinion that the proceedings would involve the disclosure of information the publication of which would be seriously prejudicial to the legitimate interests of the company.[2]

It was held by Plowman J in *Re Jermyn Street Turkish Baths Ltd*[3] that the personal representative of a member who has died may present a petition without being registered as a member where the oppressive conduct complained of took place during the member's lifetime or since his death. The decision has been doubted by Gower,[4] but seems to be in accordance with the scheme of the Principal Act, under which the personal representative is treated as the successor of the member without being registered as a member himself.[5]

1. Rules of the Superior Courts.
2. S 205 of the Principal Act.
3. [1970] 3 All ER 57.
4. P 667.
5. See para 19.13 above.

26.19 It should finally be noted that the alternative remedy is only available where the court is satisfied that it will bring to an end the state of affairs of which the petitioner complains. If this cannot be achieved, it may be necessary to wind up the company on the 'just and equitable' ground.[1] This was the course taken by Gannon J in *Re Murph's Restaurants Ltd*[2] where he came to the conclusion that a restaurant business had been operated by three persons on a basis of mutual trust and confidence, that this basis had completely disappeared and that the company could not be kept in being on the basis on which it had originally been established.

1. See para 34.10 below.
2. Unreported; judgment delivered 31 July 1979.

Part seven

Administration of the company

Chapter 27

The directors

27.01 The separation of ownership and control is a central feature of company law. The company is owned by the members, but its activities are controlled by persons who act on their behalf and who are called 'the directors'. It is important to bear this distinction in mind, even though in Ireland in a significant number of private companies the distinction is a theoretical one, the members and the directors being one and the same.

The directors of today are the legal descendants of the trustees of the deed of settlement who were a feature of the companies formed before the modern legislation.[1] They act as agents on behalf of the members and they also stand in a fiduciary relationship to them, i.e. they owe the members a duty to act in good faith in the interests of the company as a whole. They are not in the strict sense of the word trustees, since they are quite entitled to take risks in the conduct of the business which a trustee, who is expected to act in a cautious and conservative manner, would not be entitled to take. But they are undoubtedly trustees of assets which come into their hands as directors to this extent: if they misapply the assets they will be liable to the company for any loss it suffers in precisely the same manner as a trustee who similarly misapplies the trust property.[2]

1. See para. 2.05 above.
2. *York & North Midland Rly Co v Hudson* (1853) 16 Beav 485.

27.02 The articles of association usually provide that the day-to-day management of the company is to be carried on by one of the directors, who is called the *managing director*. His position should be distinguished from that of the *chairman* of the board of directors, who frequently also acts as chairman of the meetings of members.

In addition, articles frequently provide for directors who are to be *life* or *permanent directors*. In the case of a public company, such directors may still be removed by an ordinary resolution of the company; but in the case of a private company, they cannot be so removed.[1] This is a major difference between Irish and English law: in the latter jurisdiction the security of tenure of life directors of private companies was removed by the 1948 Act. In the case of a public company, the only effect of giving directors a special label, such as 'life' or 'permanent' is that they do not automatically retire by rotation and offer themselves for re-election, as is the case with other directors.

The articles also sometimes provide for a 'governing' director. It is not clear what legal significance, if any, is added to the office by such an adjective.

1. S 182 of the Principal Act.

27.03   Every company, public and private, must have at least two directors.[1] The law is thus not the same as in England where only one director is required in the case of a private company. Every company must also have a *secretary*, who may be one of the directors. A body corporate may not be a director:[2] here again the law differs from England where there is no such prohibition. While there is a statutory minimum number of directors, there is no statutory maximum.

The first directors of the company must be named in a statement delivered to the Registrar pursuant to s 3 of the 1982 Act. In addition, in the case of private companies, it is usual for the articles of association to name the first directors. The articles invariably provide for the method of appointment and retirement of directors.

In the case of a company limited by guarantee—which is usually formed for the purpose of carrying on some charitable or non-profit-making activity—it is common to entrust the management of the company to a committee or council elected by the members rather than to a board of directors. All the rules set out in this chapter apply to the members of such committees and councils, since s 2 of the Principal Act defines directors as including

'any person occupying the position of director by whatever name called.'

1. S 174 of the Principal Act.
2. S 176 of the Principal Act.

Appointment and retirement of directors

27.04   The subsequent directors of the company must be appointed in the manner provided by the articles: if no method of appointment is prescribed, they must be elected by the members in general meeting. Unless all the members present at the meeting agree to it, it is not permissible to propose the election of two or more directors by a single resolution.[1] This is to ensure that the members are not presented with a 'slate' of candidates, some of whom they may approve of and some not, obliging them to elect or reject them all. (It may be noted that in Ireland the prohibition on such composite resolutions extends to all companies, whereas in England it is confined to public companies.)

Where the articles provide that additional directors are to be appointed by the board of directors, the company in general meeting has no power to make such appointments: it can, however, amend the articles by special resolution to give itself such power.[2] The articles sometimes provide for the appointment by the directors of alternate directors, i.e. directors who may act in the place of the directors when they are absent. Such alternate directors, when their appointment takes effect, have in law the same status as the directors whom they replace.

The articles usually provide that the directors shall have power to fill casual vacancies in their number (article 98). This enables the directors to fill any vacancy other than one that arises through a director retiring by rotation or through the expiration of the period for which he was to hold office.

1. S 181 of the Principal Act.
2. *Blair Open Hearth Furnace Co v Reigart* (1913) 108 LT 665.

27.05   A director does not have to own any shares in the company. The articles sometimes provide that the directors are to hold a specified number of shares known as qualification shares. Where this is the case, s 180 of the

Principal Act requires the director to obtain the necessary share within two months after his appointment or within such shorter time as the articles may specify.

The articles usually provide for the automatic vacation by a director of his office on the happening of certain events. Thus article 91 provides that he is to vacate office if inter alia he

(a) becomes of unsound mind;
(b) resigns his office by notice in writing to the company;
(c) is convicted of an indictable offence; or
(d) is absent from meetings of the directors for more than six months without their permission.

Removal of directors

27.06 The directors of the company may be removed at any time by ordinary resolution of the company in general meeting. This crucial power of ultimate control is given by s 182 of the Principal Act and cannot be removed or abridged by the articles. It is, as we have seen, subject to one major qualification in Ireland: directors of private companies holding office for life cannot be removed under the section. Extended notice—i.e. at least 28 days notice[1]—must be given of any resolution to remove a director under the section and notice of the resolution must be sent to the director concerned, who is then entitled to be heard on the resolution at the meeting. This is so, whether or not he is a member of the company. He is also entitled to make representations in writing to the company when he receives a notice of such a resolution, but they must be of reasonable length. Provided that they are received in time, the company must state that such representations have been received in any notice of the resolution given to members and must send a copy of them to every member to whom notice of the meeting is sent. If they are not received in time, or if the company fails to send them to members, the director is entitled to require them to be read out at the meeting. There is also a provision designed to ensure that the rights conferred by the section on directors are not abused to secure 'needless publicity for defamatory matter': the court, on the application either of the company or of any person who claims to be aggrieved, may declare in such circumstances that the representations need not be sent out or read at the meeting and may require the director concerned to pay the company's costs.

1. See para 25.13 above.

27.07 A director whom it is sought to remove from office may also be employed by the company. His removal from office does not mean, however, that his employment with the company is automatically terminated. This is of particular importance in the case of the managing director, who will very often have a written service contract with the company. It would appear indeed from an *obiter dictum* of Walsh J in *Glover v BLN Ltd*[1] that in the case of a managing director the court may infer the existence of a contractual relationship even where there is no actual contract. It follows that where a managing director is dismissed, he will be entitled to damages if he can prove that his dismissal was a breach of the contract, express or implied, between himself and the company. This is made clear by s 182 (7) which provides that

'Nothing in this section shall be taken as depriving a person removed thereunder of compensation or damages payable to him in respect of the determination of his appointment as director or compensation or damages payable to him in respect of the determination of any appointment terminating with that as director...'

Moreover, it was held in *Glover v BLN Ltd* that where a managing director has a service contract for a fixed term which provides for his dismissal before the expiration of the term for misconduct, the contract may be read subject to an implied requirement that any inquiry into such misconduct and any determination made as to such misconduct observes the requirements of natural justice, or 'fair procedures', to use the term more often employed in Irish cases today.[2] Thus in *Glover*'s case, the plaintiff, who was a technical director of four companies, had a service contract which provided that he could be dismissed without compensation if guilty of any serious misconduct or serious neglect of his duties which in the unanimous opinion of the directors of the holding company injuriously affected the business or property of any of the group. In the High Court, Kenny J found that there had been in one respect serious misconduct on the plaintiff's part but that, as he had not been given notice of the charges against him, his dismissal was invalid. The finding as to serious misconduct was not challenged in the Supreme Court and that court also found that his dismissal was invalid.[3] Unlike the High Court judge, however, the majority did not base their conclusion on the fact that the plaintiff was the holder of an office: it was sufficient that the plaintiff was employed under an agreement which necessarily imported the concept of 'fair procedures' into any dismissal procedures. Walsh J invoked Article 40.3 of the Constitution, saying

'Public policy and the dictates of constitutional justice require that statutes, regulations or agreements setting up machinery for the taking of any decisions which may affect rights or impose liabilities should be construed as providing for fair procedures.'[4]

1. [1973] IR 388 at 427.
2. See para 33.03 below.
3. O'Dalaigh CJ, Walsh J; Fitzgerald J *dissentiente*.
4. At p 425.

27.08   The dismissal of a director who is an employee of the company may also afford him rights under the Unfair Dismissals Act 1977. This provides for the payment of compensation to an employee who is unfairly dismissed and for his re-instatement in his position if the tribunal adjudicating on his complaint considers that appropriate. It also provides for his re-engagement, where that is appropriate, in an equivalent position. Presumably in the case of a managing director, re-instatement would not be possible without the consent of a majority of the members, having regard to the provisions of s 182 of the Principal Act. 'Re-engagement' (e.g. as general manager but not as managing director) would presumably be available as a remedy in an appropriate case.

27.09   It should also be noted that there is nothing to prevent the articles from conferring on the board of directors the power to remove one or more of their number from office. Where such a power is given, the director may be removed, not only by a resolution of the company, but also by a valid resolution of the board of directors. This is made clear by s 182 (7) which provides that nothing in the section is to be taken as derogating from any power to remove a director which may exist apart from the section.[1]

1. Cf *Lee v Chou Wen Hsien* [1985] BCLC 45.

Remuneration of directors

27.10 A director has no right as such to remuneration for acting as director. The articles usually provide, however, for the determination by the company in general meeting of the remuneration to be given to the directors (article 76).

The amount of the remuneration is a matter for the company and it does not have to be paid out of profits.[1] But if a director accepts remuneration in excess of what is authorised by the articles, he commits a misfeasance and can be compelled to repay the amount of the excess to the company or its liquidator.[2]

The Principal Act also contains strict requirements as to the disclosure of the amount of the remuneration—and other payments to directors—in the annual accounts.[3]

The articles usually provide that the remuneration is to be deemed to accrue from day to day. It follows from this that where the director's employment is determined during the course of a year, he is entitled to an apportioned part of his salary for the part of the year during which he was a director. Where the articles contain no such provision, there is a divergence of view as to whether the remuneration is to be apportioned, but the better view would appear to be that in such circumstances the Apportionment Act 1870 applies and the remuneration should be apportioned.[4]

1. *Harvey Lewis's Case* (1872) 26 LT 673.
2. *Re Oxford Society* (1887) 35 Ch D 502.
3. See para 30.17 below.
4. Palmer, vol. I, 61: 38-40.

27.11 The articles usually provide for the payment of expenses to directors· (article 76). Such a provision is of particular importance in the modern company, because of the relief afforded to income tax payers in respect of such expenses where they are 'wholly, exclusively and necessarily' incurred in the performance of duties as directors.[1] The usual provision is that the directors may be paid all travelling, hotel and other expenses properly incurred by them in attending and returning from meetings of the directors and general meetings of the company or in connection with the business of the company. Again the amount of such expenses paid must be disclosed in the accounts.[2]

1. Income Tax Act 1967.
2. Para 30.17 below.

27.12 There is no prohibition on the making of loans by the company to the directors. If the company makes such a loan, there is no requirement as to the rate of interest or indeed as to the payment of any interest by the director. Clearly this unrestricted power to make loans to directors is capable of serious abuse, but Cox considered that changes in the law were impractical and the Principal Act followed this recommendation. It is, however, one of the areas with which amending legislation is virtually certain to deal.[1] Loans to directors have been unlawful in England except in limited circumstances since the 1948 Act.

It should be noted, however, that the Principal Act contains stringent requirements as to the disclosure of such loans in the annual accounts.[2]

1. See para 2.26 above.
2. See para 30.18 below.

Powers and duties of directors

27.13 The powers of the directors are those which the company has delegated to them. If, as is usually the case, the articles provide that the directors may exercise all the powers of the company which are not by the Acts or the articles required to be exercised by the company in general meeting (article 80), the delegation is unrestricted, and the board of directors can do whatever the company could do. they cannot, of course, do anything which is illegal or *ultra vires*, any more than the company in general meeting can.

It follows that the company cannot, in general meeting validly set aside an action taken by the directors within the powers conferred on them by the articles. Equally the company cannot itself in general meeting take any step which by virtue of its articles it has delegated to the directors.

27.14 But although the directors, once the powers have been delegated to them, can do anything which the company can do, this does not mean that the company cannot ultimately control the directors, if it wishes. In the first place, the company may always amend the articles of association by special resolution so as to circumscribe the powers of the directors in any way it thinks fit. In the second place, the company may always by ordinary resolution remove all or any of the directors except a life director. And even in the case of a life director, he can always be removed if there is a majority sufficient to effect the necessary amendment of the articles.

27.15 We have seen that directors occupy a fiduciary position towards the company. This means that they must always act in good faith in the interests of the company as a whole. The test in other words is subjective: if the directors genuinely believe that what they are doing is in the interests of the company as a whole, the court will not interfere with their decisions even though they might appear objectively to be detrimental to the company.[1]

The duty is owed by the directors to the company as a whole and not to the individual shareholders. This was first established by the leading case of *Percival v Wright*.[2] A director purchased shares from a member and did not disclose to him that the directors were aware that negotiations were in progress for the purchase of all the shares at a higher figure. When the member sought to make the director account for the profit on the shares, it was held by Swinfen Eady J that he could not succeed: there had been no breach of duty on the part of the director to the *company*. If, however, the directors can be regarded in a particular transaction as acting on behalf of individual shareholders, i.e. if they are in effect acting as the agents of individual shareholders, they will owe them a duty to act in their interests.[3]

Since the duty is owed to the company as a whole, it it not fulfilled where the directors act in the interests of a section only of the members.[4] Nor is it sufficient to act in the short term interests of the company alone without regard to its long term interests on the basis that the duty is confined to the existing body of members: the directors must take into account the long term and short term interests of the company.[5]

1. *Re Gresham Life Assurance Soc* [1872] LR 8 Ch 446 at 449.
2. (1902) 2 Ch 421.
3. *Allen v Hyatt* (1914) 30 TLR 444.
4. 'Report of the Second Savoy Hotel Investigation', HMSO, June 1954; *Gaiman v National Association for Mental Health* [1971] Ch 317 at 330.
5. Ibid.

27.16 The duty is owed to the members of the company alone. The directors owe no duty to the employees of the company to have regard to their interests. This, one of the most widely discussed lacunae in modern company law, has been abriged to some extent in England by s 46 of the 1980 Act which requires the directors to have regard to the interests of the employees as well as of the members in discharging their functions.[1]

1. See para 2.26 above.

27.17 The powers conferred on the directors by the articles, however unrestricted the language used, may only be used for the purposes for which they are conferred. Thus, the power to issue shares in the company may not be used by the directors for the purpose of maintaining their control, or their friends' control, of the company or in order to defeat the wishes of the majority of the shareholders.[1] The directors may genuinely believe that by ensuring their future dominance over the company, they are also securing its well-being, but that does not entitle them to use the power to issue shares for a purpose for which it was not intended, i.e. the maintenance of their control, as distinct from one of the purposes for which it is conferred, e.g. the raising of new capital.

An example is afforded by *Nash v Lancegaye (Ireland) Ltd*,[2] the facts of which have already been stated.[3] In that case Dixon J set aside an issue of shares which he found had been made by a majority of the directors with a view to ensuring the continued control of the company by a particular family.

It has also been held in England that the directors cannot use the power to issue new shares as a means of blocking a takeover bid of which they disapprove but which a majority of the shareholders wish to accept. In *Howard Smith Ltd v Ampol Petroleum Ltd and Another*,[4] the directors of a company called R.W. Miller (Holdings) Ltd were held to have acted unlawfully when they used their powers with this in view. More than 50 per cent of the shares in Millers were owned jointly by Ampol and another company, Bulkheads Ltd. Ampol made a takeover bid, which was rejected, and this was followed by a takeover bid at a higher figure by Howard Smith Ltd. Ampol and Bulkheads then issued a joint statement that they would not co-operate in any takeover by Howard Smith or any other firm. The directors riposted by allotting a sufficient number of new shares in the company to Howard Smith to make them majority shareholders.

Lord Wilberforce, giving the advice of the Judicial Committee of the Privy Council, said that the mere fact that the issue was not needed for the raising of new capital did not of itself make it an unlawful use of the directors' powers. But the powers were nonetheless being used for an improper purpose, i.e. the transfer of power to a new majority of shareholders. The case could no doubt have been decided on the basis that the powers were being used for a purpose for which they were not conferred, as in the *Lancegaye* case and the earlier English decision of *Hogg v Cramphorn*,[5] Lord Wilberforce, however, took the view that the use of the power in this instance was improper not merely because it was being used for a purpose for which it was not intended but because its use in the manner impugned violated a fundamental principle of company law, i.e. the constitutional separation of powers between the shareholders on the one hand and the directors on the other. The directors could not by the issue of new shares abolish the position of the majority.

1. *Punt v Symons & Co* [1903] 2 Ch 506; *Piercy v S Mills & Co* [1920] 1 Ch 77.
2. (1958) 92 ILTR 11.
3. Para 26.08 above.
4. [1974] AC 821.
5. [1967] Ch 254.

27.18 It is always open to the directors of a private company to ward off an attempt by outsiders to take over the company by using their powers to refuse to register transfers. Provided the directors exercise the discretion given to them in this area by the articles in good faith in what they believe to be the interests of the company, their decisions will not be set aside by the court.[1] In the case of many private companies of a relatively small and intimate nature—what are sometimes called quasi-partnership companies—the very basis of the company may be the confinement of the business to a relatively small number of people, such as, for example, the members of a family. In such a case, a refusal of the directors to register transfers to outsiders will be peculiarly difficult to challenge.

1. See para 19.03 above.

27.19 It should be remembered that there are now important statutory restrictions on the powers of the directors to issue shares. These have already been explained in Chapter Eight; it is sufficient at this point to recall that the directors cannot now exercise the power of the company to issue shares unless they are authorised so to do by
    (a) the company in general meeting, or
    (b) the articles.
  Moreover, where the company is so authorised, the authority will expire at the end of five years from the date on which it is conferred, unless it is renewed by a resolution of the company in general meeting.
  In addition, the shareholders of the company have now a right of pre-emption when new shares are being issued.

27.20 The directors owe a duty to the company to exercise *skill* and *diligence* in the discharge of their functions. This is a general principle, but the courts in a succession of cases of which the most important is still the decision of Romer J in *City Equitable Fire Insurance Company Limited*,[1] have broken it down into a number of sub-propositions, most of them tending to limit or modify the extent of the duty owed by directors.
(a) A director need not exhibit in the performance of his duties a greater degree of skill than may reasonably be expected from a person of his knowledge and experience. Thus a person who is appointed a director without possessing any particular knowledge or expertise which might be useful in the conduct of the company's business cannot be held responsible

for any loss the company may sustain as a result of his lack of knowledge or expertise. A director of a life insurance company, for example, who is not an actuary or a physician cannot be expected to have the knowledge or skill expected of those professions.[2]

(b) A director cannot be held responsible for errors of judgment as such. The day to day conduct of business demands that risks be taken on occasions. The law does not expect infallibility from directors or from anyone else and if a director makes a decision in what he genuinely believes to be the best interests of the company, the fact that it subsequently proves to be mistaken (frequently with the benefit of hindsight) will not of itself be a ground for setting it aside.[3]

(c) A director is not bound to give continuous attention to the affairs of his company. In particular while the failure of a director to attend board meetings with reasonable regularity is a breach of his duty to take care, he is not under a duty to attend *every* board meeting.[4] Moreover, what constitutes 'reasonable regularity' will depend very much on the circumstances of the particular case. The position of the managing director is, of course, obviously different. In the case of other directors, intermittent attention only to the affairs of the company is required, and the mere failure of a director to attend a number of board meetings will not of itself render him liable for some irregular action taken by the board in his absence.[5] In England, many persons are appointed to boards simply because they possess a title, and the practice is not unknown in Ireland, where it is also quite common to find persons appointed to boards because they are well known public figures. Clearly, the specialised attention which such directors are expected to give to the affairs of the company will be less than the attention expected of directors with a distinctive knowledge or expertise.

(d) A director is in general justified in leaving duties to be performed by another official of the company where such duties may properly be left to such an official having regard to the provisions of the articles and the exigencies of the business. In the words of Lord Halsbury LC in *Dovey v Cory*[6]

> 'The business of life could not go on if people could not trust those who are put into a position of trust for the express purpose of attending to details of management.'

There is one qualification to this principle. A director will not be able to escape responsibility where there were grounds for suspicion as to the official concerned.[7]

(e) Negligence need not be 'gross negligence'. A director will be liable for negligence in its ordinary sense. It was at one time said that a director was only liable for what was called 'gross negligence', but it is clear from later decisions[8] that this is not so and that the standard to be applied is the one generally applicable to all types of negligence, i.e. a failure to take reasonable care in circumstances where the director was under a duty to take care.

---

1. [1925] Ch 407.
2. Per Romer J in *City Equitable Fire Insurance Co Ltd*, above.
3. *Re Brazilian Rubber Plantations and Estates Ltd* [1911] 1 Ch 425 at 3 437.
4. *Perry's Case* (1876) 34 LT 716.
5. *Marquis of Bute's Case* [1892] 2 Ch 100.
6. [1901] AC 477 at 486.
7. *City Equitable Fire Insurance Company Limited* (above) per Romer J at 429.
8. *Re Brazilian Rubber Plantations and Estates Ltd; City Equitable Fire Insurance Company Limited* (above).

Contracts by directors with company

27.21 Because a director is in law in a similar position to a trustee or agent for the company, he cannot enter into a contract with the company, and any contract which he enters into with the company is liable to be set aside, unless it is authorised by the articles. The articles usually contain a provision enabling directors to enter into such contracts.[1] It is also usual to provide that a director is not to vote in respect of any contract or arrangement in which he is interested, directly or indirectly, and that if he does vote his vote is not to be counted; nor is he to be counted in the quorum for the meeting.[2] But in the case of a private company, such a restriction is usually dispensed with.[3]

1. Article 85.
2. Article 84.
3. Article 7. Part II.

27.22 It is accordingly possible for a director to enter into a contract with his company which will not be set aside, provided the requirements of the articles are met. The Principal Act, however, requires that the director should disclose the nature of his interest in such contract or proposed contract at a meeting of the directors. The relevant provisions are to be found in s 194, which also requires, in the case of a proposed contract, the disclosure be made at the meeting of the directors at which the question of entering into the contract is first taken into consideration. If the director was not interested in the contract at the date of that meeting, the disclosure must be made at the next meeting held after he becomes so interested. Where he becomes interested in the contract after it has been made, the disclosure must be made at the first meeting after he has become so interested. The section also provides for the adequacy for its purposes of a general notice by a director to the effect that he is a member of a specified company or firm and is to be regarded as interested in any contract entered into by the company thereafter with that company or firm. A director who fails to comply with the section is liable to a fine not exceeding £500.[1]

The section also provides that a copy of every declaration of interest and notice given is to be entered within three days in a book kept for that purpose. It must be open for inspection without charge to the directors, members, auditors and secretary of the company at the registered office. It must also be produced at every general meeting of the company and at any meeting of the directors where a request for its production is made in sufficient time by one of the directors. The company and every officer in default is liable to a fine of £500 for non-compliance with this requirement, and the court may compel an inspection or production of the book where it has been refused.[2]

1. S 194 of the Principal Act, as amended by s 15 of the 1982 Act.
2. Ibid.

Liability of directors to account to company for benefits

27.23 Directors being in the eyes of the law in the position of trustees for their company are subject to the same limitations as conventional trustees so far as deriving any profit or benefit from their trust is concerned. It follows from this, of course, that they are liable to account for any bribe they may receive but they are also liable to account for any secret benefits they obtain as a result of their positions, whether they take the form of commissions, cash or whatever. Moreover, if a director makes a personal profit as a result of a transaction which he would not have received were it not for his position as a director, he will also be liable to account for it to the company.

The leading case on the topic is the House of Lords decision in *Regal (Hastings) Ltd v Gulliver*,[1] which graphically illustrates the unbending attitude of the law towards benefits acquired by directors from their position. The company owned one cinema and the directors decided to acquire two others with a view to selling all three as a going concern. A subsidiary company was formed with a view to taking a lease of the other two. In order to provide the subsidiary with sufficient paid up capital to satisfy the lessors, the directors took up a number of shares in the subsidiary company themselves. They then sold their shares in both the company and its subsidiary. The sale of their shares in the subsidiary realised a profit for them, and when the new owners of the company became aware of this, proceedings were instituted against the directors by the company claiming that the profit belonged to the company. There was no suggestion that the directors had acted in anything other than good faith, or that what they had done was other than for the benefit of the company: had they not agreed to take up shares in the subsidiary, the lease would not have been granted to the subsidiary on the strength of the capital which the company itself was in a position to subscribe. The company's action failed for these reasons in the court of first instance and in the Court of Appeal, but the decision of the latter court was reversed in the House of Lords. It was held that where directors during the course of their management of the company avail of their opportunities and special knowledge and as a result obtain a profit, they must account to the company for that profit, even though there was nothing improper in what they did and the company did not suffer as a result.

But where the company in general meeting approves of the action of the directors, they will not be accountable. And it would also appear that directors may be entitled to retain such profits where the company did not itself avail of the opportunity given to it to make the profit for itself, the information made use of by the directors was not confidential and the transaction giving rise to the profit was not related to their position as directors.[2]

1. [1942] I All ER 378.
2. Gower, pp 597–598.

Remedies against directors

27.24 Where a director has been guilty of negligence in the conduct of his office, he is liable to the company for the damage which results. This liability may be enforced against him in the ordinary way by an action brought by the company. It will be remembered, however, that under the rule in *Foss v Harbottle*, such an action must be brought by the company itself and cannot in general be maintained by a group of shareholders.[1]

1. See para 26.02 above.

27.25 Where the director has been guilty of some breach of trust or where he has derived some benefit from the company for which he is liable to account, the company may enforce their rights against him either by a common law action or in proceedings claiming equitable relief such as a declaration, injunction or an account, as may be appropriate.

27.26 Apart from these remedies, a special remedy is available against a director when the company is wound up. Under s 298 of the Principal Act, the court may compel any director who has misapplied or retained or become accountable for any money or property of the company or who has been guilty of any misfeasance or breach of trust to repay or restore the money or property. This remedy—known as 'misfeasance proceedings'—is considered in more detail in Chapter Thirty-Four below.

Relief from liability as director

27.27 Directors are entitled as agents of the company to be indemnified by the company in respect of any liabilities incurred by them in the management of the company's business. In addition, it was usual for the articles to exempt the directors from liability for any losses sustained by the company other than those incurred as a result of their 'wilful default' or actual dishonesty. Section 200 of the Principal Act, however, provides that any such provision is to be void except in relation to liability incurred by the director in defending criminal or civil proceedings in which he succeeds or is acquitted or in connection with an application under s 391 of the Act in which he obtains relief from the court. That latter section enables the court to relieve any officer or auditor of the company from liability for any negligence, default, breach of duty or breach of trust, where
  (a) the officer or auditor has acted honestly and resonably, and
  (b) it appears to the court that, having regard to all the circumstances, he ought fairly to be excused.

Meetings of directors

27.28 ʇThe management of the company is vested in the board of directors and decisions affecting its management must accordingly be taken, generally speaking, at properly convened and regularly conducted meetings of the board.ʃThe articles usually provide, however, for the appointment by the directors of one of their number to be managing director (article 110) and for the entrusting to him of such powers exercisable by them as they think fit (article 112). Moreover, the articles usually provide that a resolution signed by all the directors entitled to receive notice of a meeting of directors is to be as valid as if it has been passed at a meeting duly convened and held (article 109).

27.29 The requirements as to the convening of meetings, the quorum for such meetings, voting, the election of a chairman and the general conduct of the meeting are all usually dealt with in the articles. They normally provide that the directors,
  'may meet together for the despatch of business, adjourn and otherwise regulate their meetings as they think fit.' (Article 101.)
They also usually provide that a director may, and the secretary shall on the requisition of a director, convene a meeting at any time. (Ibid). The normal provision as to a quorum is that it is to be fixed by the directors and, if not so fixed, is to be two (Article 102). If the articles so provide—and they

generally do —the continuing directors may act notwithstanding any vacancy in their number. They may also stipulate, however, that where the directors are insufficient in number to constitute a quorum, they may only meet for the purpose of increasing their number to the number necessary for a quorum or for the purpose of convening a general meeting of the company but for no other purpose (article 103).

27.30 Every director is entitled to be given notice of a meeting and the notice must be given within a reasonable time. The only exception is where the director is abroad: it is usual to provide in the articles (article 101) that the directors may resolve not to give notice of meetings to directors absent from the state who are normally resident in the state, but even without such a provision, it is probably not necessary to give notice to directors so absent.[1]

1. *Halifax Sugar etc Co v Francklyn* (1890) 59 LJ Ch 593.

27.31 A meeting of which due notice is not given or at which a quorum is not present is irregular and its decisions will not be valid. It must be remembered, however, that under the rule in *British Royal Bank v Turquand*, an outsider dealing with the company will not be affected by such an irregularity of which he has no notice since it is part of the 'indoor management' of the company of which he is not presumed to be aware.[1]

1. See para 11.15 above.

27.32 Where the directors of a company wrongfully exclude one of their number from their proceedings, he has a right of action against them, at all events where he has a proprietary interest in the company in the form of shares. This was so decided by Budd J in *Coubrough v James Panton & Co*,[1] distinguishing an earlier English decision of *Harben v Phillips*.[2] In that case the director could only be removed by an extraordinary resolution of the company and the other directors did not have a majority sufficient to remove him.

Extraordinary resolutions were abolished by the Principal Act but the articles may still provide for the appointment of life directors. In such a case, a special resolution amending the articles could be necessary before the directors could be removed, and if the other directors did not command the necessary majority, the decision in *Coubrough v James Panton & Co* could still be applicable.

1. [1965] IR 272.
2. (1883) 23 Ch D 14.

27.33 Minutes must be kept of the proceedings and meetings of directors.[1] The provisions applicable to the keeping of minutes of meetings of the company are also in general applicable to minutes of meetings of directors.[2]

1. S 145 of the Principal Act.
2. See para 25.24 above.

Publication of information relating to directors

27.34 The Principal Act requires the company to keep available for inspection at its registered office the following registers:
   (1) A register of directors and secretaries;
   (2) A register of directors' shareholdings.

There is no equivalent to s 26 of the English 1967 Act requiring every company to make available for inspection by the members the terms of service contracts with its directors.

27.35 The register of directors and secretaries is dealt with in s 195. It must contain the following particulars relating to each director:
(1) his present Christian name and surname and any former Christian name and surname;
(2) his usual residential address;
(3) his nationality, if not Irish;
(4) his business occupation, if any; and
(5) particulars of any other directorships of bodies corporate incorporated in the state held by him.
The company must send to the Registrar a return in the prescribed form containing the particulars specified in the register within 14 days after the appointment of the first directors of the company. Particulars of any change in the directors must be sent within 14 days of the change.

27.36 The register must be open to inspection by any member of the company without charge during business hours (or such time as the company may impose provided that not less than two hours' inspection in each day is allowed) and to any other person on payment of a small fee. If an inspection is refused, the company and every officer in default is liable to a fine not exceeding £100. The court may also order an inspection of the register.[1]

1. S 195(10) and (11).

27.37 The register of directors' shareholdings is dealt with in s 190. It must also be kept at the registered office and must in addition be produced at the commencement of the annual general meeting and be open and accessible during the meeting to any person attending the meeting.

The register must show in relation to each director the number, description and amount of any shares in or debentures of the company or any other body corporate which is a subsidiary or holding company of the company or a subsidiary of the company's holding company which are held by or in trust for him or his spouse or any child of his or of which he or they have the right to become the holders. It need not, however, show shareholdings in a wholly owned subsidiary of the company. Where any shares or debentures change hands, the register must show the date and the price or other consideration.

To guard against evasion of the section, the definitions of 'director' and 'shareholders' is drawn in extremely wide terms. Any person in accordance with whose directions the directors of the company are accustomed to act is deemed himself to be a director. A person is deemed to hold shares or have an interest or right in or over them where he has an interest jointly or in common with any other person or a limited, reversionary or contingent interest or an interest as the object of a discretionary trust. A person is similarly deemed to be a shareholder if a body corporate other than the company holds the shares and its directors are accustomed to act in accordance with his directions; or if he is entitled to exercise, or control the exercise, of one-third or more of the voting power at any general meeting of that body corporate.

There are similar provisions relating to the inspection of the register as are

248

contained in the case of the register of directors. There is also provision for penalties in the event of a default by the company in complying with the section.

Section 193 (1) requires every director to give notice in writing to the company as soon as may be of such matters relating to himself and his spouse and children as may be necessary for the purposes of s 190. Any person who fails to comply with this requirement is liable to a fine not exceeding £500.[1]

Section 190 does not apply to a private company where all the members of the company are directors.

1. S 193(4) as amended by s 15 of the 1982 Act.

27.38 Section 196 of the Principal Act requires certain particulars of directors to be given in all business letters in which the company's name appears. The particulars, which must be legible, are:

(1) the present Christian name, or the initials thereof, and present surname;

(2) any former Christian names and surnames; and

(3) his nationality, if not Irish.

The Act does not apply to companies registered under the 1908 Act which were registered before 23 November 1916 (the date of the coming into force of the Registration of Business Names Act 1916). The Minister may also exempt companies from the obligations of the section if he thinks it expedient so to do. If a company makes default in complying with the section, every officer who is in default is liable on summary conviction to a fine not exceeding £125.[1] No proceedings may be instituted, however, without the consent of the Minister.

1. S 196(4) as amended by s 15 of the 1982 Act.

Restrictions on becoming a director

27.39 There are four categories prohibited by law from being directors of companies:

(1) undischarged bankrupts;[1]

(2) a body corporate;[2]

(3) the auditor of the company (or of its holding company or of any of its subsidiaries);[3]

(4) a person prohibited by an order made under s 184 of the Principal Act from being a director of any company.

An order made under s 184 may be made where a person is convicted on indictment of any offence in connection with the promotion, formation or management of a company or any offence involving fraud or dishonesty, whether in connection with a company or not. In such a case, the court may, on the application of the Director of Public Prosecutions, order that the person concerned shall not be a director of any company without the leave of the court. He may be similarly prohibited from being concerned with or taking part in the management of any company either directly or indirectly. There are similar provisions enabling such an order to be made on the winding up of a company where a person has been found guilty of fraudulent trading.[4]

A person who acts in contravention of an order made under s 184 is liable on conviction to imprisonment for a term not exceeding two years or to a fine not exceeding £2,500 or both or on summary conviction to imprisonment for a term not exceeding six months or a fine not exceeding £500 or both.[5]

1. S 183 of the Principal Act.
2. S 176 of the Principal Act.
3. S 162(5)(a) of the Principal Act, as subsituted by s 6 of the 1982 Act.
4. See para 34.86 below.
5. S 184(5) as amended by s 15 of the 1982 Act.

27.40 As we have seen, there are indications that impending legislation may include provisions intended to strengthen the prohibitions on undesirable categories of persons becoming directors of companies.[1]

1. Para 2.26 above.

Chapter 28

The secretary

28.01 Every company formed under the Acts is required to have a secretary. He may be one of the directors; but it should be noted that where something is required or authorised to be done by a director and the secretary, such as the execution or witnessing of a document, it cannot be done by the same person acting both as director and as, or in the place of, the secretary.[1]

1. S 177 of the Principal Act.

Functions of secretary

28.02 The functions of the secretary are not defined by the Acts. They are, however, clearly administrative rather than managerial. The secretary is normally the person responsible for ensuring that the company complies with the requirements of the Acts, and it is accordingly a reasonably onerous position. He will be expected to attend to the following matters in particular:
  - (a) keeping charge of the register of members, register of directors and secretaries, register of debentures and register of directors' shareholdings;
  - (b) making the annual return to the Registrar;
  - (c) keeping the minutes of general meetings and of meetings of the board of directors;
  - (d) notifying the Registrar of any alterations in the memorandum and articles;
  - (e) giving notice to members of meetings;
  - (f) furnishing the Registrar with particulars of charges entered into by the company.

Appointment of secretary

28.03 The secretary may be named in the memorandum or articles of association. It is more usual, however, for him to be appointed by the members of the company or the directors. He must in any event be named in the statement now required to be delivered to the Registrar with the memorandum by s 3 of the 1982 act. Unlike the auditors of companies, there are no professional qualifications required of a secretary. The position may be occupied by a body corporate, and it is quite common for companies to avail of this power to appoint a firm of accountants or consultants to act as

251

secretary. The Principal Act also provides that anything required or authorised to be done by or to the secretary may be done by or to any assistant or deputy secretary capable of acting, if the office of secretary is vacant or there is no secretary capable of acting.[1]

1. S 175(2).

Implied authority of secretary to act on behalf of the company

28.04   A secretary may be expressly authorised to enter into a particular transaction on behalf of the company, in which case it will be binding on the company. He may also bind the company by entering into a contract which is within his apparent authority as secretary, whether it has been expressly authorised or not.[1] Thus, it would normally be regarded as within his authority to enter into contracts relating to the administrative aspect of the company's affairs, such as the management of its office. He would not normally be regarded as having authority to enter into ordinary commercial contracts for the purchase of materials, the placing of orders, etc. His position in this context should be contrasted with that of a managing director who has implied authority to enter into a wide range of commercial contracts.[2]

1. See para 11.11 above.
2. Ibid.

Chapter 29

The annual return

29.01 Every company formed under the Acts, public or private, limited or unlimited, is obliged to make an annual return to the Registrar setting out certain matters specified in the Principal Act.[1] This is one of the most important requirements of the law applicable to such companies, because the basis of that law, as we have seen, is that the public should have access to the details of the ownership, finances and officers of companies granted the privilege of incorporation. The information furnished on incorporation may be completely inadequate in this context: the subscribers to the memorandum, for example, are frequently two nominees inserted by the solicitors or accountants who prepare the memorandum and articles and who have no real connection with the company. If a company has complied fully with the requirements of the Acts, a more accurate picture of its real nature may be gained from a study of the annual returns, the register of members and directors and the register of directors' shareholdings and dealings.

Unfortunately, the strict requirements of the Acts as to the making of returns are repeatedly flouted in Ireland. They oblige the company to make the return within a specified time of the annual general meeting and set out in great detail the matters to be included. But many private companies simply ignore the relevant provisions and the penalties imposed by the Acts for non-compliance are not much of a deterrent. Now, however, the Registrar is empowered by s 12 of the 1982 Act to strike companies off the register which are in default in this area and has availed of this power in a number of instances. It is to be hoped that this will lead to a more rigid adherence to the requirements of the Acts in the future.

1. S 125-129 of the Principal Act.

Matters to be included in the return

29.02 The information required to be set out in the return differs depending on whether the company has a share capital or not. In the case of all companies, it must include
  (a) the address of the registered office;
  (b) where the register of members is not kept at the registered office, the address where it is kept;
  (c) where the register of debenture holders is not kept at the registered office, the address where it is kept;
  (d) a statement of the total indebtedness of the company in respect of all mortgages and charges required to be registered under s 99 of the Principal Act;

253

(e) the same particulars relating to directors and secretaries as are required to be contained in the register of directors and secretaries.[1]

In the case of companies having a share capital, the following information must also be given:

(a) a summary of the share capital, distinguishing between shares issued for cash and issued as fully or partly paid up otherwise than in cash;

(b) a list of the members of the company and those who have ceased to be members since the last return;

(c) the number of shares held by each member and (in the case of a private company) details of shares transferred since the last return;[2]

The detailed provisions as to such information are set out in Part I of the Fifth Schedule to the Principal Act. Part II contains the form in which the return must be made. In the case of the share capital, it is necessary to show:

(a) the amount of the capital and the number of shares into which it is divided;

(b) the number of shares taken up to the date of the return;

(c) the amount called up on each share and the total of calls received and calls unpaid;

(d) the total commission paid in respect of any shares or debentures;

(e) the discount allowed on the issue of any shares or so much of it as has not been written off; and

(f) the total of shares forfeited.

The list of members must give their addresses and occupations. It is to be made up as of the 14th day after the annual general meeting for that year. Where the company has given all the required particulars as to members and transfers of shares in its returns for the previous five years, it is only required to give details of new members, persons ceasing to be members and shares transferred since the last return. If the names of the members are not set out in alphabetical order, there must be an index for easy reference.

1. See para 27.35 above.
2. S 125 of the Principal Act.

Documents to be annexed to the return

29.03 The following documents must be annexed to the return in the case of public companies:[1]

(a) a written copy certified by a director and the secretary to be a true copy of the balance sheet laid before the annual general meeting of the company held during the period to which the return relates (including any document required to be annexed to the balance sheet);

(b) a copy similarly certified of the reports of the directors and auditors accompanying such balance sheet; and

(c) where the balance sheet is in a language other than English or Irish a translation in English or Irish certified in the prescribed manner to be a correct translation.

1. S 128 of the Principal Act, as amended by s 15 of the 1982 Act.

29.04 If the balance sheet did not comply with the requirements of the Acts at the date of the audit, the necessary additions and corrections must be incorporated in the copy annexed to the return.

Where the company fails to comply with these requirements, the company and its officers who are in default are liable to a fine not exceeding £500.

29.05 Private companies are entirely exempted from the requirement to annex the balace sheet and directors' and auditors' report to the annual return.[1] This remarkable feature of Irish company law survived the enactment of the Principal Act, presumably because Cox had recommended that there be no change in the law. The exemption may, however, be removed or at least substantially modified in the near future, when effect is given to the Fourth EEC Directive.[2]

The following companies are also exempted from this requirement:

(a) an assurance company which has complied with s 7 (4) of the Assurance Companies Act 1909;

(b) a company not having a share capital which is formed for an object that is charitable and is under the control of a religion recognised by the State under Article 44 of the Constitution and which exercises its functions in accordance with the laws, canons and ordinances of the religion concerned;

(c) a company not having a share capital and formed for charitable purposes which the Commissioners of Charitable Donations and Bequests for Ireland by order exempt from the requirement either altogether or for a limited period.

The second of these exemptions is a curious survival. The provisions of Article 44 referred to were deleted as a result of a referendum in 1972. Professor J. M. Kelly has raised the question as to whether the relevant provision could be read as though the reference to being under the control of a recognised religion was deleted, or whether this would distort the intention of the legislature.[3]

It is thought that so to read the provision would be to distort the legislative intent, which was clearly to confine the privilege to those religions then recognised by the Constitution. Professor Kelly points out that to give effect to the legislative exemption as it stands would be to perpetuate the discrimination in favour of specified religions formerly enshrined in the Constitution and would be of dubious constitutionality. It is thought that the provision in its present form is invalid having regard to the constitutional guarantee that the State will not enact laws which discriminate between religions and is in any event unnecessary in view of the power given to the Commissioners for Charitable Donations and Bequests for Ireland to exempt charitable bodies from the requirement as to a return. The opportunity should be taken in the next amending Act to remove the provision.

1. S 125 (4) of the Principal Act.
2. See para 2.24 above.
3. *The Irish Constitution*, 2nd edn p 674.

Certificates to be sent by private company with return

29.06 A private company must send with its return the following certificates signed by a director and the secretary:

(a) a certificate that the company has not, since the date of its last return, or in the case of a first return since the date of incorporation, issued any invitation to the public to subscribe for shares or debentures of the company;

(b) where the number of members exceeds 50, a certificate that the excess consists wholly of persons who under the Acts are not to be included in reckoning the number of 50, i.e. employees or former employees of the company.[1]

1. S 129 of the Principal Act.

Default in making return

29.07 The return must be completed within 60 days after the annual general meeting for the year and the company must forthwith forward to the Register a copy signed by a director and the secretary. If the company fails to comply with these requirements, both the company and every officer in default is liable to a fine not exceeding £500. Proceedings in relation to such offences may be brought and prosecuted by the Registrar.[1]

An additional power was conferred on the Registrar in the event of a default by a company in relation to the return by s 12 of the 1982 Act.

If a company has failed for three consecutive years to make a return, he may write to it (by registered post) inquiring whether the company is still carrying on business and stating that, if an answer is not received within a month, a notice will be published in *Iris Ofigiuil* with a view to striking the company off the register. Unless he receives all the outstanding returns within one month, he may publish in *Iris Ofigiuil* and send by registered post to the company a notice stating that at the end of one month from the date of the notice, the name of the company will be struck off the register and the company dissolved, unless cause is shown to the contrary or all outstanding returns are made. At the expiration of the month the Registrar, unless cause has been shown to the contrary, may strike the name of the company off the register and must then publish a notice to that effect in *Iris Ofigiuil*. Upon publication of the notice, the company is dissolved. The liability of the directors, officers and members continues, however, and the jurisdiction of the court to wind up the company is unaffected.

There is provision for an application to the court by the company or any creditor or member of the company who feels aggrieved by its having been struck off. Such an application must be made within 20 years of the publication of the notice in *Iris Ofigiuil*. The court, if satisfied that the company was at the time of striking off carrying on business or otherwise that it is just to make the order, may order that the name of the company be restored to the register. Upon an office copy of the order being delivered to the Registrar the company is deemed to have continued in existence as if its name had not been struck off. The court may also give such directions as seem just with a view to placing the company and all other persons in the same position as if the company had not been struck off.[2]

1. S 127 of the Principal Act, as amended by s 15 of the 1982 Act.
2. Note that the provisions of the section are without prejudice to the general power of the Registrar to strike a defunct company off the register under s 311 of the Principal Act. That section contains similar machinery entitling the Registrar to strike off a company where he has reasonable cause to believe that it is not carrying on business.

Chapter 30

Accounts and audit

30.01 Until the Principal Act came into force in 1964, there was no legal obligation on Irish companies to keep proper books of acounts. This is not to say, of course, that such books were not kept in practice: any careful businessman would recognise the importance of keeping a proper record of all the firms's finances on a day-to-day business. But the absence of any express requirement of the law in this area gave rise to understandable concern. The Principal Act introduced major changes in the law: for the first time, all companies formed under the Acts were expressly required to keep proper books of account and there were important new provisions as to the information to be included in the accounts which are laid before the members.

At the time of writing, it is widely anticipated that amending legislation is imminent which will implement the Fourth EEC Directive. This will almost certainly end the total exemption of private companies from the requirement to annex the balance sheet and profit and loss account to their annual return. In future, only small and medium sized companies and possibly subsidiaries of EEC parent companies may be exempted from those requirements. In addition the new legislation is expected to introduce more stringent requirements as to what must be disclosed in accounts, including details of accounting policies and methods of valuation of assets and details of operating costs.

30.02 In considering the requirements of the Acts in this area, it is necessary to distinguish between the basic records which companies are obliged to maintain and information which companies are required to prepare and in some instances, publish.

Companies are required to maintain books of account in which are recorded, on a day to day basis, the finances of the company. The directors are charged with the responsibility of preparing a balance sheet and a profit and loss account to be laid before the members annually in general meeting.[1] This balance sheet will be prepared from the books of account of the company and can be viewed as the means by which the directors render an account to the shareholders of their financial stewardship.

In practice, many companies will prepare balance sheets and profit and loss accounts at more frequent intervals than a year for internal use in managing and controlling the enterprise. In addition, it is now normal practice to produce at regular intervals budgets, cash flows and other such information as part of the internal management control system.

The auditors are required to report to the members on every balance sheet and profit and loss account laid before the members annually and to frame their report in accordance with the requirements of the Seventh Schedule to the Principal Act. To that end, they will carry out an examination of the books of account and other financial records of the company.

30.03 There are special provisions as to the preparation of 'group' accounts' in the case of companies having subsidiary companies, i.e. companies either owned or effectively controlled by them.

Books of account

30.04 Every company is required by s 147 of the Principal Act to keep proper books of account. These must relate to
(a) all sums of money received and expended by the company and the matters in respect of which the receipt and expenditure takes place;
(b) all sales and purchases of goods by the company;
(c) the assets and liabilities of the company.
The section also requires the books to be kept so as to give 'a true and fair view of the state of the company's affairs and to explain its transactions'. The phrase 'a true and fair view', which recurs in this part of the Principal Act, has never been further defined. Nor does the Act go into the minutiae of the nature of books of account—cash ledgers, cheque journals, etc— which are to be kept. The concept of books of account has developed with modern technology. In many companies the bound ledger has been replaced by a computerised system with the information maintained on magnetic tape or disc and printouts provided on computerised stationery. The sensible course to follow is to ensure that, whatever records are kept, they record the transactions in such a way that they can be understood and traced through the system at a later stage.

30.05 The books of account must be kept at the registered office of the company or such other place as the directors think fit. They must be available for inspection by the directors at reasonable times. Where they are kept at a place outside Ireland—as they may be—accounts and returns must be sent at intervals not exceeding six months to a place in Ireland where they must be open to inspection by the directors at all reasonable times. Such accounts and returns must disclose with reasonable accuracy the financial position of the company and enable the balance sheet and profit and loss account of the company to be prepared in accordance with the Principal Act.

There are penalties provided for directors who fail to take reasonable steps to secure compliance by the company with the requirements as to keeping books of accounts or who by their own wilful acts are the cause of the company being in default. They are liable on summary conviction to imprisonment for a term not exceeding six months or to a fine not exceeding £500 or both.[1] But where a person is charged with failing to take reasonable steps to secure compliance, it is a defence to prove that he had reasonable ground for believing, and did believe, that a competent and reliable person was charged with the duty of seeing that the requirements were complied with and was in a position to discharge that duty. Moreover, a person may not be sentenced to imprisonment unless the court is of the opinion that the offence was committed wilfully.

1. S 147(6) of the Principal Act, as amended by s 15 of the 1982 Act.

30.06 In addition, where the company is wound up, there are provisions for penalties if proper books of account have not been kept. Section 296 of the Principal Act provides that is such books have not been kept throughout the period of two years immediately preceding the commencement of the winding up, or the period between the incorporation of the company and its winding up, if that is shorter, every officer in default is liable to penalties. He is liable on conviction on indictment to imprisonment for a term not exceeding two years or to a fine not exceeding £2,500 or to both or on summary conviction to imprisonment for a term not exceeding six months or to a fine not exceeding £500 or to both. It is a defence if the officer shows that he acted honestly and that in the circumstances in which the business of the company was being carried on, the default was excusable.

For the purposes of this section, there is a more detailed definition of what is meant by 'proper books of account'. They must include
  (a) books containing entries from day to day in sufficient detail of all cash received and cash paid;
  (b) where the trade or business has involved dealings in goods, statements of the annual stocktaking and (except for ordinary retail sales) goods sold and purchased, giving details of the buyers and sellers sufficient to identify them or enable them to be identified.

As we have seen, proposals for new legislation now under consideration are understood to include provisions imposing personal liability for the debts of an insolvent company on the officers where proper accounts have not been kept.[1]

1. See para 2.26 above.

30.07 Records required to be kept under s 147 must be preserved by the company for a period of six years after the dates to which they relate.

The annual accounts

30.08 The directors are required by the Principal Act to prepare, or have prepared, a balance sheet and profit and loss account which they must lay before the annual general meeting of the company. To these documents must be attached the directors' report and auditors' report. The information contained in the annual accounts must include the information specifically set out in the Sixth Schedule.

In practice, information is often provided in the annual accounts additional to that specified by the Schedule. The overriding requirement is that the balance sheet give a true and fair view of the company's affairs at its year's end and the profit and loss account a true and fair view of the profit or loss since the last accounts. This requirement may involve supplying information additional to that required by the Schedule. It may even, in very exceptional circumstances, involve departing from those requirements. However, the need so to depart will arise only rarely. Moreover, while the decision as to whether such a departure should be made is ultimately one for the directors, the auditors must also decide whether it is necessary in order to give a true and fair view before they make an unqualified report.

As we have seen, there has been no judicial definition of the expression 'true and fair' and no indication of what the distinction is between 'true' and 'fair'. There may, moreover, be more than one 'true and fair' view of any given situation. It is probably safe to say, as a general rule, that annual accounts which do not contain any material error, are not misleading in any material manner and comply with generally accepted accountancy standards will meet the 'true and fair' requirement.

Statements of Standard Accounting practice are issued from time to time by the Consultative Committee of Accounting Bodies which represents the major accountancy institutions. These statements set out approved methods of accounting for application to all financial accounts which are intended to give a true and fair view of the financial position and profit or loss. Members of the professions represented are required to use their best endeavours to ensure that these standards are observed or, where they are not, that significant departures from them are disclosed or noted in the accounts.

It should also be remembered that methods of financial accounting change from time to time. New accounting standards are issued and established standards reviewed and up dated with the object of improving them in the light of new needs and developments.

30.09   There are a number of specific items which must be disclosed in the annual accounts which are specified in the Sixth Schedule. Failure to comply with these will not necessarily mean that a 'true and fair view' has not been given. But the auditors must state in their report whether the annual accounts comply with the disclosure requirements of the Schedule and accordingly where, for any reason, particular items are not disclosed, the auditors must mention this specifically in their report.

The Schedule divides the disclosure requirements between those relating to the balance sheet and those relating to the profit and loss account. In practice, much of the disclosure is made, not on the face of the balance sheet or the profit and loss account, but in separate notes which must be treated as being an integral part of the annual accounts.

Under s 395, the Minister has power to add to the matters to be stated in the annual accounts, but so far this power has not been exercised.

The balance sheet

30.10   A company's balance sheet, as we have seen,[1] sets out the capital and reserves of the company and the manner in which they are represented by the assets of the company. It has been repeatedly emphasised that it is not designed to provide a reliable guide to the worth of a company. Essentially it is a historic document intended to indicate the extent of the investment of the shareholders in the company and how that investment has been employed. Moreover, its utility as a guide to the company's worth is further affected by the fact that, in the case of fixed assets, their value in the balance sheet may be stated at the cost of acquisition, although the current value may be higher as a result of inflation. However, the concept of prudence dictates also that such assets be written down to their realisable value if this is lower than cost.

1. Para 13.02 above.

30.11   Although these limitations on the informative nature of the balance sheet must always be borne in mind, it remains a highly important document and one in respect of which the Principal Act sets out various detailed requirements which must be observed by all companies. Again the fundamental rule is that the balance sheet must give 'a true and fair view of the state of affairs of the company as at the end of its financial year'.[1] While, as we have seen, there has been no judicial definition of the words 'true and fair'—and no indication of what the distinction is between 'true' and 'fair' in this context—it is a safe general rule that a balance sheet which observes accepted accountancy standards will be regarded as complying with this particular requirement of the Acts. Those standards may, of course, change from time to time: thus, in recent years the problem already adverted to as to the effect on the valuation of assets of inflation has given rise to much discussion in accountancy circles. The Sandilands Committee in England recommended in 1975 the adoption of what has come to be called 'current cost accounting', but accounts prepared either on the current cost basis or the traditional method will comply with the requirement of the Prinicpal Act, in the case of any company.

1. S 149(1) of the Principal Act.

30.12 It is not intended to set out in detail the requirements of the Sixth Schedule, which should be consulted where necessary. Some of its more important features, however, deserve mention.

(1) *Reserves and provisions.* Reserves are one of the items in the balance sheets of companies which have tended to evoke controversy, since the manner in which these are treated can distort the company's true financial position. It is not surprising to find that the Schedule contains detailed requirements in this area.

The distinction must be observed between 'provisions' and 'reserves.' These expressions are defined by para 27 of the Sixth Schedule. Broadly, 'provisions' means any amount written off or retained by way of providing for depreciation, renewals or diminution in the value of assets, or retained by way of providing for any known liability the amount of which cannot be determined with any substantial accuracy. In this context, liability includes expenditure which has been contracted for and all disputed and contingent liabilities.

Any amount in excess of what is necessary for the requirements just mentioned is deemed to be a reserve and not a provision. Thus an amount set aside for the purchase of new property or to meet unknown contingencies would be considered as a reserve.

Unless it is restricted from doing so by the articles and provided the requirements of s 45 of the 1983 Act (which are discussed in detail in the next Chapter) are observed, a company is free to distribute by way of dividend part or all of its reserves. However, in practice most companies retain some or all of the reserves for future working capital requirements and to provide a safety net should the company get into difficulties.

(2) *Fixed and current assets.* The Schedule requires these to be distinguished in the balance sheet. This can present difficulties, since different views may be taken as to whether particular assets should properly be regarded as fixed or current. Thus, investments in property may be treated as fixed assets by some companies, while others may prefer to treat them as current, particularly if it is intended to realise them at an early date. The English Act of 1967 recognises this difficulty by providing for a third category of 'assets that are neither fixed or current', but there is no such provision in the Principal Act.

(3) *Value of fixed assets.* The Schedule provides that the amount of these

261

may be either their cost of acquisition or the amount based on actual valuation, less in either case the amount written off since the date of acquisition or valuation for depreciation or diminution of value.

One of the methods by which hidden reserves could be built up was by inserting an excessive figure in the balance sheet for the depreciation of fixed assets. The Schedule requires that where any amount written off or retained by way of providing for depreciation, renewals or diminution in value exceeds that which in the opinion of the directors is reasonably necessary for the purpose, the excess is to be treated as a reserve and not a provision.

Profit and loss account

30.13 The title of this document is almost self-explanatory. It is a statement of the profits or losses of the company since the last such statement, made up to a date which must not be more than nine months before the meeting at which it is presented. As we have seen, such a statement must in every case be annexed to the balance sheet and presented to the annual general meeting of the company in each year. Again the Sixth Schedule sets out detailed requirements as to the profit and loss account, which it is unnecessary to set out *in extenso*. It should, however, be noted that there is no requirement, as there is in England, to specify the turnover of the company in the profit and loss account.

Exceptions for certain companies

30.14 Certain types of companies are exempted from the general require-ments of the Sixth Schedule as to balance sheets and profit and loss accounts. First, banking and discount companies are exempted, such companies being defined as companies which satisfy the Minister that they ought to be so treated as banking and discount companies. Second, assurance companies are exempted where they are subject to the requirements of the Insurance Acts 1909 to 1983 and comply with the requirements of those Acts as to the preparation and deposit with the Minister of a balance sheet and profit and loss account. Third, companies of certain types are exempted if they belong to a class prescribed for that purpose by the Minister.

Other requirements as to accounts

30.15 The Principal Act requires certain documents to be annexed to the balance sheet.[1] They are:
  (1) the profit and loss account;
  (2) a report by the directors; and
  (3) the auditor's report.
The directors' report is 'on the state of the company's affairs', and it must state the amount (if any) which they recommend should be paid by way of dividend and the amount (if any) which they propose to carry to reserves. It must also deal, so far as is material to the appreciation of the state of the company's affairs, with any change during the year in the nature of the company's business or the business of any of its subsidiaries or in the classes of business in which the company has an interest. It must also contain a list of

the company's subsidiaries and of companies in which the company has a shareholding in excess of 20 per cent carrying voting rights. The report must be signed on behalf of the directors by two of their number.

If a director fails to take all reasonable steps to comply with the requirements of the Principal Act as to the report, he is liable on summary conviction to imprisonment for a term not exceeding six months or to a fine not exceeding £500.[2] It is a defence for the director to prove that he had reasonable ground to believe and did believe that a competent and reliable person was charged with the duty of seeing that the provisions of the Act were complied with and was in a position to discharge that duty. Moreover, a person may not be sentenced to imprisonment unless the court is of the opinion that the offence was committed wilfully.

1. S 157 of the Principal Act.
2. S 158(7) of the Principal Act, as amended by s 15, of the 1982 Act.

30.16 The Principal Act also requires particulars of the directors' salaries and other payments to them to be given in the accounts or in a statement annexed thereto.[1] The particulars required are:

(1) the aggregate amount of the directors' emoluments;
(2) the aggregate amount of directors' or past directors' pensions;
(3) the aggregate amount of any compensation to directors or past directors for loss of office.

'Emoluments' includes sums paid by way of expenses allowances insofar as those sums are charged to income tax. They also include benefits received by directors otherwise than in cash (which must be valued in money terms) and contributions paid in respect of them to pension schemes. The sums paid by way of compensation for loss of office which must be shown in the accounts include sums paid in respect of the loss of any office in the company and in any subsidiary.

Particulars of the relevant salaries and other payments must be given whether the sums are paid by the company, its subsidiaries or any other person. If the requirements of the Acts are not met, the auditors must include in their report, so far as they reasonably can, a statement giving the necessary particulars.

1. S 191 of the Principal Act.

30.17 The Principal Act also requires particulars of loans to directors to be given in the accounts.[1] The accounts must show the amount of any loans made during the company's financial year to:

(1) any director of the company;
(2) anyone who after receiving the loan became a director during that year; and
(3) any company in which the directors (or any of them) own more than 20 per cent of the shares carrying voting rights.

The loan must be shown in the accounts whether it is made by the company itself or one of its subsidiaries, or by some other person under a guarantee or security provided by the company or a subsidiary. The requirement extends to loans repaid during the year and outstanding balances from loans in previous years must also be shown. There are exceptions for loans made in the ordinary course of business by a company whose business includes the lending of money and loans not exceeding £2,000 made by companies to their employees in accordance with a standard practice.

Where these requirements are not met in the accounts, the auditors must give the particulars (so far as they reasonably can) in their report.

1. Section 192, Principal Act.

30.18 The directors are also obliged to give notice in writing to the company of such matters as may be necessary for the purpose of enabling the company to give particulars in the accounts of salaries and other payments to directors and of loans to directors.[1]

1. Section 193, Principal Act.

30.19 Every balance sheet and profit and loss account of a company must be signed on behalf of the directors by two of the directors. Where it is either issued, circulated or published unsigned, the company and every officer in default is liable to a fine not exceeding £500. This does not preclude the company, however, from issuing, publishing or circulating a fair and accurate summary of the balance sheet and profit and loss account where the full document has been signed.[1]

1. Section 156 Principal Act, as amended by s 15 of the 1982 Act.

Group accounts

30.20 The requirement that a public company should send copies of its accounts to the Registrar with the annual return imposed by the 1908 Act was rendered significantly less effective by the fact that no such obligation rested on a private company which was a subsidiary of the public company. This anomaly was first tackled in England in 1929 but it was not until the enactment of the Principal Act that there was any attempt to deal with the problem in Ireland. That Act required *holding companies*, as they are called, to incorporate in their own published accounts the financial position and results of their *subsidiaries*, i.e. companies which are effectively owned or controlled by the holding company. These *group accounts*, as they are called, must normally take the form of consolidated accounts showing the state of affairs of the entire group comprising the holding company and all its subsidiaries.

The significance of these requirements in Ireland is somewhat reduced by the fact that private companies which are holding companies are not required to prepare group accounts. This is in accordance with the recommendation of Cox and is not illogical, having regard to the exemption of private companies from the requirement to send accounts to the Registrar with the annual return. However, such private companies must in practice comply with the Statement of Standard Accountancy Practice relating to group accounts. Moreover, since it is virtually certain that the total exemption of private companies from the obligation to send accounts to the Registrar will end when legislation complying with the Fourth Directive is enacted,[1] it may be assumed that they will then be subjected also, to some degree at least, to an obligation to prepare group accounts.

1. See para 30.01 above.

30.21 In general terms, a company is regarded as the subsidiary of another company if it is either owned or controlled by that company. Section 155 of the Principal Act sets out the specific circumstances in which a company is regarded as a subsidiary for the purpose of the Acts. A company is treated as a subsidiary of another company if any one of the following conditions is met:

(1) the other company is a member of it and controls the composition of its board of directors;

(2) the other company holds more than half in nominal value of its equity share capital;

(3) the other company holds more than half in nominal value of its shares carrying voting rights.

In addition, where the company is a subsidiary of another company which is in turn a subsidiary of a third company, the company is also a subsidiary of the third company.

The expression 'equity share capital' has a special meaning for the purposes of the section. It refers to the issued share capital excluding any part of it which does not carry the right to participate beyond a specified amount in a distribution whether of capital or by way of dividend. Thus preference shares entitling the holder to no more than a fixed dividend would not form part of the equity share capital for this purpose.

There are special provisions dealing with shares held in a fiduciary capacity or by nominees.

30.22 In certain circumstances a holding company may be dispensed from some or all of the requirements as to group accounts. Where it is itself a wholly owned subsidiary of another company, it need not present group accounts at all. Moreover, the accounts need not deal with a subsidiary of the company if the directors are of the opinion that

(1) it is impractical or would be of no real value to the members of the company, in view of the insignificant amounts involved, or would involve expense or delay out of proportion to the value to members of the company, or

(2) the result would be misleading.

Where the directors are of this opinion in relation to all the subsidiaries, there is no obligation to present group accounts at all.[1] However, there may be a requirement under Standard Accounting Practice to prepare group accounts for the accounts to give a true and fair view.

Where a company does not prepare group accounts it remains under an obligation to give certain information as to its subsidiaries in its accounts. These requirements are set out in the Sixth Schedule and can be summarised as follows:

(1) the reasons why subsidiaries are not dealt with in group accounts;

(2) so far as it concerns members of the holding company, the net aggregate amount of the subsidiaries' profits after deducting their losses (or vice versa) for the financial year ending with that of the holding company, both so far as they are dealt with in the holding company's accounts and are not dealt with;

(3) similar information to that contained in (2) in respect of previous years;

(4) any qualification in the auditors' reports on the subsidiaries' accounts (or note or saving in the accounts themselves which otherwise would properly have appeared as a qualification) relating to a matter not covered in the holding company's accounts and material to its members;

(5) if any of the information at (1) to (4) is not obtainable, a statement to that effect.

Where the group accounts do not deal with a subsidiary, any member of the holding company is entitled to be furnished without charge with a copy of the latest balance sheet of the subsidiary sent to its members (together with the documents which must be annexed to it) within 14 days of requesting it. If any copy required is not sent within the specified time, the company and every officer in default is liable to a fine not exceeding £500. The court may also direct copies to be sent to the member requiring them.[2]

1. S 150(2)(b) of the Principal Act.
2. S 150(3) of the Principal Act, as amended by s 15 of the 1982 Act.

30.23 Where a director fails to take all reasonable steps to secure compliance by a company with its obligation to prepare and present group accounts, he is liable on a summary conviction to imprisonment for a term not exceeding six months or a fine not exceeding £500 or both. It is a defence, however, to prove that he had reasonable grounds for believing, and did believe, that a competent and reliable person was charged with the duty of complying with these requirements and was in a position to discharge that duty. Nor may a person be sentenced to imprisonment unless the court is of the opinion that the offence was committed wilfully.[1]

The form of the group accounts must be that of consolidated accounts, i.e. accounts in which the assets and liabilities, profits and losses of the subsidiary companies and the holding company are grouped together under the appropriate headings. If the company's directors are, however, of the opinion that it will better serve the purpose of presenting the same, or equivalent information, or its better appreciation, they may prepare group accounts in a form other than consolidated accounts.[2]

1. S 150(4) of the Principal Act, as amended by s 15 of the 1982 Act.
2. S 151 of the Principal Act.

30.24 The holding company's directors are required to ensure that, except where there are good reasons against it, the financial years of each of its subsidiaries are to coincide with the company's own financial year. The Minister has power on the application or with the consent of the directors to direct that the holding of an annual general meeting, the making of the return and the submission of the accounts to the meeting be postponed from one calendar year to the next with a view to enabling the subsidiary's financial year to end with that of its holding company. A director who fails to take all reasonable steps to secure compliance by the company with the requirements as to the financial year is liable on summary conviction to a fine not exceeding £250.[1]

1. S 153 of the Principal Act, as amended by s 15 of the 1982 Act.

30.25 A private company which is a holding company need not prepare group accounts.[1] If it does not do so, however, it must furnish any member of the company who has requested it with a copy of the latest balance sheet of each of its subsidiaries which has been sent to the members of that subsidiary. The copy must be furnished without charge to the member within 14 days after he has requested it. There must be annexed to the balance sheet a copy of every document required to be annexed thereto (such as the profit and loss account) and the directors' and auditors' reports. In addition, any member of the holding company is entitled to be furnished within 14 days after he has made a request to that effect with the copies of balance sheets and annexed documents of any subsidiary laid before any annual general meeting held since 1 April 1964, the date the Principal Act came into force. The company may not charge the member more than 10p but the member is not entitled to be furnished with the balance sheet laid before an annual general meeting held more than ten years before the request. The company need not send copies of balance sheets to members if on the application of the company or any person claiming to be aggrieved, the court is satisfied that the rights in question are being abused and the court may also order the company's costs to be paid by the member making the request. If the copy requested is not sent within the proper time, the company and every officer in default is liable to a fine not exceeding £500.[2]

1. S 154 of the Principal Act.
2. S 154(5) of the Principal Act, as amended by s 15 of the 1982 Act.

Auditors: appointment, removal and remuneration

30.26 Every company must appoint an auditor or auditors at each annual general meeting to hold office until the next annual general meeting. The first auditors may be appointed by the directors at any time before the first annual general meeting and hold office until the conclusion of that meeting. The company may, however, remove such auditors at a general meeting and substitute for them persons who have been nominated for appointment by any member of the company and of whose nomination notice has been given to the members not less than 14 days before the date of the meeting. If the directors fail to exercise their powers to appoint the first auditors, the company may appoint them in general meeting and thereupon the directors' powers to appoint auditors cease.[1]

At every annual general meeting a retiring auditor, however appointed, must be re-appointed without any resolution being passed unless
(1) he is not qualified for re-appointment; or
(2) a resolution has been passed at that meeting appointing someone instead of him or providing expressly that he is not to be re-appointed; or
(3) he has given the company notice in writing of his unwillingness to be re-appointed.[2]

Extended notice—i.e. at least 28 days' notice[3]_must be given of a resolution at the annual general meeting proposing the appointment of someone other than the retiring auditors as auditor or providing expressly that a retiring auditor shall not be appointed. Where notice of such a resolution is given, the retiring auditor is given certain rights to be heard in his own defence by the meeting. The company must send him a copy of the resolution, and he may then make representations in writing (which cannot be unreasonably lengthy) to the company and request that the members of the company be notified of them. Where he avails of this right, the company must state that the representations have been received in the notice given to the members of the resolution. The company must also send a copy of the representations to every member of the company to whom notice of the meeting is sent. If a copy of the representations is not sent out because it is received too late or because of the company's default, the auditors may require them to be read out at the meeting.[4]

Where notice is given of an intended resolution to appoint some person in place of a retiring auditor and for some reason the resolution cannot be proceded with, e.g. the death of that person, the retiring auditor is not automatically re-appointed.

There is provision for an application to the court to prevent the retiring auditor's rights to make representations being abused. Where the court is satisfied that the rights are being used to secure 'needless publicity for defamatory matter', the representations need not be sent out or read at the meeting and the auditor may be ordered to pay the company's costs of the application.[5]

The directors may fill casual vacancies in the office of auditor, but while any vacancy continues, the surviving auditor or auditors may continue to act. Where at an annual general meeting no auditors are appointed or re-appointed, the Minister may appoint a person to fill the vacancy.[6]

1. S 160 of the Principal Act.
2. S 160(2) of the Principal Act.
3. See para 2 5.13 above.
4. S 161 of the Principal Act.
5. S 161(4) of the Principal Act.
6. S 160(4) of the Principal Act.

30.27   Where an auditor is appointed by the directors or the Minister, his remuneration is fixed by the directors or the Minister as the case may be. In all other cases, his remuneration must be fixed by the company in general meeting or in such manner as the company at the annual general meeting may determine. It is common practice for the annual general meeting to resolve that the auditors' remuneration be fixed by the directors.

Qualifications for appointment as auditor

30.28   The requirements as to an auditor's qualifications are set out in s 162 of the Principal Act as substituted by s 6 of the 1982 Act. It provides that a person shall not be qualified for appointment as an auditor of a company unless

(1) he is a member of a body of accountants recognised for the purpose by the Minister; or

(2) he is authorised by the Minister to be appointed an auditor either

    (i) as having obtained similar qualifications otherwise than from such a body, or

   (ii) as having obtained adequate knowledge and experience, prior to 1 April 1964 in the course of his employment by, or under the supervision of, a member of a recognised body of accountants; or

  (iii) as having, prior to 1 April 1964, practised in Ireland as an accountant.

Applications for an authorisation by the Minister had to be made not later than 3 November 1983 and this procedure is accordingly spent. The only persons now qualified are members of recognised bodies of accountants and persons who were authorised by the Minister pursuant to applications made prior to that date.

The bodies which have been recognised by the Minister are:

(a) The Institute of Chartered Accountants in Ireland;
(b) The Institute of Chartered Accountants in England and Wales;
(c) The Institute of Chartered Accountants of Scotland;
(d) The Institute of Cost and Management Accountants;
(e) The Chartered Association of Certified Accountants.

30.29   The following categories are disqualified from acting as auditors:

(a) officers and servants of the company (which would include the directors and secretary);

(b) except where the company is a private company, partners of, or persons in the employment of, an officer or servant of the company,[1]

(c) persons who are disqualified from acting as auditors of a company's holding company or one or more of its subsidiaries;

(d) bodies corporate.

1. The important saving for a private company should be noted. It was accepted at the committee stage of the bill as the result of urgent representations from some deputies as to the financial burdens which might otherwise be placed on small firms.

Status and duties of auditors

30.30 It has been held in England that an auditor appointed under the section corresponding to s 160 of the Principal Act is an 'officer' of the company.[1] It would seem, however, that while he may be regarded as an agent of the company when carrying out his duties under the Acts, such as the audit, he is not an agent for other purposes.[2]

1. *R v Shacter* [1960] 2 Q B 252
2. *Re Transplanters (Holding Companies) Ltd* [1958] 2 All ER 711.

30.31 The statutory duty of the auditors is to make a report to the members on the accounts examined by them, and on every balance sheet, profit and loss account and all group accounts laid before the company in general meeting during their term of office.[1] The matters which must be dealt with are set out in the Seventh Schedule to the Principal Act. The auditors must state:

(1) whether they have obtained all the information and explanations which to the best of their knowledge and belief were necessary for the purposes of the audit;

(2) whether, in their opinion, proper books of account have been kept by the company, so far as appears from their examination of those books, and proper returns adequate for the purposes of their audit have been received from branches not visited by them.

(3) whether the company's balance sheet and (unless it is framed as a consolidated profit and loss account) profit and loss account dealt with by the report are in agreement with the books of account and returns.

(4) whether, in their opinion and to the best of their information and according to the explanations given to them, the accounts give the information required by the Acts in the manner so required and give a true and fair view

    (a) in the case of the balance sheet of the state of the company's affairs as at the end of its financial year; and

    (b) in the case of the profit and loss account, of the profit or loss for its financial year

or, as the case may be, give a true and fair view thereof subject to the non-disclosure (which must be indicated in the report) of any matters which are not required to be disclosed in the case of banking and discount companies, assurance companies and other companies prescribed by the Minister.[2]

(5) in the case of a company which is a holding company and which submits group accounts whether, in their opinion the group accounts have

been properly prepared in accordance with the Acts so as to give a true and fair view of the state of affairs and profit or loss of the company and its subsidiaries dealt with thereby, so far as concerns members of the company, or as the case may be, so as to give a true and fair view thereof subject to the non-disclosure (which must be indicated in the report) of any matters which are not required to be disclosed in the case of banking and discount companies etc.

If the auditors are not satisfied as to any of these matters, it is their duty to make their reservations clear by making the relevant statement subject to an appropriate qualification. In deciding whether any statement should be qualified, the auditors must use their own judgment and express their own opinion: if they do so and for that purpose use the skill and care which might reasonably be expected of them as competent and careful auditors, they will have performed their statutory duty.[3]

In modern circumstances more will frequently be expected of auditors than the statutory minimum: it is now standard practice, for example, for them to furnish a commentary on the company's finances to the directors.

1. S 163 of the Principal Act.
2. See para 30.14 above.
3. Palmer, vol I, 73-06.

30.32 The auditor's responsibility is an onerous one. But, in the celebrated phrase of Lopes LJ, the law treats the auditor as 'a watchdog, not a bloodhound'[1] He must ensure that there are not errors in the accounts and that they are not in any way misleading. But he is not a detective and is not expected to approach the audit on the assumption that the company has been dishonestly managed. Perhaps the most acceptable modern statement of his responsibility is by Lord Denning:

'His vital task is to take care to see that errors be not made, be they errors of computation, or errors of omission or commission, or downright untruths. To perform this task properly he must come to it with an inquiring mind—not suspicious of dishonesty, I agree—but suspecting that someone may have made a mistake somewhere and that a check must be made to ensure that there has been none.'[2]

Thus in *Thomas Gerrard & Sons Ltd,*[3] auditors were held liable where a managing director had falsified the accounts by altering invoices and the auditors, having come across the altered invoices, failed to make sufficiently exhaustive inquiries.

The auditor is required to perform his duty with reasonable skill and care. The standard expected of him is that which would be expected of any careful and competent auditor. In modern circumstances, where both accountancy and auditing practices have become stricter, this may involve a different standard in specific areas than is suggested by the older English authorities. Thus, while Lopes LJ in the case already referred to, said that it was not the duty of the auditor to take stock—'he is not a stock expert'[4]—this would have to be treated with some caution today where a more vigilant role is expected of auditors in relation to stock-taking. Today they are expected to attend at the stock taking and make tests of the stock count and valuation.[5]

1. *Re Kingston Cotton Mill Co (No 2)* [1896] 2 Ch 27 9 at 288.
2. *Fomento (Sterling Area) Ltd v Selsdon Fountain Co* [1958] 1 All ER11.
3. [1968] Ch 455.
4. At p 289.
5. Palmer, Vol I, 73.07.

Rights of auditors

30.33 For the purpose of carrying out his duties, the auditor has a right of access at all reasonable times to the books, accounts and vouchers of the company. He is also entitled to require from the officers of the company such information and explanations as he thinks necessary for the performance of those duties. He is also entitled to attend any general meeting of the company and has the same right to receive notices and other communications relating to general meetings as the members. He is entitled to be heard at any general meeting which he attends on any part of the business which concerns him as auditor.[1]

The rights conferred by the Acts on auditors in this area cannot under any circumstances be modified or abrogated by the memorandum and articles.

1. S 163 of the Principal Act.

Liability of auditors

30.34 Where the auditor fails to perform his duties with reasonable skill and care he will be liable to the company for any damages which it may sustain as a result of his negligence.

It is also clear, in the light of modern decisions, that the auditor will be liable to any other persons who suffer damage as a result of his negligence and whom he should reasonably have anticipated would rely on his skill and care. Prior to the decision of the House of Lords in *Hedley Byrne & Co v Heller and Partners*,[1] it had been thought that an action for damages for a negligent misstatement could only be maintained by persons to whom the person making the statement owed a duty in contract or a fiduciary duty. That decision established that the liability was not so confined: if it could be shown that the person seeking information or advice was trusting the author of the statement to exercise such a degree of care as the circumstances required, where it was reasonable for him to do that, and the author of the statement made it when he knew or ought to have known that the enquirer was relying on him, the author could be liable in damages for negligence in making the statement. In *John Sisk & Son Ltd v Flinn*,[2] Finlay P made it clear that this principle applies to auditors in circumstances when they should reasonably anticipate that their skill and care in the auditing of accounts are being relied on by a prospective purchaser or investor. (In that particular case, he found that there was no evidence of negligence on the part of the auditors.) Accordingly, where a prospective purchaser or investor suffers damage as a result of a want of reasonable skill and care on the part of auditors in such circumstances, the auditor may be liable.

1. [1964] AC 465.
2. Unreported; judgment delivered 18 July 1984.

30.35 How much further the liability of auditors extends has not been judicially decided in Ireland or England, but the view has been expressed in the latter jurisdiction that

'the auditors' report will not normally involve them in liability to outsiders or to individual members who might invest in the company or otherwise act in reliance upon any incorrect statement therein, as it has not been legally recognised that annual accounts are prepared with this purpose in view.'[1]

It should be remembered, however, that there has been in recent years a wide ranging extension in the ambit of persons to whom the duty of care in tort may be owed, reflected in such decisions as *Dutton v Bognor Regis Building Co*[2] and *Anns v Merton London Borough Council*[3] which have been applied by the Supreme Court in *Siney v Dublin Corporation*.[4] These decisions appear to recognise a potential liability on the part of those who issue certificates of a particular character on which a relatively undefined category of person may rely, such as certificates by local authorities as to the safety of foundations. It may be argued in the future that if a purchaser of whose existence the local authority was unaware when it issued a certificate to a builder can successfully sue the authority where the relevant inspection was carried out negligently, there is no reason in principle why an auditor who issues a misleading report following a negligent audit may not be similarly liable to a prospective investor who relies on that report, even though he had no reason to anticipate that the accounts were being audited for anything other than the usual statutory reasons. It remains to be seen whether the courts would entertain such a far reaching extension of liability so far as auditors are concerned.

1. Palmer, vol, I, para 73.10.
2. [1972] 1 QB 373.
3. [1978] AC 728.
4. [1980] IR 400.

Chapter 31

Dividends and distribution of profits

31.01 We have seen that one of the rights of a shareholder is to be given a share of the company's profits at periodical intervals in the form of a money payment called a *dividend*. The payment of dividends is generally regulated by the memorandum and articles; but there are also certain legal principles applicable which are explained in this chapter. In particular, it is a fundamental principle that dividends cannot be paid out of the capital of the company, since this would have as its consequence an unauthorised reduction of the company's capital.

31.02 It follows that dividends can only be paid out of the *profits* of the company. But it does not follow that whenever the company makes a profit, the shareholder is automatically entitled to a dividend: the company may decide not to distribute some or all of its profits in particular year but instead to carry them to its reserves. A distinction has to be drawn, accordingly, between profits which are *available for dividend* and those which are not.

31.03 These rules governing the payment of dividends might seem reasonably straightforward. Their application in practice, however, was not so simple; in particular there was room for a wide difference of opinion as to what were profits *available for distribution*. If a company sold some of its *circulating* or *current assets*. e.g. its stock in trade, for more than they cost, the surplus was usually a profit available for distribution. But what of the sale of a *fixed asset*, e.g. a factory building? Was the surplus on such a sale a profit available for distribution? If it was, did the same result follow when there was no sale and the asset was simply revalued in the balance sheet: could such an *unrealised capital profit*, as it was called, be treated as a profit available for distribution? There were also difficulties in determining what were fixed assets and what were current assets: shares held by an investment company, for example, might reasonably be regarded as coming within either category.

There was also the question of losses from previous years and how they were to be dealt with. Could a company take its accounting year in isolation and simply set off profits against losses in that year without taking into account losses made in previous years before calculating the amount available for distribution?

31.04 The answers to many of the questions posed in the last paragraph will be found in the 1983 Act. Part IV of that Act under the heading *'Restrictions on distributions of profits and assets'* contains important new provisions in this area. In general, they are intended to implement the relevant requirements of the Second EEC Directive which was concerned, as we have seen, with the maintenance of companies of their capital.[1]

1. See para 2.22 above.

General power of company to pay dividends

31.05 Every company has an implied power to apply its profits to the distribution of dividends among its members. Such a power exists, in other words, whether or not it is conferred on the company by its memorandum or articles.[1] It does not follow, however, that a company *must* apply its profits for that purpose; as we have seen, it is perfectly entitled to carry some or all of its profits to reserves or to provide for contingencies.

1. See para 17.03 above.

31.06 The articles usually provide in what proportion dividends are to be paid as between members. As we have seen, the company is normally given power to issue preference shares which entitle the holders to the payment of a dividend—usually of a fixed percentage of the profits available for distribution—in priority to the other shareholders. Subject to any special provisions of this nature, the shareholders are entitled to participate in the profits of the company in proportion to their respective interests therein. The better view appears to be that this means in proportion to the amount actually paid up on their shares and not in proportion to the nominal value of the shares.[1]

1. Palmer, vol I, 75.02.

Declaration of dividend

31.07 A dividend does not become payable to the shareholder unless it is *declared* by one of the organs of the company.[1] There is no requirement in the Acts as to which organ is to declare the dividend, but the usual practice is to provide in the articles that it is to be declared by the company in general meeting and is not to exceed such amount as is recommended by the directors (article 116). In addition, the directors are usually empowered to pay such *interim* dividends as appear to them to be justified from the profits of the company. Such an interim dividend is to be distinguished from the *final* dividend declared by the company at its annual general meeting.

1. See para 17.03 above.

31.08 As we have seen, a dividend is only payable out of profits available for distribution, and any provision in the articles to the contrary is of no effect. In practice, the articles usually provide expressly that dividends are payable only out of profits (article 118).

Enforcing the payment of dividends

31.09 When the dividend is declared, it becomes a liability of the company and the shareholder may recover the amount by action if it remains unpaid.[1] The limitation period under the Statute of Limitations 1957 is six years from the date on which the dividend is declared and not twelve years, since it is a simple contract debt as distinct from a specialty debt.[2] If the company is wound up, a dividend in arrears has no priority over other simple contract debts.[3]

1. *Re Severn and Wye and Severn Bridge Co Rly* [1896] 1 Ch 559.
2. *Re Compania de Electricidad de la Provincia de Buenos Aires Ltd* [1978] 3 All ER 668.
3. As to preferences shares, see para 17.08 above.

Apportionment of dividends

31.10 The provisions of the Apportionment Act 1870 apply to dividends. It follows that when there is a transmission—e.g. on the death of the shareholder—during a period in respect of which dividends are subsequently paid, the dividends will be apportioned. If, for example, a shareholder leaves his shares to AB and the residue of his estate to CD, AB will be entitled to the dividends as from the date of death—from which date the will speaks—but the portion prior to the death will belong to the CD as part of the residue. It is always possible, of course, for a testator or settlor to exclude apportionment by the express terms of the will or settlement.

Dividend warrants

31.11 Payment of dividends in the case of a public company is usually made by a *dividend warrant* in the form of a printed cheque drawn on the company's bank. Tax is deducted by the company before paying the dividend, but the warrant usually has attached to it an advice note which can be presented to the Revenue Commissioners to support a claim for the refund of any tax to which the shareholder may be entitled.

Dividend mandates

31.12 It is a common practice for public companies to-day to encourage the payment of dividends directly to the shareholder's bank. This is done by a *dividend mandate* in a standard form which is signed by the shareholder and authorises the payment of the dividend into the shareholder's bank account.

Scrip dividend

31.13 A company may offer its shareholders a choice between a cash dividend and a *scrip dividend*. If the shareholder opts for the latter, he is allotted an appropriate number of ordinary shares in the company in lieu of the dividend and the shares are treated as fully paid up. In times of inflation, it is an attractive option for a shareholder and it has also advantages for the company since it eases its liquid cash position and increases its capital.

Dividends must not be paid out of capital

31.14 This, as we have seen, is a fundamental rule. It does not, however, mean that the company may only pay dividends out of profits earned in the current year. If profits have been accumulated as such—i.e. carried to reserve and not capitalised – the rule does not prevent the company from distributing them as dividend. What it does mean is that the company is precluded from paying a dividend which would be in excess of the available reserves and hence cause a loss of capital. It does not mean that losses of capital sustained in the ordinary course of business must be replaced before a dividend is declared.

Restrictions on the distributions of profits and assets

31.15   Not all 'profits' are profits available for distribution. There was formerly some uncertainty as to what were profits so available. The 1983 Act, implementing the Second EEC Directive and closely modelled on the English Act now sets out detailed requirements in this area. The Act prohibits the making of a distribution except out of profits available for that purpose and goes on to set out criteria for determining what are such profits.

It must be borne in mind that a 'distribution' of profits may take forms other than the payment of dividends and 'distribution' is accordingly specially defined. Section 51 provides that it means every distribution of a company's assets, whether in cash or otherwise, except

(1) an issue of fully or partly paid up bonus shares;

(2) the redemption of preference shares;

(3) a reduction of the share capital authorised under s 72 of the Principal Act; and

(4) a distribution of assets on a winding up.

31.16   A company's profits available for distribution within this special meaning are 'its accumulated, realised profits....less its accumulated realised losses....'[1] The profits, however, may not include profits previously utilised either by distribution or capitalisation. The realised losses do not include amounts previously written off in a reduction or reorganisation of the capital.

It will be noted that it is only *realised* profits which are available. The Principal Act provides that a capital surplus arising on a revaluation of unrealised fixed assets is not available for distribution.[2] A *realised* profit arising from the actual sale of capital assets is, however, available for distribution, provided the profit has not been previously utilised either by a distribution or a capitalisation.

Some modifications of the principles laid down by these new provisions must next be noted.

(1) Where fixed assets are revalued and a surplus arises, the difference between the depreciation charge based on the revalued amount and the depreciation charge based on the cost may be treated as available for distribution. For example, machinery belonging to the company originally costs £100,000 and is being depreciated at the rate of £20,000 annually. At the beginning of the third year, the machinery is revalued to £75,000 and the annual depreciation charge is revised to £25,000 for the remaining three years. The company is entitled to treat £5,000 (being the additional depreciation each year) as available for distribution.

(2) In determining whether a company has made a profit or loss in respect of a particular asset, the company may be in the difficulty that it has no record of its original cost: where this is the case, or where such a record cannot be obtained without unreasonable expense and delay, the cost of

276

the asset is taken to be the earliest recorded valuation available after its acquisition by the company.[4]

1. S 45(2).
2. S 149(6) of the Principal Act.
3. S 45(6).
4. S 45(7)

31.17 'Realised losses' must next be considered. Obviously a debit balance on the profit and loss account is a 'realised loss'. In addition, s 45(4) states that, subject to one important proviso, any amount written off or retained for depreciation, diminution or renewal of assets or retained as a provision for known but unquantifiable liabilities is to be treated as a realised loss. Such amounts accordingly must be treated as losses in determining the amount available for distribution and they include not only the current losses but also the accumulated losses from previous years.

The exception arises where there is a revaluation of *all* the fixed assets—or all the fixed assets other than goodwill—and provision is made for the diminution in value of any of the assets: Such a diminution in value need not be treated as a realised loss. Moreover, even when there is not a revaluation as such of *all* the assets, but the directors have at least *considered* the value of each asset, the exception applies, with an important proviso: the directors must be satisfied that the aggregate value of the assets at least equals their value as stated in the accounts. Subject to that proviso, a fixed asset may be written down in the books and not give rise to a realised loss, without the necessity for a full revaluation of all the fixed assets of the company.

Restrictions on public limited companies

31.18 When a company's assets exceed its liabilities, the balancing figure on the liabilities side, as we have seen,[1] consists of the called up share capital and reserves of the company (if reserves have been accumulated). If the surplus of the assets over liabilities is *less* than the called up share capital, it might seem contrary to principle for the company to declare a dividend. It was, however, the law prior to the 1983 Act that a company could legitimately pay a dividend in such circumstances since the share capital, although appearing on the liabilities side of the balance sheet, was not a liability of the company. Now, however, a public limited company is prohibited by Part IV of the 1983 Act from making a distribution unless the amount of its net assets (i.e. its aggregate assets less its aggregate liabilities) equals or exceeds the aggregate of its called up share capital and undistributable reserves and the distribution does not reduce the amount of those assets to less than the aggregate. This again is in pursuance of the objective of the EEC Directive which, as we have seen, is concerned with the maintenance by companies of their capital.

'Undistributable reserves' in this context means:
(1) the share premium account;[2]
(2) the capital redemption reserve fund;[3]
(3) the amount by which the company's accumulated, unrealised profits – so far as not capitalised—exceed its accumulated, unrealised losses so far as not previously written off in a reduction or reorganisation of capital;
(4) any other reserve which the company is prohibited either by statute or its memorandum or articles from distributing.

1. Para 13.05 above.
2. See para 13.11 above.
3. See para 13.12 above.

31.19 An investment company, i.e. one which does not carry on business in the ordinary sense, but simply holds and manages shares or other interests in property for the benefit of its members, may be prohibited by its memorandum or articles from distributing any capital profit, such as a profit on the sale of shares held by it. Where such an investment company is a public limited company, it would be subject to the same limitations on distributing its profits as any other public limited company, although it is subject to a special limitation not applicable to other trading companies, i.e. that it cannot distribute the profits of its trade such as profits on the sale of shares. Special treatment is accordingly provided in s 47 for such a company: it may make a distribution out of the accumulated realised 'revenue' profits less the accumulated 'revenue' losses, realised or unrealised, provided its assets are at least fifty per cent, greater than its liabilities and that the distribution does not reduce its assets below that figure.

In order to qualify as an 'investment company' for this purpose, the company must meet certain conditions:

(1) it must have given notice in writing which has not been revoked to the Registrar of its intention to carry on business as an investment company;

(2) the company's business since the date of the notice must have consisted of investing its funds mainly in securities with the aim of spreading the investment risk and giving the members the benefit of the results of the management of its funds;

(3) the company's investments after the date of the notice in any company (other than another investment company) must not have been more than 15 per cent in value of its entire investment;

(4) the company must not have retained since the date of the notice more than 15 per cent of its income from securities in respect of any financial year except in accordance with Part IV of the 1983 Act;

(5) the company must since the date of the notice have been prohibited by its memorandum or articles from distributing its capital profits.

An investment company may not make a distribution under s 47 unless

(1) the company's shares are listed on a recognised stock exchange;

(2) the company has not made a distribution of capital profits or applied any unrealised profits or capital profits, whether realised or unrealised, in paying up debentures or amounts unpaid on its issued share capital during the year immediately preceding the financial year in which the distribution is proposed to be made.

The 'relevant accounts' under the 1983 Act

31.20 In order to determine whether a distribution may be made in accordance with Part IV of the 1983 Act, and if so the amount, regard must be had to 'relevant items' in the 'relevant accounts'. The relevant accounts, as defined by s 49, are primarily the last annual accounts, i.e. the accounts prepared in accordance with the Principal Act in respect of the last financial year in which accounts so prepared were laid. Where, however, the distribution is contrary to Part IV by reference only to the last annual accounts, the relevant accounts are such accounts (called 'interim accounts') which are necessary to enable a reasonable judgement to be made as to the amount of any of the relevant items. Finally, if the relevant distribution is to be made during the company's first financial year or before any accounts are laid in respect of that financial year, the relevant acounts are such accounts as are similarly necessary (in this instance called 'initial accounts').

31.21 There are provisions requiring that, in the case of the last annual accounts and of the initial accounts, they should have been properly prepared, that the auditors should have made their statutory report and that it should have been either unqualified or qualified only in respect of non-material items. In the case of the initial accounts, a copy of them must be delivered to the Registrar. In the case of interim accounts, they must also have been properly prepared and a copy of them delivered to the Registrar.

31.22 The 'relevant items' to be taken into account in determining whether a distribution may properly be made are profits, losses, assets, liabilities, provisions, share capital and reserves.

Consequences of unlawful distribution

31.23 Where a distribution is made by a company to one of its members in contravention of Part IV of and he knows, or has reasonable grounds for believing, that it is so made, he must repay it to the company.

Chapter 32

Mergers, arrangements, reconstructions and takeovers

32.01 Circumstances frequently arise in which a company wishes to sell its business to, or merge with, another company. Thus, company A may sell its assets and undertakings to company B, with the shareholders in company A being given shares in company B. It may also be decided to dissolve company A, leaving the business of the two companies effectively merged. Alternatively, it may be decided to form a new company, C, to whom the assets of both A and B are sold. The shareholders in A and B will be given shares in C, and A and B will then be dissolved. In this case, the two companies have simply amalgamated to form a third company.

A company may also wish to obtain control of another company by acquiring the shares—or a sufficient number of them to ensure control—from the existing shareholders, the procedure usually known as a 'takeover' bid.

There are also occasions on which a company, for various reasons, may wish to reconstruct or rearrange its share capital, although there is no question of a merger or amalgamation with another company.

Finally, there are occasions when a company may wish to come to an arrangement with its creditors for the payment of the company's debts, usually as an alternative to the company being wound up.

32.02 Mergers, arrangements, reconstructions and takeovers are an essential feature of commercial activity in free market economies and the Principal Act contains various provisions intended to facilitate them. In the case of reconstructions, we have already noted the company's power to reduce its capital with the sanction of the court,[1] to increase such capital without any sanction,[2] to vary the rights attached to shares[3] and to issue redeemable preference shares.[4] Sections 201 to 203 contain specific provisions enabling amalgamations and arrangements to be carried out with the sanction of the court. Section 260 empowers the liquidator of a company being voluntarily wound up to transfer the assets of the company to another company in exchange for shares in the other company. In this instance, the sanction of the court is not required. Finally, in the case of takeovers, s 204 provides a machinery under which a dissentient minority of the company being taken over may be compelled to sell their shares to the acquiring company, where the latter has acquired 80 per cent of the shares.

1. Para 15.08 above.
2. Para 15.03 above.
3. Para 16.10 above.
4. Para 17.10 above.

32.03 The Oireachtas has also recognised, however, that the public interest may not always be served by a merger, amalgamation or takeover. Accordingly, the Mergers, Takeovers and Monopolies (Control) Act 1978 provides for the investigation by the Examiner of Restrictive Practices of mergers and takeovers in the case of companies of a certain size and their prohibition, if it appears justified from his report, by the Minister.

Arrangements with sanction of court

32.04 When a company proposes to enter into a 'compromise or arrangement' with its creditors or its members and obtains the sanction of the court to it under s 201, the compromise or arrangement is binding on all the creditors or members. The section is rarely availed of, however, in practice.[1] If the company wishes to reconstruct for the purpose of a merger or amalgamation, this can usually be done by means of a voluntary winding up. using the powers conferred on the liquidator by s 260. This avoids the necessity for an application to the court: the major disadvantage is that, in contrast to an arrangement sanctioned under s 201, it is not necessarily binding on all the members. So far as compromises or arrangements with creditors are concerned, it would seem that companies who have reached the stage where such a course becomes a possible option will normally elect for a creditors' winding up instead.

1. Only one court order under the section was delivered for registration in the year 1982, the last for which figures are available: *Report of the Department of Trade, Commerce and Tourism 1982*: Pl 1784

32.05 Before the court sanctions an arrangement or compromise under s 201, a meeting must be held of the members (or class of members) or creditors (or class of creditors) whom it is sought to bind by the proposal. It is only if three-fourths of the members or creditors present at the meeting vote in favour of the compromise or arrangement that it may be sanctioned by the court. For this purpose, the court may order the convening of a meeting of the members or class of members or creditors or class of creditors whom it is sought to bind.

Accordingly, the company may initially have to decide which class of members or creditors will be affected by the proposal, before it applies to the court for an order convening a meeting. Normally the classes that will have to be considered in the case of a proposal affecting members are the ordinary and preference shareholders; and in the case of a proposal affecting creditors, the preferential, secured and unsecured creditors. But there may be further categories to be considered and the criterion to be applied in considering whether a particular category of members or creditors constitutes a 'class' within the meaning of the section was defined as follows by Bowen LJ in *Sovereign Life Assurance Co. v Dodd*:[1]

'It seems plain that we must give such a meaning to the term "class" as will prevent the section being so worked as to result in confiscation and injustice, and that it must be confined to those persons whose rights are not so dissimilar as to make it impossible for them to consult together with a view to their common interest'.

In *Re Pye Ireland Ltd*,[2] Costello J declined to order the convening of a meeting of the company's six classes of creditors where the proposal to be considered was being opposed by one of the creditors, i.e. the Revenue. The company intended, if sanction was given, to discontinue its business as a manufacturer and distributor of television and related equipment and to sell off land which it owned over a three year period in order to pay its various creditors. The Revenue were owed a substantial sum and objected to the scheme. Costello J took the view that the Collector-General was in a special position since the debts he was seeking to collect were owed to the state and that the court should be very slow to order the holding of a meeting to consider a scheme to which he objected.

It appears that this special position for the Revenue was disclaimed by counsel when the matter was appealed to the Supreme Court and accordingly that the court did not have to express any opinion as to the correctness of Costello J's view. It was accepted that portion of the Revenue debt, amounting to one year's taxes, was entitled to priority, but since the company was willing to pay this sum the court allowed the meetings to proceed.[3] It is thought that the decision of Costello J is open to question: there seems no basis in law for according to the Revenue any special standing as a creditor other than that afforded to them under the Principal Act as a preferential creditor in respect of certain taxes.

If the compromise or arrangement is for the purpose of, or in connection with, a scheme for the reconstruction of the company or the amalgamation of two or more companies, the court may also make provision under s 203 for

 (i) the transfer of the undertaking and of the property or liabilities of one company (called 'the transferor') to another company (called 'the transferee');
 (ii) the allotting or appropriating by the transferee of shares, debentures, policies, etc. which, under the compromise or arrangement, are to be allotted or appropriated by it to or for any person;
 (iii) the continuance of legal proceedings by or against the transferee;
 (iv) the dissolution, without winding up, of the transferor;
 (v) the provision to be made for persons who dissent from the scheme;
 (vi) such incidental or consequential matters as are necessary to secure that the reconstruction or amalgamation is carried out fully and effectually.

The application should be made by special summons.[4]

1. [1892] 2 Q B 573, at p 583.
2. Unreported; judgment delivered 12 November 1984.
3. Unreported. The judgments appear to have been extempory: cf *The Irish Times*, 23 November 23 1984.
4. Rules of the Superior Courts (No 1) 1966, SI 1966/28.

32.06 Before the meeting of members or creditors or class of members or creditors is held, the members or creditors concerned are entitled to be given certain information as to the proposed compromise or arrangement. Section 202 requires a statement to be sent with every notice summoning such a meeting explaining the effect of the compromise or arrangement. It must also state any material interests of the directors, whether as directors, members, creditors or otherwise, and the effect thereon of the compromise or arrangement. If notice is given by advertisement, it must either include such a statement or a notification of the place at which, and the manner in which, creditors or members entitled to attend may obtain copies of such a statement. Any creditor or member applying for a copy of the statement in response to the advertisement must be furnished with it free of charge.

32.07 A compromise or arrangement proposed under s 201 must not be illegal and must be within the powers of the company. Subject to this, there is no limitation on the nature of the compromise or arrangement that may be sanctioned under the section. The court must, of course, be satisfied that all the requirements of s 201 have been met. It would appear that the court must be satisfied that the scheme proposed is a reasonable one, but will not decide these issues in terms of its commercial merits, these being matters for the members or creditors.[1]

1. *Re London Chartered Bank of Australasia* [1893] 3 Ch 540.

Reconstruction by voluntary liquidation

32.08 This is a method more favoured in Ireland of effecting a merger or amalgamation of two or more companies, since it does not require any application to the court. Section 260 of the Principal Act empowers the liquidator of a company being wound up voluntarily to sell or transfer either the whole or part of its business and property to another company in exchange for shares, policies or other interests in the other company. The shares, etc are then distributed among the members of the company in liquidation. The liquidator may also enter into an alternative arrangement under which the members, instead of receiving shares etc, are permitted to participate in the profits of the company to whom the business is transferred or receive some other benefit from it.

As we have seen, a company may simply merge with another company by transferring all its assets and business to it, and may avail of s 260 for that purpose. Alternatively, two companies may decide to amalgamate and form a new company, in which case again s 260 may be employed.

Unlike s 201, no application to the court is necessary. The procedure under s 260, however, suffers from one major disadvantage which does not affect a scheme sanctioned under s 201; dissentient shareholders are not bound by the reconstruction. Moreover, the position of creditors is entirely different: as we have seen, in the case of an arrangement sanctioned under s 201, all the creditors or class of creditors will be bound. In the case of a reconstruction under s 260, the creditors are not obliged to look to the company to whom the business is transferred for payment. It is true that the company may have denuded itself of some of its assets, but the liquidator must retain sufficient to meet any creditor's claim or obtain an adequate idemnity from the transferee company.[1] The creditors are further protected by a provision that, in the event of the company being wound up by the court within 12 months of the resolution authorising a reconstruction under s 260, the latter resolution is to be of no effect unless sanctioned by the court.[2]

It is important to bear in mind that a reconstruction under s 260 can only be effected during the course of a *members' winding up*. A members' winding up differs from a *creditors'* winding up in that the former may only take place where those responsible for the management of the company's affairs—usually the directors—file a declaration of solvency. Where such a declaration is filed, the members effectively retain control of the winding up. Where no such declaration is filed, control of the winding up is effectively vested in the creditors and exercised by them in most cases through the agency of a committee of inspection. Accordingly, if the liquidator wishes to carry out a reconstruction during the course of a creditors' winding up, he will generally be unable to do so without the consent of the creditors or their committee of inspection.

1. *Pulsford v Devenish* [1903] 2 Ch 625.
2. Section 260(5) of the Principal Act.

32.09 A reconstruction under s 260 may only be carried out with the sanction of a special resolution of the company. As we have seen, if the company is ordered to be wound up within a year of the passing of the resolution, it is of no effect unless sanctioned by the court.

Where a shareholder does not vote in favour of the special resolution, and serves notice expressing his dissent from the resolution within seven days, he may require the liquidator either to abstain from carrying it into effect or to purchase his shares. It may well be impossible for the liquidator, as a matter of law, to abstain from proceeding with the scheme, and in most cases the result will be that he is obliged to purchase the shares of the dissentient member. If a price cannot be agreed, it must be determined by arbitration under the procedure laid down in the Companies Clauses Consolidation Act 1845. This provides for the appointment by each party of an arbitrator who, if they cannot agree, appoint an umpire to resolve the dispute. If the arbitrators fail to appoint an umpire, the court may do so under the Arbitration Act 1954. It would appear that the valuation should be made on the assumption that the scheme was not carried out and that the company's assets were distributed in the ordinary way to the shareholders at the end of the winding up. It may be difficult in practice for the dissentient member to establish this value, particularly as it has been held that he is not entitled to examine the company's officers and that, in the absence of fraud or proven inaccuracy, he is not entitled to discovery of the books of the company.[1]

The notice of dissent must be served at the registered office of the company. If a person does not dissent, he loses the right to be paid a fair price for his shares, but he is not obliged to accept shares in the new company. Thus, if the shares in the new company are of little value and impose certain liabilities, e.g. in relation to unpaid capital, on the members, the fact that a person has not dissented does not prevent him from refusing to accept the new shares.[2]

1. *Re British Building Stone Co Ltd* [1908] 2 Ch 450: *Re Glamorganshire Banking Co, Morgan's Case* (1885) 28 Ch D 620.
2. *Higg's Case* [1865] 2 H & M 657 at 665.

32.10 It is clear that any provision in a memorandum or articles which purports to deprive a member of his statutory right to dissent from a reconstruction under s 260 is void. It is also clear that the court will not allow the rights of dissentients to be circumvented by making an order under s 201 giving sanction to a scheme which could have been carried out under s 260.[1]

1. *Re Anglo-Continental Supply Co* [1922] 2 Ch 723.

32.11 A takeover may be said to occur when one company acquires a majority of the shares in another company. This may, of course, happen as a result of an agreement between the board of directors of the two companies concerned: if the directors of the company being taken over own a sufficient number of the shares, the takeover will present few complications. The takeover which presents the most problems is the attempt by one public company to acquire the necessary majority of shares in another public company by making an offer to the shareholders in that company for the purchase of their shares at a stated figure. The offer is usually conditional upon its being accepted by a stated percentage of the shareholders: when that percentage has accepted, the offer becomes unconditional and binding upon the acquiring company. Such takeover 'bids' have, of course, been extremely comon in England for many years, but are relatively infrequent in Ireland, because of the small number of public companies. It should be remembered, however, that there can be a takeover of a private company just as of a public company and students and practitioners should be familiar with the general legal principles affecting such takeovers, whether of public or private companies.

32.12 The philosophy underlying the Acts is intended to facilitate mergers, amalgamations and takeover subject to safeguards being provided for shareholders and creditors. (The public interest is intended to be protected by independent legislation, which is considered below.) In the case of a takeover, the company acquiring the shares (called in the Principal Act and this chapter 'the transferee') will usually want to acquire at least 75 per cent of the shares in the other company (called 'the transferor'). As we have seen, a special resolution of a company to be valid must be supported by at least 75 per cent of those voting at a meeting, and some important matters may only be dealt with by means of such a resolution. Even a minority of less than 25 per cent can, however, prove an embarrassment to the transferee company, and, accordingly, with a view to facilitating a takeover which has overwhelming support from the shareholders in the transferor, s 204 enables the transferee to acquire compulsorily the shares of a dissentient minority, where not less than 80 per cent[1] in value of the shareholders in the transferor have agreed to the takeover.

1. Note that only an 80 per cent majority is required: in England, the figure is 90 per cent.

32.13 A company making a takeover can put in motion the machinery under s 204 where the scheme, contract or offer has become binding or approved or accepted in respect of not less than four-fifths in value of the shares affected. The offer must have been accepted by, and become binding on, the necessary majority not later than four months after the publication of the terms of the offer to the shareholders. The transferee then has a further two months (i.e. six months from the date of publication) within which to exercise its rights to acquire the shares of any of the dissentients. This is done by serving a notice in the prescribed form[1] on any of the dissentients who in turn may apply to the court within one month for an order setting aside the notice.

The court may set aside the notice 'if it thinks fit'. There is no guidance in the section as to what matters may properly be taken into account by the court in exercising its discretion. It is clear, however, that the onus is on the dissentient shareholder who applies for such an order to establish that the terms of the acquisition are not fair.[2] It has also been held that it is not sufficient to establish that the offer could be improved.[3] The court would not, it is thought, be concerned with the commercial merits of the takeover or its effect on the public interest and, in exercising its discretion, must naturally give great weight to the fact that at least four-fifths of the shareholders have approved the takeover.[4]

It has also been held in England that it is not sufficient to allege that inadequate information was given to the shareholders,[5] but that there is a duty on the transferee to act honestly and not to mislead the shareholders in the transferor.

A different view was taken by McWilliam J in *Securities Trust Ltd v Associated Properties Ltd and Another*,[6] where he held that the shareholders in the transferor are entitled to be given 'full particulars of the transaction, its purposes, the method of carrying it out and its consequences'. It does not appear, however, that any of the earlier authorities were cited and it may be that the decision should be regarded as confined to the facts of the particular case.

1. Form No 18, Companies (Forms) Order 1964, SI 1964/45 of 1964.
2. *Re Hoare & Co* (1934) 150 LT 374.
3. *Re Grierson, Oldham and Adams Ltd* [1968] Ch 17.
4. *Re Hoare & Co* (1934) 150 LT 374.
5. *Re Evertite Locknuts*, [1945] Ch 220 at 223.
6. Unreported; judgment delivered 19 November 1980.

32.14 What is the position if the transferee, at the time of the publication of the offer, owns shares already in the transferor? If the holding of the transferee at that time exceeds one-fifth, sub-section (2) provides that the transferee cannot exercise the compulsory purchase power unless it acquires four-fifths of the remaining shares and the accepting shareholders represent three-fourths in number of the holders of the remaining shares.

32.15 It should also be noted that the time limit for giving notice to the dissenting shareholders will remain the same, even though the time within which the shareholders in the transferor company have to accept has been extended by the transferee.[1]

1. *Musson v Howard Glasgow Associates Ltd* (1961) SLT 87.

32.16 Even if the transferee does not wish to exercise the power of compulsory purchase under s 204, it must still give the dissentients an opportunity of selling their shares. This is provided for by sub-section (4), under which the transferee, where it has acquired four-fifths in value must, within one month, give notice of that fact in the prescribed manner[1] to any shareholders whose shares have not been acquired. They in turn may then give notice to the transferee requiring it to acquire their shares. The shares must then be acquired by the transferee on the same terms as the remaining four-fifths were acquired.

1. Form No 19, Companies (Forms) Order 1964.

Compensation for loss of office on mergers etc.

32.17 The Principal Act contains provisions designed to ensure that any arrangement for the payment of compensation to the directors for loss of office on a merger, amalgamation or takeover is notified to the members and approved by them before it becomes effective. Section 187 renders unlawful the payment of any compensation to a director for loss of office in connection with the transfer of the whole or part of the company's undertaking or property, unless particulars of the proposed payment (including the amount) have been disclosed to the members and the proposal approved by the members in general meeting. The disclosure must be made to all members, whether or not they are entitled to notice of meetings and must be made before the payment is made.

Section 188 requires a director to disclose particulars of any payment made to him as compensation for loss of office in connection with a transfer of shares in the company, where the transfer results *inter alia* from an offer made to the general body of shareholders. He must take all reasonable steps to secure that the particulars are included in or sent with any notice of the offer. There is provision for a fine not exceeding £125 in the event of his not doing so and for treating any sums received by him as being held on trust for those who have sold their shares as a result of the offer.

Control of mergers and takeovers

32.18 In the case of public companies, the requirements of the *City Code on Take Overs and Mergers* will be applicable, although they have no force in law. These requirements (which are set out in full in Palmer, Vol. II) are intended principally to ensure that shareholders are given sufficient information and a reasonable time within which to evaluate the information.

32.19 There are, in addition, statutory controls on all mergers and takeovers, whether of public or private companies, where the gross assets of each of the companies involved exceeds £1,250,000 or the turnover of each is not less than £2,500,000. These are contained in the Mergers, Takeovers and Monopolies (Control) Act 1978.

Where a merger or takeover within the meaning of the Act is proposed, the Minister may refer the proposal to the Examiner of Restrictive Practices. He may then, after considering the Examiner's report, by order prohibit the merger or takeover, either absolutely or except on such conditions as he specifies.[1]

1. S 9.

32.20 The Act applies to 'enterprises' and these are defined by s 1 (1) as meaning
'a person or partnership engaged for profit in the supply or distribution of goods or the provision of services...'
The word 'person' would include a company formed under the Acts, and sub-section (1) also makes it clear that it includes a holding company.

A merger or takeover within the meaning of the Act takes place when two or more enterprises in Ireland, at least one of which carries on business in Ireland, come under 'common control'. 'Common control' in turn is defined as existing where the decision as to how or by whom each of the enterprises is managed can be made by the same person or by the same group of persons 'acting in concert'. This general definition is supplemented by a special definition in the case of companies. Without prejudice to the general definition, companies are deemed to come under common control when one company acquires
(a) the right to appoint or remove a majority of the board or committee of management of the other, or
(b) more than 30 per cent of the shares carrying voting rights in the other.
(b), however, does not apply, where the acquiring company already owns more than half the shares carrying voting rights in the other company.

It should be particularly noted that for a merger or takeover to exist, it is not necessary for one company to acquire a majority or controlling interest in another. It is sufficient if more than 30 per cent of the shares are acquired.

A merger or takeover is also deemed to take place where one company acquires assets of another company and as a result the acquiring company substantially replaces the other company in the business concerned.

In certain circumstances where companies come under common control or assets are acquired, no merger or takeover will be deemed to exist for the purposes of the Act. They are:

(1) where the person making the decisions giving rise to the 'common control' assumption is a receiver or liquidator;

(2) where the person acquiring the assets is an underwriter or jobber acting as such or a liquidator or receiver acting as such;

(3) where the companies concerned are wholly owned subsidiaries of the same holding company.

32.21 We have already seen that the Act applies only to mergers and takeovers affecting enterprises with assets or turnover exceeding the statutory figures. Where, however, the Minister is of the opinion that the exigencies of the common good so warrant, he may declare that the Act is to apply to a particular merger or takeover even though the statutory figures are not exceeded.

32.22 In order to prevent the Minister being presented with a *fait accompli* which might be difficult and complex to undo, the Act provides in s 3 for the automatic deferral of the implementation of a merger or takeover until the Minister has had an opportunity of considering whether he should make a prohibition order under s 9. Accordingly, the section provides that the title to the assets or shares concerned in the merger or takeover is not to pass until

(1) the Minister has stated that he has decided not to make a prohibition order; or

(2) the Minister has made a conditional order; or

(3) a period of three months has elapsed from the date of the notification to the Minister of the proposal or the date on which the Minister receives further information in response to a request;

whichever of these three events happens first.

Moreover, s 14 provides that an order under s 201 or 203 of the Principal Act is not to be made in respect of a merger or takeover to which the 1978 Act applies until either

(a) the Minister has stated in writing that he has decided not to make a prohibition order; or

(b) the Minister has made a conditional order; or

(c) a period of three months has elapsed from the date of the notification to the Minister of the proposal or the date on which the Minister receives further information in response to a request;

whichever of these events happens first.

32.23 The statutory machinery is set in motion by a notification in writing to the Minister of the proposed takeover or merger. Section 5 requires each of the enterprises involved and having knowledge of the existence of the proposal to notify the Minister in writing of it 'as soon as may be'. The Minister may then within one month of the notification request further information in writing from any one or more of the enterprises. A person in control of an enterprise (in the case of a company any officer) who fails to notify the Minister of such a proposal is guilty of an offence where he knowingly and wilfully permitted such a contravention of the Act, and is liable on summary conviction to a fine not exceeding £500 and on indictment to a fine not exceeding £5,000.

The next step is for the Minister to decide whether he should refer the proposal to the Examiner for investigation. Both the Examiner in making his report and the Minister in deciding whether to make a prohibition order are required to assess whether the proposal would be against 'the common good' or not. This is a somewhat elastic concept, but the Examiner is given firmer guidelines than the Minister. He is required to take into account in his investigation and report certain 'criteria' as set out in the Schedule to the Act. They are as follows:

(a) the extent to which the proposed merger or takeover would be likely to prevent or restrict competition or to restrain trade or the provision of any service;

(b) the extent to which the proposed merger or takeover would be likely to endanger the continuity of supplies or services;

(c) the extent to which the proposed merger or takeover would be likely to affect employment and would be compatible with national policy in relation to employment;

(d) the extent to which the proposed merger or takeover is in accordance with national policy for regional development;

(e) the extent to which the proposed merger or takeover is in harmony with the policy of the Government relating to the rationalisation, in the interests of greater efficiency, of operations in the industry or business concerned;

(f) any benefits likely to be derived from the proposed takeover or merger and relating to research and development, technical efficiency, increased production, efficient distribution of products and access to markets;

(g) the interests of shareholders and partners in the enterprises involved;

(h) the interests of employees in the enterprises involved;

(i) the interests of the consumer.

When the Minister has received and considered the Examiner's report, he then decides whether 'the exigencies of the common good' warrant the prohibition of the proposal either absolutely or except on specified conditions. Before doing so, he must consult with any other Minister appearing to him to be concerned, and he must also have regard to any relevant international obligations of Ireland. The order must state the reasons for its being made.

One of the conditions to which an order permitting a proposal may be made subject is one that the proposal is to take effect within 12 months of the making of the order. A conditional order may also be retrospective in its effect.

Every such order must be laid before each House of the Oireachtas and if a resolution annulling the order is passed by either such house within the next 21 days on which the house has sat after the order is laid before it, the order is to be annulled, but without prejudice to the validity of anything done thereunder previously.

Where a sale of shares is rendered invalid as a result of such deferral, the vendor is entitled to recover damages from the purchaser unless the purchaser satisfies the court that before the purported sale he notified the vendor of circumstances relating to the proposed sale which gave rise to the possibility of such an invalidity.

32.24 It should also be noted that, under Article 86 of the EEC Treaty, what is called 'abuse of a dominant position within the Common Market' by one or more undertakings is prohibited. It has been held that this article entitles the Commission to control or prohibit mergers, but its practical significance in the Irish context is limited since the dominant position must be *within the Common Market* or a substantial part of it, e.g. one of the larger member states, such as the UK or France.

Chapter 33

Investigation of a company's affairs

33.01 The Minister has, as we have seen, a general supervisory jurisdiction over companies formed under the Acts.[1] In particular, he may in certain circumstances appoint inspectors to investigate the affairs of such companies.

The powers in question are conferred by Part V of the Principal Act. The Minister is given a general power under s 165 to appoint one or more competent inspectors to investigate the affairs of a company and report on them in such manner as the Minister directs. He may do so in the case of a company having a share capital on the application of not less than 100 members or of a number of members holding not less than one-tenth of the paid up capital; and, in the case of a company not having a share capital, on the application of not less than one-fifth in number of the members.

The application must be supported by such evidence as the Minister may require for the purpose of showing that the applicants have good reason for requiring the investigation. He may also require them to give security to an amount not exceeding £50[2] for payment of the costs of the investigation.

The Minister is also empowered by s 166 to appoint inspectors for the same purpose if either the company itself by special resolution or the court by order declares that the company's affairs ought to be so investigated. He may also initiate such an investigation of his own volition if it appears to him that there are circumstances suggesting

- (i) that the company's business is being conducted with intent to defraud its creditors or the creditors of any other persons or otherwise for fraudulent or unlawful purposes;
- (ii) that the affairs of the company are being exercised in a manner oppressive to any of its members or in disregard of their interests as members;
- (iii) that the company was formed for any fraudulent or unlawful purpose;
- (iv) that persons connected with its formation or with the management of its affairs have been guilty of fraud, misfeasance or other misconduct towards it or its members;
- (v) that its members have not been given all the information relating to its affairs which they might reasonably expect.

1. Para 1.14 above.
2. The amount is clearly totally inadequate in modern conditions, but does not appear to have been increased by subsequent legislation.

Conduct of the investigation

33.02 The officers and agents of the company under investigation are obliged to produce to the inspectors all the books and documents of or relating to the company in their custody or power and to give the inspectors any assistance which they are reasonably able to give.[1] The inspectors also have power to extend their investigations to the affairs of related companies (i.e. holding or subsidiary companies) with the approval of the Minister.[2]

The inspector may examine on oath the officers and agents of the company and any other body corporate whose affairs are being examined by them.[3] They have no power to examine on oath any other persons. Where, however, they think it necessary for the purpose of their investigation, that any person should be examined on oath, they may apply to the court and the court may order the person to attend and be examined on oath in relation to any matter relevant to the investigation. The court may put such questions to the person concerned as it thinks fit and the person must answer them. He is, however, entitled to be represented by solicitor or counsel who may put such questions to him as the court deems just for the purpose of explaining or qualifying any answers he has given. Notes of the examination are to be taken down in writing and read over to, and signed by, the person examined and may be used afterwards in evidence against him.[4]

Since the person concerned is obliged to answer any questions which the court puts to him, it seems to follow that he cannot refuse to answer a question on the ground that he might incriminate himself.[5]

Section 168(3), as amended by s 7 of the 1982 Act, provides that any officer or agent of the company or other body corporate being investigated who refuses to produce to the inspectors any book or document which it is his duty to produce or who refuses to answer any question put to him by the inspectors with respect to the affairs of the company or other body corporate is guilty of an offence. He is liable on summary conviction to a fine not exceeding £500 or imprisonment for a term not exceeding six months or both, and on indictment to a fine not exceeding £5,000 or a term of imprisonment not exceeding three years or both. The original provision in the Principal Act did not provide for a trial by jury. The alteration was presumably made as a result of doubts as to the constitutionality of the original provision arising from the decision of the Supreme Court in *Re Haughey*.[6]

1. S 168 of the Principal Act.
2. S 167 of the Principal Act.
3. S 168(2) of the Principal Act.
4. S 168(4) of the Principal Act.
5. *R v Harris* [1970] 3 All ER 746. It would appear from this decision that the position is the same where the inspectors themselves avail of their power to examine an officer of the company on oath. In that case, however, it is for the court to decide on a trial under sub-s (3) whether the officer's refusal to answer is wrongful: *McClelland, Pope & Langley v Howard* [1968] 1 All ER 569n.
6. [1971] IR 217.

33.03 Other than the procedures mentioned in the preceding paragraph, the procedures to be followed by inspectors appointed under s 165 or s 166 are not laid down in the Acts. Clearly, they have a wide discretion as to how they will conduct the investigation: in particular, it will, generally speaking, be a matter for them to decide whether the circumstances warrant the holding of an oral hearing.

The inspectors do no more than investigate and report. They cannot determine the rights of any persons or make orders affecting their property or status. It would seem to follow that their powers are not judicial in nature. But although properly described as administrative rather than judicial or quasi-judicial, their functions must be performed in accordance with what has been traditionally called 'natural justice'.[1] (The phrase sometimes used today is 'constitutional justice'[2] or 'fair procedures',[3] but it is not entirely clear to what extent these concepts have extended the traditional idea of 'natural justice'.)[4]

Thus the inspectors will be bound to apply the maxim *audi alteram partem,* i.e. they must give a fair hearing to any person likely to be affected by their findings and recommendations.[5] It may also be in certain circumstances a denial of natural justice not to afford a person the following:

  (i) an oral hearing and the opportunity of cross-examining witnesses;[6]
  (ii) access to documents in the possession of another person or company concerned in the investigation:[7]
  (iii) an adjournment in order to enable him to prepare his case or defend a case being made against him;[8]
  (iv) legal representation when the seriousness of the matter in issue or the consequences for the person concerned seem to warrant it.[9]

1. *East Donegal Cooperative Livestock Marts Ltd v A-G* [1970] IR 317.
2. *McDonald v Board na gCon* [1965] IR 217.
3. *Re Haughey*, above.
4. Cf Kelly, *The Irish Constitution*, 2nd edn.
5. *Maunsell v Minister for Education and Another* [1940] IR 213.
6. *Kiely v Minister for Social Welfare* [1977] IR 267.
7. *Nolan v Irish Land Commission* [1981] IR 23
8. *Kiely v Minister for Social Welfare* [1971] IR 21.
9. *Re Haughey*, above.

Oral hearing may be in private

33.04 Since the inspectors in carrying out the investigation are not administering justice within the meaning of Article 34.01 of the Constitution, it is thought that they are not obliged to hold oral hearings in public.[1] At the same time, there is nothing to prevent them from so doing if it appears desirable in a particular case. But there may be cases where the interests of the members only of a private company are involved and those of outsiders, still less the general public, are not affected. In such cases it would seem desirable that the investigation should be held in private, if the inspectors are satisfied that damage might otherwise be done to the company.

1. *Re Redbreast Preserving Co (Ireland) Ltd* 91 ILTR 12.

Report by the inspectors

33.05 The inspectors are required to make a final report to the Minister on the conclusion of the investigation, and they must also make interim reports if directed so to do by the Minister. The Minister must forward a copy of each report to the registered office of the company, and if he thinks fit, may furnish a copy of the report on payment of the prescribed fee to any member of the company or any other company dealt with in the report or to any person whose interests appear to him to be affected. When the inspectors are appointed under s 165, he must furnish a copy of the report to the applicants for the investigation. When they are appointed by the court, he must furnish a copy to the court. He may also cause the report to be printed and published and may lay it before each house of the Oireachtas. If he presents it to the Oireachtas, the publication is privileged.

33.06   If it appears to the Minister from the report that any person has, in relation to any company under investigation, been guilty of an offence for which he is criminally liable, he must refer the matter to the Director of Public Prosecutions. If the latter considers that the case is one in which proceedings ought to be instituted and actually institutes such proceedings, it becomes the duty of all the officers and agents of the company (other than the defendant) to give him all assistance in connection with the prosecution that they are reasonably able to give.

33.07   If it appears to the Minister from the report that, in the case of any company liable to be wound up, it is expedient that it should be wound up because of the circumstances specified in s 166 (b) (i) and (ii)—which are all the grounds for appointing inspectors other than the giving of inadequate information—he may present a petition for the winding up of the company to the court, unless the company is already being wound up by the court. He may do so either on the ground that it is 'just and equitable' that it should be wound up[1] or on the grounds that the affairs of the company are being conducted in a manner oppressive to any of its members or in disregard of their interests.[2] He may also present a petition for the alternative remedy under s 205;[3] or he may present a petition both for a winding up and the alternative remedy.

1. See para 34.10 below.
2. Ibid.
3. See para 26.12 above.

33.08   If it appears to the Minister from the report that proceedings ought in the public interest to be brought by any company dealt with in the report for the recovery of damages in respect of fraud, misfeasance or other misconduct in connection with the promotion or formation of that company or for the recovery of any property of the company which has been misapplied or wrongfully retained, the Minister may bring such proceedings himself in the name of the company. He may also indemnify the company against the relevant costs or expenses.

33.09   A copy of the report is admissible in any legal proceedings as evidence of the opinion of the inspectors in relation to any matter contained in the report.

Expenses of investigation

33.10   The Minister is liable in the first instance to pay the expenses of any investigation under the Principal Act. There is also provision, however, for the repayment to the Minister of such expenses by the various persons affected by the investigation.

(i) Any person who is convicted as a result of the investigation or is ordered to pay damages or restore property may also be ordered to pay the expenses of the investigation to such extent as may be specified in the order.

(ii) Any company in whose name proceedings are brought by the Minister is liable for the expenses of the investigation to the amount or value of any sums or property recovered by it as a result.

(iii) Unless a prosecution is instituted by the Director of Public Prosecutions as a result of the investigation, any company dealt with by the report, where the inspector was not appointed by the Minister of his own volition, is liable for the expenses except so far as the Minister otherwise directs.

(iv) The applicants for an investigation are liable to such an extent as the Minister may direct, except where a prosecution is instituted.

33.11 Except where they are appointed by the Minister, the inspectors' report may, if they think fit, and must, if the Minister so directs, include a recommendation as to the directions, if any, which the inspectors think appropriate in the light of their investigation, to be given as to the payment of expenses by a company or any other person under sub-paragraphs (iii) or (iv) of para 32.10.

Powers rarely invoked

33.12 The powers conferred on the Minister by Part V of the Principal Act have rarely been invoked. Indeed the only investigation of any consequence into a company's affairs in modern times was carried out under the corresponding provisions of the 1908 Act.[1] This is presumably because where matters have reached the stage at which an investigation might be appropriate, those concerned prefer to petition for the winding up of the company or for the alternative remedy under s 205, rather than go down the lengthy and uncertain road of a departmential inquiry. It is all the more surprising in these circumstances to find that one of the proposals apparently under consideration at the time of writing for incorporation in amending legislation is the extension of the investigation procedure. It is apparently contemplated that the court, rather than the Minister, will have the power to appoint inspectors. It is also suggested that the powers of the inspectors as to the obtaining of evidence will be strengthened. It remains to be seen what form these proposals will take, but the history of the procedure under the Principal Act does not inspire much confidence in such proposals as providing a more effective remedy for abuses of company law.

There is perhaps one area in which the inspectors' powers might usefully be invoked. Concern has been expressed in recent times as to the manner in which semi-state companies appear to operate without any significant degree of public accountability or control. This is all the more worrying, having regard to the comparatively large role which such companies play in the Irish economy.[2] There may be a case for availing of the investigatory procedures of the Principal Act where such companies are concerned: it might in some circumstances be a more desirable course than the compulsory liquidation of the company, since if instituted in time (an important qualification) it might restore the company to a state of commercial well being, thus bringing to an end the state of affairs which gave rise to concern without terminating the company's existence.

1. *Enquiry into Irish Estates Ltd – Inspectors' Report*, Stationery Office, 23 October 1963.
2. See para 1.06 above.

Part eight

Winding up of companies

Chapter 34

Winding up by the court

34.01 A company may in theory live for ever. It may also, however, have its legal existence cut short in two ways: by being wound up or by being removed from the register.

Strictly speaking, it is not the winding up of the company which terminates its legal existence. That only happens when the company is *dissolved*. But winding up, as the expression itself implies, is a necessary stage in the process which leads to dissolution.

A winding up may take place for a variety of reasons: because the company has simply ceased to fulfil any useful purpose, because of strife among the members as to how it should be conducted, because it is insolvent, to name some. In each case, whatever the reason, the winding up is carried out by a *liquidator*.

In the case of insolvent companies, the winding up process is in many ways similar to the bankruptcy procedure in the case of an individual. The assets of the insolvent in each case are collected by an officer and distributed among the creditors in accordance with well established rules. Some creditors, such as the Revenue, are entitled to priority for portion of their debts over the other creditors. Secured creditors may choose to rely on their securities and not avail of any distribution in the winding up or bankruptcy.

There are also, however, important differences between the two codes. A bankruptcy is invariably carried out by a permanent officer of the court known as the Official Assignee. A liquidation is carried out by a person appointed either by the company or the court for the purpose of a specific liquidation. In a bankruptcy, the assets of the bankrupt which are available for distribution among his creditors include not merely the property which he owned but also those goods which were in his 'apparent' or 'reputed' ownership. In a liquidation, only the property actually owned by the company is available for distribution.

A winding up of a company which is solvent usually presents less problems than of one which is insolvent. In the latter case, there may be difficulties as to the rights of different types of creditors—ordinary, preferential and secured—and the liquidator may have to apply to the court for directions. The court may also be called upon to investigate the conduct of the company by the directors and other officers and to decide whether any such officer should be fixed with personal liability in respect of any of the company's debts.

34.02 There are two main forms of winding up; *by the court* and *voluntary*. As the names suggest, the essential difference between the two procedures is that in the first the winding up is ordered by the court whereas in the second the members themselves decide to wind up the company. A voluntary winding up can be either a *members' winding up* or *a creditors' winding up*.

The provisions relating to a winding up by the court (which is also sometimes called *a compulsory winding up* or *compulsory liquidation*) are contained in ss 212 to 250 of the Principal Act; those relating to a voluntary winding up (or *voluntary liquidation*) generally in ss 251 to 256; those relating to a members' winding up in ss 257 to 264; those relating to a creditors' winding up in ss 265 to 273; and those common to all forms of winding up in ss 206 to 211 and ss 283 to 313. The Rules of Court which prescribe the practice and procedure to be followed in winding up are contained in the Rules of the Superior Courts (No 1) 1966.[1] The forms to be used are contained in the Appendix to the Rules.

The High Court alone has jurisdiction in the winding up of companies.[2]

1. SI 1966/28
2. S 212 of the Principal Act: cf *Stokes v Milford Cooperative Creamery Ltd* (1956) 90 ILTR 67.

Winding up by the court

34.03 The Principal Act provides that in certain circumstances the court may order the winding up of a company on the petition of a person or body entitled under the Act to present such a petition. Such petitions are most commonly presented by or on behalf of creditors of the company.

The essence of a typical winding up by the court is that, instead of each creditor of an insolvent company proceeding to enforce his claim for payment against the company individually, a liquidator is appointed to collect the assets of the company and enforce payment of the contributions due from the members. He then proceeds to distribute the assets among the creditors of the company in the priority prescribed by the Principal Act. The Principal Act contains provisions which prevent the taking of individual actions against the company during the winding up and which render void certain dispositions of property by which a company, aware of the imminence of the winding up, might seek to defraud its creditors.

Companies that may be wound up by the court

34.04 All companies formed and registered under Part II of the Principal Act or registered under Part IX of the Act may be wound up by the court. In addition, the following companies are subject to this jurisdiction:

(i) companies formed and registered under former Companies Acts;[1]
(ii) companies registered but not formed under former Companies Acts;[2]
(iii) unlimited companies re-registered as limited companies under former Companies Acts;[3]
(iv) unregistered companies.

1. S 324 of the Principal Act.
2. S 325 of the Principal Act.
3. S 326 of the Principal Act.

34.05 Part X of the Principal Act deals with the winding up of unregistered companies. An unregistered company, in this context, does not include companies formed and registered under the Acts or under previous

Companies Acts, or partnerships, associations or companies which consist of less than eight members and are formed in Ireland. Subject to this, it includes:
  (i) any partnership, whether limited or not;
  (ii) any association; and
  (iii) any company.

34.06 Among unregistered companies which may be wound up by the courts are:
  (i) companies incorporated by special Act;[1]
  (ii) companies incorporated by royal charter (but not societies so incorporated);[2]
  (iii) foreign companies which have established a place of business in Ireland but have ceased to carry on business in Ireland;[3]
  (iv) building societies formed prior to the Building Societies Act, 1874;[4]
  (v) trustee savings banks;[5]
  (vi) friendly societies;[6]
  (vii) industrial and provident societies;[7]

1. *Re Barton-upon-Humber Water Co* (1889) 42 Ch D 585.
2. *Re Commercial Buildings* [1938] IR 477.
3. S 345(7) of the Principal Act.
4. *Re Ilfracombe Building Society* [1901] 1 Ch 102.
5. S 344 of the Principal Act.
6. Friendly societies can only be wound up compulsorily: *Re Independent Protestant Loan Society* [1895] 1 IR 1; *Re Irish Mercantile Loan Society* [1907] 1 IR 98.
7. Industrial and provident Societies, like friendly societies, can only be wound up compulsorily. See Industrial and Provident Societies (Amendment) Act 1978.

34.07 A procedure is provided by Part IV of the Insurance Act, 1936, for the winding up of insolvent insurance companies on the petition of the Minister. The Minister also has power under the Insurance (No 2) Act 1983 to apply to the court for the appointment of an 'administrator' of an insurance company which is in difficulties. Under this procedure—which has been availed of in recent times in the case of the Private Motorists' Protection Association and the Insurance Corporation of Ireland—the company is not wound up (in order to avoid its insured being left without cover) but is managed by the administrator with a view to its being restored ultimately to viability.

When a company may be wound up by the court

34.08 The grounds on which a company may be wound up by the court are set out in s 213 of the Principal Act. Of these, the most important in practice are:
  (i) that the company is uanable to pay its debts;
  (ii) that it is 'just and equitable' to wind up the company; or
  (iii) that a member is being treated in an oppressive manner or his interests are being disregarded.
In addition, the company may be wound up by the court on the following grounds:
  (i) that the company has resolved by special resolution that the company be wound up by the court;
  (ii) that the company did not commence its business within a year from its incorporation or suspended its business for a whole year;

(iii) that the number of members is reduced, in the case of a private company, below two, or in the case of any other company, below seven.

The most important grounds will now be considered in turn.

34.09 *(i) Inability to pay debts.* This is the most frequent ground for winding up. Section 214 of the Principal Act provides that a company shall be deemed to be unable to pay its debts in certain circumstances, i.e.:
   (a) where a creditor has not been paid a debt of £50 or more within three weeks after demanding it in writing;
   (b) where a judgement is unsatisfied; or
   (c) where it is proved to the satisfaction of the court that the company is unable to pay its debts.
In deciding whether it has been proved that the company is unable to pay its debts, the court will generally act on evidence that a creditor has repeatedly applied for payment without success. If, however, the company can show that there is a *bona fide* dispute as to the particular debt claimed, the order will not be made.[1]

1. *Re Gold Hills Mines Ltd* (1883) 23 Ch D 210; *Mann v Goldstein* [1968] 2 All ER 769.

34.10 *(ii) 'Just and equitable'.* The Court has a wide jurisdiction to wind up a company when it is of opinion that it would be 'just and equitable' to do so. The words 'just and equitable' are not *ejusdem generis* with the other grounds enumerated in s 213, so that the court is not restricted to grounds of a similar character to those specified in the other paragraphs of the section in exercising its discretion under this paragraph.[1] Moreover, while it was at one time usual for commentators on the section to specify categories of cases in which the court would exercise its discretion, it was emphasised by Lord Wilberforce in the leading modern English case, *Re Westbourne Galleries Ltd*[2] that the section conferred a *general* power: 'Illustrations may be used,' he said, 'but general words should remain general and not be reduced to the sum of particular instances.'

It is also clear from that case that a winding up order on the 'just and equitable' ground may be peculiarly appropriate to small private companies founded on a personal relationship involving mutual trust and confidence between the parties where that trust and confidence has broken down: cases involving the sort of business association which, as we have seen throughout this books, is by far the most common type of company in Ireland. Such a company is more akin to a partnership and indeed is sometimes described as a quasi-partnership company. Because the element of mutual trust is so important in such a company, the court, as Lord Wilberforce made clear, will not refuse relief simply because there may have been no breach of a legal obligation by the members whose conduct is impugned. It will be sufficient to ground a case for an order under the section if the petitioner can show that the other members have not acted in good faith towards him and have in the broadest sense acted inequitably.

A number of passages from the speech of Lord Wilberforce in *Re Westbourne Galleries* were cited by Gannon J in *Re Murph's Restaurant Ltd*[3] and applied by him to the facts in that case. There were only three shareholders, each of them directors, and all three were actively concerned in the management of the company. One of the three was removed from his office as director by the other two and effectively excluded from all further participation in the company. The company had been conducted on an extremely informal basis and the dismissed director had never been paid any dividend on his shares. He had given up regular salaried employment in order to devote himself full time to the company and Gannon J found that the reasons for his removal put forward by his co-directors were unconvincing. He made it clear that whether or not the legal requirements had been observed in the removal of the petitioner from office, the action of his co-directors in dismissing him amounted to a repudiation of their relationship with him. He accordingly granted an order for the winding up of the company on the 'just and equitable' ground.

1. *Re Newbridge Sanitary Steam Laundry Co* [1917] 1 IR 67.
2. [1973] AC 360.
3. Unreported; judgment delivered 31 July 1979.

34.11 Other instances where the courts have made orders on the 'just and equitable' ground are where there was complete deadlock between the shareholders[1] and where it appeared that the company's affairs required investigation by the court.[2]

1. *Re Yenidje Tobacco Co* [1916] 2 Ch 426.
2. *Re Peruvian Amazon Co* (1913) 29 TLR 384.

34.12 *(iii) Oppression of a member*. Little need be said about this ground, since the circumstances in which the court will grant relief—whether in the form of a winding up order or the alternative remedy under s 205—have already been fully discussed in Chapter Twenty-Six above.

The petition: general

34.13 The machinery of a winding up by the court is set in motion by a petition which may be presented by any of the following:
 (i) the company;
 (ii) any creditor;
 (iii) any contributory, i.e. any person liable to contribute to the assets of the company in the event of its being wound up;
 (iv) the Minister;
 (v) in the case of oppression, any person entitled to apply for an order under s 205.

The right to present a petition is a statutory right which cannot be excluded by the articles of association.[1]

A company will seldom present a petition itself, since if it wishes to wind up it can pass the necessary resolution. If the directors believe that the company's affairs require investigation by the court, however, the company should present a petition; but the company in general meeting must sanction such a petition.[2]

1. *Re Peveril Gold Mines Co Ltd* [1898] 1 Ch 122.
2. *Re Galway and Salthill Tramways Co* [1918] 1 IR 62.

Petitions by creditors

34.14 The great majority of winding up petitions are presented by creditors of the company. A creditor, for this purpose, means any person owed a sum of money by the company, whether by virtue of the assignment to him of another's debt or otherwise. The term includes a 'contingent' or 'prospective' creditor; but such a creditor must provide security for the costs of the petition and must also satisfy the court that there is a *prima facie* case for winding up.[1]

1. S 215 of the Principal Act.

34.15 A petitioning creditor who cannot get his debt paid has a right to a winding up order *ex debito justitiae*, i.e. as a matter of right.[1] But the court also has regard to the wishes of the majority in value of the creditors and if the majority objects to a winding up order being made, the court may in its discretion refuse the order. The opposing creditors must, however, show some good reason for their attitude.[2]

While the wishes of the creditors are normally of great importance, the court is not necessarily bound by them. If, for example, there are circumstances which suggest that the company's affairs ought to be investigated by the court, a winding up order will be made notwithstanding the opposition of the creditors.[3]

1. *Bowes v Hope Life Insurance and Guarantee Co* (1865) 11 HLC 389 at 402.
2. *Re P & J Macrae Ltd* [1961] 1 All ER 302.
3. *Re George Downes & Co* [1943] IR 420 at 424 per Overend J.

34.16 Section 282 of the Principal Act provides that a voluntary winding up is not to be a bar to the right of any creditor to have the company wound up by the court. If, however, the majority in value of the creditors oppose such an application, it may be refused.[1] Where the court makes the order, it has power to adopt the proceedings already had in the voluntary liquidation. Otherwise, such proceedings are void.

1. *Re Wicklow Textiles Ltd* (1953) 87 ILTR 72.

Petitions by contributories

34.17 A contributory, being a member of the company, has to show special circumstances in order to obtain a winding up order. Moreover, in order to prevent people buying shares in a company with the object of wrecking it, a contributory is precluded from presenting a petition unless

(i) the number of members is reduced, in the case of a private company to one member, or in the case of any other company below seven members, or

(ii) his shares or some of them were either allotted to him, or have been held by him and registered in his name, for at least six months during the eighteen months before the commencement of the winding up or have devolved on him through the death of a former holder.[1]

1. S 215 of the Principal Act.

34.18 If a voluntary winding up is in progress, this is *prima facie* a bar to the contributory's petition, because as a member of the company, he is bound by the wishes of the majority. But it is not an absolute bar and the court under s 282 will make the order, if it is satisfied that the rights of the contributory will be prejudiced by the continuation of the voluntary winding up.

Petition by the Minister

34.19 We have seen in Chapter Thirty-Three that the Minister is entitled to appoint inspectors to investigate the affairs of companies in certain circumstances. We have also seen that he may be obliged to carry out such an investigation where the court by order or the company by special resolution requires one to be carried out. When the report has been presented, the Minister may present a petition for the winding up of the company, if it is expedient so to do by reason of circumstances specified in the section[1] either on the 'just and equitable' ground or on the ground of oppression of the members.

1. See para 33.07 above.

Form and presentation of the petition

34.20   The peitition must state:
   (i) the incorporation of the company;
   (ii) the address of its registered office;
   (iii) the amount of its paid up capital;
   (iv) the grounds on which the winding up order is sought.[1]
   It is presented at the central office of the High Court and retained there.[2] A sealed copy is taken out by the petitioner and it and the original petition are brought to the office of one of the registrars who appoints the time and place at which the petition is to be heard. The registrar lists the petition for hearing before one of the judges assigned by the President of the High Court for the hearing of chancery matters; and he can alter the time appointed for its hearing at any time before it is advertised.[3]

1. Rules: Form No 2, Appendix M.
2. Rule 9.
3. Rule 10.

Service and advertisement of the petition

34.21   Unless it is presented by the company, the petition must be served on the company at its registered office. If there is no registered office, it should be served at the principal, or last known principal place of business of the company (if any such can be found) by leaving a copy there with any member, officer or servant of the company or, if no such person can be found there, by leaving a copy there or serving such member or members of the company as the court may direct.[1] The Rules provide for the obtaining of copies of the petition by the contributories and creditors.[2]
   The petition must be advertised in the prescribed form[3] seven clear days before the hearing, once in *Iris Ofigiuil* and once at least in two Dublin daily morning newspapers or in such other newspapers as the registrar may direct.[4] Any error in the title, the name of the company (such as the omission of the word 'limited'[5]) or the date and place fixed for the hearing may render the advertisement invalid. But a trifling error in spelling, by which no one is misled, will not invalidate it.[6]

1. Rule 12.
2. Rule 14.
3. Form No 5, Appendix M.
4. Rule 11(1).
5. *Re London and Provincial Pure Ice Manufacturing Co* [1904] WN 136.
6. *Re J & P Sussman Ltd* [1958] 1 All ER 857.

34.22 The court will restrain the publication of the advertisement by injunction, when the petition is an abuse of the process of the court.[1] Thus, where the *existence*—as distinct from the *amount*—of a debt is disputed on substantial grounds, the court will restrain the advertising (and further prosecution) of the petition; and this even though the company is insolvent.[2] But if a petitioner has sufficient grounds for petitioning, the fact that his motive may be antagonism to someone cannot render these grounds insufficient. Conversely, if he has no sufficient grounds, the petition will be an abuse of the court's process, even though its presentation is not actuated by malice.[3]

1. *Re: a Company* [1894] 2 Ch 349.
2. *Mann v Goldstein*, above.
3. *Stonegate Securities Ltd v Gregory* [1980] 1 All ER 241; *Re Pageboy Couriers Ltd* [1983] ILRM 510. Cf *Re Murph's* unreported; McWilliam J; judgment delivered 5 August 1979.

The statutory affidavit

34.23 Every petition must be verified by an affidavit referring thereto, known as 'the statutory affidavit'.[1] It must be made by the petitioner and sworn and filed within four days after the petition is presented. The Rules make the affidavit *prima facie* evidence of the statements in the petition.[2] The object of the affidavit is to prevent the abuse of filing unnecessarily long affidavits in support of the petition.[3] Allegations of fraud or misconduct in the petition, however, not only can but must be supported by a more detailed affidavit.[4]

1. Rule 13; Forms 6 and 7, Appendix M.
2. Rule 13.
3. *Re Gold Hill Mines* (1883) 23 Ch D 210 at 214.
4. *Re S A Hawken Ltd* (1950) 66 TLR (Pt 2) 138; *Re ABC Coupler and Engineering Co Ltd* (No 2) [1962] 3 All ER 68.

Notice of intention to appear

34.24 Every person who intends to appear on the hearing of the petition must serve on, or send by post to, the petitioner or his solicitor or Dublin agent at the address stated in the petition notice of his intention to do so.[1] The notice must be in the prescribed form and must be served in the manner prescribed by the Rules.[2] On the day of the hearing, a list of the names and addresses of those who have given such notice (or a statement that no notice has been received) must be handed by the petitioner or his solicitor to the registrar prior to the hearing.[3]

1. Rule 16.
2. Rule 16; Form No. 8, Appendix N.
3. Rule 17.

Affidavits in opposition

34.25 Affidavits in opposition to the petition must be filed within seven days after the publication of the last of the required advertisements; and notice of the filing of every such affidavit must be given to the petitioner or his solicitor or Dublin agent on the day on which it is filed.[1] The petitioner and the opposing deponents may be cross-examined on their affidavits, but the court has a discretion as to allowing such cross-examination.

1. Rule 18.

Withdrawal of petition

34.26   The failure of the petitioner to proceed with the petition does not mean that any other person with the appropriate standing who wishes to obtain a winding up order must start the proceedings afresh. A petitioner may consent to the withdrawal of his petition or allow it to be dismissed or the hearing adjourned. He may fail to appear at the hearing or to make any application for an order in the terms of the prayer in the petition. In any of these circumstances, the court may substitute as petitioner any creditor or contributory, who has a right to present such a petition and wishes to prosecute the petition, upon such terms as the court deems just.[1]

1. Rule 19.

Hearing of the petition

34.27   Upon the hearing of the petition, the court may dismiss it with or without costs, adjourn the matter conditionally or unconditionally or make an interim order or any order it deems just, including, of course, an order for winding up.[1] In all matters relating to the petition, the court may have regard to the wishes of the creditors and contributories and may, if it considers it expedient to do so, direct meetings to be summoned to ascertain such wishes. The procedure at such meetings is prescribed by Rules 51 to 55.

If the company is solvent, the wishes of the contributories, being the persons chiefly interested in the assets, carry most weight; if it is insolvent, the creditors.

1. S 216 of the Principal Act. If a number of petitions are presented, the order is made on the first presented: *Re Bamford* [1901] 1 IR 390.

34.28   Section 216 of the Principal Act provides that an order for winding up is not to be refused on the ground only that the assets of the company have been mortgaged to an amount equal to or in excess of those assets or that the company has no assets. It might seem at first sight that no useful purpose would be served by making the order in such circumstances, but in an appropriate case the court will do so, e.g. where the company intends to carry on business to the detriment of innocent creditors.[1]

1. *Re Clandown Colliery Co* [1915] 1 Ch 369.

The winding up order and its effect

34.29   The order is to the effect that the company be wound up by the court under the provisions of the Acts.[1] The winding up dates, however, not from the date of the order but from the presentation of the petition.[2] A voluntary winding up dates from the passing of the appropriate resolution, and when a compulsory winding up is ordered after the commencement of a voluntary winding up, the winding up dates from the passing of the resolution.[3]

It is important to bear in mind that the winding up order does not terminate the company's existence. It remains in being until the court makes an order under s 239 of the Principal Act dissolving the company.

1. The prescribed form for the order is Form No 10, Appendix M.
2. S 220(2) of the Principal Act.
3. S 220(1) of the Principal Act.

34.30 An immediate effect of the order is to render void and ineffective all dispositions of property (including choses in action) of the company between the commencement of the winding up (i.e. the presentation of the petition) and the date of the order, unless the court otherwise directs.[1] In practice, the court usually allows such dispositions to remain effective, if they are made *bona fide* and in the usual course of business.[2] Lodgments to a bank account and the drawing of cheques on it are 'dispositions' within the meaning of the relevant section.[3]

The order also renders invalid any attachment, sequestration, distress or execution put in force against the property and effects of the company after the commencement of the winding up.[4]

1. S 218 of the Principal Act.
2. *Re Burton & Deakin Ltd* [1977] 1 All ER 631.
3. *Re Gray's Inns Consolidated Co Ltd* [1980] 1 WLR 711; *Re Pat Ruth Ltd* unreported; Costello J; judgment delivered 4 February 1981.
4. S 219 of the Principal Act.

34.31 Any floating charge on the undertaking of the company created within twelve months of the commencement of the winding up is rendered invalid, unless it is proved that the company was solvent immediately after creating the charge, except to the amount of cash paid to the company in consideration of the charge, with interest thereon at the rate of 5 per cent.[1] This is an important provision, since banks and other institutions which lend monies to companies normally require such a floating charge to be created by the company to secure the advance. If a petition is presented within twelve months from the creation of the charge and a winding up order made, the charge is invalid except to the extent of monies actually advanced in consideration of the charge. The provision has been more fully dealt with in Chapter Twenty-One above.

1. S 288 of the Principal Act.

Staying of proceedings

34.32 It is essential to the nature of the winding up procedure that individual creditors should not be allowed to proceed with a multiplicity of separate actions against the company. Accordingly, the Principal Act provides that no action or proceeding can be taken against the company after the order or after the appointment of a provisional liquidator except by leave of the court and subject to such terms as the court may impose.[1]

1. S 222 of the Principal Act.

34.33 There are many instances in which the court will exercise its power to allow proceedings to be maintained notwithstanding the winding up order. Secured creditors are allowed to proceed with any action to enforce their security as a matter of course.[1] Other examples are proceedings in respect of fatal accidents under s 48 of the Civil Liability Act 1961;[2] for specific performance;[3] and for securing the fruits of an earlier action.[4] The application for leave is made by motion on notice.

1. *Lloyd v Lloyd & Co* (1877) 6 Ch D 339.
2. *Re Thurso New Gas Co* (1899) 42 Ch D 486 at 491.
3. *Thames Plate Glass Co v Land etc Co* [1870] LR 11 Eq 248.
4. *Re National Provincial Insurance Corpn, Cooper v National Provincial Insurance Corpn* (1912) 56 Sol Jo 290.

34.34 After the presentation of the petition and before the making of the order, any creditor or contributory, in the case of an action or proceedings in the High Court or an appeal to the Supreme Court, may apply to the court in which the action, proceeding or appeal is pending for a stay of the proceedings; and, in the case of an action or proceeding in any other court, may apply to the High Court for an order restraining further proceedings. The court to which the application is made can restrain the proceedings on such terms and for such period as it thinks just.[1]

1. S 217 of the Principal Act.

Costs

34.35 The costs of the petition are in the discretion of the court; but in the event of the winding up order being made, the usual practice is to give the petitioner and the company their costs. It is also usual to allow one set of costs each to the creditors and contributories supporting the petition.[1] The costs are paid in the first place out of the assets of the company.[2] If the order is refused, the petitioner may have to pay the costs of any creditors and contributories who opposed the petition. But if a petitioning creditor has actually obtained judgment for his debt and fails to get a winding up order because of opposition by the majority of creditors, costs will not usually be given against him.[3]

1. *Re Humber Ironworks Company* [1866] LR 2 Eq 15.
2. Rule 129(1).
3. *Re R W Sharman Ltd* [1957] 1 All ER 737.

Appeal

34.36 Any party affected by the winding up order, or by the court's refusal to grant one, may appeal to the Supreme Court by serving notice of appeal within twenty-one days from the date of the order.[1] When a company appeals from the making of a winding up order, it can be required to give security for the costs of the appeal.[2]

1. Ord 58, r 3 of the Rules of the Superior Courts.
2. S 390 of the Principal Act.

Statement of affairs

34.37 When the court has made the winding up order or appointed a provisional liquidator,[1] a statement must be filed in court of the company's affairs. The statement, which must be in the prescribed form[2] and verified by affidavit,[3] must show:
  (i) the company's assets and liabilities;
  (ii) the names, residences and occupations of the company's creditors;

    (iii) the securities held by such creditors and the dates when such securities were given;

    (iv) such further information as may be or as the court may require.[4]

1. For the appointment of a provisional liquidator, see para 34.48 below.
2. Form No. 13, Appendix M.
3. Rule 25.
4. S 224 of the Principal Act.

34.38 The statement is to be filed and verified by one or more of the directors at the date of the winding up order and by the secretary at that time. Alternatively, it can be filed and verified by such of the persons named in s 224 (2) as the court may direct. It must be filed within 21 days from the date of the winding up order or within such extended time as the court may for special reasons appoint. There are ancillary provisions in regard to penalties for not complying with the requirements of the section and the rights of contributories and creditors to copies or extracts from the statement.

34.39 If a person who is required to make, or concur in making, such a statement, anticipates that he will incur costs or expenses in connection with its preparation—such as, for example, accountants' or valuers' fees—he should apply to the liquidator for his sanction, submitting an estimate of the costs in question. If there is no liquidator, a similar application should be made to the court. Unless such sanction is obtained, the costs or expenses involved will not be allowed out of the assets, except by order of the court.[1]

1. Rule 26.

34.40 The court has power to dispense with the requirements as to filing a statement of affairs.[1] An application for an order to that effect must be supported by a report of the liquidator showing the special circumstances which, in his opinion, render such a course desirable.[2]

1. S 224 of the Principal Act.
2. Rule 27(1).

34.41 Unless the court otherwise orders, the liquidator must send, as soon as practical, to each creditor mentioned in the statement and to the contributories a summary of the company's statement of affairs, including the causes of its failure, and any observations thereon which the liquidator may think fit to make.[1] Where prior to the winding up order the company was being wound up voluntarily, the liquidator may, in his discretion, send the creditors and contributories an account of the voluntary winding up.[2]

1. Rule 29(1).
2. Rule 29(2).

34.42 The court may from time to time require any of the persons named in s 224 (2) to attend before the court for the purpose of giving such further information in relation to the company as the court may think fit.[1]

1. Rule 25(2).

Proceedings under the winding up order

34.43 The order must be advertised by the petitioner once in *Iris Ofigiuil* and once in each of the newspapers in which the petition was advertised, unless the court otherwise directs.[1] It must also be served on such persons (if any) and in such manner as the court may direct.[2]

A certified copy of the order is to be left at the office of one of the Examiners of the High Court within ten days of its perfection. If this is not done, any other person interested in the winding up may take this step and be given the carriage of the winding up proceedings by the court.[3]

A notice to proceed under the order must then be taken out and served on all the parties who appeared at the hearing of the petition.[4] On the return day fixed by this notice, a time is fixed for the next major step in the winding up: the proof of debts and the settling of the list of contributories. Directions are given by the Examiner as to the advertisements to be published for all or any of these purposes and generally as to the proceedings and the parties to attend thereon.[5]

1. Rule 21.
2. Ibid.
3. Rule 22.
4. Ibid.
5. Ibid.

Appointment of the liquidator

34.44 The court appoints a liquidator or liquidators to carry out the winding up. He is described by the title of 'the Official Liquidator'. He must, within twenty-one days after his appointment publish in *Iris Ofigiuil* a notice of his appointment and must deliver to the Registrar an office copy of the order appointing him.[1] If he fails to comply with these requirements, he is liable to a fine not exceeding £250.[2]

1. S 227 of the Principal Act.
2. Ibid as amended by s 15 of the 1982 Act.

34.45 The liquidator can be appointed by the court either without previous advertisement or notice to anyone or following the publication of an advertisement in the prescribed manner.[1] He is required to give security on his appointment, and the usual requirement is that he enters into a bond with two or more sureties in a sum approved by the Court.[2] The court may, however, authorise him to act as liquidator without giving security for such time as the court may fix.[3]

1. Rule 30.
2. Rule 32.
3. Ibid.

34.46 It should be noted that there is no requirement in the Acts or the Rules that the liquidator should be qualified in any manner. In practice, it is almost invariable for the liquidator to be a practising accountant and he is usually a member of one of the recognised professional institutes.

Remuneration

34.47 The court directs what remuneration the liquidator is to receive.[1] There is no scale of fees fixed for remuneration: the court considers the circumstances of the particular case and determines what is fair. The court is in no sense bound by the scales of fees fixed for accountancy work by professional institutions, although it may take such scales into account in determining what is fair remuneration if it thinks proper. In practice, the court will naturally seek to ensure that there is reasonable uniformity in the fixing of remuneration for accountancy work of similar types. In order to achieve this result, a practice has developed in recent times of appointing a creditor— usually the Revenue—to represent the general body of creditors in an inquiry into the liquidator's charges before the Examiner. The procedure is not dissimilar to the taxation before a taxing master of a successful litigant's costs. The Examiner then submits a report on the inquiry to the judge.[2]

1. S 228 of the Principal Act; Rule 47.
2. See *Re Merchant Banking Ltd*, unreported, Costello J, judgment delivered 29 April 1985.

Provisional liquidator

34.48 The court may in certain cases appoint a provisional liquidator before any winding up order is made. This will usually be done when the company's assets are in danger. He can be appointed without advertisement or notice to any party-unless the court directs otherwise and without giving security.[1]

1. Rule 15.

Resignation and removal

34.49 The liquidator may resign or be removed by the court 'on cause shown'.[1] Thus, a liquidator was removed when he insisted on acting in the shareholders' interests only, although there was no reasonable prospect of paying the debts in full and the liquidator was acting in good faith.[2]

A vacancy in the office of liquidator, however caused, is filled by the court. When the liquidator resigns or is removed, he has to deliver all books, papers, documents and accounts in his possession relating to his office to the new liquidator. He will not be released from his office until he has done so.[3]

1. S 228 of the Principal Act.
2. *Re Rubber and Produce Investment Trust* [1915] 1 Ch 382.
3. Rule 37.

Duties of the liquidator

34.50 The principal duties of the liquidator are:
  (i) to take possession of the company's assets and protect them;
  (ii) to make out lists of the creditors and contributories;
  (iii) to have disputed cases adjudicated upon by the court;
  (iv) to realise the assets;
  (v) to apply the proceeds in payment of the company's debts and liabilities in the proper priority;
  (vi) to distribute the surplus (if any) among the contributories and adjust their rights.

34.51 As soon as he has been appointed, the liquidator must take into his custody or under his control all the property and choses in action to which the company is, or appears to be, entitled.[1] should there be any interval between the making of the winding up order and his appointment, the property during that period is in the custody of the court.[2]

1. S 229 of the Principal Act.
2. Ibid.

34.52 The court may, on the liquidator's application, make an order vesting all or any part of the assets in him in his official name.[1] Unless such an order is made, the assets remain vested in the company: there is no *cessio bonorum* merely by virtue of the winding up order. If an order is made vesting any property in the liquidator, he may then institute or defend in his official name any proceedings relating to that property or which it is necessary to bring or defend for the purpose of effectively winding up the company.[2] Any other proceedings are brought by him in the name of the company.

1. S 230 of the Principal Act.
2. Ibid.

The committee of inspection

34.53 The liquidator may be supervised and assisted in the conduct of the winding up by a committee of inspection composed of creditors and contributories. If the court so directs, he must summon a meeting of creditors and contributories or separate meetings of each category in order to decide whether an application should be made to the court for the appointment of a committee and who are to be its members.[1] If separate meetings of the creditors and contributories are held and come to conflicting conclusions as to whether a committee should be appointed or as to its composition, the court can resolve the dispute.[2]

There are provisions in the Principal Act as to when the committee is to meet; as to the majority required for its decisions; and as to the resignation, forfeiture of office, removal and replacement of members.[3] It has been held that the members may not purchase the assets of the company or make a profit from the winding up,[4] without the sanction of the court.

1. S 232 of the Principal Act. For the procedure, see Rule 51.
2. S 232(2) of the Principal Act; Rule 51.
3. S 233.
4. *Dowling v Lord Advocate* 1963 SLT 146.

Meetings of creditors and contributories

34.54 There are provisions in the Acts and the Rules for the summoning by the court and the liquidator of meetings of creditors and contributories.[1] The former are called 'Court Meetings' and the latter 'Liquidator's Meetings'. The Rules prescribe the procedure for summoning such meetings, the manner in which they are to be conducted and the proof by creditors of their entitlement to vote and contain certain provisions for voting by proxy.[2]

1. S 232 and 309 of the principal Act; Rule 55(1).
2. Rules 57 to 84 inclusive.

Powers of the liquidator

34.55 Certain powers are specifically conferred on the liquidator by s 231 of the Principal Act, but the list is not exhaustive. Some of the powers—principally the carrying on of the company's business, the bringing or defending of civil or criminal proceedings, the employment of a solicitor, the settlement of claims and the making of calls—he can exercise only with the consent of the court or the committee of inspection. Without such consent, he can do the other things specified in the section, including 'all such other things as may be necessary for winding up the affairs of the company and distributing its assets'. Thus, the liquidator, without such consent, may

  (i) sell any property of the company;
 (ii) accept and make bills of exchange or promissory notes on the security of the assets;
(iii) prove in the bankruptcy of any contributory;
(iv) take out administration to the estate of a deceased contributory;
 (v) execute deeds, receipts and other documents.

But while the liquidator is entitled to sell any property of the company without the sanction of the court, it is the usual practice for him to apply to the court for its approval in the case of the sale of assets of any significant value. He is entitled to apply to the court for directions under s 260 of the Principal Act and this right is frequently availed of in the case of sales of the company's property. The procedure applicable where the property is being sold subject to the court's approval is dealt with in para 34.59 below.

34.56 The liquidator is specifically given power by s 290 to disclaim with leave of the court any property which is unsaleable or not sufficiently saleable, because of obligations attached to it, such as land burdened with onerous covenants, shares or stocks in companies or unprofitable contracts. The disclaimer, to be effective, must be made in writing within the time prescribed by the Act and he can be required to elect whether he will disclaim or not by a person interested in the property. There are ancillary provisions as to the vesting of disclaimed property, the rescission of onerous contracts and damages for their breach.

The section expressly provides that the disclaimer is not to affect the rights and liabilities of third parties except so far as is necessary for the purpose of preserving the company and its assets from liability. This means that the right of the landlord of property to recover rent from a guarantor (or the original lessee where the lease has been assigned) is not affected by a disclaimer. This was so held by Keane J in *Tempany v Royal Liver Co*[1] in which he refused to follow the English decision of *Re Katherine et Cie*.[2]

1. [1984] ILRM 273.
2. [1932] 1 Ch 70.

Position of the liquidator

34.57 The liquidator is an agent of the company with fiduciary obligations arising from his office and with statutory obligations imposed on him by the Acts.[1] If the company has not been dissolved, he may be ordered to pay damages or compensation under s 298 of the Principal Act;[2] and if the company has been dissolved, he may be sued for breach of his statutory duties.[3] It would seem that while he may be loosely described as a 'trustee' for the company, he is not in any sense a trustee for its members or creditors.[4]

1. *Re Belfast Empire Threatre of Varieties* [1963] IR 41 at 49.
2. See para 34.89 below.
3. *Smith & Sons (Norwood) Ltd v Goodman* [1936] Ch 216.
4. *Re Belfast Empire Threatre of Varieties*, above, in which *Re Uniacke* (1944) 78 ILTR 154 was not followed.

Payment in of money, sales of property and declaration of dividends

34.58 The liquidator must pay all moneys received by him into the Bank of Ireland to the account of the liquidator within seven days from their receipt and can be charged interest and disallowed his remuneration if he fails to do so.[1] He must also deposit notes, bills and other securities in the Bank as soon as they come to hand.[2]

The court may order any person who owes money to a company to pay it into such bank as the court may appoint to the account of the liquidator and all moneys and securities so paid are to be subject in all respects to the orders of the court. The Rules provide the machinery whereby this is done.[3]

The Rules provide for the signing and countersigning by the liquidator and the Examiner of cheques;[4] for the investment of moneys standing to the credit of the liquidator in their joint names;[5] and for the payment of dividends and interest into the liquidator's account.[6]

It is normal for the liquidator to be given a float account which enables him to draw cheques without the countersignature of the Examiner. He then accounts for the operation of the float, at intervals prescribed by the court, to the Examiner.

1. Rule 118.
2. Rule 119.
3. Rule 121.
4. Rule 122.
5. Rule 123.
6. Rule 124.

34.59 The Rules of the Superior Courts dealing with the sale of real and personal property with the approval of the court are applicable to sales of property belonging to a company in the course of a winding up. The conditions or contract of sale must be settled and approved by the court unless the court otherwise directs; and the court may, on a sale by public auction, fix a reserve.[1]

The court must ensure that the best price possible is realised for any property being sold; and, save where a binding contract has been entered into with its approval, it will direct the liquidator to accept a higher offer for the property even where an earlier lower offer has been recommended for acceptance by the liquidator.[2]

1. Order 51 of the Rules of the Superior Courts; Rule 125.
2. *Van Hool McArdle Ltd v Rohan Industrial Estates Ltd and Another* [1980] IR 237. dintinguishing *Re Hibernian Transport Co Ltd* [1972] IR 190.

File of proceedings

34.60 All documents in the winding up proceedings must be filed by the liquidator in one continuous file and kept by him as the court directs. Every contributory and creditor who has proved is entitled to examine the file free and take copies or extracts at his own expense. The file must be produced in court as required.[1]

1. Rule 133.

Contributories

34.61 For the purpose of getting in the assets of the company, the liquidator must obtain payment from the 'contributories' within the meaning of the Acts of the amount, if any, uncalled on their shares in the company.

The Principal Act provides that, in the event of the company being wound up, every present and past member is to be liable to contribute to the assets to an amount sufficient for the payment of its debts and liabilities and the costs of the winding up, and for the adjustment of the rights of the contributories between themselves.[1]

To this general principle, there are certain qualifications specified in s 207. The most important in practical terms is that which limits the liability of a member of a company limited by shares to the amount, if any, unpaid on his shares. In the case of a company limited by guarantee, it is limited to the amount which he has undertaken to contribute in the event of a winding up.

Past members, who ceased to be members more than a year before the winding up commenced, are also exempted. Even those who were members within the year are not liable for debts contracted since they ceased to be members and are not liable to contribute at all unless the present members are unable to make the contributions required from them under the Act.

1. S 207 of the Principal Act.

34.62 To enforce the liability of contributories, the liquidator at the time directed by the Court makes out a list of persons whom he claims to treats as contributories.[1] So far as practicable, he must observe the requirements of s 235 (3) by distinguishing between persons who are contributories in their own right and as representatives of others.[2] The list is settled by the Examiner, unless it appears to the court that it will not be necessary to make calls or to adjust the rights of contributories in which case the settlement may be dispensed with.[3]

The list is made out in two parts: 'A', consisting of the present members and 'B', of the past. A members are primarily liable, the B members being called upon to contribute only if the A members' contributions are exhausted.

Calls are to be made on contributories to the extent of their liability for the payment of any money which the court considers necessary to satisfy the debts and liabilities of the company; and, for this purpose, debts and liabilities include estimated debts and liabilities. Calls are enforced by court order. The application for the order is made by motion on notice stating the proposed amount of the call. The procedure for making calls is provided by Rules 93 to 95.[4]

1. Rule 87. A bankrupt should be placed on the list of contributories as being liable for calls, if the bankruptcy petition has been presented *before* the winding up petition. (*Re Ligoniel Spinning Co Ltd* [1900] 1 IR 250). It would seem that in Ireland a fully paid up shareholder should also be placed on the list althought the company is insolvent; *Re Hollyford Mining Co* (1867) IR 1 Eq 39. (But see *Re Consolidated Goldfields of New Zealand* [1953] Ch 689.)
2. Rule 87.
3. S 235 (2) of the Principal Act; and see *Re Paragon Holdings Ltd* [1961] Ch 346.
4. For calls generally, see Chapter Eighteen above.

Distribution of surplus assets among contributories

34.63 Subject to the payment of the creditors and of the costs of the winding up, the assets are distributed among the contributories in accordance with their rights and interests.

The surplus is first applied in repaying to the contributories the amounts they have paid up on their shares. Where it is more than sufficient for this purpose, the actual amount paid up is first returned to them and any balance left over is distributed among them in proportion to the nominal amount of the share capital held by each of them.[1]

Where the surplus is not sufficient to repay all the capital paid up, the liquidator must, if necessary, 'equalise' the amounts paid up. He does this by making calls on the contributories who have paid less than others for amounts sufficient to make all the shares equally paid up. The surplus is then distributed in proportion to the nominal amount of the share capital held by each contributory.[2]

Where, however, the articles of association provide that losses are to be borne in proportion to the amount of the capital paid up or which ought to have been paid up by the contributories, the general rule does not apply and the liquidator cannot equalise the amounts paid up by making calls.[3]

The memorandum and articles may contain other provisions modifying or excluding the general principles stated above. In construing any such provisions, it must be borne in mind that the phrase 'surplus assets' may bear different meanings according to the context in which it is used. It may mean the balance left after the creditors and the costs of the winding up have been paid; or it may mean what remains after payment of the capital paid up on all classes of shares.

1. *Ex parte Maude* [1870] 6 Ch App. 51.
2. Ibid.
3. *Re Kinatan (Borneo) Rubber Ltd* [1923] 1 Ch 124.

The creditors

34.64 The principle of limited liability means that the creditors' remedy is solely against the company. The usual object of a winding up by the court is to prevent the creditors from maintaining separate actions against the company and to provide machinery whereby all the creditors are paid so far as the assets of the company permit. Accordingly, the Acts and the Rules prescribe the manner in which they are to come in and prove their claims and the priority which certain classes of creditors are to enjoy.

34.65 The debts which can be proved are specified in s 283 of the Principal Act. All debts payable on a contingency and all claims against the company, present or future, certain or contingent, and whether ascertained or sounding only in damages, are admissible to proof against the company. A just estimate must be made, as far as possible, of the value of any debts or claims which are subject to a contingency or which sound only in damages or for some other reason do not bear a certain value.

The liquidator must reject debts barred by the provisions of the Statute of Limitations 1957 provided that the statutory period of limitation has expired before the commencement of the liquidation.[1]

1. *Re General Rolling Stock Co Ltd* (1872) 7 Ch App 646.

Application of the rules in bankruptcy

34.66 Section 284 of the Principal Act provides that in the winding up of insolvent companies, the same rules are to apply as in the law of bankruptcy with regard to:

(i) the respective rights of secured and unsecured creditors;

(ii) debts provable, and

(iii) the valuation of annuities and future and contingent liabilities.

It should be noted that the section does not mean that all the bankruptcy rules apply in a winding up. Only those which deal with the three matters specified apply. In particular, the bankruptcy rules the effect of which is to increase the assets available for the bankrupt's creditors by invalidating certain transactions, do not apply.[1] The Principal Act, as we have seen, contains equivalent provisions appropriate to a winding up.

It does mean, however, that a debt not provable in bankruptcy cannot be proved in a winding up. Consequently, claims for unliquidated damages arising otherwise than by reason of contract or breach of trust are excluded.[2] Accordingly, unliquidated damages arising from personal torts cannot be proved, unless of course judgment has been recovered for an ascertained amount of damages.

1. *Re Irish Attested Sales Ltd* [1962] IR 70.
2. Bankruptcy (Ireland) Amendment Act 1872, s 46.

34.67 The application of the bankruptcy rules means that the provisions of s 251 of the Irish Bankrupts and Insolvents Act 1857, which deal with the setting off of debts, are imported into a winding up. That section provides that where there are mutual debts owing or there has been mutual credit given by and between the bankrupt and any other person, one debt or demand can be set off against the other, notwithstanding an act of bankruptcy prior to the debts being contracted or the credit given. Only the balance after such set off can be proved in a winding up.

34.68 All debts may be set off under the section, but there must be 'mutuality'. Thus, a trustee cannot set off a debt owed by him personally to the company against a debt owed by the company to him as a trustee.[1] An unsecured debt may be set off against a secured debt under the section.[2]

1. *Re Newman, ex parte Brocke* (1876) 3 Ch D 494.
2. *McKinnon v Armstrong* (1877) 2 App Cas 531.

Procedure for ascertaining the creditors and proving their claims

34.69 In order to ascertain the creditors, an advertisement is published at such time as the court directs fixing a time within which the creditors are to send in to the liquidator particulars of their claims. This advertisement also appoints a day for adjudicating on the claims.[1]

The liquidator sets out in an affidavit the debts which he thinks should be allowed without further evidence and those which should be proved.[2] At the adjudication, the Examiner decides which debts should be allowed upon the liquidator's affidavit and which creditors should come in and prove.[3] The liquidator then gives notice to the latter of the time at which they are to attend to prove their claims.[4]

The value of contingent or unliquidated claims is to be ascertained, as far as possible, according to their value at the date of the winding up order.[5] Debts can be proved by sending particulars of the claim through the post, an affidavit not being necessary unless the liquidator and the Examiner specifically require one.[6] A creditor may come in and prove at any time before the final distribution of assets, but he cannot disturb any dividend already paid.[7]

The Examiner states the results of his adjudications in certificates.d[8]

1. Rule 96; Form No 35, Appendix M.
2. Rule 98.
3. Rule 99.
4. Ibid.
5. Rule 100.
6. Rule 97.
7. *Re General Rolling Stock Co,* above.
8. Rule 102.

Preferential debts

34.70   Certain debts set out in s 285 of the Principal Act (as subsequently amended) are given priority. Subject to this , all unsecured creditors are on an equal footing and must be paid equally. The State as such has no priority to be paid first and in full out of the assets, the existence of such a right being an aspect of the royal prerogative which did not survive the enactment of the Constitution of Saorstat Eireann.[1] Judgment creditors who have not completed execution of their judgments have no priority.[2].

Before any debts, including the preferential debts, are paid, a sum to meet the costs and expenses of the liquidation must be retained.[3] The remuneration, costs and expenses of the liquidator form part of these costs and expenses and consequently have priority over the preferential debts.[4]

The list of debts in s 285 does not provided an *order* of payment. Although they take priority over all other debts, they rank equally among themselves and if the assets are insufficient to pay them all, they must abate in equal proportions.

1. *Re Irish Employers' Mutual Insurance Association Ltd* [1955] IR 176.
2. S 291 of the Principal Act; and see *Re Leinster Contract Corpn* [1903] 1 IR 517.
3. S 285 (8) of the Principal Act.
4. *Re Redbreast Preserving Co (Ireland) Ltd* [1958] IR 234.

34.71   The debts in question include:
 (i) local rates which became due and payable within twelve months prior to the 'relevant date';[1]
 (ii) all assessed taxes, including income tax, corporation tax, value added tax and capital gains tax[2], not exceeding in the whole one year's assessment;
 (iii) sums deductible by the company as an employer under the relevant PAYE regulations, within the period of 12 months before the relevant date;
 (iv) wages and salaries (including sums due by way of commission) payable to any clerk or servant by the company for service rendered to the company during the four months prior to the relevant date;

(v) wages payable to any workman in the employement of the company (including sums payable by way of piece or time rates) within the period of four months prior to the relevant date;

(vi) holiday remuneration;

(vii) contributions payable by the company under the Redundancy Payments Act 1967 during the twelve months prior to the commencement of the winding up or the making of the winding up order;

(viii) damages for personal injuries due to people employed by the company.

A director of the company may be a 'clerk or servant' of the company within the meaning of (iv).[3]

1. In the case of a compulsory winding up, the date of the winding up order or the appointment of a provisional liquidator; in the case of a voluntary winding up, the passing of the necessary resolution.
2. Capital gains tax is included by virtue of the Capital Gains Tax Act 1975, s 51 (1), Sch 4, para 15.
3. *Stakelum v Canning* [1976] IR 314, in which *Beeton & Co Ltd* [1913] 2 Ch 279 was followed and *Re Newspapers Proprietors' Syndicate Ltd* [1900] 2 Ch 349 was not followed.

34.72 The section also provides that where a person advances money to an employer for the purpose of paying wages or salaries, the lender is entitled to the same right of priority as the employee would have had. In legal terms, the persons advancing the money (such as a bank) are *subrogated* to the rights of the employee, i.e. they stand in their shoes. It may not be easy for a bank or similar lending institution to establish that an account was opened expressly with a view to funding the payment of salaries or wages, but it was held by Plowman J in *Re Rampgill Mill Ltd*[1] that a benevolent rather than a narrow construction should be given to the section and in that case he permitted subrogation where the account had been opened to enable the company to meet its commitments and they clearly included wages due to employees. A similar approach was adopted by Carroll J in *Re Station Motors Ltd*.[2]

1. [1967] Ch 1138.
2. Unreported; judgment delivered 22 November 1984.

34.73 A further statutory right of subrogation is given to the Minister of Labour under the Protection of Employees (Employers Insolvency) Act 1984. Under that Act, the Minister is empowered to make payments to employees out of the Redundancy Fund established under the Redundancy Payments Act 1967 in respect of certain debts owed by an insolvent employer (including a company in liquidation) to his employees. The debts include arrears of wages, holiday pay and awards under various modern acts dealing with minimum notice, redundancy payments, unfair dismissal and employment equality. The Minister is given by s 10 the same right of priority as the employee would have enjoyed in respect of any of the debts.

Secured creditors

34.74 Secured creditors are creditors who have some mortgage, charge or lien on the company's property.

The application of the bankruptcy rules means that a secured creditor may adopt any of the following courses in a winding up:

(i) he may rely on his security and not prove in the winding up;

(ii) he may realise his security and, if it is insufficient, prove for the deficiency;

(iii) he may value his security and prove for the deficiency, the liquidator having the option of accepting his valuation;

(iv) he may surrender his security and prove for his debt like an unsecured creditor.[1]

A solicitor who holds a lien on documents of the company for his costs is a secured creditor.[2] A landlord is not a secured creditor, simply because he has a power of distress.[3] A creditor who has obtained a conditional order of garnishee, but has failed to serve it on the debtor before the winding up commences, is not a secured creditor.[4]

A person who executes a judgment against a company's lands or goods before the commencement of the winding up is a secured creditor; but under the provisions of s 291, he must have completed the execution before the winding up begins. The Principal Act obliges the sheriff, if required by the liquidator so to do, to hand over goods not actually sold; and when a judgment exceeds £20, the sheriff must retain the proceeds of sale for fourteen days and if he receives notice of a winding up order during that period must pay the proceeds, less the costs of execution, to the liquidator.[5] Anyone who buys goods from the sheriff in good faith acquires a good title to them, notwithstanding the winding up order.[6]

1. Bankruptcy (Ireland) Amendment Act 1872, s 63.
2. *Re Safety Explosives Ltd* [1904] 1 Ch 226.
3. *Re Coal Consumers' Association* (1876) 4 Ch D 625 at 629.
4. *Re Stanhope Silkstone Colliery Co* (1879) 11 Ch D 160.
5. S 292 of te Principal Act.
6. S 291 (3) of the Principal Act.

Leasehold property

34.75 Where a lease to a company being wound up contains a power of re-entry, the lessor may apply to the court for liberty to re-enter and the court will allow him to do so, without his having to bring proceedings.[1]

1. *General Share and Trust Co v Wetley Brick and Pottery Co* (1882) 20 ChD 260 at 266.

34.76 When the liquidator takes possession, or remains in possession, of leaseholds for the purpose of more effectively realising the assets, the lessor is entitled to payment of the rent in full as part of the expenses properly incurred by the liquidator.[1] The liquidator is then responsible for any repairs or other obligations for which the lessee is liable under the lease.[2] He may disclaim the lease with the leave of the court under s 290 of the Principal Act and the lessor can then prove for any damage he has sustained. The measure of such damage is the difference between the rent which would have been paid by the company under the lease and the rent which the lessor is likely to obtain during the unexpired residue.[3]

1. *Re Oak Pitts Colliery* (1882) 21 Ch D 322.
2. *Re Silkstone & Dodsworth Co* (1881) 17 Ch D 158.
3. *Re Hide ex parte Llynvi Coal Co* [1871] 7 Ch App 28.

Interest

34.77 The interest upon debts which carry interest ceases to run from the date of the commencement of the winding up, unless the assets are sufficient to pay all the debts in full.[1]

In order to ascertain the balance for which a secured creditor can prove after realising his security, the proceeds of the security are applied in payment of the principal sum with interest down to the date of the commencement of the winding up. He may then prove for the balance of principal and interest due down to that date as an unsecured creditor.[2]

1. *Re International Contract Co Ltd Hughes' Claim* [1872] LR 13 Eq 623.
2. *Quartermaine's Case* [1892] 1 Ch 639.

Fraudulent and undue preferences

34.78 Section 286 of the Act renders invalid as a 'fraudulent preference' any act relating to the property made or done by or against a company within six months before the commencement of the winding up if it qualifies as a fraudulent preference in the bankruptcy of an individual. This includes any conveyance, mortgage, delivery of goods, payment or execution.

34.79 For the preference to be fraudulent, it must be established that the transaction took place within six months of the commencement of the winding up and that the principle motive of the company, acting through its directors, was to prefer the creditor.[1]

The onus is on the liquidator to establish a dominant intention on the part of the company to prefer one creditor over another.[2] It is not enough to prove that there was an actual preference from which an intention to prefer is then, with hindsight, inferred. The liquidator must prove an intention to prefer at the time the payment is made.[3] But where there is no direct evidence of intention, there is nothing to prevent the court from drawing an inference of an intention to prefer in a case where no other possible explanation is open.[4] Where, however, the liquidator proves no more than a state of facts which is equally consistent with guilt or innocence (an expression used for convenience since there is no question of criminal liability) he will have failed to discharge the onus.[5]

1. S 286 (1) of the Principal Act.
2. *Corran Construction Ltd v Bank of Ireland Finance Ltd*; unreported; McWilliam J judgment delivered 8 September 1976.
3. *Re M Kushler Ltd* [1943] Ch 248.
4. Ibid.
5. Ibid.

34.80 The payment alleged to be a fraudulent preference may have benefited the person concerned only indirectly. This will not prevent it, however, from being a fraudulent preference. This frequently arises in guarantee cases: a director of the company may have personally guaranteed the company's overdraft and may then procure the repayment of the overdraft by the company with a view to eliminating his personal liability. In such a case, if an intention to prefer the director indirectly by the repayment of the overdraft can be proved, this will constitute a fraudulent preference.[1]

1. *Re Station Motors Ltd*, above.

34.81 If the transaction is void as a fraudulent preference of a person whose property is mortgaged or charged to secure the company's debt, he is to be treated in the winding up as though he was a surety for the debt to the extent of his charge or his interest in it.[1]

1. S 287 of the Principal Act.

34.82 The section is for the benefit of *all* the creditors and cannot be invoked if the result of recovering the property comprised in the fraudulent preference would be to the benefit of a section only of the creditors.[1]

1. *Ex parte Cooper* [1875] 10 Ch App 510.

Fraudulent trading

34.83 When it appears in a winding up that the company's business has been carried on by the company with intent to defraud creditors or for any fraudulent purpose, the court may declare that any of the directors who were knowingly parties to the fraud and any other person who was knowingly a party to carrying on the fraudulent business shall be personally liable for all or any of the debts of the company.[1]

1. S 297 of the Principal Act.

34.84 This section places a most important responsibility on the directors and management of a company. If they allow the company to continue trading at a time when they know it to be insolvent, they may render themselves personally liable under the section for the company's debts. If the company carries on business and incurs debts when there is to the knowledge of the directors, no reasonable prospect of the creditors being paid, it is, in general, a proper inference that the company is carrying on business with intent to defraud.[1]

1. *Re Wm C Leitch Bros Ltd* [1932] 2 Ch 71.

34.85 Normally one would expect to find a pattern of continuous fraudulent trading where an order is made under the section. Thus in *Re Aluminium Fabricators*,[1] O'Hanlon J found that the directors of a company had deliberately maintained a dual system of bookeeping in order to conceal from their auditors, the Revenue and their creditors generally the fact that they were siphoning off assets of the company for their own benefit. Hence the directors had been carrying on business fraudulently within the meaning of the section and were fixed with personal responsibility for all the company's debts.

But it is also clear that a single transaction may be enough to justify the making of an order under the section. In *Re Hunting Lodge Ltd*,[2] an application was made under the section when two directors, RP and his wife JP, had arranged for the sale of the only remaining asset of the company (the licensed premises near Limerick known as 'Durty Nelly's') to O'C, P Co being used by O'C as a vehicle for completing the transaction. The sale price was £480,000, but there was a secret arrangement for the payment of £200,000 by O'C directly to RP and not into the company's account. This money was lodged by RP in a building society in fictitious names. At the time of this transaction, the company was insolvent and when it was wound up the liquidator applied for an order under the section against RP, JP, O'C and P Co.

Carroll J held that the words 'any business of the company' in the section were not synonomous with trading; a single transaction which was entered into with the intention of defrauding the company's creditors could bring the section into operation. Since it was clear that the object of the transaction was to ensure that the sum of £200,000 was paid to RP rather than the creditors, an order could be made under the section.

1. Unreported; judgment delivered 13 May 1983.
2. Unreported; judgment delivered 1 June 1984.

34.86 It should be noted that the section is not confined to directors of the company: any persons who are 'knowingly parties' to the fraudulent carrying on of the business can be fixed with personal liability. In the case of persons other than the directors, however, mere inaction is not enough. The failure of the company's secretary or financial adviser to warn the directors of the company's insolvency and its possible consequences has been held to be an insufficient ground for the order.[1] But in *Re Hunting Lodge Ltd*, Carroll J found that not merely RP and JP were liable but also O'C and P Co on the ground that they had actively participated in the fraudulent transaction.

1. *Re Maidstone Building Provisions*, [1971] 3 All ER 363.

34.87 The judgement against the persons concerned is for a fixed sum, which then becomes part of the assets.[1] The court may also charge the liability of the directors against any security which they hold from the company; and may directly or indirectly disqualify a director from acting in the management of the companies for a specified period. A similar order can be made on the application of the liquidator or any creditor or contributory.[2]

1. *Re William C Leitch Bros Ltd (No 2)* [1933] Ch 261.
2. S 184 of the Principal Act.

Property held in trust

34.88 Property which can be identified as belonging to, or held by, the company in trust for any persons may be followed and recovered by the liquidator.[1]

1. *Re Lang Propeller Ltd* [1926] Ch 585 at 595; *Shanahans' Stamps Auctions Ltd v Farrelly and Dawson* [1982] IR 386.

Misfeasance proceedings

34.89 Section 298 of the Principal Act provides a useful summary remedy for recovering money from the promoters, directors, managers or other officers of the company which they have misapplied or have wrongfully received or for which they are accountable to the company. It can also be used when the directors have been guilty of some negligence or misfeasance for which they are answerable to the company in damages. It should be noted that the section does not create any new offence or cause of action; it simply provides a more expeditious remedy.[1]

Misfeasance proceedings have been taken when the directors have used funds of the company for objects not sanctioned by the memorandum;[2] or have paid dividends out of capital;[3] or have made secret profits;[4] or have sold their own property to the company.[5] In all cases, it must be shown that actual pecuniary loss has been caused to the company.[6]

1. *Re Irish Provident Assurance Co* [1913] 1 IR 352.
2. *Coats v Crossland* [1904] 20 TLR 800.
3. *Moxham v Grant* [1900] 1 QB 88.
4. *Pearson's Case* (1877) 5 Ch D 336.
5. *Re Cape Breton Co* (1885) 29 Ch D 795.
6. *Re SM Barjer Ltd* [1950] IR 123 at 137.

34.90 Misfeasance proceedings are brought by motion on notice. The notice must state the nature of the declaration or order which is sought and the grounds of the application. It must be served personally, together with a copy of any report or affidavit on which it is grounded, on every person against whom an order is sought not less than seven clear days before the day named for hearing the application.[1]

Misfeasance proceedings are abated by the completion of the winding up. They are not revived if the dissolution of the company is declared void under s 310 of the Principal Act.[2]

1. Rule 50.
2. *Re Lewis & Smart Ltd* [1954] 2 All ER 19.

34.91 Under s 8 of the Civil Liability Act 1961 on the death of any person, all causes of action subsisting against him survive against his estate, with certain exceptions which are not material; and consequently the estate of a decreased director can be sued in the ordinary way for any tort or breach of trust committed by him during his lifetime. But it would seem that this does not enable misfeasance proceedings to be brought against his estate.[1]

1. *Re British Guardian Assurance Co Ltd* (1880) 14 Ch D 335.

Examination by the court

34.92-34.93 The court is given power by s 243 of the Principal Act to summon before it any officer of the company or any person known or suspected to have in his possession any of the property of the company or suspected of being indebted to the company, or any person whom the court may deem capable of giving information concerning the promotion, formation, trading, dealing, officers or property of the company. This power becomes exercisable at any time after the appointment of a provisional liquidator or the making of a winding up order. The court can direct such an examination to be held in private, such a procedure not being repugnant to Article 34.1 of the Constitution.[1] The examination may be held either before the judge or an officer of the court, such as the Master or the Examiner.[2]

1. *Re Redbreast Preserving Co (Ireland) Ltd* 91 ILTR 12.
2. Ord 39, r 4.

34.94 The section provides that none of the answers of the person shall be admissible in evidence against him in any other proceedings, civil or criminal, except proceedings for perjury in respect of any of the answers. It was held by O'Hanlon J in *Re Aluminium Fabricators Ltd*[1] that this did not prevent the transcript being used in proceedings under the winding up order itself, e.g. an application under the fraudulent trading section.

1. [1984] ILRM 399.

Prosecution of officers and members

34.95 If it appears that any officers and members of the company have been guilty of offences in relation to the company, the court can direct the liquidator to refer the matter to the Director of Public Prosecutions. If the Director considers that proceedings should be brought, the liquidator and every officer or agent of the company (other than the defendant) must give him all reasonable assistance in connection with the prosecution.[1]

1. S 299 of the Principal Act.

Offences

34.96 The Act provides for the punishment of certain offences by officers of a company which is being wound up or is subsequently wound up. These offences, which include the falsification of books, concealment or removal of property and fraudulent practices relating to creditors are set out in ss 293, 294, 295 and 296 of the Principal Act. They are punishable on conviction on indictment by penalties ranging from penal servitude for a term not exceeding two years, a fine not exceeding £500 or both to penal servitude for five years or a fine not exceeding £10,000 or both. They are also punishable summarily, the maximum sentence being imprisonment for six months or a fine not exceeding £100 or both.

Termination of the winding up

34.97 When the liquidator has passed his final account, he applies to the court for directions as to the applicaton of the balance.[1] When the application, as so directed, has been vouched to the Examiner, the Examiner certifies that it has been so vouched and that the affairs of the company have been completely wound up.[2] If the company has not already been dissolved, the liquidator immediately after such certificate has become binding applies to the court for an order that the company be dissolved from the date of the order.[3] An office copy of the order is to be forwarded by the liquidator to the Registrar within 21 days from the date of the order.[4]

The dissolution may within two years be declared to have been void[5] The application for such a declaration is made to the court by motion on notice.

1. Rule 138.
2. Ibid, Form No 46, Appendix M.
3. S 249 (1) of the Principal Act.
4. S 249 (2) of the Principal Act.
5. S 310 of the Principal Act.

Chapter 35

Voluntary winding up

35.01 A company can be wound up voluntarily in the following circumstances:
- (i) if the company resolves by special resolution that it should be bound up voluntarily;
- (ii) if the company in general meeting resolves that it cannot by reason of its liabilities continue its business and that it be wound up voluntarily;
- (iii) when the period, if any, fixed for the duration of the company by the articles expires, or the event, if any, occurs on the occurrence of which the articles provide that the company is to be dissolved, and the company in general meeting has passed a resolution that it be wound up voluntarily.[1]

Of these, (i) and (ii) are by far the most common. It should be noted that where the company is wound up voluntarily because of its inability to stay in business, the necessary resolution can be passed with a simple majority and the same applies to a winding up on the rare occasions when (iii) is invoked. In any other case a three-fourths majority is required.

1. S 251 of the Principal Act.

35.02 There are two types of voluntary winding up: members' and creditors'. In a members' winding up, certain important matters (notably the appointment of a liquidator) remain under the control of the company. In a creditors', this control is transferred to the creditors or a committee representing them.

Commencement of a voluntary winding up

35.03 A voluntary winding up is always begun by a resolution of the company, but as we have seen, the form of the resolution will depend on the circumstances which give rise to the winding up. The company must give notice of the passing of the resolution by advertisement in *Iris Ofigiuil* within 14 days from its being passed. If this is not done, the company and every officer in default are liable to a fine not exceeding £125. The liquidator is deemed to be an officer of the company for this purpose.[1]

1. S 252 of the Principal Act as amended by s 15 of the 1982 Act.

Declaration of solvency

35.04 Before the resolution for a voluntary winding up is passed, the directors of the company (or where there are more than two, a majority of them) may make a declaration as to the solvency of the company at a meeting of the directors. The declaration takes the form of a statement by the directors that, having inquired fully into the affairs of the company, they have formed the opinion that the company will be able to pay its debts within a specified period, which must be not more than twelve months from the commencement of the winding up.[1]

The importance of this declaration is that it determines whether the winding up is a members' or a creditors' winding up. If no declaration is made, the winding up proceeds as a creditors' winding up. But a creditor may also apply to the court, where a declaration is made, for an order that the winding up continue as a creditors' winding up. Such an application must be made within 28 days from the advertising of the resolution for winding up and the creditors applying and those creditors supporting him must represent at least one-fifth in number or value of all the creditors. The court may make the order if it is of the opinion that it is unlikely that the company will be able to pay its debts within the period specified in the declaration of solvency.[2]

The declaration is of no effect unless it is made within the 28 days immediately preceding the passing of the resolution and is delivered to the Registrar for registration not later than the delivery of a printed copy of the resolution to the Registrar as required by s 143. (Such a copy must be delivered not later than 15 days after the passing of the resolution.) It must embody a statement of the company's assets and liabilities as at a date not more than three months prior to its date.[3]

1. S 256 of the Principal Act.
2. S 256 (3) of the Principal Act.
3. S 256 (2) of the Principal Act as substituted by s 9 of the 1982 Act.

35.05 A director who makes a declaration of solvency without having reasonable grounds for the opinion that the company will be able to pay its debts within the specified period is liable to imprisonment for a period not exceeding six months or to a maximum fine of £500 or both. If the company is wound up in pursuance of a resolution passed within the 28 days period, but its debts are not paid or provided for in full within the stated period, there is a rebuttable presumption that the director did not have reasonable grounds for his opinion.[1]

The declaration of solvency does not affect the right of the creditors of the company to have it compulsorily wound up if in fact they can prove that it is insolvent.

1. S 256 (6) of the Principal Act.

The creditors' meeting

35.06 In the case of a creditors' winding up, the company is obliged by the Acts to summon a meeting of the creditors.[1] They must also publish an advertisement giving notice of it at least once in two daily newspapers circulating in the district where the registered office or principal place of business of the company is situated. The director of the company must cause a full statement of the position of the company's affairs, a list of its creditors and the estimated amount of their claims to be laid before the meeting. They must also appoint one of their number to preside at the meeting. A maximum fine of £500 can be imposed in the event of the company or any of its directors failing to comply with these requirements.[2]

Should the meeting of the company at which the resolution for voluntary winding up is dealt with be adjourned and the resolution be passed at the adjourned meeting, any resolution passed at the meeting of the creditors is to have effect as if it were passed immediately after the passing of the winding up resolution.[3]

1. S 266 (1) of the Principal Act.
2. S 266 (6) of the Principal Act, as amended by s 15 of the 1982 Act.
3. S 266 (5) of the Principal Act.

Appointment of a liquidator in a creditors' winding up

35.07   At the creditors' meeting, the creditors and the company may each nominate a person to be liquidator of the company. If different persons are appointed, the creditors' nominee is to be the liquidator. If no person is nominated by the creditors, the company may appoint the liquidator. There is a provision that in the event of different persons being nominated as liquidators, any director, member or creditor of the company may within fourteen days after the creditors' nomination apply to the court for an order directing that the company's nominee be liquidator instead of or jointly with the creditors' nominee or an order appointing some person other than the creditors' nominee to be liquidator.[1]

On the appointment of a liquidator, all the powers of the directors cease, except so far as the creditors, or their committee of inspection, sanction their continuance.[2]

1. S 267 (2) of the Principal Act.
2. S 269 (3) of the Principal Act.

The committee of inspection

35.08   The creditors in a creditors' winding up are given important powers which enable them to supervise the actual conduct of the liquidation. These are exercised through a body called 'the committee of inspection'. The committee is appointed by the creditors at the creditors' meeting or at a subsequent meeting and consists of not more than five members. The company may, if it wishes, appoint three additional members to the committee at the meeting when the winding up resolution is passed or at any time subsequently in general meeting. But the creditors have a power of veto over any such appointment by the company and, if they so resolve, the persons thus appointed are disqualified from acting, unless the court otherwise directs. The court has jurisdiction to appoint other persons instead of those disqualified by the creditors' resolution. The number of members on the committee cannot in any event exceed eight.[1]

1. S 268 of the Principal Act.

Remuneration of liquidator in creditors' winding up

35.09   The committee of inspection fixes the remuneration to be paid to the liquidator in a creditors' winding up. If there is no committee, the creditors do so. Any creditor or contributory who thinks the remuneration is excessive can apply to the court within 28 days after it has been fixed to have it fixed by the court.[1]

1. S 269 of the Principal Act.

Appointment of a liquidator in a members' voluntary winding up

35.10   In a members' voluntary winding up, the company in general meeting appoints one or more liquidators and can fix his or their remuneration. On the appointment all the powers of the directors cease, except so far as the company in general meeting or the liquidator sanctions their continuance.[1] The passing of the special resolution that the company be wound up voluntarily is an essential preliminary to the appointing of the liquidator.

The liquidator can be appointed at the same meeting at which the winding up resolution is passed and this is the usual practice. It is not strictly necessary that the notice convening the meeting should expressly refer to the appointment of the liquidator, but it is obviously preferable that it should. In practice, the notice usually states that a named person will be proposed at the meeting as liquidator. If this resolution is not passed, the meeting can appoint another person. If there is any doubt as to the validity of the appointment, the court will usually appoint the person whom the meeting intended to appoint.

1. S 258 (2) of the Principal Act.

Powers and duties of the liquidators in a voluntary winding up

35.11   The liquidator in a voluntary winding up may exercise all or any of the powers vested in an official liquidator in a compulsory winding up. Some of these, however, may only be exercised with the sanction of a special resolution of the company (in the case of a members' winding up) or the court, committee of inspection or creditors (in the case of a creditors' winding up). They are the powers to
   (i) pay any class of creditors in full;
  (ii) make compromises or arrangements with creditors or persons claiming to be creditors or having, or alleging themselves to have, claims against the company;
 (iii) compromise calls, liabilities to calls and debts and claims between the company and contributories or other debtors or possible debtors.[1]
If there is no committee of inspection in the case of a creditors' winding up, the powers may be exercised with the sanction of the court or the creditors.

1. Section 276 (1) of the Principal Act.

35.12   All the other powers conferred on the liquidator in a winding up by the court can be exercised by the liquidator in a voluntary winding up without sanction. These include the power
   (i) to bring or defend actions in the name of and on behalf of the company;
  (ii) to carry on the business of the company so far as may be necessary for its beneficial winding up;
 (iii) to sell the property of the company;
 (iv) to execute deeds and other documents in the company's name and where necessary use its seal;
  (v) to draw cheques etc. in the company's name and on its behalf;
 (vi) to borrow money on the security of the company's assets;

(vii) to do anything else that may be necessary for winding up the company.[1]

1. Ibid.

35.13 It is in theory possible to appoint more than one liquidator, but this is very rarely done nowadays. Where more than one is appointed, the liquidators' powers may be exercised by such one or more of them as may be determined at the time of their appointment, or in default of such determination, by any number not less than two.[1] They cannot make a general delegation of their powers to one of their number, although they may delegate the execution of a particular document. When one of them dies, the survivor cannot act alone: a new liquidator must be appointed.

1. S 276 (3) of the Principal Act.

35.14 The liquidator's duty, as in a compulsory winding up, is to get in the assets of the company, pay the creditors and adjust the rights of the contributories. He is an officer of the company.

In the case of a members' voluntary winding up, if the liquidator at any time thinks that the company will not be able to pay its debts in full within the period specified in the declaration of solvency, he must forthwith summon a meeting of the creditors and lay before it a statement of the company's assets and liabilities. If he fails to do so, he is liable to a fine not exceeding £250.[1]

1. S 261 of the Principal Act, as amended by s 15 of the 1982 Act.

Meetings of the company and creditors

35.15 The liquidator may summon general meetings of the company for the purpose of obtaining its sanction to the exercise of the powers which require such sanction. He may also summon a meeting for any other purpose as he thinks fit.[1]

In the case of a members' winding up, he must summon such a meeting at the end of the first year from the commencement of the winding up and at the end of each succeeding year, or at the first convenient date within three months from the end of the year. He must lay before the meeting an account of his acts and dealings and of the conduct of the winding up during the preceding year and must within seven days after the meeting send a copy of his account to the Registrar. He is liable to a fine not exceeding £250 if he fails to comply with these requirements[2] There is a similar requirement to call a meeting of the company and of the creditors in the case of creditors' winding up and to lay before them a similar account.[3]

1. S 276 (1) of the Principal Act.
2. S 262 of the Principal Act, as amended by s 15 of the 1982 Act.
3. S 272 of the Principal Act as amended by s 15 of the 1982 act.

Remuneration of the liquidator

35.16 In a members' voluntary winding up, the company in general meeting may fix the remuneration to be paid to the liquidator.[1] As has already been noted, in a creditors' winding up, it is determined by the committee of inspection, or, if there is no such committee, by the creditors.[2]

If the remuneration is not so fixed, it may be fixed by the court, each case being considered with regard to its particular facts.[3]

1. S 258 of the Principal Act.
2. Para 35.09 above.
3. *Re Amalgamated Syndicates Ltd* [1901] 2 Ch 181.

35.17 Where the winding up resolution is set aside as invalid and the company is afterwards ordered to be wound up, the liquidator in the voluntary winding up is not entitled to be paid anything for his services as such. He is, however, entitled to reasonable remuneration for any work done by him which has been useful to the company for business purposes unconnected with the liquidation or which has been used by the official liquidator with full knowledge of the facts.[1]

1. *Re Allison, Johnston & Foster Ltd ex parte Birkenshaw* [1904] 2 KB 327.

Applications to the court

35.18 The liquidator may apply to the court under s 280 for the determination of any question arising during the course of the winding up. He may also ask the court to exercise in relation to the enforcing of calls or any other matter all or any of the powers which might be exercised by the court if the company were being wound up by the court. Such applications may also be made by any creditor or contributory of the company. The court may accede wholly or partially to the application, if satisfied that the determination of the question or the exercise of the power will be 'just and beneficial'.[1]

1. Sub-s (2).

35.19 This power, like the corresponding power conferred on receivers by s 316, is very useful and liquidators should not hesitate to make use of it if they have any serious doubts as to how to proceed. It has been held in England that the powers conferred by the corresponding section of the 1948 Act should be liberally construed.[1] On an application under the section the court may, among other things, restrain proceedings being brought against the company. (Unlike an order for the winding up of the company by the court, a voluntary winding up does not automatically prevent such proceedings being taken.) The usual course is to stay the proceedings.

An application for the examination of directors or other persons either in private or public may also be made under the section.[2]

1. Palmer, vol I, 86–19.
2. See para 34.92 above.

35.20 The liquidator may also find it necessary to apply to the court under this section in relation to calls. As we have seen, in the case of a compulsory winding up, the list of contributories and the amounts which they are required to pay are settled by the Examiner.[1] In the case of a voluntary winding up, the liquidator may settle the list himself, applying the same principles, i.e. distinguishing between present and past contributories and having recourse to the past contributories only when the liability of the present has been exhausted. If he is in any doubt about the amount which should be called up or the liability of any member he should apply to the court.

1. See para 34.62 above.

35.21 The liquidator may also find it advisable to apply to the court for a direction as to whether he should carry on the business of the company. He is perfectly entitled, however, to carry on the business without the sanction of the court and his decision will not be capable of challenge if it has been arrived at in good faith and having obtained any advice which he might reasonably be expected to seek.[1]

1. *Re Great Eastern Electric Co Ltd.* [1941] Ch 241.

35.22 The court may also make an order under the section annulling the resolution to wind up or staying all proceedings in the winding up. This may happen, for example, where the company has come to an arrangement with its creditors. Where such an order is made, an office copy of it must be sent forthwith by the company to the Registrar for registration.

Possession of books and assets and sales by liquidator

35.23 The liquidator is entitled upon his appointment to obtain possession of the books and records of the company and of all its assets. He should enforce this right without delay, and in the case of choses in action, i.e. things which can only be recovered by action and not by obtaining possession, such as book debts, he should give notice at once to the persons concerned, such as the debtors, of his appointment. If he encounters any difficulty, he should apply to he court without delay.

In the case of books and other records and documents, the person in whose possession they are may claim a lien, i.e. a right to retain possession of them until he has been paid for services rendered to the company. This may arise, for example, in the case of a solicitor, and the liquidator will usually agree to pay the amount of the costs—subject to the bill being taxed, if necessary— out of the assets which come into his hands.

35.24 The liquidator may sell all or any of the assets of the company without the sanction of the court. He should, of course, where appropriate obtain expert advice and valuations and this should always be done in the case of real or leasehold property. It is also normal to fix a reserve price in the case of such sales. The liquidator has power to execute any contracts, conveyances, etc. in the name of the company.

Removal of liquidator

35.25 The court has power under s 277 to remove a liquidator on cause shown and appoint another in his stead. The most usual ground for such an application is the possibility of a conflict of interest[1] but any misconduct on the liquidator's part will also, of course, justify the making of such an order.

1. E.g. *Re Charterland Goldfields Ltd* (1909) 26 TLR 132.

Costs

35.26 Section 281 provides that all costs, charges and expenses properly incurred in the winding up, including the remuneration of the liquidator, are to be payable out of the assets of the company in priority to all other claims.

333

Solicitors frequently require payments on account of their costs as the liquidation proceeds: where this is done, the liquidator should obtain from the solicitor an undertaking to refund any amount which has been paid by the liquidator but disallowed on taxation.

The costs of the liquidator have no priority over the claims of secured creditors. He will, however, be entitled to be paid any costs incurred by him in realising or preserving the security.[1]

1. *Re Regent's Canal Ironworks Co ex parte Grissell* (1875) 3 Ch D 411.

Final meeting and dissolution

35.27 As soon as the affairs of the company are fully wound up, the liquidator must make up an account of the winding up and call a general meeting of the company and (in the case of a creditors' winding up) a meeting of the creditors for the purpose of laying the account before the meetings and giving any explanation of it which may be necessary. The account must show how the winding up has been conducted.[1]

The meeting must be called by advertisement in two daily newspapers circulating in the district where the registered office is situated. It must specifiy the time, place and object of the meeting and must be published at least 28 days before the meeting. The liquidator must send a copy of the account to the Registrar within a week from the date of the meetings— or where they are not held on the same date, from the date of the later meeting—together with a return to him of the holding of the meetings and of their dates. If no quorum was present, it is sufficient to state that fact. The Registrar must register the accounts and return on receipt of them, and on the expiration of three months from their registration the company is deemed to be dissolved.

The court may on the application of the liquidator or any other person who appears to the court to be interested make an order deferring the date at which the dissolution is to take effect until such time as the court thinks fit. The person who obtains such an order must send it to the Registrar for registration within 14 days from its being made, and if he fails to do so is liable to a fine not exceeding £50.

If the liquidator fails to call the general meeting of the company or meeting of creditors he is liable to a fine not exceeding £250.

As in the case of a winding up by the court, the dissolution may within two years be declared to have been void.[2]

1. S 263 (members' winding up) and S 273 (creditors' winding up) of the Principal Act, as amended by s 15 of the 1982 Act.
2. S 310 of the Principal Act. See para 34.97 above.

Winding up under supervision

35.28 The 1908 Act provided a procedure for the winding up of companies 'subject to the supervision of the court'. This enabled a voluntary winding up to continue, but under the court's supervision. An order for winding up under supervision had the same effect as a compulsory winding up order in relation to proceedings against the company: they were automatically stayed by the order. It was, however, rarely invoked in practice and both Cox and Jenkins recommended its abolition, a recommendation which was implemented by the Principal Act.

Appendix

Re: Bray Travel Ltd and Bray Travel (Holdings) Ltd

The Supreme Court: Henchy J, Kenny J, and Hederman J.   13 July 1981

Appeal from Order of Costello J.

HENCHY J.

This is an important case. Obviously it is going to be extended over a period of time. It is desirable that the liquidator should be given directions. The court considers it necessary to dispose of the interlocutory matter today. The case is only at the stage that a plenary summons has been issued. Subsequent to the issue of the plenary summons a notice of motion was issued. On that motion Costello J made an order in which he granted an interlocutory injunction restraining until further order the companies from disposing or dealing with their assets without the permission of the official liquidator.

In these circumstances two questions arise. First, whether it was open to Costello J to form the view that the whole of the group of defendants and the associated companies formed an interlocking economic unit which should be dealt with as one for the purposes of the interlocutory application.

Secondly, whether the balance of convenience required that the defendants be restrained from dealing with the assets.

The starting point is that each individual company is a separate person in the eyes of the law and entitled to the standing that goes with it. The modern trend has been to go behind the facade and look at the reality. See *Smith Stone and Knight v Birmingham Corporation* [1939] All ER 116; *D H N v Tower Hamlets* [1976] 1 All ER 462; *Jones v Lipman* [1962] 1 All ER 442 and the recent decision of Costello J in the *Power Supermarket* case.

In the Power Supermarket case Costello J said:

'It seems to me to be well established from these as well as from other authorities (see *Harold Holdsworth & Co. Ltd v Caddies* [1955] 1 All ER 725; *Scottish Co-operative Wholesale Society Ltd v Meyer* [1959] AC 324 that a court may, if the justice of the case so requires, treat two or more related companies as a single entity so that the business notionally carried on by one will be regarded as the business of the group, or another member of the group, if this conforms to the economic and commercial realities of the situation.'

335

In my opinion that sums up the tests as applied in *Gough on Restitution*. Prima facie there is a case to be made for the companies in this case to be treated as a single economic entity.

The court selects the person to liquidate and to carry out the task of liquidating but the task of liquidation cannot be carried out merely by reference to the affairs of the company in liquidation where the company was so closely linked with others as to be part of a single entity. The companies are distinguishable in that there are separate books and separate premises: nevertheless there is an inextricable nexus, so that it would be unreasonable to ask the liquidator to liquidate one company without regard to the associated companies.

I would adopt the views expressed by Costello J which I have quoted above.

I would uphold the injunction.

Even if one does not rely on the concept of a single entity there were transactions of a questionable nature. There was a dealing in shares that suggests that they passed at an undervalue. That would be a good case for a tracing order.

I would affirm the order.

KENNY J.

I too would affirm the order. Bray Travel Ltd is in liquidation by the court. The statutory documents filed show that it is grossly insolvent. There is a deficiency of £500,000. The company has seven subsidiary companies. (He referred to the relationship between the companies as set out in para 4 of Mr Gribbon's affidavit).

I am satisfied that the order of Costello J was justified. The liquidator has a fair case to present that he will succeed in establishing that the companies are one economic unit or reality.

There is a tendency over the last forty years to look at the reality. The accounts of group companies are now required to be consolidated.

Secondly the order might be upheld on the tracing principle. The property was sold at a gross undervalue. The liquidator may be entitled to trace. The liquidator's concern at present is that the property should be preserved. If I were the High Court Judge I would have granted the injunction. I would dismiss the appeal.

HEDERMAN J.

I would dismiss the appeal for the reasons mentioned by Henchy J and Kenny J.

Index